The
# Major Neuroses
and
# Behavior Disorders
in Children

MELITTA SPERLING, M.D.

# MELITTA SPERLING, M.D.

# The
# Major Neuroses
## and
# Behavior Disorders
## in Children

JASON ARONSON, NEW YORK

Library of Congress Catalog Card Number: 73-17747
ISBN: 0-87668-124-0
Sperling, Melitta
    The Major Neuroses and Behavior Disorders in Children
© 1974 Jason Aronson, Inc., New York

# CONTENTS

# Foreword

Dr. Melitta Sperling was a brilliant and dedicated psychoanalyst who was widely known for her clinical acumen and skills. She had a special knack for identifying lacunae in the therapeutic applications of psychoanalytic technique, especially in regard to psychosomatic problems and the psychopathology of children. Focusing on these relatively neglected areas, her psychoanalytic contributions were consistently based on carefully reported and studied clinical material that enabled her to develop and demonstrate sound therapeutic principles based on clinically supported psychoanalytic formulations.

Throughout her work, she maintained an unwavering search for therapeutic results based on sound techniques. Her clinical experience was remarkably broad, and she made significant contributions to the psychoanalytic and psychotherapeutic techniques related to problems as diverse as ulcerative colitis, phobias, sleep disturbances, enuresis, obsessional neuroses, deviant sexual behavior, and childhood schizophrenia—among many others.

Her lucid clinical papers are a remarkable demonstration of

the rich rewards that a sensitive clinician can derive from the mutual interaction between clinical observations, theoretical constructions, and advances in technique. Her work vividly demonstrates the unique and essential role that classical psychoanalytic therapists play in generating vital insights into some of our most puzzling psychiatric syndromes.

Dr. Sperling's work demonstrates the unmatched value of an approach to their resolution that is founded on classical psychoanalytic principles—principles to which she adhered to the very end of her remarkable and rewarding career.

ROBERT J. LANGS, M.D.

# Introduction

I began my psychoanalytic training after practicing pediatrics and general medicine for nearly ten years. This background may account in part for my special interest in child analysis and psychosomatic medicine. Of the nearly fifty years of my medical practice, the last forty have been devoted exclusively to the practice and teaching of psychoanalysis, child psychiatry, and psychosomatic medicine.

In 1940 I established, with the help and support of the late Dr. B. Kramer, then Chief of the Pediatrics Department at The Brooklyn Jewish Hospital, a psychoanalytically oriented child psychiatric clinic. I directed this clinic and the prenatal mental hygiene clinic which I established several years later, for fifteen years. There I began the psychoanalytic treatment of children suffering from a variety of psychosomatic diseases, such as ulcerative colitis, mucous colitis, psychogenic diarrhea, skin diseases, bronchial asthma, allergies, migraine headaches, petit and grand mal epilepsy, etc. In the treatment of these children I introduced the method of simultaneous treatment of mother

xi

and child. This method proved to be not only a very successful therapeutic aid but a research tool that led to new insights into the dynamics of the mother-child relationship, not only in psychosomatic diseases but also in children with severely disturbed behavior, including child psychosis.

I studied the vicissitudes of the mother-child relationship in a great variety of clinical syndromes and found that the quality of this relationship was the most important factor in the child's choice of mechanisms of defense and of his illness. The case materials selected for this volume will illustrate these dynamics as well as the therapeutic techniques that have made it possible to modify or even to resolve this pathological relationship in operation.

In 1948 I started the teaching of psychosomatic medicine as well as psychoanalytic child development and child psychiatry at the Department of Psychiatry of the State University, Downstate Medical Center. In 1949 I became a charter member of the Psychoanalytic Association of New York and of the Division for Psychoanalytic Education at the State University of New York, Downstate Medical Center, where I became a training and supervisory analyst at the Adult and Child Analytic Faculties and a clinical professor of psychiatry. More than thirty years ago I introduced the teaching of psychoanalytic child psychiatry to pediatricians and physicians of various specialties in courses under the auspices of the joint committee of postgraduate education of the Kings County Medical Society.

My interests and contributions in child analysis and child psychiatry have covered a wide range. My investigations into sleep disturbances and phobias of children, which began early in my analytic career, developed into the most comprehensive and systematic studies of these syndromes in children. Deviate sexual behavior in children was another area of interest to me and led to the investigation of such behavior through the simultaneous treatment of mother and child. Other behavior disorders, such as psychotic behavior and childhood schizophrenia, were another area of research. The psychoanalytic treatment of character disorders, borderline cases, and perversions was an area of great interest for me also in adult patients.

In my teaching of child analysis and child psychiatry I felt the need for a textbook of child psychiatry that would be based on psychoanalytic insights. Such a book should use the fundamental findings from psychoanalytic child psychology and the clinical experiences gained in the practice of child, adolescent, and adult analysis which I had the good fortune to be able to combine. It should consider the basic psychological factors in the psychopathology presented by the individual child, that is, not the symptomatology per se but the basic personality disturbance underlying the symptoms. It should consider as dynamic factors the level of fixation and regression, the quality of the mother-child relationship, the unconscious meanings to the child of the traumatic events in the past and of the present situation, and the personalities of the parents, with particular emphasis on their mutual neurotic needs and on the role they have assigned to the child in satisfying these needs.

A sleep disturbance, for instance, is not a disease but a symptom, which, like many other symptoms such as phobias and enuresis, can occur in a variety of psychiatric disturbances ranging from neurosis to psychosis. The approach and prognosis will be different in each case, and a proper assessment of the situation and a strategic treatment plan are essential. (This and similar aspects will be dealt with in the various sections.) Here lies my major objection to behavioral and other therapies, which deal only with the symptoms and do not take into consideration the personality of the patient, and which pretty much deny the existence of the unconscious, the most powerful force in human behavior, healthy or sick. This volume is an attempt to fill this need.

## Concepts and Therapeutic Techniques

Child analysis was invented as a method to treat the inhibited anxious neurotic, not the uninhibited, impulsive, manifestly aggressive child. Neurotics suffer from unconscious internal conflicts between the ego and superego, with guilt feelings. The child with behavioral problems is in conflict with his environment.

That is, the neurotic suffers from his neurosis, while the child with a behavior disorder tries to make others suffer. In order to make such a child amenable to insight therapy it is necessary to transform him into a neurotic and to induce him to internalize conflicts and aggression. This can be achieved only if the child can form a new object relationship, different from that which he has with his parents, with his analyst-therapist. Under the influence of the new object relationship the internalized aggression can be sufficiently libidinized so that it can be used constructively for more adequate functioning—in other words, a proper fusion between the destructive aggression and the libidinal self-preservative drives can take place.

Simultaneous analysis of mother and child permitted a new approach to the study of the development of the ego and the superego and of object relationships. It made it possible to detect very early the deleterious effects of certain pathological attitudes of the mother in the relationship to her child. The mother or the person who functions as the mother to the young child is the auxiliary ego of her child in early infancy and sometimes even beyond. She is also the model for his superego later on. She is in charge of weaning (acceptance of separation and of changes) and of toilet training, that is, acquisition of sphincter control, which at this stage of development equals instinctual control. Her own neurotic, characterological or psychotic disturbances will impinge very early upon her child and interfere with his development. The overanxious mother, the obsessional compulsive, and the mother with depression is unable, because of her own neurosis, to apply sensible advice. Therefore, an approach based on psychoanalytic insight, confronting the mother with her unconscious conflicts concerning her child, is not only the most effective therapy for both the mother and her child but is also the best prophylaxis for the child's future development. This can be accomplished in many cases in brief psychoanalytically oriented therapy, provided the analyst-therapist understands the situation, has the ability to establish a rapport with the mother and shows tact and empathy in his handling of her and of her child. Numerous illustrations of such situations are to be found in this volume.

The problems are more severe in those cases where the parent and in particular the mother suffers from character disorders. Here narcissism, ambivalence, and need for omnipotent control are most prominent. Especially in cases of mothers with perverse tendencies there is often an indiscriminate use of the child for the satisfaction of such needs. There is generally little consideration of the child's individuality, his own personality and needs. There is also usually much inconsistency in the handling of the child, ranging from overstimulation and seduction to rejection and deprivation. These attitudes foster a similar characterological development of the child. Illustrations for this can be found in Parts 5 and 6 in this volume.

Obesity, thumb-sucking, and other habits, addictive and impulsive behavior in general, indicate the problems these children have in the area of instinctual and of self-control (see Chapter 24). One motive for the writing of this volume was to share with analysts, psychiatrists, and therapists my clinical experiences with such patients, accumulated in a lifelong practice, in the hope that their patients may derive some benefit from it. When I speak of "analysis" here, I do not mean classical analysis, where the patient lies on the couch and is seen five times weekly. In patients with character disorders, changes in technique are necessary. With children we rarely do classical analysis, but allow them a certain freedom in the office. With young children the technique of treating the mother alone is often most effective and often sufficient. In older children with characterological and behavioral disorders, preparatory treatment of the child is replaced by preparatory treatment of the mother, so that she can accept and cooperate in the treatment of her child. A positive relationship and a therapeutic alliance with the mother are important prerequisites for a successful outcome of the treatment of such children. It also shortens the duration of the treatment of the child and insures that the child will stay and will maintain the gains made in treatment. Illustrations are frequent in this volume. Even in adult patients with character disorders it is inadvisable to insist upon the classical method, with the patient on the couch and the analyst silently behind him. Such patients have often to be treated sitting up and facing the analyst. One adolescent girl during a phase of her treatment would frequently dance around the office singing, or she would sit on the floor or desk testing me, to see if I would become annoyed and consider her crazy for acting that way. She had always been able to annoy her mother and to provoke her into calling her crazy with this behavior. The approach with these patients is active and goal-directed. We begin with the interpretation of the masochistic aspect of the behavior, of the damage done to oneself and of the high price. One has to be careful not to fall into the trap and take the role of the controlling parent to whom the patient will deny satisfaction, or whom he will tease as he felt that he had been teased. The behavior of the patient resembles that of the parent: at first gratifying and then disappointing or gratifying at the price of submission and thus of control. It is important to mobilize in the patient a motivation for wanting to please himself and to help him create a realistic ego ideal. In some cases we have to begin with the analysis of the superego, without devaluing the parents. It is important to convince the patient that he does not have to be like the parent with whose negative aspects he is identifying.

Some amount of repetition seems unavoidable in a presentation such as this. I have tried to use it advantageously, as an opportunity to present various aspects of the same patient in different contexts. This has helped me, and I hope will also help the reader to get a better general view of the patient's total psychopathology and development in treatment and over the years. As can be seen in the material, I had long follow-ups with many of my child patients, and in some cases—particularly three "hopeless" schizophrenic children—I have been able to assist them with problems in their adult life and with their own children. A review of the case material from various aspects approximates what actually happens in the treatment process. The reaction of a patient to an important interpretation given early and repeated later in treatment is usually quite different. Some react as if they had never heard it before: "Why didn't you tell me this before?" or "If you had told me this a year ago I would have scratched your eyes out." It takes time until a new insight is fully accepted, integrated and properly applied. I and many other analysts, I am sure, have had similar experiences in supervision. Since these are all learning processes this is not surprising, and repetition may not only not hurt but may even be useful.

# CLASSICAL PSYCHOANALYSIS AND ITS APPLICATIONS

A series of books under the editorship of Robert J. Langs, M.D.


LANGS, ROBERT—"The Technique of Psychoanalytic
Psychotherapy" *Vol. I and II*

KESTENBERG, JUDITH—"Parents and Children"

SPERLING, MELITTA—"The Major Neuroses and Behavior
Disorders in Children."

GIOVACCHINI, PETER—"Psychoanalysis of Character
Disorder"

KERNBERG, OTTO—"Object Relations Theory in Psychoanalysis."

NAGERA, HUMBERTO—"Female Sexuality and the Oedipus
Complex"

MEISSNER, WILLIAM—"The Paranoid Process"

HOFFER, WILLIE—"The Early Development and
Education of the Child"

The
# Major Neuroses
and
# Behavior Disorders
in Children

MELITTA SPERLING, M.D.

# PART 1

# THE MOTHER-CHILD RELATIONSHIP

# 1
# The Clinical Effects of Parental Neurosis on the Child

## Disturbances in the Mother-Child Relationship

The earliest indication of a disturbed mother-child relationship usually manifests itself in a disturbance of the vital functions of the child, such as food intake, sleep, excretion, and respiration. There are sometimes severe disturbances of these functions for which no apparent reason or remedy can be found, and which are of more serious significance than the mild and transitory disturbances encountered during the developmental phases. In these cases, superficial psychotherapy, reassurance, advice, or manipulations are ineffectual. It would seem that only interpretations exposing the unconscious motivations and conflicts of the mother are helpful. This can often be accomplished even in brief contacts with the mother. With young children, treatment of the mother alone is often sufficient to dissolve the pathologic relationship. Such indirect treatment is the only method by which infants or preverbal children can be treated successfully. In the very young, even severe psychosomatic disorders are still reversible if something is done to alter the disturbing relationship between mother and child.

Feeding and eating disturbances are the earliest and most frequent psychosomatic disorders in children. They are the first indications of something amiss in the mother-child relationship, and seldom reach the child analyst or child psychiatrist. The following is an example.

CASE 1.   The mother of a five-month-old infant was referred to me by a pediatrician who had recognized that the mother's psychologic problems were the cause of the child's symptoms. The situation was as follows: The woman had given birth to a healthy, well-developed eight-pound boy whom she breast-fed in the hospital. She experienced much anxiety and worried that she might not have enough milk and urged the doctor to prescribe a formula to have on hand at home in case breast-feeding should prove insufficient. At home she began to add the formula after each feeding. She would wake the child when he fell asleep after breast-feeding and force the bottle upon him. When he began to vomit after each feeding, she consulted a pediatrician, who advised her to stop the additional feedings. She did not accept this advice. As time went on, the child refused to take the breast, continued to vomit, and developed colic. She consulted another pediatrician, who advised her to starve the child for some time until he could take food again. At this the mother became panicky, abandoned any schedule, and was obsessed by only one desire, i.e., to get food into the child. The child was losing weight rapidly, and she again consulted the pediatrician who referred her to me.

I learned from the mother that she had not wanted this child, and particularly not a boy. She had wanted to end the pregnancy, which was not planned for, but her husband would not agree. She feared that something would happen during birth or that the child would be born dead. She had a twelve-year-old daughter who had never presented any difficulties to her. Psychoanalytic investigation revealed that she had unconsciously identified her son with her younger brother, who had died in infancy when my patient was five years old. She had always felt guilty over the death of this brother, without having been conscious of her death wishes against him. She had, by the force of repetition-compulsion, reenacted with her own child this unresolved conflict with her brother. Awareness of this helped her to accept the baby as her son and restored her ability to feed and care for him properly (Sperling, 1954).

The progressive development of a severe feeding disturbance arising from a distorted mother-child relationship and the therapeutic approach which takes into consideration both partners of this relationship are illustrated by the following case, in which mother and child were treated by me in concomitant analysis.

CASE 2. When Ann started psychoanalytic treatment, she was four years of age. She had been referred to me (but not brought in) when she was three because of severe and persistent vomiting, anorexia, and abdominal cramps with periodic episodes of diarrhea for which no organic cause could be found. A year later, when the child developed an intense phobic attachment to her mother, refusing to allow her out of her sight, the mother acted upon the referral.

In the treatment of the mother I learned that prior to Ann's birth she had had an obsessional concern regarding her husband, who suffered from mild diabetes. Her attitude toward him had changed markedly upon the discovery of this condition, as had her entire behavior. She could not work, developed a sleep disturbance, and found it impossible to concentrate on anything except her husband's condition. As soon as Ann was born she completely lost her anxious preoccupation with her husband's ailment and devoted herself exclusively to her baby. Soon after the child's birth, she thought that Ann was not taking enough food; she changed the formula and increased the number of feedings, with the result that at seven weeks of age, Ann developed anorexia, vomiting, and diarrhea, for which she had to be hospitalized. After a short stay in the hospital, she was discharged and put on a diet and new formula. Her symptoms continued and she was hospitalized again at eleven months of age. Her condition, however, remained unchanged up to the time she began treatment with me. At the age of four, she had not been given any solid foods but was still on a formula elaborately prepared and fed to her with a spoon by her mother. The mother maintained that only she knew how to prepare the child's food and how to feed her. Up to the time treatment began, Ann had vomited with every feeding.

Analysis of the mother revealed that Ann's intense need to hold on to her mother was a reflection of the mother's inability to let her out of her sight even for a moment. She was in constant dread over the child. She did not permit her to taste candy or solid food for fear that she would choke on it instantly. Even when Ann had been in need of glucose because of the acidosis caused by her continuous vomiting, the mother could not carry out the doctor's suggestion to allow her to suck on a lollipop.

Ann's mother was the youngest of five children and had been a particularly demanding and possessive child. She had to have her way and would threaten suicide if her mother did not comply immediately with her wishes. To her mother's illness and death when she was an adolescent she had reacted in a way which she could not understand before her analysis. During the illness, she had been so concerned about her mother that when the doctor came, he had to attend to her first. Throughout this period, she had a rapid pulse and could neither eat nor sleep. On the day of her mother's death, she heaved a sigh of relief, ate a complete meal, and had her first sound sleep. She had never realized how dependent she had been nor aware of the way in which this dependency had expressed itself in her possessive and controlling behavior. In retrospect, she could understand her intolerance of the suspense created by her mother's illness, a situation over which she had no control. She accepted the death as something that she had wanted to happen in order to put an end to the agonizing uncertainty. Her reaction could also be understood as a defense against an impending depression and as an attempt to maintain her fantasy of omnipotence.

She had carried over her dependency to her husband, whom she controlled similarly to the way she had her mother. When he developed a mild diabetic condition she became extremely disturbed, reacting to his illness as she had to her mother's. As soon as Ann was born, she transferred this relationship from her husband to the child, keeping the baby in a state of complete dependency.

After she had gained some understanding of her need to control her child completely, she began to relinquish her hold on Ann to some extent. The latter reacted to this not only by giving up her phobic clinging, but also, to her mother's surprise (and frustration), by demonstrating a strong desire for independence. When the child first began her play analysis, she insisted on having her mother with her in the playroom and continually asked her permission for everything we did. She apparently understood and accepted my interpretations regarding her insecurity in relation to her mother—casually injected—because, on her fourth visit, she decided to come into the playroom by herself. Leaving my office that day, she said to her mother: "I don't want you to come in with me into the playroom anymore. I have a much better time without you." This was a big step forward in Ann's life, as well as in her mother's. Throughout the previous year, Ann had refused to remain with anyone but her mother, not even accepting her father or the nursemaid who had been with her since infancy.

About six months after the beginning of treatment, an episode occurred which illustrated the interplay between the unconscious of the mother and her child and the way in which an immediate phobic reaction of the child could be induced by the mother's unconscious needs. At the time when this occurred, Ann's condition had improved to the extent that she had given up clinging to her mother and was playing outdoors with other children. She had also been asking for some solid foods—bread, fish, meat— which she would eat when her father or grandmother were in the house but not at her regular mealtimes when her mother fed her. She had also completely stopped vomiting. All of a sudden, there was a relapse into the phobic cling- ing and refusal of any solid food. In the session with the mother, it was revealed that this had set in on the day after the mother's visit to her gynecologist for a checkup. During her pregnancy with Ann, the mother had undergone a gynecologic operation and there was some question as to whether she should or could have another child. She had seen this doctor once before, more than a year ago, and the day after that, as she distinctly remembered, Ann's phobic behavior had started. On her way to the doctor this time, she had thought about this and wondered whether the same would happen again. At the doctor's she found out that she could not have another child. After discussing this, the mother was able to recognize clearly that she had been unwilling to let go of Ann and that the fleeting thought she had had about a recurrence of Ann's symp- toms had expressed her unconscious wish for her daughter to remain attached to her.

The morning after this session the mother said to Ann in a casual way: "I am going shopping now and Mary [the maid] will take you out this morning." Instead of clinging, crying bitterly, vomiting, and complaining of abdominal pain as she previously had whenever her mother attempted to leave her, Ann accepted this suggestion very readily. Her mother was now able to realize that it was actually she who clung to her daughter and experienced difficulty in leaving her, and now that she was determined to let go of her, Ann was accepting it without disturbance.

It was difficult for the mother to surrender her food control, even though she permitted the child more freedom now in other areas. When Ann began to bombard her mother with questions as to when she would have "regular food," the mother felt guilty but could not accede with ease to the child's request. She understood that this meant setting Ann free, allowing her normal independence. Ann, in turn, was testing her mother constantly during this period. Often she would come and tell her that she had cramps, and would carefully watch for her reaction. On one occasion, she was sucking hard candy at home, something which she did in every one of our play sessions, but which she had not yet done at home. She suddenly made a noise, as if she was choking, and watched her mother's face very closely. When the mother remained calm ("It does take a lot out of me," the mother would tell me), Ann said: "Don't you hear? I am choking!" The mother replied: "You're a big girl now and you know how to suck a candy." Ann continued to test her mother for some time before she was convinced that this change in the mother's attitude was a real one (M. Sperling, 1954).

Eating disturbances in young children can be severe and, in some cases, can be regarded as somatic equivalents of depression (Chapter 23). Anorexia nervosa and pernicious vomiting in older children and adolescents are always serious conditions, and a pathologic mother-child relationship is an important factor in these cases (M. Sperling, 1968b).

# 2

# Indirect Treatment of Psychoneurotic and Psychosomatic Disorders in Children

Indirect treatment I would define as a method whereby the neurosis of the child is influenced so decisively through the psychoanalytic treatment of the mother, that the neurotic conflict of the child in relationship to the mother can be resolved. This is different from guidance of mothers, where the environmental changes are effected by suggestion and direct manipulation, while the basic relationship between child and mother remains unchanged, unless the child is treated directly. In indirect treatment, the emphasis in the treatment of the mothers is upon the unconscious elements motivating their attitude toward the particular child.

In this chapter, I am dealing with cases in which direct treatment was not applicable for two primary reasons: first, because these children refused to accept psychiatric treatment; secondly, because it was not possible to bring the child for therapy because of physical incapacity. Also, the three cases selected for presentation are those of older children—aged twelve and a half to fifteen at the start of treatment—suffering from conditions that one would usually not consider suitable for indirect therapy. The severity of their conditions had necessitated hospitalization in each case; all three had left the hospital unimproved and with a bad prognosis unless they could be treated psychiatrically. Since the conflict of these girls seemed to center upon their mothers, the attempt was made to resolve these conflicts by treatment of the mothers.

Miriam's parents consulted me about her when she was twelve and a half years of age. They had been worried about her behavior for several years. An only child, she was a shy, withdrawn girl who had no friends and who was seclusive, preferring to stay at home. Occasionally, she had outbursts of severe temper in which she would become highly abusive of her parents, especially of her mother. She did well scholastically but in this sphere also she occasionally lost interest. Her parents had hoped that she would outgrow this behavior but when it became more marked, they became disturbed. Miriam's parents were both professional people. Although not relaxed in the interview, the father related well and did not appear to be a seriously handicapped person. The mother, however, hardly spoke a word and was obviously ill at ease, blushing and perspiring heavily throughout the interview.

Miriam, a physically well-developed girl, resembled her mother in stature and manner. She moved and talked slowly with sudden quick movements indicating a great deal of repressed energy. She was very distrustful and exercised caution not to reveal anything in the interviews. I saw her at the end of the school term when Miriam was preparing to leave for camp. My understanding with the parents had been that I would see Miriam a few times to evaluate her condition and to make suggestions regarding treatment which, if indicated, was to start in the fall. In the four sessions with her, she began to warm up a bit, expressing some resentment about her mother. She told me, for instance, that the mother had given away her dog, whom she loved dearly, because the maid would not tolerate it in the house; that the mother never planned anything in which her wishes were considered. Both parents were usually very busy. When the mother came home, she was tired, or had a headache. On Sunday, they would occasionally visit relatives with whom Miriam was bored. She was apprehensive about going to camp, preferring to spend the summer with her parents at a place where there were no children of her own age. She was finally persuaded to go to camp when it was impressed upon her that her mother needed a vacation. She had been in camp twice and had been very unhappy both times. She was appealed to by her parents as "a big girl" and since the camp owners were friends of her parents, she agreed to go.

I interpreted Miriam's feelings regarding camp to her parents and suggested that they should not send her. They could not accept the suggestion and the changes involved in it for them, however. They felt confident that this time Miriam would make a good adjustment in camp.

I heard from Miriam again in the fall. Her father had called me several times during my own vacation. When I saw him, I learned that Miriam was in a hospital with an undiagnosed illness that had originated in camp. At first, it was suspected that she might have contracted infantile paralysis because she had difficulty in moving her arms and in walking. She had no temperature, however, and examination by various consultants finally ruled out this diagnosis. In the hospital, which specialized in joint diseases, she received physical therapy but her condition grew steadily worse and finally a psychiatric consultant was called. After examining her, he declared in her presence that there was nothing wrong with her and that she was suffering from conversion hysteria. Miriam reacted to this by becoming completely immobilized and from then on had to be carried on a stretcher to and from the treatment room. Transfer to a psychiatric hospital was advised because there were no further indications for physical therapy. Miriam was very disturbed and insisted that she be taken home or she would never get well. The father was at a loss in this situation and asked my advice. I learned from the father that Miriam had had two accidents in camp. First, she sprained her wrist, after which she had difficulty in moving her arm, and ceased participation in games and play activities. Later, on the way to the swimming pool, she caught her foot on a nail. From then on, she had difficulty in walking, did not go swimming, nor would she leave her room. The father came up to see her finally but the mother never did. By this time, Miriam was very unhappy and practically immobilized, so that her father took her home. The mother also had to break up her summer vacation and come home. Because it had been so difficult to care for Miriam at home, and since no diagnosis could be established, she had been hospitalized.

Miriam refused to see me, and even had she agreed, it was not feasible because she could not walk. In view of her negativistic attitude and refusal to accept psychiatric treatment in a hospital or by me, I advised the father to take her home, provided that the mother would agree to take a leave of absence from her profession to care for Miriam under my guidance. Under these circumstances, it seemed to me best to work through the mother. With feelings of great apprehension and annoyance, the mother accepted my suggestion. I arranged to see her every other day.

Miriam had the time of her life. She behaved like a baby and was treated accordingly, demanding the complete attention of her mother. She would throw pillows around the room, talk and play with her mother in a babyish manner, demand her mother's jewelry, which she would put on and keep with her in bed. She had to be fed and carried like a baby. It was an important step forward when Miriam asked to be taken downstairs, after a few weeks. At first, this had to be done with the complete support of the mother on whom she leaned with all her weight. (The mother noticed, however, that on many occasions when she turned away, Miriam was quite able to stand up by herself.) After several weeks, Miriam began to show interest in books, asked about the children in school, spoke of going out to participate in a forthcoming birthday party at the home of a relative. But she demanded that the mother accompany her and promise to carry her if necessary. The mother had to put her into the car, take her there (i.e., if she could not walk) and bring her back home. When returning from the party, Miriam noticed a boy—a schoolmate of hers—and whereas heretofore she had leaned heavily on her mother as if unable to walk by herself, she now ran quickly up the stairs by herself.

Miriam now asked for a particular schoolmate to come to see her, began to show interest in schoolwork, and announced to her mother that she planned to return to school in the near future and would allow her mother to resume her work. Miriam returned to school at the beginning of the new term. Although she had missed a full term of school, she was able to catch up with her work.

Miriam is now seventeen and has had no recurrence of this behavior. According to the mother, she is much happier and a more pleasant girl with whom to live and leads an active social life.

Although it is not possible to give a detailed account of the analysis of the mother, I feel it essential to the understanding of this case to briefly relate its significant features. The mother, previous to treatment, had never really spoken about herself to anyone, not even to her husband. She had not wanted any children, moreover not so soon after her marriage. She had definitely not wanted a daughter. Miriam was an accident. It was her husband's fault. He had "tricked" her into it and she resented both the child and her husband. She had been very unhappy throughout her childhood. Her mother, a sick woman who was treated as an inferior being by her husband, later developed a manifest manic depressive psychosis and had to be institutionalized where she died. My patient herself felt very inferior to her brother and father. She would have liked to have chosen her father's profession but he discouraged her by making it clear that he did not think girls in general and she in particular had the intellect for it. She was very shy, had no friends, and never spoke up in groups.

She was very efficient in her work and received recognition for her abilities, but could not participate actively in discussions or meetings.

When Miriam was born, she stayed home with her until the child was one and a half years old. Actually, she had done this upon her husband's prompting only and felt that the maid could have done just as well as she. She recalled that upon her return to work, Miriam refused to look at her or speak to her when she came home in the evening. Miriam continued in this behavior quite consistently and it would seem that she never forgave her mother for having deserted her. It would seem to me that the camp experience reactivated Miriam's frustration connected with this early separation from the mother. At camp, she had been very unhappy and had suffered two accidents with no attention shown her by her mother who, in fact, had not even come up to see her once. This had apparently touched off the feelings of her earliest childhood, when she felt deserted by her mother. Regression to the early infantile stage, to the time when her mother had cared for her, therefore, seemed to be the way in which she could get her mother to repeat this experience for her. Miriam thus managed to achieve her unconscious purpose through illness. The mother perceived that this was Miriam's way of forcing her to do that which she had always rejected—namely, be a mother to her, and she resented the arrangement accordingly.

These feelings were interpreted in discussion with the mother and demonstrated to her as they arose in the current situation. The mother was quite unable to recognize the child's needs and to gratify them at this belated date without help. It was an interesting experience to observe the keenness with which Miriam sensed her mother's feelings and the immediacy of her reactions. At the time when the mother was especially eager to return to work, Miriam, who had already improved, suddenly lapsed back into the behavior shown at the onset of her illness. When the mother accepted her lot with greater patience and understanding and for the first time showed genuine interest in her daughter, the child responded with gratitude.

Prior to the analysis, the mother had been unable to look at Miriam without bringing up strong fears concerning her sanity.

This proved to be a projection onto the child of her fears about herself. The projection was a defense mechanism which served to protect her from recognition of her fears about herself. When the mother was able to accept Miriam on a rational basis, a decisive change in Miriam's behavior took place. It was then that Miriam indicated her willingness to return to school, which meant to set her mother free.

It was clear that the mother was afraid to bring into the analysis her feelings about her husband and to discuss her marital relationship with me. On the surface, the relationship seemed to be one of mutual acceptance; however, it was obvious that she was transferring to her husband all the hostility and hatred which she had felt for her father and brother. I felt it would be too dangerous to stir up feelings that could be satisfactorily resolved only in a comprehensive analysis. The mother had made it clear to me, however, that she was concerned only with the understanding of her relationship with Miriam and with helping her. As soon as Miriam returned to school—after about three and a half months—the mother discontinued her treatment and returned to work. I later learned from the mother that Miriam was doing consistently well, that she was functioning much better than previously, but that her attitude regarding psychiatric treatment was still a negative one. I felt that this was a reflection of the mother's rejection of analysis. The mother, it seems to me, did not really want to know herself. She was harboring an intense hostility and hatred stemming from her unresolved relationship with her father and brother and transferred to her husband. In view of this intense hostility and paucity of genuine feeling for people, I would regard her as a latent psychotic. Nevertheless, her treatment enabled her to accept Miriam on a rational basis instead of having to avoid her phobically because Miriam had symbolized to her (in projection) the "insane" part of her own personality. Because of her mother's complete rejection of her, Miriam had not been able to establish emotional relationships with people and had remained fixated on an early infantile level (pregenital), to which she regressed in reaction to disappointment. Only through the analytic treatment of the mother was it possible to establish this new relationship between them which opened to Miriam the path for further (normal) development.

Harriet came to me for psychiatric treatment when she was thirteen years of age. Her mother reported that for a period of six months prior to referral, she exhibited sudden outbursts of temper, excitement, screaming, breaking and throwing things out of the window, etc. In one of these attacks, she tore hair out of her head and tried to bite and scratch anyone who came near her. She was considered a possible schizophrenic by a psychiatrist who saw her at that time. With the repetition of these attacks, she was placed in a psychiatric hospital, where she stayed for two months. In the hospital, she did not have temper trantrums, was friendly and well poised. She was correctly oriented for time, place, and person, and performed well on all tests. Physical and neurological examination revealed no abnormalities. EEG findings were reported as "consistent with psychopathic personality." In the first months after admission, she had made many demands on the nurses, and showed some compulsive features, such as protecting her toilet articles with cleansing tissues, wanting to sleep on the bed covers instead of between the sheets. These symptoms subsided, however, and she became insistent upon going home. Voluntarily, she began to decrease her food intake in an effort to effect discharge from the hospital. Finally, she persuaded her parents to take her home and was discharged against advice with a diagnosis of "psychoneurotic reaction with phobic-compulsive features: prognosis without treatment—bad; with treatment—fair."

In subsequent interviews with the mother, I learned that Harriet had always been a self-willed, demanding child. Although she was an unplanned baby, the mother maintained that she had accepted her well nonetheless. She was a thumb-sucker up to her eleventh year and enuretic until her tenth year. She had had temper tantrums at a preschool age and she had always been a behavior problem. She argued and fought so with her younger brother (three and a half years her junior) that he had to be sent to a boarding school when Harriet was eleven and a half years of age.

Harriet's father had been in the army for several years and it was apparent that the child resented his return. At the age of eleven, she first began to show fears of illness and death, becoming especially apparent immediately after her girl friend died of an acute illness. On seeing a moving picture on cancer, Harriet exhibited marked fear that she might develop the disease. This fear of cancer was aggravated by the cancer publicity program in school and one day she tore a poster from the wall to avoid seeing it in the future.

She began to menstruate at twelve and a half and seemed to take the event calmly. According to the mother, Harriet had been prepared for it. At that time, the child told her mother that the school hygiene teacher had instructed the children that one out of five of them would die of cancer. She reported the teacher as saying that the children would die when they went to sleep and that, if the Lord wished it, He revived them. After this, Harriet began to stay up late, feared sleep, and wanted a light on in her room. She tried to prevent her parents from leaving her alone in the house. She also tried to avoid going to school and one day openly refused to go. At about this time, too, she developed compulsive hand-washing and feared that the dishes were unclean. Several weeks later, she refused to leave the home at all, and declined food, fearing it was poisoned. She began to complain that her vagina felt dirty and open. She refused to wear clothes below the waist. She would not sit on a chair without spreading a clean towel on it first. She questioned her mother whether a boy the age of her brother could impregnate a girl. At about this time, her states of excitement and her temper outbursts became increasingly severe. Several outbursts lasted for hours at a time. Usually the precipitating event was obscure but on some occasions, it followed a minor frustration, e.g., not being permitted to listen to a favorite radio program.

During these attacks, she seemed well aware of her conduct and once briefly interrupted one of them to explain a comic strip to her mother. In one attack, she wrote an obscene word on the bathroom door.

The first time she had an attack, her mother found her in the bathroom where she had wrecked most of the bathroom fixtures. She was crying, "Help me, mother. Do something. I feel so dirty." She stood with her legs wide apart, complaining that her vagina felt wet.

Prior to Harriet's admission to the hospital, she had been in a sanitarium, where she had behaved well. She had promised her parents that if they took her home she would make daily visits to the psychiatrist recommended by the sanitarium. After the first visit, however, she refused to return to the psychiatrist's office. While in the hospital, she had again pledged to accept psychiatric treatment, inducing her parents to take her to the country for the summer. She was very difficult there and the mother had to meet all her demands in order to keep her calm. On her return, she visited the psychiatrist who referred her to me. She was told that I would help her get a tutor since she was concerned about catching up with her school work, in which she had fallen behind.

Harriet was a delicate-looking, pretty girl, very carefully groomed. She made it clear to me that she felt perfectly well, that she had no fears or difficulties and did not consider herself in need of psychiatric treatment; that she had come and would continue to come only because of her parents' insistence. I learned that she had had some school difficulties and was concerned about her grades, for in spite of her high IQ (128), she did not perform well. She was upset especially because the girl with whom she had been in competition was now ahead of her in school and was primarily concerned with gaining quick advancement to outstrip her rival. I arranged to see her twice a week, suggesting that I might be helpful to her in some way. She spoke a great deal about horses and declared that if she had her choice, she would live on a ranch where she could ride all day. She had persuaded her father to rent a horse for her and twice a day, he had to take her to the stable. She envied her brother, at boarding school, where the boys wore attractive uniforms. She openly said that she would have much preferred to be a boy. (She strenuously rejected any suggestion of boarding school for herself, however.) At the same time, she derived great satisfaction from the attention paid her by boys and showed a high degree of insecurity and sensitivity in her relations with them. Thus, she became very depressed when, during a visit to her brother's school, a certain boy paid no attention to her and at another time she was overexhilarated by some small flattery on the part of another boy.

Her mother had to accompany Harriet to my office. She resisted getting up in the morning and dressing in order to keep her appointment. After five sessions, Harriet declared that she saw no reason for treatment since she felt fully capable of handling her own affairs, and was doing well in her studies. Her father, sensitive to the stigma of psychiatric treatment, agreed with her only too readily.

The impression I gained of Harriet was that of a highly narcissistic and psychopathic personality, in which some unsuccessful attempts were being made at establishing a compulsion neurosis. I recognized that the parental attitudes continued to be a vital factor in the production of Harriet's behavior. Since modification would have to be effected in their attitudes, I realized the need to work with and through the mother. The mother readily accepted my suggestion, indicating that she always felt that something was wrong in the way Harriet had been handled. Since her husband never agreed to a policy of greater firmness and consistency with the child, the mother had not asserted herself.

Shortly after Harriet stopped coming to see me, the father phoned to tell me that she was having a severe temper tantrum. Unless he would buy her a horse immediately, she threatened to break things and to expose him to the neighbors. (The father had promised to buy her a horse

when she was in the hospital.) I interpreted to the father
that he could not live in constant fear of Harriet and of
what she might do. His main fears centered upon a possible need for a future hospitalization, in view of his promise
never to commit her again. I advised him to talk with Harriet and to explain the situation to her—that his financial
position did not permit the purchase of a horse and that if
she behaved uncontrollably, he would have to hospitalize
her. The father had originally been advised not to frustrate
Harriet and to fulfill all her wishes. These suggestions were
readily adopted by him because being lenient with her fell
in line with his own needs. He had always contended that
his wife was too strict with her. There was no unity
between the parents regarding the child. Aware of this,
Harriet took full advantage of the situation.

With the father's decision in favor of a firmer management of Harriet, his apprehension about handling future
situations was considerably lessened. This change in his
attitude indeed had a beneficial effect on Harriet. She realized that the tables were turned and that she could no
longer rule her father by threats and temper tantrums.

In the therapeutic sessions with the mother, I learned of the
unsatisfactory nature of the marriage, that she was disappointed
in her husband, particularly because he disagreed with her on the
handling of the children. From the time of her birth, she had
always considered Harriet "like" the father. In retrospect now,
she could understand why she had not handled Harriet differently when she could have done so. It had been her way of demonstrating her disapproval of her husband to him. Through Harriet, she could show him how immature, indulgent, uncontrolled,
inconsiderate she considered him to be. Harriet was not a wanted
child and the mother had had many obsessional fears regarding
her when she was an infant. In her own adolescence, the mother
had exhibited compulsiveness, and also reaction formations stemming from her unresolved conflicts about masturbation, her femininity, and also feelings about her parents and sisters. Her
unconscious objection to her own femininity she had projected

onto her daughter and had not realized that this was her true reason for rejecting Harriet. She had also passed on to Harriet her own unconscious fears about masturbation, menstruation, and sexual functions.

To compensate for the absence of genuine interest in Harriet, the mother established the pattern of giving her material things, in this way fostering the child's unreasonable demands. As the mother gained insight into herself and achieved acceptance of Harriet, their relationship improved considerably. This was apparent in Harriet's responses to her mother. Formerly, the child had rejected suggestions or advice given by the mother and had been demanding and abusive to her. She now became rather considerate of her mother and spontaneously offered to help her in the house, and frequently asked her advice. She returned to school, caught up with her work, and even gained an extra term in the interim.

On days when Harriet was frustrated with her mother, she would not get up in the morning, and would refuse to go to school. However, when her mother would speak to her, she usually changed her mind and was able to maintain a rather good school record. Harriet had never had any close friends. At this time, although it was difficult for her to make friends in school since most of the students were older than she, she socialized well. She gave up horseback-riding and developed another hobby to satisfy her exhibitionistic needs—namely, ice-skating. The brother came to live at home and I learned from the mother that Harriet accepted him well. The family as a whole was a much happier one, and according to the mother, whom I saw on occasions, Harriet at fifteen and a half years old was leading the normal life of an adolescent girl.

In conclusion, I would say that in the analysis of the mother, which lasted over a year, it was recognized that she had projected her own conflicts about her femininity upon Harriet; and that her rejection of Harriet was tied up with this and with her identification of Harriet with the objectionable features of her husband's personality. She had transmitted to the child her own unconscious fears about menstruation, masturbation, and sexual functioning. The mother's fears, due to lack of acceptance of her own femininity, were reactivated with the advent of Harriet's menstruation, inducing a panicky response in Harriet. Harriet was obviously confused in her sexual orientation, because she did not have an adequate object for feminine identification. Through resolution of the mother's rejection of her own femininity, she became a suitable object of identification for her daughter and made it possible for Harriet to resolve her pregenital fixation and to develop normally.

Helen came to me when she was about fifteen years of age, following a nine-month period of illness. Her illness started with a cold shortly before her fourteenth birthday, which she had had to spend in bed. She continued to have a low-grade fever, developed severe anorexia, and vomiting so that she could hardly eat anything. She vomited even fruit juices and was losing weight rapidly. In four weeks, she lost about ten pounds. The attending physician could not diagnose her condition, nor could he prescribe an effective therapy. Helen's mother, desperate about the anorexia and weight loss, accepted the doctor's suggestion of hospitalization. In the hospital, where the child underwent a series of tests and examinations, no diagnosis could be established. She continued to have a low-grade fever, but was able to eat and stopped vomiting. She was discharged after several weeks. As soon as she came home again, her anorexia became pronounced; she could not eat and vomited the food when her mother finally would coax her into eating. The mother was in a panic and again Helen was hospitalized. Hospital examinations yielded no positive findings. During her stay there, however, she was able to eat and gained some weight. After several weeks, she was discharged and the mother advised to take her to the country, where she was left in the charge of a relative. Helen still suffered a low-grade temperature—up to about 101— and, although able to eat, she did not gain weight. After a short stay, she insisted upon returning home but as soon as she was back, the cycle repeated itself. By this time, her parents were deeply worried and they decided to again hospitalize her, anxious to find out what caused her condition. In another hospital now, all findings were negative again and after several weeks, she was discharged from this third hospital with a tentative diagnosis of rheumatic fever. She came now under the care of a pediatrician who suspected a psychogenic element in her illness and referred her to me.

Helen accepted referral to me on the basis that I decide whether she could return to school in her present physical condition. I saw her three times and I realized that she would not accept treatment at present because of her relationship with her mother. While the mother seemed eager for Helen to start therapy, it could be seen that her over-anxiousness actually concealed opposed unconscious desires and it was to these that Helen was reacting. I learned from the mother that on the day Helen discontinued her visits with me, they had quarreled; for as soon as Helen awoke that morning, the mother had begun to remind her of her appointment with me. The episode ended when Helen agreed to keep this particular appointment, but she made it clear that it would be her last one. I did not exert pressure upon Helen. We agreed that she could return to school and that should she experience any difficulty, she would contact me. Without her knowledge, I had arranged with the mother for psychoanalytic therapy for herself, because this seemed the best way in which to help Helen at present, a way in which, also, Helen could be made amenable to direct psychoanalytic treatment in the future.

I learned from the mother that Helen was grateful that I had not insisted on her coming for psychiatric help, and that she was progressing well. In the first two months of school, she had gained about twenty pounds and now weighed 126 pounds, while her lowest weight during her illness had been 100. She had also made a number of friends in school, both boys and girls, and had lost her low-grade fever. I had arranged with the mother that Helen was not to be coaxed by her but rather should be allowed to take her food herself and to eat her luncheons in school. Helen also had made up with her girl friend with whom she had broken off shortly before the onset of her illness and she spent very little time at home.

The mother revealed very strong guilt feelings regarding Helen's illness. She felt intuitively that the child's condition was in some way related to her, although she did not know how, and had expressed this feeling to the treating physician. It was actually through the mother's prompting that the case was finally referred to me. She had been very much aware of the fact that Helen had been able to eat and that her condition improved whenever she was away from home and that she stopped eating and began vomiting whenever she returned. But she could not understand this, for Helen was her only child and she had always given her much attention and care. Until Helen had been about thirteen, they had been very close to one another. At that time, Helen had begun to detach herself from the mother and became almost inseparable from her girlfriend Rita. The mother now blamed herself for having broken up this friendship and was able to connect it with the onset of Helen's illness. The mother had thought that Helen's friend was not a good influence on Helen but in the course of the treatment, she came to understand that she had actually resented the friend for taking Helen away from her. Helen would do whatever the friend told her and would disregard her mother's opinion.

The mother, the oldest of a family of six children, had been burdened with the care of the younger children and was very bitter about the frustrations of her own childhood. She felt that she had never received any attention, and resented the lack of her educational opportunities and that she had to go to work at a young age when she would have preferred to continue her schooling. She felt especially disappointed and frustrated with Helen because Helen did not appreciate all she was doing for her. When Helen was younger, the mother had been very indulgent of her to the extent of infantilizing her. And now she had become very critical of her, nagging and calling her "lazy" and "spoiled" and disapproving of everything that Helen did. She was able to recognize her ambivalent feelings regarding Helen and understood that she had been treating Helen as she herself would have wanted to be treated by her own mother and that she expected Helen to respond with submissiveness and dependence. With the mother's increasing ability to recognize her need for this exaggerated control, which had caused her complete disregard of Helen's individuality, Helen was enabled to resolve her conflict. This conflict was centered upon whether to hold on or to let go of her mother, a conflict which she had acted out somatically in her symptoms.

The mother, who was in psychoanalytic treatment with me for a year and a half, was able to understand and resolve her guilt feelings, which stemmed from her unconscious need to keep Helen dependent on her. The guilt had manifested itself in her anxiety over Helen's illness and in her inconsistent handling of her. At this point, she allowed Helen to assert herself.

I had an opportunity to learn more about this relationship and to verify that these were the psychodynamics in Helen's illness when Helen came for treatment herself at the age of sixteen and a half. Helen at nineteen became engaged. It may be of interest to learn that as a reaction to Helen's engagement, the mother returned for additional psychoanalytic therapy, because of the reactivation of a severe insomnia.

## Discussion

Indirect treatent, a term taken from the child guidance field (Lowrey, 1939, 1948) and representing a method in which modifications in the environment are effected as part of the treatment process with the child, is here used to denote psychoanalytic treatment of the mother undertaken because of her role in the child's illness.

A distinction is here to be made between the concept of indirect treatment where changes are effected through guidance, suggestion, and supportive therapy of the mother and in which conscious material is interpreted, as compared with indirect treatment involving the mother in psychoanalysis in which deep unconscious conflicts are resolved.

The preventive value of psychoanalytic treatment of the parents in handling childhood neurosis has been stated by Freud in his *New Introductory Lectures* (1933). The work of Anna Freud shows how necessary she finds it to include the parents, particularly the mother, in the treatment plan (1928). The role of the mother in the neurosis of the young child and the interplay of unconscious forces between them has been generally recognized by child analysts. A. M. Johnson (1949; 1944), S. Szurek (1942), and others in their work with adolescents found that they had to treat the mothers together with the children in difficult cases.

From the material presented in the three cases here, the mother emerges as the decisive factor in the environment; around her personality the child's illness is produced. The psychodynamics in the illness of these three adolescent girls points up that they were reacting violently to the pressures of puberty because they were caught in arrested emotional development and were acting out pregenital relationships. In other words, these girls who were able to sublimate in certain areas of their personality (e.g., intellectual) were dominated to a very high degree by their pregenital attachment to their mother and had to be reached in treatment through the mother just as if they were in reality young children.

In recognition of the oedipal conflict as the nuclear pattern in neurosis, treatment was focussed on the mother so that she could provide a more adequate release for the normal genital development of the child. Where the mother herself has not accepted her own femininity, she obviously cannot be an adequate object of identification for her daughter. In the situation where the mother's detachment from the child is keenly felt as rejection, the psychosomatic illness of the child represents a regression to a period of life, namely, infancy, when dependency was equated with love. Also, where the mother is struggling with a need for absolute control over the child, her wish can be gratified in the form of the child's complete loss of independence through physical illness. That such attitudes on the part of the mother are unconscious is obvious; the underlying conflicts reflected in these attitudes are deeply repressed and have to be interpreted; e.g., in the case of Miriam, the mother's fear of her own insanity was projected onto the child with an accompanying loss of affect, and interpreted by the child as complete rejection. The psychoanalytic treatment of the mother in my cases made it possible for the child to resolve the acute conflict and furthermore, by changing the *unconscious* attitude of the mother in relation to the child, made the mother acceptable as an object for identification. Considering the role which proper identification plays in personality development, we can appreciate the fact of turning the mother into a suitable object for identification, particularly in the case of a girl.

In a child, as well as in an adult, we know from experience that personality changes and relief from neurotic conflicts can be brought about only through a personal analysis. However, the child, even in adolescence, may be considered *in statu nascendi* and therefore capable of responding to a basic shift in the psychological equation, that is, where the mother's own increased maturity enables the child to emerge from the pregenital relationship with her and to take the necessary steps in growth, involving appropriate identification and superego formation, with independence from the parents.

One must reckon with the mother's twofold resistances in indirect treatment: first, against understanding of her own unconscious, and then against the recognition of the effects of her own attitudes upon the child. However, this understanding of her own unconscious and its effects upon the child enables the mother to function towards the child in many situations as if she were the analyst herself.

It was possible, through psychoanalytic treatment of the mothers, to resolve the principal conflict of these girls, which centered upon their mothers, and which had expressed itself dynamically in the various clinical pictures that these patients presented.

The method of indirect treatment, as described here, whereby the psychoanalytic treatment of the mother is aimed to establish a satisfactory relationship with the neurotic child, I consider a valuable addition to our methods of technique. In cases where the child refuses treatment for himself, it is invaluable and eventually renders the child amenable for direct treatment.

# 3
# Children's Interpretation of and Reaction to the Unconscious of Their Mothers

In this chapter I shall attempt to demonstrate with material from the simultaneous analyses of severely disturbed children and their mothers that the symptoms of these children represented their responses to their mother's unconscious wishes. Neurotic reactions, as well as strangely eruptic behavior (to all outward appearances psychotic), could be understood as an unconscious answer to an unconscious wish of the mother for the child to act in this particular way. Neither mother nor child was aware of the underlying unconscious motivations.

This phenomenon, the production of neurotic behavior or illness in the child, in response to the "unconscious" of the mother, could impress one as a process brought about by telepathy or thought transference. Close analytic observation of mother and child, however, made it possible to explain these phenomena psychologically as the carrying out by the child of an unconscious wish of the mother. This wish was transmitted to the child by some clues in the mother's demeanor to which the children in my cases showed great sensitivity.

We know that between mother and child there exists a kind of preverbal communication and that infants are aware of changes in facial expression, shades in voice tone of their mothers, etc. In a film, M. Fries demonstrated the infant's extraordinary sensitivity to the mother's feelings, of which the mother herself may be unaware, but which are perceived by the infant, e.g., in the way he is being held by his mother. Where the mother, owing to her own emotional arrest, has an exaggerated need to keep her child in a highly dependent state, this sensitivity is maintained by the child in dealing with his mother. It is as though the child were in a prolonged infancy and continued to communicate with the mother in this primitive way. The wishes of such mothers have to be carried out because the child has not been allowed to sever its dependent ties in normal growth and because the often intense mental cruelty of the mother (evidenced openly or in the ambivalent attitude) makes it mandatory that the child carry out her unconscious wishes. The child in such a case very often does not react to the manifest content of the mother's verbalizations, which seem appropriate to the situation, but reacts instead to their unconscious intent. I should like to illustrate this with some case material.

A very inhibited mother had unconsciously identified herself with her five-year-old daughter, Laura, whom she used for the vicarious satisfaction of her own sadistic impulses. Laura had a difficult time with the children in kindergarten because of her provocative behavior. Actually she liked these children and wanted to be friends with them but antagonized them upon unconscious instigation by the mother. As a result they called her "naughty Laura" and reported her to the teachers, etc. The mother herself had always been a model child. One day Laura behaved very badly toward the maternal grandmother and her mother's only sister, saying hateful things to them. This was very unusual, because Laura, her grandmother's favorite, had always treated her with affection. The mother, who in her analysis was just then beginning to become conscious of her hatred toward her mother and sister, was very much startled and believed Laura to be reading her mind. When she reproached the child for her behavior, Laura said, "But you hate them and you really wanted me to tell them this." For the mother, this only confirmed Laura's telepathic abilities. But when she asked her, "What makes you say this?" and Laura casually answered, "I heard you talk to them on the telephone, mummy, and I could hear that you hated them," the mother suddenly understood how her own unconscious reflected itself in her daughter's behavior.

I should like to report two episodes from the analyses of a mother and her four-year-old daughter, Ann, who suffered from a severe phobia and psychosomatic symptoms.

Ann had been a feeding problem since birth. At four years she was still on a liquid diet—a formula elaborately prepared and fed to her by her mother. Up to the time when treatment started, there had not been a single meal without retching and vomiting. Ann had, since infancy, also suffered from periodical diarrhea and abdominal cramps. At three years of age she suddenly developed a phobia. She would not let her mother out of sight, refusing to stay with anyone else, even with her father or nursemaid. In the analysis of the mother it was revealed that she had an extreme need for complete control over the child. This was a result of her own unconscious dependence stemming from her relationship with her own mother. After Ann's mother had gained insight into her behavior and was able to relinquish her hold upon the child to some extent, Ann stopped vomiting and clinging to her. In her play analysis at the same time, Ann had been acting out her fears connected with growing away from her mother and becoming independent.

Suddenly she relapsed into her old symptoms without any apparent reason. In the analysis of her mother it was learned that Ann's relapse had set in on the morning after the mother had visited her gynecologist for a check-up. On the way home from the doctor the mother had the fleeting thought that Ann might have a recurrence of her phobia, because she remembered that Ann's phobia had originally started almost one and a half years ago, on the day after she had visited the same doctor. At that time he had advised her against another pregnancy because of a gynecological condition. With the mother's understanding and resolution of her unconscious wish for Ann to cling to her and to remain an infant for ever, Ann's symptoms disappeared as suddenly as they had set in. It was an instructive experience for the mother to find that the next morning when she casually said to Ann, "I am going shopping now and the maid will dress you and take you out," Ann accepted this very pleasantly, while the day before she had clung to her mother hysterically, vomited and complained about cramps at any attempt of the mother to leave the house.

Ann also suffered from car-sickness to the degree that she would not ride in the car at all. The car-sickness had set in suddenly together with the phobia when Ann was three years old. She had become so frightened then that she screamed when she approached the car. In the analysis of the mother, it was learned that at the time Ann's car-sickness had started, the mother had been extremely apprehensive with Ann in the car, continually asking her whether she felt nausea, wanted to vomit and the like, and that this behavior had been due to her unconscious wish to prevent Ann from riding in the car and thus excluding any possibility of Ann's having an automobile accident. The mother's unconscious wish for Ann not to be able to ride in the car had been transmitted to the child through her anxiety. After the mother had worked this through in her analysis (the car-sickness had not been discussed with Ann at all), Ann was able to ride in the car without any symptoms. In fact she enjoyed going on long rides with her father and it took a good deal more work with the mother to help her accept Ann's growing independence.

It would seem to me of interest to report some fragments

from the analyses of a manic-depressive mother and her five-year-old son, referred for treatment because of his psychotic-like behavior. Both mother and child were highly intelligent and capable of fine psychological understanding and both were in analysis for over three years.

In the analysis of the mother it was revealed that, unconsciously, her son represented to her her brother, born when she was five years old and killed in an accident when she was twenty-eight. After her brother's death she experienced a manic phase and decided to have a child to make up to her mother. Paul was born prematurely—almost exactly on the day of her brother's death anniversary —and was named after her brother. Up to the age of two and a half, while being raised by a nursemaid, his behavior was not conspicuous. When the mother suddenly discharged the maid and took care of him, Paul, who had been toilet-trained, began to wet and soil himself and became very spiteful and difficult to manage. He became more and more destructive, with unpredictable outbursts. One day when he was about four and a half years of age while his mother was talking on the telephone and so presumably did not notice, Paul swallowed ten thyroid tablets. This happened shortly before his mother decided to accept referral for treatment of him. The physician whom she called several hours later, when Paul was in a highly agitated state, as much as accused her of intentions of murder.

In her analysis the mother remembered that at about the age of six she herself had attempted suicide by drinking a poisonous liquid and was saved only because she was given immediate aid. That Paul had complied with his mother's unconscious wish to kill him was substantiated in later analysis. Only then his reaction was somewhat different. One evening when Paul was already in bed he asked his mother for a drink. She went into the kitchen, where she could not make up her mind what to give him—plain water, milk or cherry soda, and so she came back carrying three glasses. Paul looked at his mother and then at the three glasses. He drank the plain water. She felt very uncomfortable afterward—she was alone with him as his father was away on a business trip—and she decided to visit a neighbor after Paul fell asleep. While sitting there she suddenly recognized the reason for her discomfort— she was afraid to be alone with Paul because of her wish to harm him. At times such impulses would intrude into her consciousness in the form of obsessional thoughts, e.g., when she once bought a very large tea-kettle she found herself thinking that it could hold enough water to scald Paul. (Incidentally, her brother had been burned to death.)

Whenever Paul's father was away on business trips, Paul became especially destructive and provocative at home. In his play analysis at such times he would play the game, "The Witches have come back from Witches' Land." He resorted to much magic and day dreaming, and yet in spite of the supernatural powers which he attributed to himself his feeling was that he could not win out against the witches. His behavior could be understood as compensatory to an overwhelming feeling of helplessness and fear of his mother's sadism. He was extraordinarily sensitive to her facial expressions, which were not at all in keeping with what she was saying, and the shades in the tone of her voice. This was brought out on innumerable occasions. At a later phase in his analysis, when he was able to express this awareness openly (instead of acting it out) he would sometimes say, "This is the angry face you make," and like a mirror he reflected her mannerisms, of which she herself was completely unaware—the hanging lip, or the way in which she chewed the inside of her cheeks, the lip biting, finger pointing and cracking, etc. Just when Paul, who had started to attend a private school and had begun to feel more secure there, was walking to school by himself and playing with the children in the street, the mother made a swift decision to buy a private home out of the school district and in a neighborhood where there were no playmates for Paul. She rationalized that she did it for Paul so that he could be happier with a basement and a garden to himself.

In her analysis she could understand that she had acted out her vengeance on Paul and me, because I had prevented her from leaving her husband and thus taking Paul away from his father. There was a period then during which Paul refused to go to school. This was overcome through work with the mother by making her sufficiently aware that she did not want him to go, although consciously she was over-anxious for him to go. Paul himself had rationalized his behavior by telling me a story about a famous American writer who had never gone to school at all but had always stayed at home with his mother. His mother had told him this story. It was obvious that Paul understood his mother's motives, and, although he rebelled against them consciously, unconsciously he still felt compelled to comply with them. One day when she reproached him for hanging on to her and for not having any friends, he said, "If you really wanted me to have friends, why did you move away from X?"

Once Paul threw roller skates out of the window of the car, while his mother was driving. "I don't know why I did it," he told me with a grin. "I guess Dilly Dan pushed me." Dilly Dan was a fictitious character whom Paul had introduced into the play analysis. According to Paul, Dilly Dan was a naughty little boy who pushed Paul into acting explosively. In her analysis, however, the mother could recognize that she had wanted Paul to behave destructively in order to show him up to his father and the little girl with whom Paul had been trying to make friends and who were present in the car. Similarly, when the director of the school and Paul's teacher came for dinner one evening, Paul broke most of the glasses and china, wildly throwing all the pots and pans out of the dish closet. His mother watched the spectacle without interfering, rationalizing her non-interference to her flabbergasted onlookers by saying that she did not want to hinder Paul because she felt that he should be allowed to "express himself freely." In the analysis she understood that actually she had wanted him to carry on in this way because the director and his teacher liked him and because she did not want him to remain in this school.

She was extremely jealous of the relationship between Paul and his father, which unconsciously reminded her of her brother's relationship to her father. She therefore resented her husband's minding of Paul in the morning and insisted that it be left to her. There were scenes in the morning after Paul refused to get out of bed and wash and dress himself, when she felt that only by using force could she manage him. He would then mess and spill, smear toothpaste over the mirror, play with the razor blades, stuff the soap and towels into the toilet and bathtub.

One day the following incident occurred: Paul, in the bathroom, urinated at his mother, who stood there and did nothing, but when he flooded the bathroom, she got furious and beat him severely, shaking and cursing him. He said to her, "Why didn't you stop me?" And when his mother remained silent, he continued, "You really want me to do these things or you could stop me." This behavior of the mother was very reminiscent of the early part of his treatment, when Paul, who had been very amiable in the play session, as soon as he came into the waiting-room and saw his mother, would become very wild, and sometimes would spit into his mother's face. On such occasions, she sat there with a frozen smile and did nothing to stop him. (This was left to the analyst.) Her fury came out later, when there was no apparent reason, and then Paul would say to her, "But this doesn't call for so much anger."

In the analysis she remembered that whenever her little brother had been left in her care, he used to be very difficult and destructive, but when he was left with the neighbors, they would tell her mother what a nice boy he was. Recognition of her need to force Paul, and its origin, enabled her to gain some control over it, and resulted in a very remarkable change in Paul's behavior. He got up in the mornings, dressed all by himself, was cheerful and co-operative, so that one day his mother remarked to me, "I never gave him a chance before."

At a later phase of their analysis—Paul had made considerable progress by then—his class one day put on a play in which Paul took part for the first time. He had played his role expertly and his mother praised him very much. That evening when she asked him to do something, Paul stalled and took refuge on his bed. She felt herself becoming impatient when she said, "Come on now, get off that bed and do what has to be done."

"I will not," he replied. "If I get off this bed, you'll beat me and slap me and hurt me."

"Why, Paul? Whatever makes you say that?" she asked.

"Oh, *you* know," he said. "You have been furious with me ever since I was so good in the play this morning."

In the analysis of the mother that same morning, it had been brought out that although she had felt very proud of Paul, unconsciously she had resented his success, which, because she still identified him with her brother, had aroused her profound anger toward him.

Story games which Paul used to play with his mother at a later phase in the analysis reflected the changes in their relationship. In these games the bad mother was dead and he was happy and free, while in the witches' game before, he could never win out despite his magical powers. I should like to report the mother's verbatim account of one of these games and also to add that Paul's seemingly fantastic accusations against the bad mother were basically justified. At the start of his analysis Paul would incessantly play games in which he was tying and locking up dolls. I learned from the mother that Paul had frequently been tied with a rope to his chair in kindergarten and also locked up. Upon advice, the mother had a bolt made to his door and used to lock him up when he displeased her. When he was three and a half years old and once made a bowel movement on the carpet in his room, she got so angry that she stuck his face into it. Her cleaning woman at that time had said to her, "You are not a mother or you couldn't do that."

This is the account of one of their games:

PAUL: I must be a boy who has just come here to live with you. I must be very happy. Tell me a name that means very happy.

MOTHER: Felix. That's French and it means happy.

PAUL: Okay. I'm Felix. You see the reason I came to live with you here is that my mother died—and my house is all empty—and I had to find somewhere to live and so I came to live with you.

MOTHER: Well, we'll be very happy to have you, I'm sure. My son Paul has always wanted to have a brother like you and I'm sure he'll be delighted.

PAUL: Okay. My mother died. She was a terrible woman. She was a Fascist. In fact, she was a friend of Hitler's. If she hadn't died, I'd have killed her anyway. She was cruel to men. She never wanted to let them live. She killed my father. And she wanted to kill me.

MOTHER: Why, Felix, she sounds frightful. What dreadful things could she have done to you to make you feel this way about her?

PAUL: My mother used to torture me. She used to tie me up.

MOTHER: How old were you when she tied you?

PAUL: She always did it to me. She also locked me into my room. And she took everything away from me that I liked. She even didn't want to let me go to school.

MOTHER: Well, now you will see the fine school my son Paul goes to; he goes to X——— school.

PAUL: Yeah, she didn't want *me* to go to that school. But let me tell you something. I'm strong. I could have killed her many times, but I didn't want to. Now that she's dead, I'm having her jewel box packed with some of her things and they're going to be sent here to me. Boy, I'm glad she's dead!

## Discussion

In "Dream and the Occultism," (New Introductory Lectures on Psycho-Analysis, 1933), Freud, in discussing telepathy and thought transference, stated that unconscious wishes about to emerge into consciousness are those which are most suited for thought transference. It was my aim to demonstrate that the unconscious and preconscious wishes of the mothers in my cases transmitted themselves to the child through some concrete signs which could be received by the child through ordinary sensory perception (visible, audible or touch).

It would seem to me that in the case of Burlingham (1935), cited by Freud in his paper, in which no psychological explanation could be found for the child's reading his mother's mind as it were, a similar situation may have existed to that in my cases. The child may have been observant of minute indications unconsciously given by the mother. In cases where this close rapport exists, the child may react to apparently insignificant details lost sight of by others.

Children in this type of relationship with their mothers often make observations like paranoids who notice everything and who interpret it in reference to themselves. Exaggerated and distorted as such paranoid productions may appear at first glance, one can, in a study which includes both the child and the mother, detect that the child is not merely reacting to a fantastic image but to a real persecutor, namely his mother. This paranoid quality is especially marked in cases where the mother rejects the child because she unconsciously identified this child with a hated object from childhood (sibling or parent) or with a hated part of herself. For the child in such a situation it is vitally important to observe his mother closely and to employ omnipotence and sadism as his weapons in the struggle with the mother. Although these children rebel in the form of behavior deviations—neurosis, psychosis or psychosomatic illness—at the same time they carry out the unconscious wishes of their mother as if given a command.

Only in simultaneous analytic work with mother and child can this sensitive synchronization be understood and resolved. Treatment of the child alone in such cases does not reveal those forces to which the child is reacting nor does it make growth possible unless the mother can give up her own infantile strivings, which are reflected in the child's illness.

# PART 2

# SLEEP DISTURBANCES IN CHILDREN

# 4
# Sleep Disturbances in Children

## Introduction

Anxiety is the first sign of a developing neurosis. In young children it may not show itself as manifest anxiety but by affecting important functions such as sleep. What kind of a neurosis or behavior disturbance or psychosis the child will develop later depends on the age of the child, the nature of the trauma, the premorbid personality, the quality of object relations, and many other factors. This chapter deals with the clinical syndromes studied systematically and arranged in accordance with the developmental stages of the child. Early detection and proper assessment of the total situation are important factors, not only for correct diagnosis and treatment, but also for the prevention of a more malignant development later.

In any discussion of disturbances of sleep—whether of children or adults—it would be advantageous to define first the function of sleep. In *The Interpretation of Dreams* (1900) Freud made a revolutionary explanation of the phenomena of sleep and dreams, which, although the subject of persistent research, had for many centuries remained enigmatic. Freud (1920) introduced into the phenomenon of sleep an active principle—namely, the *wish* to sleep, that is, voluntary withdrawal from reality into sleep. If for neurotic reasons the wish to sleep is either absent or turned into its opposite, we meet with a neurotic sleep disturbance. He showed (1936) that the most common cause of interference with the wish to sleep is anxiety, stemming from repressed impulses and wishes and representing fear of a breakthrough of such impulses and wishes during the state of sleep. Freud attributed to dreaming an essential sleep-protecting function. By disguised expression of repressed wishes and impulses in a compromise between wish and defense against it, the dream serves the purpose of drive discharge during sleep and protects sleep against disruption by anxiety-evoking unconscious impulses.

It is of particular interest that most recent psychophysiological research into the phenomena of sleep and dreaming seems fully to confirm Freud's early assumption (Dement, 1964; Fraiberg, 1959). The findings of dream-deprivation experiments are particularly interesting in this connection. Serious personality changes and even psychotic episodes have been shown to occur in subjects who had been deprived of dreaming either by forced awakening, total sleep deprivation, or suppression of dreaming by certain drugs. This would indicate that dreaming is not only an essential nocturnal psychological activity, as Freud assumed, but perhaps even a physiological necessity.

Jekels (1945) pointed out that sleep on its deepest level represents a danger to the existence of the conscious ego. Awakening, according to Jekels, is not merely a passive occurrence but is achieved actively and with the help of the dream. He ascribed to the dream the function of serving as the waker of the sleeping ego. Dreams, therefore—and this was also proposed by Freud (1920)—have, above and beyond their function of providing hallucinatory wish-fulfillment and of guarding sleep, a more basic function: to awaken the sleeper from sleep and to provide a transition from the sleeping to the waking state. Under ordinary circumstances dreams facilitate a gradual transition from sleeping to waking. Under extraordinary circumstances—when there is an acute danger to the sleeping ego, either for physiological or psychological reasons—the dream has the functions of *abruptly* awakening the sleeper. This is usually accomplished by a nightmare or an anxiety dream, an aspect of dreaming dealt with more fully later in the discussion of pavor nocturnus.

Here again present-day experimental research into the phenomena of sleep and dreaming are most interesting. This research has established that dreaming with its hallucinatory and especially visual imageries takes place during REM (Rapid Eye Movements) sleep and "that during these phases a quasi waking level of physiological activity is attained, which does not occur in any of the other sleep stages" (Fisher and Dement, 1963, p. 116).

I should like to quote from the paper by Jekels (1945) the following passage because it seems to me that this might help us to utilize more adequately the meaning of dreams for our study of sleep disturbances in children:

> It also seems to me that the delicate and cautious process of restitution is evidence of the tendency to protect sleep as much as possible, a tendency to which the wish fulfilling tendencies of the dream may contribute their share. I do not think that the main objective of this function of the dream is to be the guardian or keeper of sleep. It appears rather that the main task of this function consists in its opening up the deepest wells of the life instinct—the wells of infantile sexuality—thus contributing all the libidinal cathexis necessary for the restitution process. [pp. 184–85]

## General Remarks

The subject of neurotic disturbances of sleep was reviewed by Fenichel and others in a symposium in 1942. In his discussion Fenichel reemphasized that for complete fulfillment of the function of sleep, tensions must be excluded from the organism. These tensions may be determined by external physical discomforts or by psychological conflicts. Impairments of the function of sleep were, he believed, encountered in every neurosis. That sleep disturbances are sometimes relatively slight, Fenichel explained by his observation that some neurotics had learned to render innocuous by secondary measures sleep-disturbing stimuli emerging from repression. He found "that the sleep-disturbing effect is greater for those involved in acute repressive conflicts than for those who have learned to avoid struggles by means of rigid ego attitudes." Both incipient failure of repression and intensely experienced affects—especially sexual excitement without gratification—apply particularly to insomnia in certain phases of childhood.

No systematic studies of neurotic sleep disturbances of children have yet been made; this study represents such an attempt. I have arranged, therefore, the clinical material to be presented in accordance with the phases of the psychosexual development of the child. The basic and characteristic conflicts of each developmental phase are reflected in sleep disturbances that may be considered as typical of each phase. Each successive phase adds its own characteristics to the sleep disturbances of the preceding phases, if the sleep disturbance has not been treated or has not subsided on its own accord.

The occurrence of mild and transient sleep disturbances during the oedipal phase (between three and five years of age) can be considered a typical feature of childhood in our culture. The severer disturbances of this phase, however, especially the acute exacerbations leading to persisting sleeplessness, are pathological phenomena indicative of serious emotional disorder. A persistent sleep disturbance during this phase can be considered to be the manifestation of an infantile neurosis of the child. There is a definite analogy between these sleep disturbances and the traumatic neuroses of adults with regard to genesis, dynamics, and treatment. This and other aspects of this type of sleep disturbance will be discussed in more detail later in the chapter.

I consider a better knowledge of sleep disturbances in children important not only for the purpose of appropriate immediate therapy, but even more so for prognostication of later neurotic illness and for prevention of such illness. I wish particularly to emphasize that disturbances of sleep in children are the first reliable signs of emotional conflicts, and that this symptom precedes any other overt indication of such conflicts in the behavior of the child.

## Sleep Disturbances in Infancy

### *The Oral Phases of Development During the First Year of Life*

A peacefully sleeping infant is the essence of relaxation and tranquillity. It seems inconceivable that infants should suffer from neurotic insomnia, rather than from sleeplessness incident to illness, pain, hunger, and other physical discomforts. Because infants normally require a great amount of sleep, a prolonged and severe interference with it in a very young child should be considered to be of serious import, even in the absence of other signs of distress. The organism of the infant is dependent upon its environment for protection from too intense stimulation, which creates in the infant states of excessive tension. According to Freud (1936), "The flooding with excitation of an organism without adequate defenses is the model for all later anxiety." Anxiety is the most frequent cause of sleeplessness in children, as it is among adults. Unless the physical and emotional needs of the infant are reasonably gratified, or until its physical and psychological tensions are relieved, it cannot achieve sleep sufficient for its requirements. As it is not possible to explore the sources of the infant's anxiety directly, it is necessary to examine carefully not only the infant but even more so its environment, particularly its mother and her feelings regarding her child, in the search for the sources which provoke and maintain the state of tension in the infant. Rarely is a psychiatrist or psychoanalyst consulted for such a sleep disturbance in an infant. This is the domain of the pediatrician, and having been a pediatrician myself before training in psychoanalysis I have had rich clinical experience with this problem pediatrically. It is only by chance that I had occasion to see a few cases of severe sleep disturbance in infants in my analytic practice. I should like to present two cases in order to illustrate and to discuss the dynamics and management of such a situation.

In one case, the maternal grandmother was my patient and in her analysis she frequently spoke of her grandchild, an infant of four months. She and the entire family were very much disturbed by the fact that the baby cried incessantly, particularly at night, and could not be calmed, even with sedatives. The many pediatricians who had examined the child—even with X-rays—could neither find a cause for this behavior nor suggest an effective therapy. The grandmother, applying some of the insight and understanding which she had gained from her analysis, arrived at the conclusion that the baby cried and could not sleep because it was very unhappy. "She sighs like an old person," my patient would tell me, "and food has to be forced into her and then she vomits it up. I don't think she wants to live." Her daughter, the mother of the infant, lived at my patient's house and depended entirely upon her parents, who had not allowed her to marry the father of the child, whom they considered a fortune hunter. The infant's mother came to see me upon my patient's suggestion; she was very frank about her feelings regarding the baby. In the beginning, she had hoped that because of her pregnancy her parents would allow her to divorce her husband and marry the father of the child. When she realized, however, that they would not agree to this and when she also recognized that this man was a highly irresponsible individual, she would have liked to have an abortion. But she was afraid to do so because of her parents and because of the advanced stage of pregnancy. In the hospital she would have liked to place the baby for adoption but had not dared because of her parents' opposition. Now she felt that the infant was to blame for her unhappiness. She could not look at the child; she could not pick her up and could hold her only with great repugnance. She was aware that the baby's nurse was rather forceful with the infant but this did not trouble her; it would be better if the baby were dead anyway. She could not discuss these feelings with her mother, although she felt that her mother also did not accept the child. Her father was so angry that he had not even seen the child yet. Being a genuinely warm person who felt frustrated and bitter about the outcome of her love affair, she was able to accept the interpretation that she was projecting her responsibility for her unhappiness onto the child, and was able to overcome her rejection of the baby. The effect of the change in the mother's feelings upon the child was most impressive. Within a short time, her restlessness disappeared; she was able to sleep and her eating also improved considerably. Contributing factors, it would seem, were also the changed attitudes of the grandparents, who began to show affection for the child. Since no other treatment had been instituted and in fact all medication had been withdrawn, the sudden and marked change in the infant's behavior may justifiably be attributed to the change in the attitude of the environment toward the infant, particularly that of the mother (M. Sperling, 1949b).

In the second case, the mother of a six-month-old girl reported that the child was waking up many times during the night, crying incessantly; even when held by her mother it was difficult to quiet her. During the day her sleep was very restless, and she would frequently awaken screaming and anxious. The child's mother was an overanxious person, who was beginning to show signs of emotional strain that were believed to be caused by the child's insomnia. Investigation proved, however, that the mother's emotional condition was the cause and not the result of the child's sleeplessness and that the mother actually prevented the child from sleeping. Her overconscientiousness about the child was a disguise for her unconscious hostility. She had a fear that something would happen to the child during sleep and she was constantly watching her. She would listen over the crib to determine whether the infant was breathing and became very apprehensive when it was quiet. She would then fuss with the bedclothes until the child awoke, which provided her with a reason for taking the child out of the crib. To advise that the child be permitted to sleep was useless because of the severity of the mother's neurosis that was affecting the child in this way. Treatment of the mother provided an opportunity to follow up the development of this child for two and a half years. The marked improvement of sleep corresponded with changes in the mother's feelings toward her child (M. Sperling, 1955a).

## The Role of the Mother-Child Relationship in the Genesis of Infantile Sleep Disturbance and the Role of Such Disturbances in the Etiology of Severe Emotional Disturbance in Childhood

The importance of the mother-child relationship for the emotional development of the child is now generally accepted as a fundamental factor of child psychology. The deleterious effects of a disturbed mother-child relationship have been described from direct observation by investigators such as Fries (1945), Ribble (1943), Spitz (1946), to name only a few. The method of simultaneous psychoanalytic treatment of disturbed children and their mothers that I introduced twenty years ago has opened up new insights for the understanding and treatment of emotional disorders in children (Chapters 3, 9, 13, 21; M. Sperling, 1951). This method permitted me to study (and to modify) the modes of this interaction between mother and child and the subtle ways in which the mother's unconscious feelings are transmitted, as well as the child's specific pathological responses. The two cases of infantile sleep disturbance just reported and the material to follow are illustrative examples of the role of such a disturbed mother-child relationship in the etiology of early sleep disturbance of the child. There are no references in the psychoanalytic or psychiatric literature to the role of infantile sleep disturbance in the etiology of severe emotional disturbance in later childhood except for my own contributions to this subject (see also M. Sperling, 1949b). I have pointed out there, and I am stating again here, that I consider a severe neurotic sleep disturbance in infancy a rather ominous symptom that may be the first and only clinical indication of a psychotic development in later childhood. Adequate assessment of such a sleep disturbance in its incipience, and proper management of such a case, may forestall a malignant later development. I had occasion to treat a considerable number of children with severely disturbed behavior in whom sleep disturbance in infancy had been the only manifest neurotic feature of the early life. The atypical behavior and other manifestations appeared only much later. I should like to present some case material pertinent to this issue:

CASE 1. Fred was nine years old when he was referred to me because of his strange behavior. After a short period of observation, it became evident that Fred's mother, herself a latent schizophrenic, was in need of treatment and unable to cooperate sufficiently to make it possible to treat the boy in his home environment. He was hospitalized, and while he was receiving psychotherapy in the hospital I worked with his mother. I learned that Fred had had very severe sleeping difficulties, practically from birth. During the first year of his life his mother had had to carry him in her arms almost all night every night without being able to quiet him. Later he suffered from frequent nightmares. According to his mother, Fred had been difficult to manage from infancy but it was at about the age of six when he started school that his peculiarities became most apparent. His sexually uninhibited attitude toward his mother also became apparent then. He shared the parental bedroom and often was in bed with his mother who, on the one hand, was seducing him and, on the other, was very unpredictable and often openly sadistic toward him. While we can only speculate upon his early (first year of life) sleep disturbance, considering it as a result of the intense—psychotic—anxiety stemming from his oral sadistic impulses (this boy later showed definite paranoid trends with severe anxiety), we are on certain ground when we interpret his later sleep disturbance as a defense against overwhelmingly strong sexual-aggressive impulses toward his mother and murderous impulses toward his father. One day, prior to his admission to the hospital, Fred remarked while walking with his mother: "Don't we look like husband and wife? If you want me to, I could kill father." To sleep in such a situation meant to expose himself to the danger of being overcome by his impulses and of carrying them out in a state of impaired consciousness. That this was psychodynamically so was corroborated by the change in the nature of his sleep disturbance as a result of his treatment and separation from his home environment. Fred's sleep, on his admission to the hospital, had at first been severely disturbed, but after a stay of several months there he was able to sleep through the night comparatively well. During his weekend visits home, however, he had a very difficult time in falling asleep and developed a ritual. After he went to bed, he would start a discussion with his mother saying, for instance, "I will fall asleep now. Is it all right?" If she said that it was all right, he would not be satisfied and would reply that she should have answered something else. No matter how she responded to his question, he was not satisfied and it soon became obvious that this was a means by which he wanted to keep her and himself awake. At a later point, he was able to explain to his mother what had forced him to act in this way: "At first, I was afraid that I might die in my sleep and so I had to stay awake. But then I was afraid that you might die in your sleep and so I had to talk to you to make sure that you were still alive."

Fred, because of his belief in his magical powers, expected the immediate fulfillment of his destructive wishes, and he tried to cope with them in a way similar to that of the compulsive neurotic. This case illustrates the importance of voluntary withdrawal from the outside world as the active dynamic element in the onset of sleep. In a state of depression and in states of acute influx of aggressive destructive impulses with a decrease in object cathexis, sleep is intentionally avoided because it would mean destruction of the object world and of oneself. According to

Simmel (1942), in certain neurotic, prepsychotic, and psychotic states such a danger to life seems to exist from within and sleep has to be avoided for that reason.

CASE 2. Mike, a boy of six and a half, was referred by the school because of his infantile behavior, which was so disturbing that he had to be expelled. From earliest infancy Mike, because of a severe sleep disturbance, had been given sedatives, with little effect. According to his mother, he had not slept at all during any night of his first year of life. Between one and two years of age he became very destructive and unmanageable, but then his sleep improved. At the age of three, he again suffered from insomnia, from which time on he slept with his mother. In this case also, aside from the very pronounced infantilization, the results of maternal seduction were obvious. His mother sometimes allowed Mike expression of his impulses with little restraint and at other times imposed upon him severe deprivations. This inconsistency led to a pathological ego and superego development. The clash with the outside world and society occurred when he entered school. In the treatment, Mike was aggressive toward me, in an openly sexual manner jumping at me, trying to poke at and to touch my genitals. Dolls he would grab, pull their legs apart, and poke between the legs. He would pull their arms out, poke at their eyes, tear their hair off, and then throw them to the floor, seeking to smash them completely with his feet.

I learned from the mother that, during this period of his treatment, his sleep had improved remarkably. This could be explained by the fact that Mike was releasing his sadistic impulses during his play sessions. During part of the anal phase, that is, from age one to two, Mike had had a period of comparatively undisturbed sleep. This, as we will hear later when discussing the role of the anal phases in the etiology of sleep disturbances of children, is not what one would have expected in this case. The explanation for this was found in the fact that Mike's mother had allowed him discharge of anal sadistic impulses freely. But she had severely restricted any open expression of phallic (sexual) behavior and of masturbation. At the same time she was overstimulating Mike by overexposure and close physical contact (taking him into bed with her) and thus increasing his sexual tensions.

It is known that the outbreak of a severe neurosis, and particularly of a psychosis, is often preceded by an acute disturbance of sleep. Simmel (1942) raised the question: "Is it not conceivable that the start of a schizophrenic process might be at least associated with a disturbance of the temporary ability to regress by means of sleep?" In this connection again the findings from recent sleep deprivation experiments are of particular interest (Murray, 1959). This would mean that under the pressure of intense, repressed sexual and destructive impulses sleep has lost its economic function of serving as a refresher for the ego and has to be avoided because of the danger of an imminent psychotic break. It is known that an individual may wake from sleep, or rather from a dream, with a full-fledged psychosis. The struggle between the psychotic ego, which wants only sleep and which has a strong tendency to regress to its prenatal condition, and the nonpsychotic ego can be observed in latent psychotics and particularly in depressed patients. Such patients have a difficult time awakening and getting out of bed in the morning. There is a continuous struggle between the ego, which wants to awaken and to turn toward reality and the object world, and the other part of the ego which wants to sleep and to turn away from reality.

It is characteristic that such a sleep disturbance initiating a psychosis may show itself resistant to sedatives, even when given in large doses. Illustrative is the case of a twelve-year-old boy in whom the outbreak of an acute schizophrenic episode of a paranoid type was preceded by severe insomnia, which had lasted many months and resisted all sedation. This boy not only did not sleep but avoided going to bed. He would walk through the apartment all night long, spending most of his time in the kitchen where he could keep the light on without disturbing his sleeping parents and sister. This acute and intense insomnia had occurred at the time when his only sister, nineteen years old, had become engaged and was soon to be married. Ralph, my patient, had shared his sister's bedroom since he was a little boy. Not only had he shared the room with her, but he had often slept in the same bed with her. When he was ten and had been away with his mother and sister in the country he had shared their room, and he had also had a short period of insomnia then. He had behaved very strangely at this time and was heard mumbling obscene words to himself. He had always been a somewhat peculiar boy, impressing people as mentally retarded (which he was not). He kept to himself, had no friends, and showed an infantile attachment to his mother. His mother rejected him openly; she had not wanted a second child and not a boy. Ralph had been a great disappointment to her. In his case, also, the outstanding feature in his early infancy was a sleep disturbance. Ralph had to be hospitalized and sleep had to be induced by the intravenous use of hypnotics.

The topic of sleep disturbance and psychosis will be taken up again in the discussion of pavor nocturnus and sleep phobias.

## Sleep Disturbances During the Anal Phases of Development Between Ages One and Three

Freud (1930) ascribed the genesis of neurosis in man to the repression of primitive drives, a factor indispensable for the process of civilization. During the short span of its second and third years, the child in our culture has to accomplish the amazing feat of being transformed from a primitive being into the little citizen of our homes and nurseries. During this period toilet training is at its height or completed, and repression of anal-erotic and anal-aggressive impulses takes place even if toilet training has not been instituted prematurely or harshly. During this period mild sleep disturbances of a transitory nature are therefore a rather common occurrence. Whenever such repressions are excessive and abrupt and additional traumatic experiences aggravate the situation, the effect will be reflected immediately in more severe disturbances of sleep. Additional traumata may be the birth of a sibling (which often prompts the mother to accelerate the training of the older child), surgical operations, and other severe illnesses. Emotional overstimulation and seduction are particularly traumatic because they prematurely stimulate phallic impulses and thus reinforce anal conflicts and intensify the child's repressive struggles.

B. Bornstein (1935) demonstrated that a two-and-a-half-year-old child's fear of lying down to sleep was the result of an acute fear of soiling the bed during sleep, which had been reinforced by premature phallic impulses. A similar instance in a child of eighteen months was reported by Wulff (1927). In this case it was of particular interest that the child's sleep disturbance was relieved through counseling the parents about their handling of the boy's toilet training, that is, by advising the parents to relax their demands for abrupt suppression of anal impulses. More recently S. Fraiberg (1950) reported similar observations of sleep disturbance in children during the anal phases of development. These psychoanalytic observations are confirmed by the studies of behavioral psychologists. A. Gesell (1943), in his behavior profiles based on large-scale studies of small children, considered sleep disturbance at this age (from fifteen to thirty months) as one of the developmental features of the period.

## Management

In the early stages, before the sleep disturbance has fully developed, treatment may be very rewarding. Very good results can often be obtained indirectly by guidance of the mother. It is necessary to provide substitute gratifications and outlets for anal-erotic and anal-sadistic strivings through physical activity and appropriate play such as smearing (playdough), tearing, cutting, coloring, etc. It is also necessary to advise mothers to relax their demands for too early and too rigid cleanliness and conformity. In this area one has to be careful to avoid the pitfall of going to the opposite extreme by not setting any standards for performance. I should like to illustrate this aspect of faulty habit training as it specifically relates to faulty sleeping habits by citing two somewhat extreme cases of this kind, one of a nearly two-year-old and one of a ten-year-old child.

CASE 1.   The mother of a twenty-two-month-old boy consulted me because of his severe insomnia from birth; it had become progressively worse. From the history and my observation of the boy's behavior, it was clear that the mother had overindulged him. She had been afraid to allow him to cry at night because her husband became angry when his sleep was disturbed. She had resorted to hiring someone to sit with the child throughout the night. She was desperate because all these measures, including sedatives, were not effective. The boy screamed so loudly during the night that the neighbors complained. She then decided to take care of the child herself but soon felt exhausted and unable to cope with this problem. While the mother was giving the history, holding the boy in her lap, he was trying to prevent her from talking, obviously annoyed with me because I was diverting his mother's attention from him. The mother was clearly afraid of him and was capitulating to him, although she seemed at the same time to be annoyed with him. When I told him in a firm tone to keep quiet and to allow his mother to talk, the effect startled his mother. He suddenly became quiet, looking at me open-mouthed, but he did not cry. His mother had told me that he was rather a friendly child, very active and demanding, seldom crying during the day. When I suggested that she let him cry through several nights without attending to him, she raised the objection that even if her husband permitted it, the neighbors would have her evicted. I assured her that I would give her a certificate to the effect that she had taken this course of action upon medical advice, and that if her husband objected she should board him with friends for several nights. This soon proved successful and during the past three years the boy has been sleeping peacefully. This case is a disturbance of sleep from faulty training. That it was rather easily corrected was a consequence of the early age of the child and the fact that the mother was not seriously neurotic.

CASE 2.   A ten-year-old girl suffered from chronic and severe insomnia to such a degree that she scarcely slept throughout the night. She would fall asleep toward dawn and then could not be awakened. Her father held her while her mother dressed her; when she finally got to school— usually an hour late—she would fall asleep. The school recommended psychiatric consultation. The parents and the pediatrician believed that the child's condition was organic and were skeptical about psychotherapy. The mother told me that the girl had been a very small baby with so "tiny" a stomach that she believed that she had to feed her hourly during the night. By the age of two she would consume a quart of milk in the course of the night. The father had formed the habit of playing with the child while she was awake during the night. When the mother felt that the child was strong enough to do without these feedings, she found that the girl would insist upon having her bottle, clinging to it all night even when it was empty. Sedation, corporal punishment, deprivations had no effect and only contributed to making her a serious problem. She had also, it transpired, shared the parental bedroom from infancy up to her tenth year. She was still usurping her mother's place in the parental bed with the father. The mother slept on a cot.

Returning to the problem of managing such sleep disturbances in children during the anal phases of development, I want to point out that at this stage the counseling of the parents is often the most effective therapeutic factor, one which also has a preventive value not only for the specific symptom of sleep disturbance but also for faulty character development. Even when the anxiety resulting from the repressed anal impulses has already led to reaction formation and compulsive traits of character in the child, treatment at this early age is comparatively simple and effective.

The practice of taking a child into the parental bed, as a means of restoring sleep disturbed by nightmares, serves only to provide an additional source of overstimulation for the child whose disturbance of sleep itself indicates its inability to cope with its aggressive and sexual impulses. It has the effect of adding fuel to the fire. The remedy is usually to eliminate the source of the overstimulation, which very often emanates from a mixture of parental prohibition and seduction. (A case in point is that of Freddie, Chapter 5.)

## Sleep Disturbances During the Oedipal Phase Between Three and Five Years

The oedipal phase is the classical period of sleep disturbance in children. During this age, from about three to five, almost every child experiences a transient period of disturbed sleep. While most children can surmount this temporary disturbance, we find that some develop a permanent disturbance of sleep, often of a rather severe character. In most of these cases, a very similar setting is found. These are children who, on the one hand, are exposed to sexual overstimulation, often bordering on seduction, by their parents. On the other hand, these same parents, and with boys especially the father, do not allow overt expression of sexual impulses and by their behavior increase castration anxiety and the conflicts of the oedipal phase.

The repression of the oedipal wishes and the conflicts about infantile masturbation with the resulting fears of castration are reflected in the specific sleep disturbances of this age. In most cases they are mild and temporary, with occasional nightmares and difficulty in falling asleep.

The circumstance under which such disturbances become chronic and pathological I have found always to be a defeat of the child's task of renouncing its oedipal strivings. Faulty parental attitudes are an important factor. Particularly harmful is the suppression of any overt manifestation of sexual feelings, sexual curiosity, and jealousy in the child, with concomitant overstimulation and seductive behavior toward the child. This is seldom done in a way which is manifest to the parents, but is sensed as seduction by the child who reacts to it. Maids, governesses, relatives are often agents of gross excesses in such pathological over-stimulation of children.

The onset or exacerbation of difficulty with sleeping is often attributed to such various external sources as television, movies, unusual excitement, or frightening experiences. Although many children are exposed to these experiences, only a few react to them in this particular way. The fact that only some individuals exposed to the same stimulus develop a traumatic neurosis is an indication that the trauma has activated repressed experiences from the past in those who have a latent predisposition. Precipitating traumata are the birth of a sibling, surgery, or illnesses which are interpreted as castration by the child. The following cases will illustrate this.

CASE 1. A six-and-a-half-year-old boy had been preoccupied with fears of death for a year and a half. He had had no experience of death in his family. He would cry before going to bed because he was afraid he might die. When finally he fell asleep he would soon wake up in fear. This had become progressively worse. At five years of age, when driving past a cemetery, it was explained to him that this was a place where dead people were buried; that their bodies slept there forever while their souls went up to heaven. His mother described him as a model child, who was greatly attached to her and very considerate of his baby brother, one and a half years old.

Very soon, during sessions of play therapy, an intense repressed hostility and death wishes toward his brother became evident. This brother had become the immediate rival for the affection of his mother at a time when the boy found himself in the difficult situation of having to renounce the mother as the oedipal love object. His unconscious death wishes against the brother-rival had gained reality with the discovery that there was a special place from which dead people did not return. Fearing he might be punished in like manner for his evil intent, he saw in going to sleep an acute danger which was associated in his mind with death. The mother had in many ways fostered his unhealthy attachment to her, at the same time putting a premium on the repression of aggressive and sexual behavior. Release and working through of these impulses in play therapy and modification of the attitude of the mother resulted in a striking improvement in the boy's sleep within a short time.

CASE 2.   Frank, six and a half years old, had suffered from severe nightmares and difficulty in falling asleep from the age of four and a half. The reason for seeking treatment at this point was an acute exacerbation of the sleep disturbance, owing to an experience in school. The teacher had discussed fire prevention in class, and had given the children a questionnnaire to be filled out by the parents. The boy, becoming preoccupied with the fear that there would be a fire in the house, refused to go to bed, walked through the house to see that the gas was turned off and that everything was under control. The mother was also concerned because he was rather timid, did not play with other boys, and was not attentive in school.

Early in his analysis Frank would run out of the office several times during each session to see whether his mother was still in the waiting room and to present her with love letters which he either dictated to me or managed to write himself. When later he was convinced that he could reveal his true feelings, he vented an intense resentment against both parents, which proved to be connected with having witnessed the primal scene during his nocturnal wanderings and with the birth of his sister when he was two. Clinging to his mother was a reaction-formation to unconscious hostility, and his possessiveness of her was his way of taking her away from the father and the sister. The intensification of the sleep disturbance was the result of repressed, dangerous, aggressive impulses to set the house on fire when everybody was asleep and he himself not fully awake.

## Sleepwalking (Somnambulism) and Allied Phenomena and their Relation to Neurotic Insomnia

The two cases of acute sleep disturbance just cited are a good illustration of the neurotic type of oedipal sleep disturbance. Both children had a relatively well-functioning ego and superego and were able to handle the intensification of their oedipal conflicts, their aggression, and their sibling rivalry by repression. They were able to maintain repression of these impulses during the day without manifest disturbance of their behavior. They were able consciously to tolerate the intrusion of derivatives of their repressed impulses in disguised form—in one case the fear of death and of dying and in the other case the fear of fire and of burning—that is, they were able to tolerate a certain amount of anxiety without symptom formation and impairment of their functioning. Sleep, however, to both these children, because they were in a state of acute and abrupt repression, represented a danger, of a breakthrough of these repressed impulses during the state of sleep. They defended themselves against this danger by neurotic insomnia, that is, by trying to stay awake and by awakening fully with the help of anxiety dreams when these repressed impulses threatened to overcome the sleeping ego.

I would like to compare the behavior of these children with that of children who sleepwalk. The essential difference is that the sleepwalking child is only partially, that is, motorically, awake during the sleepwalking, while the child with neurotic insomnia is fully awake during its nocturnal activities, whatever these may be—getting out of bed, walking through the house, going to the bathroom, parents' bedroom, etc. In contrast to the sleepwalking child, who has amnesia for his nocturnal activities, the child with neurotic insomnia never leaves the house during his nocturnal wanderings; he is at all times fully aware of his actions and has complete recall of the events of the night.

Sleepwalking is an insufficiently understood and inadequately studied phenomenon in children. It is by no means a rare occurrence; to the contrary it is found rather frequently and often in combination with night terrors (pavor nocturnus). I should like to present some clinical material to be used as a basis for the investigation of the dynamics of sleepwalking and for study of the differences and similarities in the dynamics of this syndrome and neurotic insomnia as well as of the prognostic significance and treatment of this type of sleep disturbance.

Sleepwalking children are rarely brought for treatment because of the sleepwalking unless it is very excessive or associated with night terrors. Treatment is usually sought because of other symptoms such as behavior difficulties, school problems, etc. I have found that sleepwalking children as a rule suffer also from coexisting psychosomatic symptoms, especially from so-called allergic conditions such as hay fever, bronchial asthma, migraine headaches, petit mal, epilepsy. Neither these psychosomatic symptoms nor the behavior problems, however, are regarded as related to the sleepwalking by untrained observers.

CASE 1. Walter was twelve and a half when he was referred for treatment because of behavior and learning difficulties. Although he was a boy of superior intelligence, he had consistently failed in most of his subjects but was not left back because the public-school rules did not allow this. His parents felt that the best way to handle him was to deprive and punish him. His mother seemed particularly annoyed with him and the father claimed that she behaved in a rather uncontrolled fashion with the boy. I learned from Walter that he was in the habit of waking up several times at night and that he also was an occasional sleepwalker. His habit of waking up nightly and going to the bathroom was considered as quite normal by his parents, and since the sleepwalking happened infrequently, they attributed no significance to it. Walter's analysis revealed that he was sexually highly overstimulated and that this, to a very large extent, was the basis for his difficulties. In working with the mother it was found that she had unconsciously identified Walter with her younger brother, who had died of acute appendicitis at the age of eight. Walter's mother, who had been an adolescent when this happened, blamed herself for her brother's death because she had prevented her mother from calling a doctor in time by saying, "You don't call a doctor for a bellyache." She seemed to have some concern about her son's sleep disturbance, as indicated, for example, by the following remark: "My brother had nightmares and used to sleepwalk and people say that children who do that die young. I was worried about Walter for that reason and calmed down only when he passed the age of eight." It was at that time, also, that she gave birth to a little girl and turned her attentions to the baby. Until the early part of his analysis Walter's home environment continued to be a sexually overstimulating one. His mother took showers with him, there was a great deal of sexual play with his little sister, and an unusual physical closeness with the father.

The analysis of his nightmares revealed many homosexual fantasies, e.g., he was run over, crushed by a truck, attacked from the rear, etc. He had had some actual homosexual experiences with boys at camp. At home he would walk around in the nude and sleep in the nude, but he was very much concerned about exposing his body to boys. He claimed that they teased him because he did not have pubic hair and because he looked "girlish." Walter had complete amnesia for his sleepwalking. On many occasions he had endangered himself seriously while sleepwalking and leaving the house. Once in the middle of the night he was found, sitting in a parked car by a passing motorist, who brought him home. His many perverse and aggressive incestuous impulses could be brought to the fore and worked with therapeutically only after he had stopped sleepwalking.

CASE 2.    Harry was nine years old when brought for treatment for a severe school phobia. In the course of treatment it was found that he also suffered from a sleep disturbance that had preceded his school phobia, and that he had been sleepwalking during the past year. He also suffered from psychosomatic symptoms, beginning with bellyaches and diarrhea, and now was sneezing and coughing in a manner suggestive of an incipient bronchial asthma.

During the past year he had had on a few occasions nocturnal convulsions suggestive of epileptic seizures. The parents, and particularly the father, did not seem to be concerned with any of these symptoms but interested only in getting Harry back to school as quickly as possible. The father had unsuccessfully tried every means himself, including severe corporal punishment and deprivation, before reluctantly accepting psychiatric treatment, which he considered a treatment for weaklings. The father had had an unusually close relationship with Harry from infancy and had been instrumental in Harry's developing severe reaction formation against anal impulses at an early age. Both parents had been overconcerned when he was little. They had lost one child before Harry was born and another infant when he was two years old. It was apparent that the father was trying to shape Harry into some kind of idealized image of himself. Harry was the only child until age five, when a sister was born.

Harry developed a severe sleep disturbance followed by the school phobia and other symptoms after his father returned home from an absence of two years. Harry was then six years old. The psychological records, including a Rorschach taken when Harry was eight and a half years old, showed that he was struggling with tremendous repressed aggression and lived in terror of being overwhelmed by his impulses. A tendency to withdraw had been noted, but there were no concrete evidences of disturbed thinking or deterioration of reality testing at that time. Clinical exploration indicated that a rapid deterioration of personality had taken place in the intervening half-year. Harry appeared close to a psychotic break. His nightmares were of such intensity and vividness that he would awaken confused, unable to differentiate between dream and reality. More recently the feeling of reality of his dream images carried over to the daytime. He had amnesia for his sleepwalking. He also had brief lapses of memory during the day that seemed to be the beginning of petit mal. His father had found him on many occasions in the paternal bedroom (the parents slept in separate bedrooms) in the middle of the night. Harry seemed unresponsive, staring at his father, seemingly unaware of his surroundings and actions. His nightmares dealt with violence and death, something terrible happened in them, somebody was getting killed. He had difficulty recalling them and appeared very frightened when talking about them. He had a recurrent nightmare that appeared to be a link to the sleepwalking. This dream dealt with the disappearance of his father; there was a devil in it, and an explosion.

It was found that there was very close physical contact between Harry and his parents, the father being alternately seductive and sadistic. The mother was still bathing him and cleaning him after bowel movements. There was an enormous intensification of both positive and negative oedipal strivings, which had to be abruptly repressed because of the intense aggression and murderous impulses against the father. Because of his intense unconscious aggression his castration anxiety was of psychotic proportions. He was turning in masochistic (homosexual) submission toward the father in reality. At the same time he was trying desperately to cope with his repressed homosexual and suicidal impulses. This was expressed in the sleep disturbance at night and the school phobia by day. The various somatic symptoms served as emergency outlets for his destructive drives. His main mechanism in dealing with his instinctual drives was to externalize the internal and therefore inescapable danger which he was trying to accomplish by sleepwalking at night and in the school phobia during the day. (For discussion of the interrelated dynamics of sleep disturbance of this kind, phobia, and paranoia, see Chapters 7 and 9).

When Harry's panic lessened and he was apparently accepting me as his therapist, the father, I believe, threatened by this, withdrew him from treatment and placed him in a military school. The father, who appeared to me to be a borderline case with marked depressive and paranoid trends, was inaccessible to any psychotherapeutic intervention. I felt that under the circumstances separation from the sick father was therapeutic in itself.

CASE 3. Bill was also nine years old when he was referred to me because of night terrors and sleepwalking. I shall limit myself here to the discussion of his sleepwalking and come back to this case in the chapter on pavor nocturnus. Bill was the youngest child in the family and the mother's pet boy. He was very much overprotected by her and kept away from boyish activities. Because of frequent nightmares, which he had had from an early age, he had been allowed to come into the parents' bedroom and into bed with his parents. He could never fall asleep when his mother was not at home and, on such nights, he would either go to bed in the parents' bed or wake up shortly after he had gone to sleep and walk into their bedroom while in a sleeping state. The father did not dare to oppose his wife, but did not quite agree with her upbringing of the boy, thought him sissyish and would have liked him to be more aggressive and "a fighter." The family standards regarding manners were very high and perfect behavior was required. On the other hand, the mother exposed herself freely to the boy when dressing or bathing and treated him as the "innocent little boy." Bill's acute increase in night terrors and sleepwalking between ages eight and nine could be understood as a direct reaction to his parents' being out evenings more frequently than they had in the past. The mother had rationalized her overconcern for Bill in this way: before Bill was born, she had suddenly lost a son at the age of eight from an acute respiratory infection. Bill, too, suffered from frequent colds and he had hay fever; and for these reasons the mother had been staying at home most of the time, afraid to leave him, although there was a grandmother, a maid, a sixteen-year-old daughter, and another son ten years older than Bill in the house. When Bill had passed the critical age of eight, the mother became more daring and often left the house. It was then that his night terrors and sleepwalking increased to such an extent that his parents could no longer overlook them. The referring pediatrician who had seen him in several attacks gave me the following description: Bill would either be sitting in his bed, gesticulating and talking, or jumping around on his bed, as though fighting with somebody. Frequently he would jump out of bed, walk around, turn on the water, and perform imaginary fights. When his parents found him near the staircase one night, just attempting to walk down, they became sufficiently alarmed and accepted the pediatrician's suggestion for psychiatric treatment.

In the treatment, Bill at first could not remember anything about his nocturnal activities. After some time he was able to recall some nightmares in which he found himself lost or in danger or—as in one of his nightmares—walking straight into a lake. As treatment progressed he began to remember some of the events which took place during his night terrors and the sleepwalking. The main theme was fights with his father; they would have duels in which he triumphed over his father. He also talked in his sleep and would say, for example, "get into reverse," "this tackle isn't good." There was a special sensation attached to his sleepwalking which was always present. It was a feeling that the person toward whom he was walking was coming closer and closer to him and was becoming enormously big. This was very frightening to him. There would seem to be some connection between this sensation and the sensation that epileptic patients experience in their aura. However, Bill did not suffer from petit mal, epilepsy, or headaches.

## Discussion

From approximately thirty children in whom sleepwalking was a symptom, I have selected these three cases because they highlight certain features which I consider typical of this condition. In my case material the number of boys was far greater than that of girls. It seems to me that this is not an accidental finding but that this type of sleep disturbance may actually be more frequent among boys because of its relation to castration fear. Striking in these cases is the similarity in parental attitudes characterized by a two-faced morality. Under the guise of paren-

tal concern these parents permitted themselves release and gratification of pregenital (perverse) impulses of an exhibitionistic,
voyeuristic, coprophilic, sadistic nature, at the same time prohibiting any overt expression of such impulses in their children. This
leads to a pathological ego and superego development of the
child, a subject that I shall discuss further in the section on
pavor nocturnus. I consider this as a specific etiologic factor in
the development of sleep disturbance associated with sleepwalking. The oral phases of development are usually satisfactory in
these cases, but beginning with the anal stage there is a progressive pathological development with intensification during puberty and adolescence. These children, in contrast to those who
suffer from neurotic insomnia, do not have a latency period. The
difference lies in the different character structure and the different mechanisms of defense against instinctual drives they use.
The child with neurotic insomnia, by awakening fully from the
dream, does not permit himself any acting out of forbidden or
dangerous impulses in reality. The child with pavor nocturnus
and sleepwalking by not awakening fully and by continuing the
dream, as it were, permits himself to act out in disguise some of
these impulses in reality. I would put the differential emphasis
between these two groups on *action*. The sleepwalking child
needs to act out in reality, without being fully aware of his
impulses and actions and with amnesia for them. There is a similarity between this behavior and that of acting-out patients and
perverts. The child with neurotic insomnia, very much like the
neurotic patient, can accept fantasy gratification instead of
acting out of impulses in reality.

The dynamic situation—and this is important for therapy
—in cases of sleepwalking is similar to the situation encountered
in patients with character disorders and acting-out behavior. As
in sleepwalking, so in this type of acting out, repressed memories
are not admitted to consciousness and the patient acts them out
in some disguised way in real life, without being aware of the
meaning of his behavior. In these cases the patient is able to
admit these memories to consciousness and to tolerate them,
that is, actually remember them instead of acting them out, only
after some amount of analysis and with strengthening of the ego.

In sleepwalking the urge for discharge of these impulses is even stronger, while the pressure of the superego does not permit this because the impulses are of a homosexual and sadistic nature and often of a criminally perverse nature. It is of interest that in all these children death, and especially their own death, played a great part in their emotional lives. In most of these cases the children were actually a replacement for a dead child, which in the fantasy of the patient meant that, were it not for the death of the sibling, his parents would not have wanted him and he would not have been born. This may contribute to an intensification of the self-destructive drives in these children. The sleepwalking child is awake bodily but he refuses to awaken fully and to assume awareness of and responsibility for his actions. The urge to act out destructive impulses seems to be particularly strong and the ability to tolerate anxiety, that is, some awareness of these impulses, very low. It is not coincidence, in my opinion, that these sleepwalking children had psychosomatic manifestations also, such as asthma, hay fever, allergy, and in one case convulsions; this is, rather, another indication of their inability to tolerate tension and their need for immediate—that is, somatic —discharge of their threatening impulses.

Sadger (1920) has emphasized the fact that for the sleepwalker the motoric awakening of the lower extremities is characteristic. The legs are used for running away from a danger. Actually, sleepwalkers have a tendency to leave the house. A tenyear-old sleepwalking boy had once walked to a neighbor's house in the middle of the night. He thought that his parents were not at home, he said later. Actually, his parents and little sister were all in their beds sleeping. It is erroneous to assume that the sleepwalker is completely unaware of his environment. In this case the boy had very strong destructive impulses directed toward the entire family and in his state it was safer not to acknowledge that they were all fast asleep but to leave the house for their protection, as it were. At another time his parents had found him, again in a sleepwalking state, busying himself at the gas range, where he had already turned on the jets. He also suffered from persistent headaches and violent attacks of sneezing, which had been diagnosed and treated as hay fever. In the analysis, these symptoms revealed themselves as the distorted and somatically converted expression of severe chronic anger against his stepfather, who would often punish him severely by beating and deprivation. Similarly to Harry, this patient too appeared overtly submissive toward his stepfather while his aggressive and homosexual impulses were expressed in his symptoms.

In conclusion, it would seem that the danger from which the sleepwalker wants to run away is an internal one, namely, the succumbing to deeply repressed, intense sadistic, and perverse impulses, which is turned into an external danger similarly to the mechanism used in the dream and in phobias. The close dynamic relation between these conditions and other (hysterical) states of amnesia and epileptic fugues would seem to me to be explicable also on this basis (L. J. Sachs, 1957).

## Typical Fears Associated with the Sleep Disturbances of the Oedipal Phase and Some Remarks on Management

There are typical fears associated with the sleep disturbances of this phase, such as fear of attack, injury, death. These are expressions of the child's fear of punishment for masturbation and his castration anxiety. Typical also are fears of monsters, ghosts, burglars, robbers, kidnappers. These fears on closer investigation reveal themselves as projections of the child's own aggressive impulses directed toward the parents or sibling rivals. The case of six-and-a-half-year-old Dick may illustrate this.

Up to the age of five, Dick had been the only child and, according to his parents, a model one. He was rather timid and passive, openly afraid of his father. He also showed signs of a beginning compulsion neurosis. He had had frequent nightmares from about the age of three. During the last year, his sleep had been very disturbed and he would come into his parents' bedroom at all hours of the night with signs of great fear. For this reason, prior to the time he started treatment, the boy had been sleeping with his mother while the father slept in the boy's bed. He had fears of the dark, could not stand any noise during the night, and constantly talked of burglars, robbers, and kidnappers. When he was five, a sister had been born and his parents were delighted with his wonderful attitude toward the baby. The acute exacerbation of his sleep disturbance and his many fears, however, revealed themselves in the analysis as the result of strong sadistic impulses directed toward his sister and mother—at whom he was angry for having had the baby. His fears of burglars, robbers, and kidnappers were a projection of his own aggressive impulses and wishes regarding his sister, whom he would have liked to be kidnapped, and his father, whom he wanted to rob of the mother.

Dick's case lends itself also for a brief discussion of some basic principles in the treatment of such sleep disturbances. His anxiety dreams and his night and daytime fears, his timid and effeminate behavior, and his learning inhibitons were related to the excessive repression of aggressive and sexual impulses. In the treatment of the neurotically inhibited child there is inevitably in the course of the treatment a transitory phase of freeing of these repressed impulses from the symptoms in which they are expressed, namely, sleep disturbance and fears. This therapeutic reeducation of the child should preferably be carried out in conjunction with the parents, so that they do not enforce immediate repression of the freed impulses that the child in the course of his therapy will learn to sublimate, that is, to use constructively. In order to get the child ready for this a part of his neurosis and character deformation has to be removed in therapy.

The analyst or therapist has to be able to establish a relationship with the child that enables the child to make a positive identification with his therapist in the important therapeutic aspects and to be willing to accept discipline from him. Only then, will the analyst be able to convey the feeling to the child that he can tolerate his destructive impulses in consciousness without having to act them out instantly. There seems to be a naive belief that psychoanalytic therapy with a child is permission given by the analyst to the child to act out all of his impulses. If this were so, such a therapy would certainly not only not help the child, but would increase his internal and external difficulties. Being at the mercy of his impulses, he would only get into more serious conflicts with his environment in his attempts to act them out. The child must feel that the analyst, while understanding his urges and his need to release them, will stand by and not let him be overwhelmed by them. If the child does not feel safeguarded in this way by his analyst, he will be anxious and distrustful, looking upon the analyst as a person who seduced him into being "bad" and thus getting him into conflict with himself and his environment. The child always, and rightly so, interprets complete permissiveness on the part of the adult as weakness, and as a result may become increasingly destructive in order to test how far he can go without being stopped. Every analyst has had the experience when treating children that his permissiveness is felt as a threat by the child. The child, like the adult patient, wants the analyst to be as afraid as the child himself is of his impulses so that the analyst will not insist upon bringing these dangerous impulses to the fore. The analyst must not fail in this test; it is this specific experience that so many children have never had in actual life with their parents, who are afraid of their child's impulses.

Dick's parents were compulsive personalities with very high standards. His training had been strict and discipline in his case meant to deny the *existence* of any "badness." After he realized that he did not need to impress me with his gentlemanlike manners and that I neither approved nor disapproved of his actions, his behavior changed very much in the playroom. He began not only to throw things around but insisted that he could hurt me and that I had to pick everything up for him. While it was necessary to allow him to bring to the fore and to release his repressed aggressive impulses, at the same time his behavior had to be interpreted and it had to be made clear to him that I was not his mother, whom he wanted to abuse and punish for sleeping with father and having the baby. It was necessary to insist that he not deliberately destroy things, and that he help me clean up the mess. It was also necessary to guide the parents so that they should not restrict him too severely as they had before but yet not allow unrestrained behavior. It is the acceptance of the existence of these feelings in the child without condemnation which is essential, and not the permission to act out such impulses. To the child such permission means that he is not able to control his impulses, if he is aware of them. Therefore, these children operate with excessive repression and denial of such impulses and become overly "good," passive, and generally inhibited. The child has to learn to tolerate his impulses in consciousness and to acquire control over them, instead of either acting them out in reality or repressing them. This is only possible with parents who are tolerant of such feelings in their children but not of such behavior. Dick, for instance, had never been allowed to smear or to play with finger paint. He had had a very strict period of bowel training with abrupt repression of anal erotic and anal sadistic impulses. It was then that his sleep disturbance began, and became intensified during the oedipal phase with repression of sexual impulses and masturbation. The birth of the sister was an additional trauma that acutely aggravated his sleep disturbance.

Dick's parents, because they felt guilty for having restricted him severely in the past, now tended to go overboard in the opposite direction by not setting any limits and by encouraging release of destructive impulses instead of offering more suitable indirect outlets. This phase of treatment could be managed successfully with the parents. Dick, who remained in treatment long enough after his sleep disturbance had cleared, was able to work through and to consolidate his "new" personality.

There is a general tendency to misinterpret psychoanalytic principles and to mistake an intermediary phase of treatment for the goal of treatment. In treating sleep disturbances in children one should be aware of the fact that the sleep disturbance is a symptom of the child's neurosis and one form in which the child expresses his neurotic conflicts. It is inadvisable to limit treatment to the removal of the presenting symptom only (in this case the sleep disturbance) because the neurotic conflict, if left unaltered, will seek expression in other symptoms and behavior. It is also sometimes not desirable to remove the sleep disturbance too quickly because some parents bring the child for treatment only for the inconvenience that the child's sleep disturbance causes them and when other measures have failed to stop it. Such parents will withdraw the child from treatment as soon as the sleep disturbance clears, that is, during the intermediary stage, without giving the child a chance to finish treatment.

Five-and-a-half-year-old Roy is such an example. He came for treatment because of a severe sleep disturbance which had become increasingly worse, so that hospitalization was being considered for him. He suffered from nightmares and night terrors and kept his parents up most of the night. His nightmares revealed rather openly his death wishes for his parents; usually both his parents would be killed in them or disappear in a sewer, etc. Roy would awaken in great fear and, to make certain that they were still alive, he would keep them up with him for the rest of the night. He was afraid to fall asleep because of these nightmares and for that reason refused to go to bed altogether. Roy shared his parents' bedroom from birth. He was resentful of both parents—of his mother who was overstimulating him sexually in many ways, and of his father for being very strict with him and for having intercourse with the mother. As soon as Roy was able to bring to the fore his repressed (sexual and sadistic) impulses, his sleep disturbances cleared up and his parents, mainly concerned with his disturbed sleep and the night terrors, withdrew him from treatment. One rather amusing feature from Roy's treatment indicates that he was in the transitory phase. One day he came to my office with a baseball bat, which he put down beside him while we played a game of cards. When I asked him why he needed the baseball bat, he said, "To hit you over the head in case you win." He had become outwardly aggressive during this phase of the treatment. That his parents had not given us a chance to work through this liberated aggression was one of the reasons for my regretting his too quick "recovery."

I have no follow-up on Roy, but I would be inclined to think that he continued in the direction of externalizing his aggression, of which his parents at that point apparently were more accepting than of the sleep disturbance. I consider the type of sleep disturbance associated with night terrors, from which Roy suffered, as an indication of a serious personality disturbance, which may become fully manifest in puberty and adolescence. Another case in point is Ruth (see Chapter 5).

## Pavor Nocturnus*

Pavor nocturnus is so frequently encountered in children that pediatricians and parents have come to regard it as a phenomenon of childhood, to be placed in a category similar to certain daytime fears considered typical in children.

If we consider the fact that the wish-fulfillment tendency of the dream is to be observed in young children in an almost undisguised way, the occurrence of a pavor nocturnus is a somewhat surprising finding. We assume that in children the ego and the superego are not so strongly opposed to the demands of the id as in the adult, and will permit fulfillment of frustrated or warded-off wishes to come through in the state of sleep, with little or no objection.

What then causes children to suffer from the sleep disturbance known as pavor nocturnus?

I should like briefly to review some of the known theories on this subject first, before discussing my findings of my psychoanalytic investigations of pavor nocturnus in children. In *The Interpretation of Dreams*, Freud (1900) makes brief reference to this subject, stating that pavor nocturnus is a nocturnal anxiety attack with hallucinations occurring frequently in children, the anxiety being a result of the warded-off and distorted sexual impulses. In accordance with Freud's view, Jones, in his fundamental work *On the Nightmare* (1931), considers pavor nocturnus in adults as a form "of anxiety attack essentially due to intense mental conflict, centering around some repressed component of the psychosexual instinct."

* Some of this material is taken from the paper, Pavor Nocturnus, *J. Amer. Psa. Assoc.*, 6 (1958), 79–94.

Since pavor nocturnus is essentially a phenomenon of child-hood, it is a matter of some surprise that the psychodynamic fac-tors have been almost exclusively reconstructed from adult analy-sis, and that its investigation thus far has not been approached more directly through study in children. A case reported by J. Waelder (1935), that of a seven-year-old boy who had pavor nocturnus, corroborated Freud's concepts of the sexual nature of warded-off instinctual wishes in the genesis of pavor nocturnus. M. Klein (1932) stressed the role of aggressive impulses in pavor nocturnus. Waelder and others who have observed pavor noctur-nus in children are impressed with the phenomenological differ-ences between this manifestation in children and the nightmare syndrome of the adult; Waelder in fact considers pavor noctur-nus essentially a childhood phenomenon (1935).

The pavor nocturnus of childhood as I have studied it in children of all ages, from two years to adolescence, has manifes-tations that do not occur in the nightmare of adults. Jones (1931) considers three features as essential characteristics of the adult nightmare: (1) agonizing fear; (2) a feeling of oppression with a sense of suffocation; (3) the feeling of utter helplessness and paralysis. These features, although present at times in chil-dren, are in many cases missing from the pavor nocturnus picture of childhood. In fact, in most cases, the pavor nocturnus in chil-dren is characterized by hypermotility rather than by the paral-ysis characteristic of the adult. In her detailed account of the psychoanalysis of the seven-year-old boy, Waelder describes the pavor nocturnus attacks in which the boy would suddenly awaken, sit up in bed, cry out, scream, thrash about with his body and arms as if he were fighting. He was obviously acting out a dream, and although he was talking and moving about, he was neither completely awake nor actually asleep. In this case, psychoanalytic study of the pavor nocturnus brought out another major difference between pavor nocturnus in children and night-mare in the adult, namely, the adult's vivid recall of the content of the nightmare, and the child's retrograde amnesia for the pavor nocturnus attack. In some cases, adults' nightmares may have a recurrent theme and, in a way, remain with the patient during his waking state as a conscious memory. Although this type of behavior does occur frequently in children, the pavor nocturnus in which there is hypermotility and retrograde amnesia is decidedly characteristic of children.

On the basis of clinical observations and dynamic considerations I suggest a differentiation between three types of pavor nocturnus in children. I would like to discuss their clinical criteria, their etiology and their dynamics as well as the prognostic significance of this symptom for the future development of the child.

*Type I*: Pavor nocturnus with hypermotility, psychoticlike behavior during the attack, and retrograde amnesia for it.

*Type II*: Characterized by a sudden onset of pavor nocturnus dramatically following a specific trauma. This type is, from the etiologic, phenomenologic, and dynamic points of view, closely related to the traumatic neurosis of the adult. In fact, this type of pavor nocturnus may be regarded as representing the initial phase of the traumatic neurosis of the child, and might well be referred to as the traumatic type of pavor nocturnus.

*Type III*: Characterized by the occurrence of nightmares with varying contents during sleep, from which the child awakens fully, in anxiety, and with a vivid and often lasting memory of the contents of the dream. Often the parents may not even be aware that their child suffers from this type of pavor nocturnus, because these children frequently lie awake in anxiety for many hours during the night, but do not disturb their parents' sleep. These children suffer comparatively "silently," as it were, while the children of the first group are rather noisy during the attack and always manage to awaken and to disturb the parents. This form of pavor nocturnus may be called the neurotic type. It is most closely related to nightmare syndromes of the adult. In this group also belong the milder and transitional forms of Types I and II.

In Type I, the psychotic type of pavor nocturnus, there is an early and insidious onset, with marked intensification during the anal and particularly the oedipal phases. Both the positive and negative oedipal strivings are highly intensified, with repressed murderous impulses toward both parents, and there is a progressive course during latency, extending into puberty. These children grow up in an atmosphere of varying degrees of continuous sexual overstimulation by one or both parents, older siblings, or other adults in the child's environment; e.g., they are permitted to witness or even to participate in all kinds of sexual intimacies between their parents. They usually share or have shared the parental bed or bedroom for long periods of time. These parents use the child for gratification of their own perverse sexual needs (coprophilic, exhibitionistic, voyeuristic, sadistic, homosexual) with various rationalizations, while the child's overt sexual expressions and activities are repudiated, often in peremptory and cruel fashion. This two-faced moralistic attitude of the parents leads to a pathological development of the superego with specific structuring of it, namely, a "split of the superego." The mechanism of the splitting of the superego was first described by M. Klein (1948), who considered it to be a mechanism "analogous to and closely connected with projection." Otto E. Sperling (1929), using the same term, developed his concept of the "split of the superego" from the psychoanalytic study of perversions in adults. He found that part of the superego of these patients not only condoned but, in fact, demand the patient's perverse behavior. The corrupted superego of the child, prevented from unification and consolidation by the inconsistencies of his parents, is not opposed to the breakthrough and acting out of the forbidden impulses in a state in which the child is not asleep and yet not fully awake. The dynamics of this type of pavor nocturnus would bear out the validity of Simmel's ideas (1942) concerning the relation of sleep and psychosis. Simmel stressed the disturbance in psychotic states of the ability to awaken during the day. There is a great similarity between this dream state with motoric awakening in pavor nocturnus and certain psychotic states.

Pavor nocturnus, Type I, can be considered as a psychotic episode occurring under the special condition of sleep; it is limited to the nighttime and is without recall of the events of the night. The interrelation of the pavor nocturnus of this type with somnambulistic states, petit mal, fugue, states of amnesia, and psychosis has been pointed out in the section on somnambulism. It is beyond the scope of this chapter to do more than point to the possible transitions between these states. One factor of paramount importance should be emphasized here: the prognostic significance of this type of persistent pavor nocturnus for a later psychotic development. Conversely, any study of psychotic behavior in children bears inquiry into the incidence of an earlier pavor nocturnus pattern, as we have seen in general with sleep disturbance in infancy.

Two clinical examples may illustrate these points.

CASE 1.   Nine-year-old Bill, whose sleepwalking has been discussed in an earlier chapter, is of particular interest because his development was followed up to adulthood. He was treated by the writer from age nine to eleven and then again from age fifteen to seventeen and a half, and seen for shorter periods until age twenty, at which time he started full analysis, which terminated after three years. His was a typical case of pavor nocturnus, Type I, with early onset, and severe exacerbation during latency and into puberty. All the factors that I consider of etiological significance in such cases were found in almost pure culture in the case of Bill, aggravated by a particularly neurotic mother, a seductive father, and a brother older by ten years. In his pavor nocturnus attacks Bill would be sitting in bed, talking and gesticulating, or jumping around and engaging in imaginary fights. Invariably he would end up in his parents' bedroom and remain there for the rest of the night. In treatment, he succeeded in lifting the amnesia for some of his pavor nocturnus attacks, especially one in which he was dueling with his father.

Since the pavor nocturnus attacks had ceased and the boy appeared to be functioning very well, the parents considered him cured and discontinued treatment when he was eleven years old. Bill was seen by the writer again at the age of fifteen. According to his parents, he had done very well until he became excessively preoccupied with his violin and wanted to quit school. His loss of interest in his studies was the primary concern of his parents, who were unable to appreciate the boy's serious condition. However, they consented to further treatment.

Bill was withdrawn and distrustful; he appeared very close to a psychotic break. The analysis of his nightmares, of his sadomasochistic fantasies, of his preoccupation with sexual crimes and criminal perverts, and of his fears of homosexuality brought great relief of his panic. The summary of the Rorschach taken when Bill was sixteen years old states: "On the whole, the impression is of a very bright, gifted boy, who is suffering from a paranoid schizophrenia. There is no danger of immediate overt psychotic breakdown, but the schizophrenic process would seem progressive and pervasive." While I did not share the pessimistic prognosis based on the Rorschach and the opinions of consulting psychiatrists, this Rorschach is here cited in support of my belief of the close interrelation of the pavor nocturnus, Type I, with psychosis.

At seventeen and a half, Bill was well enough to go to an out-of-town college and function in a college community. At twenty, analysis was suggested so that he could work out many unresolved problems, especially his latent homosexuality and his relationship with women. The outbreak of a frank psychosis in early adolescence in this case had been prevented, I am convinced, through the earlier treatment; it is my belief that the final outcome of untreated severe cases of pavor nocturnus of Type I is psychotic development. I have a twelve-year follow-up on Bill. He has been able to choose and to pursue successfully a difficult professional career. He is married, the father of two children, and leads a very satisfactory life.

CASE 2. I should like to cite briefly a case of pavor nocturnus type in another nine-year-old boy whom I did not treat but whose mother was in analysis with me for several years. Her analysis, undertaken for reasons unrelated to her son's disturbance, disclosed a particularly intimate relationship between the boy and herself. She would think of him as her "little husband" since he looked like her husband, and was lovingly attached to her, while she felt that her husband, who suffered from a chronic depression, was often detached and distant. Arnold was apparently accorded some privileges of a husband by his mother; he could lie down with her and fondle her breasts, tell her what to wear and how pretty she looked. She expressed annoyance about Arnold's excessive masturbation in her presence.

Arnold would awaken during the night, cry, and fail to recognize his environment. When he was three-and-a-half years old and a brother was born, there was an increase and intensification of the pavor nocturnus attacks. When he was five years old, the parents consulted a child specialist, who reassured them and did not advise treatment. At the time the analysis of his mother began, his pavor nocturnus attacks were frequent and frightened his mother. He appeared to be very agitated, would jump out of bed, run around, often saying, "He'll kill us if he finds us in the nest. I'll kill him." He was not awake and did not recognize his environment and would fall asleep when his mother would lie down with him. For these attacks, he had complete amnesia. In the analysis of the mother it was found that the reference to the "nest" was a fantasy which the mother apparently shared with her son, a phenomenon which H. Sachs (1942) has described. She would repeatedly dream of herself and the members of her family as birds in a nest or in a cage. She had a fantasy in which she imagined herself as a little bird in a nest fed by the mother bird. In actuality, Arnold and his mother owned a pair of parakeets and together cared for them.

The mother was particularly impressed with the marked changes which took place in her son's total behavior concomitant with her analysis. During the first year of her analysis, his pavor nocturnus attacks had stopped completely. The mother had remained in analysis until Arnold was eleven-and-a-half years old. He is now thirteen and his development seems to have proceeded very satisfactorily.

That a nine-year-old boy with pavor nocturnus, Type I, was so decisively influenced by the analysis of his parents (his father was also undergoing analysis at that time) is a suggestive observation which raises one very important question and sheds light on another. Is it possible to bring about a decisive change in the structure of the superego of a nine-year-old child indirectly by changes in the behavior of his parents? In this case, it was particularly the behavior of the mother who, for neurotic needs of her own, had from his earliest infancy seduced the boy into a highly pathological relationship with her which had been changed through analysis.

The phenomenon which this case helps to explain is the following: it is a common experience that the pavor nocturnus attacks of young children may be brought to an end without treatment by the mere fact that the parents carry out consistently the advice not to take the child into bed with them. Friedjung (1924) reported such experiences first. This phenomenon cannot be explained only by the elimination of overstimulation. My impression is that these children are keenly aware of their parents' true feelings and that they cannot be followed by lip service. They interpret and react to the change in the parental attitude not only as the parents' decision to set limits for the child but to set limits for the parents as well. Children need the example of a firm, honest, and consistent superego. In the case of Bill, the analyst had no or little contact with the parents, who were patently unwilling to modify their behavior in any way. In the case of Arnold, the analytic work was with the parents only.

I consider pavor nocturnus, Type I, characterized by hypermotility, hallucinations, and retrograde amnesia, to be a specific childhood phenomenon, which does not occur in this form in adults. There is an insidious onset and progressive development into puberty, at which time serious character disorders, perversions, or even psychotic states may become manifest. The most important etiological factor is chronic sexual traumatization. From a dynamic point of view I consider the structure of the superego as the most significant factor in these cases. I have referred to this as a "split in the superego." The pathologically intensified pregenital sexual and the phallic impulses are permitted by the superego to break through and to be acted out in the disguise of the pavor nocturnus attack. Sleepwalking, which as we have seen is often associated with pavor nocturnus Type I, is the form of sleep disturbance which in some cases may be continued into adulthood. I am referring in this connection again to the interrelation of this symptom with fugue states, states of amnesia, and certain psychotic states.

The second type of pavor nocturnus, the traumatic type, is characterized by a sudden onset following an acute trauma such as surgery, sickness, accident, death in the family, birth of a sibling, etc. There seems to be a definite analogy between the pavor nocturnus of these children and the traumatic neurosis of adults. This type of pavor nocturnus occurs in children of all ages and is characterized by fitful sleep, crying out during sleep, frequent awakening in anxiety from a dream which represents a repetition of the original traumatic situation, and a need, especially in younger children, to cling to the protecting parent. Very often, this phobic clinging is carried over to the daytime.

I shall deal with this type of pavor nocturnus more fully here because the findings from the treatment of these children would seem to me to provide a better understanding of the traumatic neurosis in adults. I would like to recapitulate briefly some concepts of traumatic neurosis developed by Freud in *Beyond the Pleasure Principle* (1920).

According to Freud, the traumatic neurosis is the result of a breakthrough of the stimulus barrier. The fact that of those exposed to the same stimulus only some individuals develop traumatic neurosis, while others do not, is an indication that the trauma has activated repressed experiences from the past in those who have a latent predisposition. An outstanding characteristic of traumatic neurosis, at least in its early phases, is the tendency of the patient to relive the traumatic situation in nightmares. Freud considered these dreams to be an exception to the theory of dreams, which is based on the principle of wish-fulfillment. In fact, this phenomenon of recurrent nightmares in traumatic neurosis is used by him in support of the concept of repetition compulsion. Freud explained that the function of such dreams is to help to bring about, by repetition in the dream of the traumatic situation, a belated mastery of the stimulus, the lack of which has caused the traumatic reaction in the first place.

In my opinion, it is difficult to conceive that, for the purpose of mastery, there would be a recall of a danger situation that could not be mastered in the waking state, during sleep when the ego and superego are least prepared to cope with it. To the child in the posttraumatic state, when both the narcissistic equilibrium and his object relationships are profoundly disturbed, sleep, due to its withdrawal from reality and from the real objects, may itself come to represent a danger situation—the danger of permanent loss of reality. While the memory of the trauma can be warded off during the day when the mother is present and when motility and other outlets are available, its intrusion cannot be avoided during sleep. In fact, in some cases, the state of sleep itself, because of the immobilization and the separation from the mother, becomes associated with the traumatic situation and may be feared and avoided because of this. It would seem to me that the revival of the traumatic experience in the nightmare has the function of precipitously awakening the sleeper and bringing him back to the reality which, painful though it may be, is preferable to the intolerable psychic state that results from the imminent danger of being overwhelmed by the original trauma. Jekels' concept (1945) of the function of the dream as a waker and of awakening as an active process seems especially applicable here. When the continuation of sleep and dreaming becomes a threat to the maintenance of the psychic and possibly of the physiological equilibrium the nightmare serves as the abrupt waker. To be overwhelmed by one's own impulses equals loss of control of one's self, which in turn equals loss of one's mind and loss of reality. By awakening, the sleeper now actively extricates himself from the traumatic situation (relived in the dream) over which he had no control and which he suffered passively when it occurred in reality. Awakening thus represents both mastery of the trauma by actively interrupting the traumatic situation of the dream and an attempt to reestablish the shattered narcissistic equilibrium by securing the protective presence of the love object (mother).

The traumatic effect of an experience comes mainly from two sources: (1) the feeling of complete helplessness provoked by the traumatic situation; (2) the specific meaning that the experience holds for the child. In this connection, Otto E. Sperling's psychoanalytic work with adult cases of war and civilian traumatic neurosis (1950a) is of particular interest. He found that the traumatic effect of the experience derived from the fact that these patients had interpreted the trauma as a command of their superego—parent(s)—to submit to the ego-alien wishes, such as enemy propaganda, illness, or even death. This concept of "the interpretation of the trauma as a command" proved to be particularly applicable to the behavior of the children with traumatic pavor nocturnus that I treated.

The traumatic type of pavor nocturnus is characteristic of the early phases following a traumatic experience, before definite symptom formation has set in. Eventually these children will develop similar sequelae to those studied in treatment of the traumatic neuroses of adults. There will be neurotic, psychosomatic, or psychotic disorders, depending upon age, level of fixation, degree of disturbance in object relationship, and other factors.

The case of a four-year-old child, in whom this type of pavor nocturnus could be observed *in statu nascendi* and resolved in the acute phase, might serve as an illustration.

Olga developed an acute pavor nocturnus and a very serious anorexia following a tonsillectomy. This child had been very carefully prepared for the operation. Her mother was with her until she was taken into the operating room. Olga remained in the hospital for only one day, during which the mother was with her most of the time. I saw Olga two weeks after the tonsillectomy when she was in very poor physical condition, had lost weight, refused food, even liquids, and hospitalization because of dehydration was considered. She had nightmares in which she screamed. "Don't, I won't, I can't, no, no, I don't want to leave this room," and screamed for her mother. She would wake up five or six times a night, go into her parents' bed, saying that she was frightened. She appeared depressed, withdrawn, and negative, and clung to her mother. At the age of eight months Olga had exhibited fears of dogs, fire engines, noises, and moving objects. At that time, she had been abruptly weaned from the breast and bottle, transferred to her own room, and toilet training had been instituted. Still she developed well until the time her brother was born, when she was not quite three years old. At three and a half, she was sent to nursery school. She seemed to accept the separation from her mother, but became a "finicky" and dawdling eater. She seemed to be quite attached to her brother and was heard on several occasions expressing the wish to have a genital like his. Olga's case is very similar to that of two-year-old Linda, described in Chapter 9. Linda developed an acute pavor nocturnus following the birth of a brother. A few months prior to this, Linda had been placed in treatment with me because of a peculiar kind of sleep disturbance: recurrent attacks of nocturnal paroxysmal tachycardia. The relation of nocturnal psychosomatic "attacks" and sleep disturbance will be taken up briefly later in the chapter. The birth of the brother and the onset of the pavor nocturnus occurred while I was on vacation. Play analysis revealed intense repressed oral-sadistic impulses directed against her mother and baby brother. It further revealed that she had interpreted in retrospect a tonsillectomy she had undergone at eighteen months as an oral castration and punishment by her mother for her oral-sadistic impulses.

Olga, through her play and by verbalization, revealed that she too had interpreted the tonsillectomy as a punishment for oral-sadistic wishes (directed toward her mother's breast and her brother's penis) and had experienced it as an oral castration inflicted upon her by her mother.

This was brought out very instructively in a game with a clay doll. She was the mother, the analyst was the sister, Olga, and the doll was the baby brother. On one occasion, she got angry with him, grabbed him, hit him, saying that he was dirty and naughty. She then bit off his head, and was furiously cutting his neck with a knife, saying that her tonsils had been cut out by a lady doctor. The analyst restored his head and also put back his little clay penis.

which Olga had removed several times before, without any interference. When she again took it off, I asked her casually, "What's that?" She said, "A little nothing." I said, "But this is something. It is his little penis." She got very angry and said that he had to have his appendix taken out. She prepared him for the operation which she performed by cutting his belly and pulling out clay representing the appendix and the contents of his belly.

That the anesthesia had been a particularly traumatic experience was brought out in her play and in her nightmares. The "No, no" and "Don't" in her nightmares expressed her struggle against being overcome by the anesthetic against her will, an event she had been unable to prevent in reality, but from which she could escape by waking up when she relived it in the nightmare. The experience of being overwhelmed by the anesthetic and made unconscious against one's will would seem to be the prototype for the fear of being overwhelmed by one's own impulses and to lose control and contact with reality. In this connection, the case of an eleven-year-old girl, who had had a tonsillectomy at age ten, is of particular interest. She remembered her dream while under anesthesia. She saw colored circles running around. She tried to push them around the corner, but she couldn't. A mocking voice said, "Rhoda, you are going crazy." This was her interpretation of anesthesia as the command, "You must be crazy, must die." She was terrified. She didn't want to cry, but she had to when she came to. Since then she had a funny feeling in her dreams. It was like being in another world and feeling that she could not come back as she had thought that she would not come back from the anesthesia. She came for treatment because of her strange and withdrawn behavior. She had once tried to choke herself by grabbing her neck with both hands. In Olga's case the preparation for the operation, the covering of the eyes, and the anesthesia were a very important part of the surgical game and repeated with precision again and again. She did not know what tonsils actually looked like and was relieved when it was shown to her by shaping them from clay. She said, "Oh, just two little balls."

There was a complete resolution of the pavor nocturnus and the anorexia following the release and interpretation of this material in Olga's play sessions where she had been doing actively to the clay doll (her brother) what she had suffered passively in reality. For Olga, the tonsillectomy had been the ultimate trauma in a series of traumata, experienced by her as oral deprivations, inflicted by the mother (abrupt weaning, early toilet training, and birth of the brother, who was being nursed and who had a penis). Thus, Olga's chronic disappointment in her mother suffered an acute exacerbation at the time of tonsillectomy, to which her mother took her and which was performed by a lady doctor. Her acutely intensified oral aggressive impulses had to be repressed abruptly by her severe superego, and this led to the pavor nocturnus, the anorexia, and the total behavior which resembled a depression. Olga had interpreted the tonsillectomy as a command by her mother (superego) not to eat the breast-penis and to accept the punishment (castration). She responded to it with the exaggerated unconscious obedience characteristic of the traumatic neurotic.

In conclusion, I should like to emphasize again that Type II of pavor nocturnus can be considered the traumatic neurosis of childhood, from which the later sequelae—neurotic, particularly phobic, psychosomatic, or psychotic manifestations—develop. The onset is sudden, often dramatic, following a final trauma in a series of narcissistic injuries. Under the impact of the trauma the aggressive impulses are intensified. Because the trauma is interpreted by the child as a command of the superego to submit —that is to be sick, to die—these impulses are turned against the self.

The third group, the neurotic type of pavor nocturnus, does not need to be dealt with extensively here. It is a frequent phenomenon of an episodic or recurrent nature in children and has its origin in the conflicts of the oedipal phase. To this group also belong the sleep disturbances of the oedipal phase discussed in preceding chapters. The concepts developed on the nightmare of the adult by Jones (1931) apply to this type of pavor nocturnus in children.

The superego permits the dangerous and forbidden impulses

that are warded off during the day to come out during sleep in the disguise of the dream, but insists upon immediate waking up when there is a danger that the ego might be overcome by these impulses and carry them out in reality. The child awakens fully in anxiety, and with a vivid recall of the contents of the nightmare, which may become a lasting memory. It can be revived later in life, either in its original or in somewhat changed form.

## Nocturnal Psychosomatic Symptoms, Enuresis and Soiling

The occurrence during the night of a psychosomatic disturbance that awakens the sleeper is a form of sleep disturbance that occurs in children and adults. I am not concerning myself here with psychosomatic diseases in which nocturnal attacks are a frequent occurrence—e.g., bronchial asthma or ulcerative colitis—but what I have in mind are the cases in which the child wakes up in the middle of the night, feeling sick, nauseated, or having severe stomach cramps which often necessitate calling a doctor. This occurs repeatedly and examination does not reveal any organic causes for these symptoms. I should like to illustrate this with one case:

Eight-and-a-half-year-old Erna was referred for treatment because she suffered from many fears and although she did not wet herself during the day, she always had damp panties. From the age of four, she had had recurrent attacks at night in which she would wake up with a severe stomachache, often so severe that a doctor had to be called. During treatment, we learned that Erna still shared her parents' bedroom. Her parents thought that, aside from her attacks, she was a sound sleeper, but actually she very often had been up at night and had witnessed parental intercourse many times. She had many fears of a sexual nature. She was afraid to walk up the stairs alone, even in broad daylight, fearing that a man was following and would attack her. She had very sadistic rape fantasies and her damp panties were a result of her constant sexual overstimulation. Her parents were rather annoyed with my suggestion to remove Erna from their bedroom. When they finally did, her mother asked me whether she could sleep in the same room and bed with Erna, rationalizing that she had to have this type of a bed because of her backache. On this occasion, I learned that the mother was frigid, always objected to intercourse, and had used Erna, in a way, as a protection against her husband's approaches. Erna's idea of intercourse was that of assault and rape; for this was really what it amounted to between her parents. Analytic investigation revealed that, in that symptom, Erna was putting herself in her mother's place, being penetrated by the father, but instead of pleasure, she was experiencing excruciating pain and fear as a punishment for such wishes, which are taboo in the unconscious.

In a similar situation, another patient, a boy of five, also had stomachaches but his was not a conversion symptom; it was intentional and he was simply faking. "If I say that I have a stomachache," he told me, "my parents get up. Mother makes tea for me. They fuss around and I wind up in bed between them." This boy was achieving consciously and deliberately what other children achieve only through a symptom at the cost of anxiety and suffering, namely, to separate the parents and prevent their intercourse at night.

It would seem to me that the cases of enuresis and soiling or diarrhea at night also belong to this group. While we cannot really consider enuresis as a sleep disturbance, since the enuresis serves as a vehicle for the discharge of tensions and thereby rather makes sleep possible, it may be of interest to learn something about the sleep behavior of children when they are treated because of their enuresis. In my experience most of these cases during their treatment have a transient period of disturbed sleep with nightmares preceding the giving up of the enuresis. Many mothers have told me of their observation of how restless the child's sleep becomes at a certain period of treatment, while this same child during the enuretic phase had been a very sound sleeper. Some children actually stay up for part of the night to make certain that they will not wet. This struggle takes place only as long as the child unconsciously still wants to wet. Once this is worked out in the treatment, these children can sleep very soundly and not wet—e.g., Jean was eight when, after a year of analysis, she decided that she could give up enuresis. Frequently her mother would overhear her say in her sleep, "I won't do it. No, I won't" (see Chapter 17).

## Sleep Phobias, Sleep Rituals, Habitual Waking Up

A frequent form of sleep disturbance is a sleep phobia. A certain amount of sleep phobia is a factor in most sleep disturbances. In the more pronounced cases, the children not only want their mothers to be at home but the mother has to lie down with the child until he falls asleep. The child will often wake up in the middle of the night to make sure that mother is still there and go looking for her through the house and stay awake if she is not at home. Usually these children also show phobic traits and a phobic attachment to their mothers during the daytime. This is indicative of their repressed hostility and death wishes against their mother. This hostility and resentment against the mother stems as we have already seen from the same two main sources —the oedipal situation and sibling rivalry. I would like to give one example.

CASE 1.   Six-year-old Miriam would refuse to go to sleep without her mother and would physically resist any attempt of her mother to leave her bed by holding tightly to her mother's breast. This she had done since the birth of her little brother when she was three and a half. She had severe nightmares with the typical content of being pursued by wild animals who wanted to devour her, thus revealing her own very strong oral-sadistic impulses. By holding on to her mother, she was not only taking her away from the brother who slept in the parents' bedroom but also from the father. To separate her parents was one of the aims which she achieved with the sleep disturbance. When I interpreted to Miriam her sadistic behavior toward her mother and her possessiveness of her, Miriam became very angry and said, "I won't let you take my mother away from me. I am going to have her in bed with me when I want to, or I'll have so many headaches in the morning that you won't know what to do!" She often complained about headaches in the morning and used this as an excuse for staying home from school. She was able, however, after having understood this behavior to relinquish her hold upon her mother to a considerable extent.

CASE 2. In the case of twelve-year-old Charles, who suddenly developed a sleep phobia, we were able to study the dynamics very clearly before he had a chance to combat it by compulsive mechanisms. Usually such an acute sleeping phobia is the result of an acute defensive conflict due to a sudden increase or mobilization of aggressive impulses. In his case, a traumatic experience preceded the onset of his phobia. He had witnessed by chance the suicidal jump of a woman from a window. He reacted to it immediately with disturbance. That night he was afraid to go to sleep and, since his condition did not improve but became increasingly worse, he was referred for treatment. In his treatment, it was found that this experience had mobilized his own suicidal impulses; that is, he was afraid to go to sleep lest he be overcome by the impulse to jump out of the window during the night. But he also had—and this was at the basis of his conflict—the unconscious impulse to throw his younger brother out of the window, as he had seen the body of the woman being flung through the window. Not to go to sleep was a defense against being overcome by such an impulse.

Compulsive neurotic rituals of children aimed at counteracting their repressed impulses are common and well known; for instance the need to have bedclothes arranged in a certain way, to have something placed under the pillow, or as one of my patients, a twelve-year-old girl did, to have all her shoes lined up in a row near her bedside. These children often spend part of the night rearranging the objects and go into a panic when anyone moves any of them.

Thirteen-year-old Ernest, who suffered from intense castration fears reactivated and intensified by several traumatic experiences, developed a rather unusual sleep ceremonial: Sleepless for many months, he had finally devised an ingenious contraption which made it possible for him to fall asleep for several hours at least during the night. He had attached one end of a string to the knob of his door and the other end to his wrist. To the middle of this string, which went over a chair, he had attached a penknife. He had figured it out very accurately that when anyone who was six feet tall (his father) opened the door, the pull of the string would release the knife which would then directly hit the penis of the person who walked in.

Six-and-a-half-year-old Barry suddenly developed the following sleep ritual: every night, he was found sleeping on the floor on the doorstep of his mother's bedroom. In his case, this was a very sensible action, as we found out. His father had left the family several months ago, and Barry had often heard his mother say that she was so fed up with everything that it would be best for her to leave also. By placing himself in front of her door, Barry, in a very effective way, planned to prevent his mother from carrying out her threat. Consciously, Barry had not been aware of why he had to sleep in this fashion.

The habit that some children have and that often continues into adulthood—of awaking at a certain time or several times during the night to go to the bathroom—is in most cases a result of the particular methods of toilet training. It is a form of sleep disturbance which yields easily to explanation of its cause (see Chapter 16). Children often like to delay going to sleep and will use all kinds of delaying tactics. Very often the reason for stalling is a rather harmless one. The child is still full of energy and wants to participate in the family activities. These children as well as those with milder transitory sleep disturbances during the anal and oedipal phases present no real management problems.

This chapter focusses on the psychopathology and the differential diagnostic criteria of the more severe neurotic sleep disturbances in children, in the hope that early detection and proper assessment will enhance not only our therapeutic but even more so our preventive efforts with children.

# 5
# The Diagnostic and Prognostic Significance of Children's Dreams and Sleep

My interest in sleep and dream phenomena of children is of long standing (see Chapters 4, 5, 6; M. Sperling, 1949b, 1955a). I was fortunate in having had the opportunity to follow up some of the cases which I had treated or evaluated at a very early age and to test the reliability of my predictions made then. This chapter incorporates some of these experiences and observations from the treatment of severely disturbed children and adolescents in whom specific sleep disturbances had been prominent features of childhood. The treatment of children suffering from enuresis, petit mal, epilepsy, and various psychosomatic disorders such as bronchial asthma, ulcerative colitis, mucous colitis, etc., provided insight into the interrelated dynamics of dreams, sleep, and nocturnal somatic symptoms.

The findings from the psychoanalytic investigation of sleep disturbances in children and especially of the phenomena of pavor nocturnus, are of particular interest. In Chapter 4, I described Type II of pavor nocturnus in children, which is characterized by recurrent nightmares leading to abrupt waking up, as "the traumatic neurosis" of childhood, and expressed the belief that the nightmare, contrary to being a guardian of sleep and serving belated mastery of traumatic experiences, has the function of waking the sleeping child abruptly and fully because the progressive increase of anxiety during sleep represents an acute danger to the sleeping ego.

The situation is different in Type I pavor nocturnus. Here the child does not fully awaken and the confused delusional dream state continues even though the child may be out of bed, walking or talking, that is, motorically awake. I have described this type of pavor nocturnus as an episodic, psychotic-like attack limited to the nighttime and the special conditions of the dream state.

The findings from the recent dream and sleep research by Charles Fisher (1969) in New York are of particular interest for the understanding of pavor nocturnus and nightmares. He found that the most severe nightmares with behavior resembling pavor nocturnus Type I in children (his studies are with adults) do not occur during the REM periods, that is during the superficial stages of sleep associated with dreaming, but during Stage 4, which is the period of deepest sleep. Awakening from these severe nightmares is sudden, the subject appearing to be dissociated, confused, hallucinating, and unresponsive to the environment. Brain waves show a waking alpha pattern but the subject is nevertheless not fully awake. Fisher found that there is a relationship between the depth of sleep and the severity of the nightmare: the deeper the sleep, the more severe the nightmare. According to Fisher, the REM dream seems to have a mechanism that modulates anxiety, while the Stage 4 nightmare seems to indicate a massive failure of ego functioning and is more like a brief, reversible, psychotic attack which seems to resemble the pavor nocturnus Type I sleep disturbances in early childhood.

Neurotic sleep disturbances in infancy, that is, sleep disturbances for which no external or internal physical explanation can be found, are by no means a rarity. Because infants normally require a great deal of sleep, and in view of the findings from psychophysiological sleep and dream research concerning the effects of prolonged sleep and dream deprivation, a persistent sleep disturbance in a very young child should be considered to be of serious import, even in the absence of other signs of distress. Because it is not possible to explore the dream life or the sources of the infant's sleep disturbance directly, it is advisable to investigate the mother's feelings about her child in search for the sources which provoke and maintain such a state of tension in the infant. Rarely is a psychiatrist or psychoanalyst consulted for a sleep disturbance in an infant. This is the domain of the pediatrician and here is an added indication for the desirability of educating pediatricians to the awareness of the role of the mother-child relationship in the etiology of neurotic sleep disturbances in young children. I have had an opportunity to learn about and to intervene in several such cases of infantile sleep disturbance in the treatment of the mother, and in one case, in the treatment of the grandmother of the child (M. Sperling, 1949b).

I have treated a considerable number of children for severely disturbed behavior, in whom sleep disturbance in infancy had been the only manifest neurotic feature of the early life. The atypical behavior and other manifestations appeared later (see Chapter 21). The youngest child whom I could study and treat for severe sleep disturbances in play analysis was two years old (see Chapter 9).

Linda from the time of infancy, had suffered from sleep disturbance and attacks of paroxysmal tachycardia which occurred during the night. The sleep disturbance became more intense after a tonsillectomy at age one and a half and the birth of a brother when she was two years old. During this time she began to have recurrent nightmares. She would wake up screaming, confused, and hallucinating, sometimes looking for fish on her pillow who wanted to bite her, or screaming that a kitty or dog was biting her. In play analysis, intense oral-sadistic impulses directed against her mother's breast and her brother's penis were brought to the fore. She had been weaned abruptly at nine months and toilet trained before her brother's birth. She had had a tonsillectomy at one and a half, which she had experienced as an oral castration inflicted upon her by her mother.

Linda developed fears of dogs and cats, of noises, the dark, and of being alone. The nightmares during sleep and the daytime phobias were an indication that this child felt in danger of being overcome by her threatening impulses. Her nightmares, her paroxysmal tachycardia, and her phobias were an indication that she was defending herself against ego disintegration. The concomitant psychoanalytic treatment of her mother was an important factor in the successful outcome and in preventing a psychotic development.

A persistent sleep disturbance in a young child with recurrent nightmares is an indication that the child's ego is struggling against overwhelming anxiety. If no relief is forthcoming, there will be ego impairment resulting from crippling defenses, leading to phobias, psychosomatic illness, or even psychosis.

I should like to illustrate such a situation with one example. Four-year-old Ruth suffered from a persistent sleep disturbance with recurrent nightmares, especially about a spider in her bed who threatened to take her to the hospital. This was the earliest indication of a schizophrenia with marked paranoid trends, which she developed at age eight and a half. As with Linda, in this case as well, the mother had rejected her child from birth because of her sex. Ruth too had been weaned and toilet trained early and had had a tonsillectomy before the age of two which she had experienced as an oral castration inflicted upon her by her mother. She had experienced the birth of a brother at age two and of another brother at age eight, when she had a recurrence of the sleep disturbance with nightmares followed by the onset of the manifest psychosis as a loss of mother-breast-penis. Ruth too was struggling against overwhelmingly strong oral and anal-sadistic impulses, while suffering from intense breast and penis envy. However, her mother was not available for treatment and the brief play analysis at age four brought about a subsidence of the sleep disturbance, but not a change in the child's personality structure nor in a modification of the mother-child relationship (M. Sperling, 1949b). Although it had been insufficient to prevent the psychotic development during puberty, this early intervention was an important factor in rendering Ruth amenable to treatment. She was treated successfully for her psychosis from age nine through adolescence (Sperling, 1955d). This case is cited in order to emphasize the necessity for adequate assessment of such a sleep disturbance in a young child.

During the anal phases, repression of anal-erotic and anal-sadistic impulses takes place. Whenever such repressions are excessive, abrupt, or aggravated by additional traumatic experiences, the first indication will be a disturbance of sleep. According to O. Fenichel (1942), impairment of the function of sleep is the first indication of repressive conflicts, before the individual has learned to avoid struggles by means of rigid ego attitudes, that is, before definite mechanisms of defense and specific symptoms are formed. The prognosis of such sleep disturbances is good and they can usually be handled indirectly by advising mothers to relax their demands for too early and too rigid cleanliness and conformity. In this area, however, one has to be careful of the pitfalls of mothers going to the opposite extreme whereby they set virtually no standards of performance. Substitute gratification and outlets for anal-erotic and anal-sadistic drives through physical activity and appropriate play should be provided. B. Bornstein (1935), Fraiberg (1950) and Wulff (1927) have described such cases.

However, my experiences from analytic work with children suffering from pavor nocturnus and sleepwalking (see Chapters 4, 5; and M. Sperling, 1969a), from deviate sexual behavior (see Part 5), from enuresis (see Part 6), and from various psychosomatic diseases such as bronchial asthma (1963), mucous colitis (1950c), ulcerative colitis (1969b), petit mal, and epilepsy (1953b), etc., as well as the work done with severely disturbed or psychotic children (Chapter 21), have taught me that the role of the anal phases in character and symptom formation is not yet sufficiently considered. During the anal phase, separation conflicts are activated and anal drive and ego development as well as locomotion make their expression possible. Unresolved separation conflicts of the anal phase provide the pathological basis for particularly intense oedipal conflicts. The development during this phase has a decisive influence upon the vicissitudes of the aggressive drives, of narcissism, ambivalence, and bisexuality. The ambivalence, omnipotence, and narcissism that become associated with anal processes and sphincter control may thus become the most important vehicle for control of impulses in general. Conflicts about sphincter control may become equated with control of impulses, that is, of internal reality as well as control of mother and external objects, that is, of external reality, and may also be used for the symbolic expression of separation conflicts. Children of this age will evidence their separation problems in sleep difficulties, fear of the dark, and fear of being alone. This was expressed by a little girl who when put to bed, said "talk to me, Mommy, then it won't be so dark." Some children need substitutes in the form of special toys to take to bed with them. An exaggerated need and attachment to such articles may be an early indication of childhood fetishism (Chapter 15). Other children may show their separation conflicts more manifestly by clinging and holding on to their mothers physically, at bedtime.

If, however, expression of anal impulses and of aggressive drives is severely restricted and at the same time the child is excessively stimulated by anal manipulations and by visual exposure and close body contact, a climate is created which is conducive to the development of pavor nocturnus Type I. This type of pavor nocturnus has in most cases an insidious onset during the anal phases, reaching a climax during the oedipal phases when character maldevelopment and symptom formation are beginning to appear as indications of the child's struggle with overwhelmingly strong sexual and aggressive impulses. Because we rarely see the initial stages of this type of sleep disturbance, and because of the prognostic significance it holds for future character and personality development, I should like to discuss and to illustrate such a situation with two cases, one of a young child and one of an adolescent in whose analysis the early sleep disturbance could be reconstructed.

The case of three-year-old Freddie, who at the age of one and a half had begun to have nightmares and occasional night terrors, came to my attention during the treatment of his mother, and could be managed indirectly by modifying his mother's handling of him. Freddie appeared to be too much concerned with cleanliness and showed the beginnings of food and sleep rituals. His mother was preoccupied with anal functions and frequently used suppositories and enemas for herself as well as for Freddie. At age two he had shown a tendency to have temper tantrums which his mother had quickly suppressed. She did not allow him any overt expression of aggression. Freddie also had indulged in a form of anal masturbation by sticking his finger into his anus. This behavior subsided when his mother was able to curtail her preoccupation with the anal functions of her son. She had been in the habit of taking him into bed with her as the "only way" to get him to sleep after he awakened from a nightmare. The practice of taking the child into the parental bed as a means of restoring sleep disturbed by nightmares serves only to provide an additional source of overstimulation for the child whose disturbance of sleep is an indication of his inability to cope with his (aggressive and sexual) impulses. The fact that Freddie's mother remained in therapy during his oedipal phase development was most beneficial for him. In this case the early intervention through the mother had proved of therapeutic and preventive value.

Twelve-year-old Lenny was referred for severely disturbed behavior and an incapacitating mucous colitis. From the age of three, he had suffered from a sleep disturbance with nightmares. He would awaken in the middle of the night and look for his mother. This became more intense during the oedipal phase when his mother would have to lie down with him and hold his hand and promise that if he should die, she would die with him. With the onset of an overt school phobia and episodic nocturnal diarrhea, his sleep disturbance improved. He developed the full-blown mucous colitis during puberty following a recurrence of the sleep disturbance which reflected the resurgence of the unresolved oedipal conflicts and his masturbatory struggle (M. Sperling, 1950c). During the phase of his treatment when he had given up the mucous colitis symptoms (severe cramps and non-bloody diarrhea), he had a transitory return of the sleep disturbance with nightmares. One recurrent nightmare of an Egyptian "mummy" was particularly frightening and informative. The specific fears caused by this nightmare related to the fears of the anal phase, specifically the fear of separation and death which now served to express his castration fears and feminine wishes. Touching the mummy was fatal because there was a curse that anyone who touched the mummy had to die; it also made the mummy disappear, which was particularly frightening. He had many hypochondriacal fears of a paranoid nature, being especially afraid of poisoning, injections, illness, surgery, etc. He had stopped masturbating and regressed to the anal level of sexuality. The colitis symptoms served both the gratification of and punishment for his aggressive and pregenital sexual wishes.

The occurrence or recurrence of a sleep disturbance with nightmares is a typical phenomenon observed during the treatment of children with psychosomatic disorders, such as asthma, colitis, epilepsy, etc. It occurs during the phase of treatment when the child is giving up the psychosomatic symptoms which had provided the needed instant release of the threatening impulses via somatic channels. The character and content of the nightmares and dreams during this period express the child's specific fears and fantasies and are a key for the understanding of the dynamics of the specific somatic symptoms in each case. This aspect of the dream and fantasy life of children with psychosomatic disorders has been dealt with in detail in the published accounts of these respective syndromes (M. Sperling, 1950c, 1953b, 1963, 1969a, and many others not listed here). Enuretic children with persistent enuresis usually develop a sleep disturbance with nightmares, for the first time in their lives, during the phase of treatment when they are giving up the enuresis. In these cases the enuresis had served the immediate discharge of their impulses, thus protecting them from a sleep disturbance. During a transitory phase in their treatment, enuretic children may keep themselves up deliberately for many hours during the night in order to prevent themselves from having nightmares or bed-wetting. This is true also for children with psychosomatic disorders and is an indication of their intolerance toward anxiety and impulses which had been released previously in somatic symptoms or enuresis. This intolerance to anxiety and tension is an important differential diagnostic criterion between these children and those who suffer from a neurotic sleep disturbance. I shall return and elaborate on this subject after a brief discussion of neurotic sleep disturbances during the oedipal phase.

The repression of the oedipal wishes and the conflicts about infantile masturbation, with the resulting fears of castration, are reflected in the sleep disturbances of this phase. In most cases these are mild and transitory with occasional anxiety dreams and difficulty in falling asleep. There are typical fears associated with these sleep disturbances. Dreams deal frequently with attack, injury, or death. These are expressions of the child's fear of punishment for masturbation and his castration anxiety. Typical also are fears of monsters, ghosts, burglars, robbers, kidnappers, etc. These fears on closer investigation reveal themselves as projections of the child's own sexual and aggressive impulses directed toward the parent or sibling rivals. While the occurrence of mild and transient sleep disturbances during the oedipal phase can be considered almost a typical feature in our culture, the more severe sleep disturbances of this phase, especially acute exacerbations leading to acute sleeplessness, and anxiety dreams, are pathological phenomena. A persistent sleep disturbance during this phase, in the absence of other symptoms, can be considered a manifestation of the infantile neurosis of the child. From the dream and sleep behavior, it is possible to make a differential diagnosis between neurotic or other more serious psychopathological development of the child. This differential diagnosis is important for the therapeutic approach and for prognosis and prevention. I should like to present a clinical vignette of a neurotic sleep disturbance and then compare it with that of a more serious sleep disturbance in a child of the same age, using this as a basis for the discussion of the similarities and differences in the genesis and dynamics between these sleep disturbances and between the prognostic significance and therapeutic approach.

Six-and-a-half-year-old Bobby had had a mild transient sleep disturbance between ages four and five. For the past year and a half his sleep disturbance had become more intensified; he had difficulty in going to sleep and when he fell asleep he would frequently wake up in anxiety. His mother described him as a model child who was very attached to her and very considerate of his baby brother, one and a half years old. Bobby had frequent dreams about cemeteries and dead people getting out of their graves and coming to fetch him. He was preoccupied with fears of death although he had had no experience of death in his family. He would sometimes cry before going to bed because he was afraid he might die in his sleep. Therapy revealed that his oedipal conflicts had been complicated and intensified by repressed hostility and death wishes toward his brother who had become his immediate rival for his mother's affection at a time when he was at the height of his positive oedipal conflict. Once, when he was five years old and driving past a cemetery with his parents, it was explained to him that this was a place where dead people were buried. Also, about that time he had been warned about playing with his penis.

Bobby is a good illustration for the neurotic type of oedipal sleep disturbance. He had a relatively well-functioning ego and superego and was able to handle the intensification of his oedipal conflicts, his aggression, and his sibling rivalry by repression. He was able to maintain repression of these impulses during the day without manifest disturbance of his behavior, and was thus able to tolerate a certain amount of anxiety without symptom formation and impairment of ego functioning. However, because he was in a state of acute repression, sleep represented the danger of a break through of these impulses (Fenichel, 1942). He defended himself against this danger by neurotic insomnia, that is, by trying to stay awake or by awakening *fully* with the help of anxiety dreams when these repressed impulses threatened to overcome the sleeping ego. He had full recall of the events during the time of the night when he was up and was fully aware of his environment and actions. In fact, he rarely got out of bed or disturbed his parents. He was more or less a "silent" sufferer.

The essential difference in the sleep behavior between the child with neurotic insomnia and the child with pavor nocturnus Type I (and sleepwalking) is that the child with neurotic insomnia awakens fully from sleep and has complete recall for the events of the night, while the child with pavor nocturnus and sleepwalking is not fully awake and has a retrograde amnesia for his nocturnal activities. The child with neurotic insomnia, by awakening fully from the dream, does not permit himself to act out forbidden or dangerous impulses in reality, while the child with pavor nocturnus Type I, by not awakening fully and by continuing the dream in a partially awake state, permits himself to act out in disguise some of his impulses in reality. I would put the differential emphasis between these two groups on *action*. The child with pavor nocturnus Type I and sleepwalking needs to act out in reality without being fully aware of his impulses and action, and with amnesia for them. The dynamic situation, and this is an important factor in the treatment of children with pavor nocturnus and sleepwalking, is similar to the situation in patients with character disorders and acting out behavior. There is also a striking similarity in parental attitudes and early childhood experiences found in the histories of patients with character disorders and acting out behavior. These children are exposed to overstimulation and inconsistency on the part of the parents. The oral phases of development are usually more satisfactory, but beginning with the anal phase, there is a progressive pathological development with intensification during puberty and adolescence. These children in contrast to those who suffer from neurotic insomnia, do not have a satisfactory latency period. An important difference is the different character structure and the different mechanisms of defense against instinctual drives used by these children. The urge to act out impulses is particularly strong and the ability to tolerate anxiety, that is, some awareness of these impulses, is very low. This explains the frequent association of pavor nocturnus Type I with psychosomatic symptoms, which serve as emergency outlets, or the replacement of this type of sleep disturbance by psychosomatic symptoms.

I would like to illustrate such a situation with the brief vignette of six-and-a-half-year-old Charlie. Charlie was referred for treatment because of a school phobia, which manifested itself mainly in somatic symptoms. He was always sick and tired in the morning and his mother would dress and feed him breakfast in bed. Charlie would vomit every morning either before leaving the house, or on the way to school or in school. He finally refused to go to school at all. Although he was a very bright child, his performance had been poor. From about age three he suffered from pavor nocturnus Type I. He would wake up during the night appearing fearful, confused, and unresponsive to his environment, seemingly in a dream state. He would walk into his parents' bedroom and get into bed with his mother. Occasionally he would talk during this state, sometimes saying "I hate you all; I hate this house. I want to leave," and actually attempt to walk out of the house. In the mornings he was tired and sleepy and had complete amnesia for the happenings of the night. During the past year, the pavor nocturnus attacks were less frequent, although Charlie had now developed a severe cough which kept him and his parents up for most of the night. The cough had been diagnosed as allergic but did not respond to medication. He would never go to bed when his mother was not at home and would often sleep with his clothes on. His daytime behavior had become increasingly disruptive and demanding and because of his phobias and abusive behavior toward other children, he was a rather isolated child.

Both parents showed marked anal fixations. His mother overcompensated for her rejection of him by overindulgence but did not allow him appropriate expressions of aggression. She was very controlling and restrictive. Her treatment revealed that she had unconsciously encouraged his phobia by her overprotection and overanxiousness and that he had been used by her for the acting out and gratification of some of her own unconscious needs. Charlie had accommodated his mother in these areas and retaliated by his disturbing and demanding behavior. Unlike Bobby, he was not a silent, but in fact a very noisy sufferer. Preparatory treatment of his mother was necessary in order to modify her relationship with Charlie and to make him amenable to therapy. As is typical for such cases, Charlie was not brought for treatment for his pavor nocturnus and sleepwalking, but under the pressure of the school, for his school phobia and behavior.

Children with pavor nocturnus and sleepwalking are rarely brought for treatment because of these symptoms unless their behavior is endangering their own or their family's safety and even then, rarely before school age. Treatment is usually sought because of other symptoms, especially behavior difficulties, school problems, or phobias. Responsible in part for this is the belief of parents, shared by pediatricians, that children outgrow pavor nocturnus and sleepwalking and therefore do not require treatment for these symptoms. This belief is supported by the fact that pavor nocturnus Type I is usually given up during puberty or adolescence. However, parents and pediatricians do not know what my extensive and long experience with children suffering from this type of pavor nocturnus has taught me—namely, that it is given up in exchange for severe character and personality disorders and other behavior and symptoms which neither the patient nor his environment relate to the preceding sleep disturbance. Frequently, these children suffer from so-called allergic conditions such as persistent coughing, hay fever, bronchial asthma, headaches, petit mal, etc., sometimes coexisting and sometimes replacing the pavor nocturnus. These symptoms and the pavor nocturnus Type I are indications of the severity of the pregenital fixations and conflicts. The character structure of these children is predominantly anal with marked ambivalence, bisexuality, tendencies to homosexuality, sadomasochism, and other deviations.

Although Charlie came for treatment at age six and a half, his character psychopathology was already so severe that it required long therapy (under my supervision) and preparatory as well as concomitant treatment of his mother (with myself). His father had also been in analysis with another analyst.

I have now a nineteen-year follow-up on patient Bill, reported in Chapter 4. He was treated for pavor nocturnus and sleepwalking from ages nine to eleven; he was seen again at age fifteen when he was close to a psychotic break. His psychological records, including Rorschach, at that time indicated that he was suffering from a paranoid schizophrenia. That he was amenable to analysis, I attribute, as in the case of Ruth, to his previous therapy. From age twenty to twenty-four he had more analysis to work out his latent homosexuality and other related problems. He is married, has children, and is pursuing a professional career. I am citing this case here to emphasize again the prognostic significance of this type of sleep disturbance.

I have stressed in particular three features as differential diagnostic criteria for pavor nocturnus Type I. One, the fact that the child is only partially awake and behaves as if in a dream state; two, hypermotility, whether the child is in or out of bed; and three, retrograde amnesia. These features are manifestations of strong regressive tendencies and indications of impairment of the ability to wake up fully, as well as a tendency to *act out* impulses in reality. This behavior points to a possible connection with psychotic states. Simmel's (1942) ideas concerning the connection of sleep and psychosis are of interest here. Simmel makes the point that in psychotic states there seems to be a disturbance of the ability to awaken fully during the day. Apparently there is a similarity between the dream state, with partial awakening during the night in pavor nocturnus Type I, and some psychotic states. Observations from recent experimental sleep research would seem to validate my conclusions concerning the difference between pavor nocturnus Type I and other sleep and dream states which have been drawn from clinical psychoanalytic work with children during the past twenty-five years.

Broughton (1968), a neurologist, reported that in most of the subjects studied, bed-wetting, sleepwalking, and nightmares of the type described by me as pavor nocturnus Type I, occurred during sudden arousal from slow wave Stage 4 sleep. He observed an increase in physiological activity, mental confusion, and retrograde amnesia in these subjects. He was particularly impressed with their decreased response to light and concluded that these sleep disturbances are essentially "disorders of arousal." Unfortunately, however, the drawback with physiological research is the unfamiliarity and often the resistance to psychoanalytic thinking and methods of the researcher. Broughton's explanation for these phenomena is a purely physiological one; he attributes it to predisposing physiological changes in the body. Because he observed little or no mental content on the subjects, he jumped to the conclusion of a "psychological void." He attributed the terror and confusion in this type of nightmare victim to the increase in his heartbeat, rather than to the anxiety which in my opinion causes both the acceleration in physiological activity and the nightmare, with the confusional state following it. Here the superiority of the psychoanalytic method of investigation is unquestionable.

In the psychoanalytic treatment of children suffering from pavor nocturnus, sleepwalking, bed-wetting, and other related symptoms, I have succeeded in lifting the retrograde amnesia while restoring the memory and the psychic content of the nocturnal attacks (Chapters 4, 17; M. Sperling, 1969a). In this connection, the psychoanalytic work with patients suffering from psychosomatic diseases, in particular, migraine headaches, altered states of consciousness, petit mal, and grand mal epilepsy are of interest (M. Sperling, 1953b). With these patients too, analysis succeeded in lifting the amnesia for their petit mal and even grand mal attacks. That it is possible in psychoanalytic treatment of psychosomatic patients to uncover the fantasies converted into and released in the somatic symptoms has been amply demonstrated (M. Sperling, 1950c, 1963, 1969b). In fact, the combined physiological and psychoanalytic study of the various sleep states and the phenomena associated with them may well prove a source not only for a better understanding of dream and sleep mechanisms, but perhaps also for the still "mysterious leap from the mind to the body," and the transformation of psychic content into physiological activity and vice versa.

I have described Type II pavor nocturnus as the traumatic type. Here the onset is sudden, often dramatically following an acute trauma. Such a trauma may be surgery, accident, illness, death in the family, birth of a sibling, etc. This type can occur in children of all ages and is characterized by fitful sleep, crying out during sleep, and waking up in anxiety from a nightmare which may represent a repetition of the traumatic situation which preceded the onset of this sleep disturbance. This type of pavor nocturnus is analogous to the traumatic neurosis of adults and can be considered as the traumatic neurosis of childhood. The revival of the traumatic situation during sleep leads to anxiety, and the continuation of sleep under these circumstances would be dangerous. The nightmare in this situation functions as the abrupt waker and the mastery lies in waking up and escaping the traumatic situation in the dream that the child had been unable to escape and to master in reality. In most cases, waking up from this type of pavor nocturnus is accompanied by relief, in contrast to the behavior in pavor nocturnus Type I. This, as well as the acute onset and transitory character, is an important differential diagnostic criteria. It is of therapeutic and especially of preventive significance that in traumatic neurosis there is a characteristic incubation period during which sleep is disturbed in this specific way, before the onset of manifestly disturbed daytime behavior. The case of four-year-old Olga, who developed an acute severe sleep disturbance and anorexia following a tonsillectomy, will be recalled (Chapter 4). The child had been having repeated nightmares in which she would cry out, "No, no, don't!" Olga had been adequately prepared for the surgery except for the anesthesia, and in her nightmares she relived the struggle against being overcome by the anesthesia against her will, an event which she had been unable to prevent in reality and from which she could escape by waking up when she relived it in her nightmares. It was possible in a few play sessions to reconstruct the meaning which the traumatic events that had caused this behavior had for her and to free her from her symptoms. She has remained well and symptom-free in a long follow-up.

However, in an already traumatized child, an additional trauma may have the effect of profoundly disturbing the object relationship and the balance between the libidinal and aggressive drives. These will be experienced as particularly dangerous during deep sleep when the regressive tendencies threaten to overcome the weakened ego of the child. These tendencies have to be counteracted with emergency speed and measures and the sudden and excessive increase in the cardiorespiratory rate and other physiological hyperactivity are indications of the mounting anxiety. Fisher (1969) in his research has described how the subject of such a nocturnal attack awakens from deep sleep (Stage 4), when his pulse rate was 60, suddenly with a pulse rate of 150, sweating, agitated as if in great danger. This is exactly how some children with the traumatic type of pavor nocturnus feel and behave. They call in panic for their mother and want to be held and comforted. They may be confused for a while, still under the spell of the nightmare, but they awaken fully and have recall of the nightmare and the events of the night, as was the case with Olga.

In the cases of two-year-old Linda and four-year-old Ruth, the traumatic effects of the tonsillectomy for which both children had not been prepared was added to an already severe sleep disturbance, thereby contributing to its intensification, but they too were able to remember the nightmare and the events of the night.

Following a traumatic experience, children should be encouraged to verbalize and to abreact their feelings in order to protect them from permanent consequences. After the incubation period, that is, with the subsidence of the acute sleep disturbance, some changes in the child's daytime behavior may appear. These changes, depending on the premorbid personality of the child, may vary from mild phobic to more severe neurotic or somatic reactions.

An adolescent boy whom I treated for severe school phobia and paranoid distrust comes to mind. In this case, the crucial traumatic experience occurred at age four, when he had to undergo surgery for which he had not been prepared at all. In fact, his mother, afraid that he would not go to the hospital, had misinformed him. The sleep disturbance following this experience went unnoticed and the subsequent changes in his personality and behavior, in addition to a tendency to develop severe headaches, had not been related to this traumatic experience by him or by his environment. In his analysis it was found that he still suffered from disturbed sleep with episodic nightmares and intense destructive impulses of both a homicidal and suicidal nature.

Sleep disturbances of childhood, like other early established behavior patterns, are frequently carried over into adulthood, contributing to the high incidence of neurotic insomnia among the population.

Type III of pavor nocturnus, the neurotic type, has its origin in the conflicts of the oedipal phase and is phenomenologically and dynamically similar to the nightmare syndrome of the adult. The concepts about the nightmare of the adult developed by Jones (1931) apply in some measure to this type of pavor nocturnus in children. Here the superego permits the dangerous and forbidden impulses that were warded off during the day to come out during sleep in the disguise of the dream, but insists upon immediate waking up when there is a danger that the ego might be overcome by these impulses. This type of nightmare occurs episodically, and the child awakens fully in anxiety and with a vivid recall of the contents of the nightmare which may become a lasting memory. It can be revived later in life either in its original or in somewhat changed form.

Here again, Fisher's research and thinking are most interesting in validating and explaining clinical observations. He states that despite the fact that the REM period is generally characterized by considerable cardiorespiratory activity, anxious REM dreams seem to be accompanied by a motor paralysis that limits physiological reactions to anxiety, and further, that this process keeps a person asleep or prevents too great a disruption should he awaken. He also states that it appears that the REM dream has a mechanism which modulates anxiety by abolishing or diminishing physiological responses. He found that spontaneous awakenings with reports of anxious mental content can occur at any time of night in any of the four stages of sleep, but that the most severe nightmares take place during the period of deepest Stage 4 sleep. On the basis of these findings, one would be inclined to think that the neurotic type of pavor nocturnus is associated with the REM period of sleep, while the traumatic and psychotic type is associated with the periods of deep sleep.

## Summary and Conclusions

In this chapter I have been concerned mainly with three aspects of children's dreams and sleep:

One, to establish and to investigate further the relationship of these phenomena with developmental phases and conflicts. My investigations have revealed the importance of the pregenital phases and preoedipal relationships in the genesis of sleep disturbances in children, and in particular the role of anal phase development and conflicts in the genesis of pavor nocturnus Type I. I have expressed my belief that this type of sleep disturbance may be the first indication of serious pathological character and personality development. I have also re-emphasized the prognostic significance of a persistent severe infantile sleep disturbance.

Two, as indicated by the title, I have been particularly concerned with the practical, clinical aspects of these phenomena and their application in assessing existing pathology and predicting, or if possible preventing, future psychopathology in children. For this reason, I have tried to define especially some of the differences between neurotic sleep disturbances and those of the type of pavor nocturnus I and II in children.

Three, I have attempted to correlate psychoanalytic sleep and dream research with findings from recent experimental research of these phenomena (Broughton, 1968; Fisher and Dement, 1963; 1969; Dement, 1964).

While experimental research is important in enhancing our knowledge of the physiology of the processes of sleep and dreaming, psychoanalytic investigation is essential for the understanding of the mental processes involved.

# 6

# Dream Symbols and the Significance of Their Changes During Analysis

The analysis of dreams has remained a most rewarding tool in the analytic workshop, often permitting the assessment of the analytic situation at once.

Some patients use dream symbols which appear to be specific for them and especially suitable to express their basic fantasies. This applies particularly to recurrent dreams that deal with the basic wishes and conflicts of the patient.

My observations refer to such recurrent dreams with specific dream symbols, and this study concerns itself particularly with the changes which these "typical" symbols undergo in the course of the analysis. These changes and the time of their occurrence appear to have a specific significance and could be considered as typical phenomena in certain types of patients. Fragments from the analyses of three patients serve to illustrate my observations.

CASE 1 concerns a sixteen-year-old boy, whose psychological records indicted that he suffered from a progressive schizophrenic process with an unfavorable prog-

nosis (paranoid schizophrenia). In spite of superior intellectual endowment, he was a complete failure in school. For a
considerable period of his analysis he related recurrent
dreams which dealt with stone statues. He remembered
having had such dreams in earlier childhood, particularly
one dream which recurred frequently during his analysis. In
this dream he would see two giant stone statues that were
moving slowly toward him. He was frightened in the dream
since there was the danger that a statue might tumble on
him and crush him. He would wake up from this dream in
great fear. In another recurring dream he possessed a
magic wand, and by waving it he could transform people
into stone.

In a screen memory he saw himself in a baby carriage
in a large room of stone or marble. He was looking up at
the ceiling from which marble statues were hanging down.
This patient had an excellent and very vivid memory of his
early childhood. He remembered that his mother used to
take him in the baby carriage to the neighborhood bank
and leave him in the tremendous lobby while transacting
her dealings at the bank teller's window. This bank lobby
reminded him of the room in the screen memory.

The anxiety of being crushed by the stone statues
above him was much better concealed in this conscious
memory than in the recurrent dream. In this connection the
(astonishing) fact that this patient had actually never left
the parental bedroom is of interest. Even during the early
part of his analysis he would frequently get into bed with
his parents, who thought nothing of having their sixteen-
year-old son in bed between them. His parents were very
neurotic, elderly people, for whom their only child was a
source of instinctual gratification. His father called him,
"my beautiful redcheek." He liked to caress his son's
cheeks and to fondle his neck and back when he was sitting behind him watching TV. My patient had surprised his
father masturbating many times. When his father caught
him masturbating at thirteen, he told him that this was very
dangerous. He showed him a book which stated that masturbation could cause brain damage and stupidity.

The character of his dreams changed dramatically in the course of his analysis. The stone-statue dreams were followed by a period during which he repeatedly dreamed about wooden horses. These horses moved and appeared very awkward. Then followed a period of dreams of wild animals, especially wild horses and big apes. These dreams were very turbulent and disturbing to him. He would, in an occasional fit of temper, shout and scream or smash a soap dish in the shower, while the water was running and he could not be heard by anyone in the house. It became obvious that he conceived of himself, as he did of his parents, as wild and uncontrollable beasts. This behavior could be understood as a belated reaction to primal-scene experiences. As a child he had transformed his parents into stone statues and made himself into some kind of an automaton.

Following this phase of analysis, during which his feelings had been mobilized, there were manifest changes in his behavior and approach to people, which had become much more human.

The changes in dream symbolism described above had by far preceded the clinical manifestations. The nature and extent of his emotional immobilization and disturbance in object relationship revealed in these dreams could be dealt with fully only later in his analysis after some of his paralyzing fears had been exposed and diminished. The growing transference relationship and trust in his analyst led to a gradual defrosting of his feelings and to the changes in affect and object relationship.

CASE 2 concerns a twelve-year-old boy, who suffered from latent schizophrenia. In school he would spend most of his time drawing science-fiction cartoons. This preoccupation he continued at home, where he kept to himself and did not play outdoors or with other children. He had a very active fantasy and dream life, which took him completely away from his problems. He had recurrent dreams of colliding celestial bodies, gigantic explosions and catastrophies occurring in the universe, millions of miles away from earth. No living creatures or life of any sort appeared to be present in these dreams. They dealt exclusively with distant planets and enormous destructive forces of supernatural dimensions. In reality he lived in a very turbulent environment, where frequent violent (physical) fights were going on between his parents.

In the course of the analysis certain modifications occurred in his dreams. The events of these dreams were still projected into the universe and onto other planets but now dealt with a certain type of monster. These monsters were neither people nor robots, but originated from plants. They were gigantic, incapable of feelings, very treacherous and destructive. They threatened to invade the earth. He had seen a horror movie, *The Thing*, which had apparently served as a model for this particular plant-monster dream. It is of interest in connection with this presentation to note that, although prototypes for monsters had been available to him long before, he had not used them until now. It would seem that, by a specific selectivity, a choice in the available symbolic expressions is made when the patient is ready for the use of these symbols.

This particular mechanism of the schizophrenic to dehumanize and to project himself and his conflicts onto the universe is well known from the Schreber case (Freud, 1911). A variation of this mechanism, the projection onto machines—the "influencing machine" V. Tausk called it (1919)—has been dealt with in children by Rudolf Ekstein (1954) and also by L. J. Sachs (1957). This presentation, however, is concerned primarily with the phenomenon of the changes of dream symbolism during analysis and the prognostic significance of these changes. Unfortunately, no further changes in the dream symbolism of the second patient could be observed because his analysis terminated at this point (after eleven months). His father had died suddenly and his mother, who had assumed full custody over him (her only child), withdrew him abruptly from treatment. She had been opposed to his analysis and yielded only under the pressure of her husband. She had always thought that the boy should be placed outside the home.

There is a dynamic similarity in the symbolic expressions which these two patients used, originally as well as in the changes effected by analysis. Both patients, because of the specific needs of their disease (schizophrenia), had to block their affects and to withdraw cathexis from the real objects. The withdrawal of cathexis was much more extensive in the second patient, who had to externalize and displace his conflicts altogether from living creatures and the earth. As a young child, he had had violent temper tantrums. This violence, reflected in the catastrophic events of the universe, if experienced consciously and released in motor action, would have meant the immediate destruction of his object world and himself. At the start of his analysis he felt totally unable to deal with real feelings and people.

The analysis of the first patient was successfully terminated when he was twenty-one years old. Nine years later he was married, working in his chosen profession, had a child, and seemed to function satisfactorily.

CASE 3 concerns a thirty-six-year-old woman in analysis because of a psychosomatic ailment (ulcerative colitis). Only one fragment of a certain phase of her analysis will be used for this presentation. This phase of her analysis was characterized by a striking change in dream symbolism. Preceding this phase, she had had a variety of dreams, mainly dreams in which primitive natives, who had to be subdued, symbolized the dangers of her own primitive, repressed impulses. This was followed by a prolonged period of analysis during which the patient produced many dreams which dealt almost exclusively with birds. In this series of dreams there were various types of recurrent dreams. In one recurrent dream a bird (she actually owned a bird) was in perpetual danger of being destroyed, usually by a cat, and was rescued by her at the last moment. In another type of dream, the bird's claws had to be clipped because they were dangerous to others. There were dreams in which she compared her bird with that of her mother's; usually her bird was bigger, had brighter feathers, and a larger beak. There were frank sexual dreams about a male bird impregnating the female by placing a drop of sperm next to the female's genital. Particularly frightening was a dream in which a bird lover showed her his birds. In the dream she touched a bat and, although she did it very gently, the bat bit her finger. She had never believed stories about bats flying into women's hair. She liked birds; in fact, her father had been a bird lover and had kept birds.

No full analysis of these dreams nor the patient's problems can be given here, except to state that it became apparent that she was expressing specific infantile sexual fantasies of a predominantly phallic character through this bird symbolism. The symbol of the bird was overdetermined and, in accordance with the level of these fantasies, as *pars pro toto*, also represented herself, her husband, the analyst, and other significant people. In one dream a helpless bird, whose feet were screwed to the bottom of the cage, represented her husband, whom she would have wanted to be castrated and to be her captive. It also represented herself, because she felt in her marriage like a bird in a cage.

When the castration complex and her fears of the penis emerged into consciousness, again a very dramatic change in dream symbolism occurred. Her sleep became disturbed and she had frank anxiety dreams dealing with spiders who were biting and drawing blood. It is not my intention to deal any further here with the analysis of this patient (M. Sperling, 1960), except to indicate that this change in dream symbolism expressed a basic change in the patient's feelings. The analysis had reactivated her early childhood sleep disturbance and her earliest and most deeply repressed oral sexual (homosexual) fantasies. What is of particular interest here is the use of specific dream symbolism during a specific phase of analysis and the change of dream symbolism concomitant with the change of the dominant fantasies. The bird symbolism as well as the spider symbol had been available to her at any time during her analysis. It came into use, however, at that phase of her analysis when it became the specific symbolic expression of her specific fantasies and conflicts mobilized by analysis at that time. The bird became the specific symbol for her phallic (bisexual) fantasies and conflicts, and the spider for the oral (homosexual) ones.

## Summary

The aim of this chapter was to draw attention to two phenomena:

1.   The specificity of dream symbolism for certain patients, particularly in recurrent dreams, which deal with the basic conflicts and fantasies.

2.   The fact that these changes in dream symbolism during the analysis precede the changes in the patient's conscious feelings and fantasies and are therefore of considerable prognostic significance.

# PART 3

# PHOBIAS
# IN CHILDREN

To some extent what has been said about sleep disturbances holds true also for phobias. Phobias are a step further in the development of a more organized neurosis from a sleep disturbance or anxiety state. Obsessional compulsive and conversion mechanisms are used defensively in phobias. The association with, the alternation of or the replacement of phobias by psychosomatic syndromes are frequent occurrences and have to be taken into consideration when treating patients with psychosomatic diseases or probias. These aspects have been dealt with in my work with psychosomatic diseases and phobias. Obsessional compulsive defenses and phobic mechanisms themselves often cover up an underlying psychotic personality structure, usually one with paranoid trends. A cautious procedure in removing these defenses in such patients is indicated.

# 7

# School Phobias: Classification, Dynamics and Treatment

School phobia is actually one variety of the group of phobias. A systematic study of the phobias, which constitute the most widely encountered neurosis in children and adults, is still lacking. The classical concepts, valid to this day, were developed by Freud (1909a) almost sixty years ago in his account of the indirect treatment of Little Hans. According to these concepts, a phobia is the neurosis of the oedipal phase and deals with castration anxiety and the conflicts of this phase.

The analytic study of young children has enabled child analysts to observe directly phobic manifestations in children of preoedipal age (B. Bornstein, 1935; Wulff, 1927). In my analytic work with children of preoedipal age (see Chapter 9), I could study the sources of anxiety which led to the onset of phobia before the oedipal phase. It is my impression that pregenital impulses and pregenital fixations are of major significance in this neurosis. In the treatment of psychosomatic patients, children as well as adults, I found that there is a dynamic interrelation between the psychosomatic symptoms and phobic behavior, often with an alternation between the somatic manifestations and the overt phobic behavior. This is the case particularly in mucous and ulcerative colitis and in bronchial asthma (M. Sperling, 1950c, 1952b, 1955c, 1961, 1963).

I have come to consider phobias as a neurosis which is related to the anal phase of instinctual development, and even more specifically to the anal-sadistic phase. A new version of the earlier conflicts about separation appears at and belongs to the anal phase of development (roughly between ages one and a half and three). It is during this phase that the motor equipment necessary for active separation—walking away from mother—develops, and when the ambivalence conflict concerning the anal instincts is at its height. It is the conflict of whether to hold on or to let go of feces (unconsciously equated with objects). During the oral phases there is only passive dependence because the child lacks the equipment for initiating any active separation from the mother in reality.

I would suggest classifying the phobias as being midway between the obsessive-compulsive and the hysterical neuroses, but closer to the first. The main mechanisms of defense in phobias and in obsessive-compulsive neuroses are similar—namely, displacement, isolation, and projection. In 1909 Freud described a mechanism characteristic of phobias, i.e., the externalization of an instinctual internal danger, which then can be avoided as an external danger. The high degree of ambivalence and narcissism, the persistence of the fantasy of omnipotence, and the exaggerated need for control are characteristic pregenital (anal-sadistic) features of this neurosis, and provide the link with other pregenitally fixated disorders (character disorders, certain perversions such as fetishism) and with psychosomatic diseases, especially with asthma and colitis. In all these conditions, separation anxiety is a crucial issue, and its persistence interferes with a satisfactory resolution of the oedipal conflicts.

From this it follows that school phobia has to be considered a psychoneurosis in the true sense; that is, that it is based on unconscious conflicts and fantasies and that the reasons a phobic child gives for his behavior are rationalizations, while the true reasons are unknown to him. Although this concept is shared by many workers in the field (Coolidge et al., 1960; A. Freud, 1965; Greenbaum, 1964; Johnson et al., 1941; Kahn and Nursten, 1962; E. Klein, 1945; Suttenfield, 1954; Talbot, 1957; Waldfogel et al., 1957), it is essential to emphasize this very strongly because there is the temptation to treat a school phobia with a commonsense approach, such as reassurance, reasoning, persuasion, reward or punishment. It should be obvious that none of these can really be effective or have *lasting* results, although it may be possible to bring a child back to school by any of these means. I am aware of the importance of inducing a phobic patient to return to the phobic situation as soon as possible; the aim of treatment, however, cannot be limited to this goal. It is our responsibility not only to bring the phobic child back to school, but also to make it possible for the child to remain in school without *too much* anxiety. An inordinate degree of anxiety interferes with the child's ability to function properly and inadvertently leads to other pathological behavior and symptoms, which, because they may not be as apparent and disturbing as is the school phobia, may go unnoticed at first and not be regarded as consequences of the school phobia by the child's environment. Psychosomatic manifestations are frequent substitutions for school phobias; "real" illness is a "legitimate" reason for absence from school.

It is unfortunate for school-phobic children that many of those who professionally deal with them do not seem to realize that a phobia is a neurotic illness, often more painful and crippling than a "real illness," and that bringing the child back to school "by hook or crook" is not the answer (Eisenberg, 1958; Leavitt, 1964; Waldfogel et al., 1957). Serious characterological and other maldevelopments are the consequences of untreated or poorly handled school phobias.* I shall deal with this aspect of the problem further in the discussion of the treatment of chronic school phobias.

For the purpose of choosing the most expedient approach to the management of school phobias, it is necessary to differentiate

---

* In this connection, a report by Garvey and Hegrenes (1966) is pertinent, because it exposes the fact that these authors believe that the removal of the symptom is identical with the elimination of the neurosis iteslf.

between acute and chronic school phobia and between a common or induced school phobia; moreover, the child's age must be taken into consideration: whether the onset of the phobia occurs in prelatency, latency, or adolescence.† As far as adolescence is concerned, it includes not only high school but also college students. The onset of a school phobia in college students is not a rare occurrence; it may be masked by other symptoms, especially by somatic manifestations of various kinds and characterological symptoms, and may culminate in a "mental breakdown." At any rate, whatever the overt symptoms may be in each case, the underlying dynamic factor is the inability to accept separation from a parent figure and to function independently away from home. The purpose of leaving school and returning home is usually achieved, even if only temporarily.

*Acute school phobias* can occur at any age, during any time of the year, not necessarily at the start of school or after school vacations. There is usually no history of prior school-phobia behavior. In all cases of acute school phobia, I favor a direct and analytic approach, regardless of age. I am aware of the fact that this is not always possible and that such children can be and are brought back to school by other approaches. In Chapter 8, I explain why I consider an analytic approach in acute cases particularly important; I shall briefly recapitulate here some of the salient points:

In the acute school phobia, it is often possible to detect, in one or in a few interviews, the unconscious significance of the precipitating event and to interpret it to the child. The traumatic event is usually one that represents a danger to the child's ability to control reality; that is, a danger of loss of control over a situation or object (usually the mother). In the final analysis this extreme need for control reveals itself as a wish for control over life and death, and the fear of the phobic patient (child or adult) as a fear of death. The precipitating event may be real or feared illness or death of a parent or a person unconsciously representing a parental figure, or illness or an accident, or surgery

† In this context, the chapters on "Assessment of Pathology" in *Normality and Pathology in Childhood* by A. Freud (1965) are particularly relevant.

performed on the child, which to the child has the meaning of having barely escaped death. In other words, the event represents an acute separation threat and, to the child predisposed to phobia by its fixations to the anal-sadistic level, has the meaning of impending death (of the parent or of the child himself). The fixation to the anal phase has other implications: object relationships are highly ambivalent, the narcissistic orientation has persisted, and so has magical thinking (omnipotence of thought), which means that the child equates his unconscious death wishes with actual reality.

I consider an acute school phobia as a "traumatic neurosis with school phobia as the presenting symptom." The intense anxiety caused by this trauma leads to an increase in the need for magical control (control over life and death), which the child is attempting to achieve by the phobic behavior.

Seven-year-old Peter's school phobia began suddenly one day in school during assembly. He became panicky and ran home looking for his mother. The next day he was reluctant to go to school. In school he became panicky and ran home again. This repeated itself, and after a few days he refused to go to school at all. When I saw him he had been out of school for nearly three weeks. In retracing the circumstances under which he had his first anxiety attack in school, I learned that it had occurred in assembly when he heard the teacher play the piano. He suddenly felt "funny," very sad, and had an irresistible urge to see his mother. He associated the music with a funeral, and more specifically with the funeral of a neighbor, a lady who had committed suicide while her child was in school. For the purpose of bringing him back to school it was sufficient to make him aware of his fear that this could happen to his mother and to link it with the unconscious wish by remarking casually that boys sometimes when they are angry have such wishes and are afraid that they might come true. His phobia cleared up immediately.

There was a rather strong probability that Peter might have

sensed the depressive mood of his mother and that his sudden phobia was also a sort of realistic protection for her. Chapter 8 shows that it is possible to bring an acutely school-phobic child back to school rather quickly by this method, which to some extent might even have a preventive effect and forestall the development of a later insidious neurosis. Exposure of the unconscious death wishes results in a devaluation of the magical qualities attached to unconscious thought processes.

It is important to differentiate this type, the traumatic or common type of acute school phobia, from what I would call *"induced" school phobia.* "Induced" school phobia is not an infrequent occurrence, especially in younger children. From the point of view of a differential diagnosis, the most significant factor is the absence of a manifest external precipitating event (which by its unconscious meaning for the child has such a traumatic effect) in the "induced" phobia, in contrast to the "common" acute school phobias. The onset of acute, induced school phobia is a much less dramatic event than that of an acute traumatic school phobia, because in the first case we are dealing with a more insidious traumatization of the child owing to the pathological parent-child relationship. "Induced" school phobia can also occur at any time during the school year. In these cases we usually find indications of some phobic behavior in the past; therefore, even if such a child is brought for treatment as soon as the school-phobic behavior becomes more apparent, we are really not dealing with the acute onset of the phobia any longer. In these cases, because of the neurotic needs of the person, usually the mother (but not too infrequently also the father), who induces the phobic behavior of the child, the indirect approach through therapy of the parent—especially with young children—is not only preferable but imperative. The real acute phase of such an induced school phobia one gets to see only accidentally, in which case it may be possible to resolve it *in statu nascendi.* I would like to give an example of an acute, induced school phobia in a five-year-old boy.

The inducer, in this case, was the father, who was in

analysis during the time when John developed an acute school phobia. Mr. J. was very distressed about the situation and blamed himself for his son's phobia, thinking that he was the cause of it because he had not devoted enough time to his son. John now was clinging to his father, and requested that he stay home with him and not go to work. He could not give a reason why he did not want to go to kindergarten, which he had previously attended willingly. In fact, he said that he liked the teacher, and that the children were okay. Attempts to get him to school failed. Even when his mother could get him into the car and take him to school, John refused to enter the school. In this case, my knowledge of the father's personality and of the family dynamics made it possible to understand the development and meaning of the child's phobia and helped to resolve it rather quickly through the help given to Mr. J. in his analysis.

Mr. J. had been a phobic person since childhood, but had managed to cover up his phobia rather cleverly by manipulating his environment. His wife, apparently because of her own needs, lent herself to play in with the patient's phobia. She was always at home taking care of the house and children. At the time of the acute onset of John's phobia, Mrs. J., as a result of her husband's analysis, had become much freer and was even considering beginning some activities which would take her away from the house for brief periods of time. John was the youngest of three children and the only boy, and there had been talk about having a fourth child. Manifestly, this was a strong wish expressed by Mrs. J., but Mr. J.'s analysis revealed that it was unconsciously intended by him as a means of tying her to the house and limiting her newly regained mobility, so that he was very ambivalent about whether to impregnate her or not. The patient himself was at a critical phase in his analysis, which at that time dealt with the core of his phobia, i.e., the early relationship with his mother displaced onto his wife and, in the transference, onto his analyst. He seemed to come closer to a resolution. He had begun to drive alone and to go places by himself, and he had even taken a plane trip recently. (He had never traveled anyplace before and had always managed to have someone go along with him in the car.) He felt trapped in the analysis; giving up the phobia meant giving up magical control and revolving the infantile tie with mother (his wife and his analyst), that is, to finish his analysis. The deepest meaning of the phobic relationship, as I see it, is to maintain the infantile tie with mother forever, that is, the avoidance of any change, any termination. In the final analysis, this equals the avoidance of accepting the reality of death.

My patient had always identified himself with John. He felt that John looked like him. He also thought that John was rejected by his mother as Mr. J. had felt rejected by his own mother. He had always been closer to his father. He looked like his father and felt that his father preferred John among all the grandchildren. Analysis revealed that at this critical point in his analysis Mr. J. had passed on his phobia to his son. He continued the phobic relationship with John by playing the part of the solicitous father. This was a piece of clever acting out. Instead of resolving his phobia, Mr. J. arranged for a phobic relationship with his son. This could be convincingly and effectively interpreted to him. He became aware that by his anxiety and overconcern about John, he had been transmitting to John his unconscious wish for the phobic dependence. The most startling thing for Mr. J. was what he called John's paradoxical reaction. Without any intervention from the outside, there had been a dramatic change in John's behavior. John, who previously had been whining and fearful in the morning, reluctant to get dressed and to leave the house, now was as happy as a lark, more carefree and relaxed than before the onset of the phobia. This change occurred when Mr. J. was able to disengage himself from his pathological involvement with John and to treat him more casually. The child responded with immediate relief, and directed his interest back to his playmates and outside activities. The extra interest, devotion, and time given to him by his father had apparently been correctly interpreted by John as a premium for his compliance with his father's unconscious wishes.

Certain aspects of Mr. J.'s analysis during this period are of particular interest for the further understanding of the phenomenon of induced school phobia. These aspects dealt with Mr. J.'s relationship with his father, which he had conspicuously neglected in his analysis. He had always considered his father the more independent and the more considerate parent and had had a manifestly positive relationship with him. The conscious hatred and hostility he felt for his mother had occupied a large part of his analysis. He now remembered that his father would often belittle the mother in his presence and that he would tell on his mother to his father. His father used to take him on his business trips and have him sit for hours in the car waiting for him. The patient had insisted on looking at this as a proof of love and had never before admitted to himself that he felt that his father was phobic and inconsiderate and was using him as a tool in his phobic manipulation. To admit this would have meant to acknowledge the same concerns in himself. He could now understand that he had been trying to do the same with John.

John's phobia served many functions in his father's mental life and in the family's neurotic needs. At this point I want to mention only the following:

1.   In identification with John, Mr. J. could maintain his own phobia, the maintenance of which was threatened by the analysis.

2.   Mr. J. perpetuated with John the relationship he had had with his own father; that is, he transformed what he had experienced passively into an active experience; he did with John what had been done to him by his father.

3.   The phobic child also could substitute for the fourth child, the new baby, by fulfilling the purpose of limiting the freedom of the parents.

4.   John's phobia served Mr. J. as a punishment of his wife (mother) and analyst because he implied that Mrs. J.'s rejection of John and, in the transference, my rejection of the patient,

caused John's phobia. It was as if he said: "My wife is a bad mother to John and you are a bad analyst to me." He clearly manifested this attitude by assuming the role of the good father with John—being even better than a mother. He felt, and it would seem that Mrs. J. shared this feeling, that John's behavior exposed her as he had exposed his own mother by his behavior in childhood. A further significant meaning which he brought out in the analysis was that now I would have to treat John for his school phobia so that I really had nothing to gain by insisting that he finish his analysis. In this way, the relationship with me (the tie with mother) would not terminate but would continue through John and forever.

I would now like to illustrate the dynamics and the handling of a case of induced school phobia in a child of latency age.

Six-year-old Ann developed a phobia at the start of the first grade in school. According to the mother, Ann had gone to nursery and kindergarten without too much difficulty.

Mrs. A. related that on the first day of school they met a little boy on the way to school who was crying, "I don't want to learn the ABC's. I don't want to go to school." Mrs. A. was disturbed by this, but to her surprise Ann went into the auditorium of the school willingly. The mother started to wink at her and wave good-bye, whereupon Ann wanted to come over to her mother, but was prevented from doing so by the teacher. In fact, two teachers grabbed her. Mrs. A. brought Ann to school the next day, and since the line had not yet formed, she brought Ann to her classroom and stayed with her until the other children came. She noted that Ann was uneasy. Ann did not mix with the other children, and she cried when her mother left. The next day Mrs. A. did not take Ann to school. When she came for treatment, Ann had been out of school for two weeks.

The mother thought that Ann's phobia was related to a baby sitter they had had a few weeks prior to this incident.

Ann never stayed with anyone in the family, not even her father or the maternal grandmother. With the exception of her mother, Ann would stay only with a baby sitter who lived on the same floor. Several weeks before, when this girl was not available, the mother hired another baby sitter. Mrs. A. seemed to have strong feelings about this girl, whom she described to me in great detail. Mrs. A. was shocked when Ann, who knew this girl, accepted her readily. A week later when this girl came again, Ann was very upset and did not want her to stay. Although Mrs. A. had no special plans for tht evening, she insisted that the baby sitter stay with Ann. Ann threatened to vomit, but the mother left her. However, Mrs. A. returned immediately because she felt that she should not have left and found that Ann had vomited. The vomiting was then repeated for several nights, Ann getting up at the same time each night and vomiting.

I then learned that Ann had had a period of nightly vomiting when she was about eleven months old, and that the pediatrician had implied to the mother that she must be doing something wrong with the child. Ann would vomit only during week nights when the house was quiet and she was alone with her mother. Mr. A. was working nights at that time. On weekends, when the house was full of people, the child never vomited. When Ann was about three or four she was very active and often said, "I want to play on the street. I want to go there. I want to do this by myself." Yet at night she always clung to her mother, who had to come into Ann's bedroom innumerable times. This would end up with the mother becoming angry, yelling, and spanking Ann.

When I pointed out to Mrs. A. that it appeared to me that she was overconcerned with Ann and seemed to be holding on to her tightly, she said, "She's my only child. I am now married fourteen years, and I had to wait seven years until I could conceive." When I remarked that she seemed to want an exclusive relationship with Ann, into which nobody was to intrude, not even her own mother or husband, she said, "Ann is crazy about her father, but she wouldn't stay with him alone. In fact, he doesn't want to stay with her, because he wouldn't know how to handle her." She then related that Ann was willing to stay with her father or even to go out with him provided her mother stayed at home. Ann had to know where her mother was and that she would find her in the same place. In her second interview, Mrs. A. traced the onset of Ann's phobic behavior back to the time when Ann was ten months old and Mrs. A. had left her with a baby sitter for the first time. It was then that the vomiting, which the doctor had diagnosed as purely emotional, began.

The mother felt that the intensification of the phobia occurred after the last baby sitter had stayed with Ann. Since then, Ann had been getting up nightly and would not stay with her father or grandmother in the evening, though she did not mind doing so during the day when she knew where her mother was. On several occasions Ann had recently wanted to come into her mother's bed, and although Mrs. A. knew that she should not accede, she gave in to Ann's demands.

After the second interview I suggested to Mrs. A. that she take Ann back to school. She reported that Ann refused to go into the school building, but when Mrs. A. said, "Then let's go home," Ann became angry at her. Ann did not want to go home and stayed in school. Then there was a holiday after which Ann refused to go back to school. Mrs. A. wondered whether she should do homework with Ann or put her into a private school so that she could stay with her in school. She talked of the close relationship she had with Ann. She then began to talk about her marriage and her feelings about her husband. Her husband had a very bad temper, he became very upset when he had to stay with Ann because he had to clean her up after she vomited. There were frequent scenes between them. At this point Mrs. A. began to cry and then related that she had been unhappy when she got pregnant after seven years. She did not like the child. She was melancholy.

Everything in the house appeared strange to her. Previously she had never stayed much at home; she did not even cook at home, they always ate out. She thought that she had finally become used to having the child. Last winter Ann had had the whooping cough and Mrs. A. had been with her constantly. During this and the next interview Mrs. A. became increasingly aware of her own need for Ann's phobia, which kept Mrs. A. from running away and leaving her husband. She had suffered from a chronic untreated depression since the birth of Ann. Although after the third interview Mrs. A. was able to convey to Ann that she no longer needed Ann as a protection and Ann returned to school promptly and without any fuss, I felt it necessary to refer the mother for psychotherapy, both for her own sake and to make sure that she did not fall back on Ann for security.

In this connection an experience with a patient whom I treated successfully for a severe school phobia when she was an adolescent is of interest. I saw this patient again eleven years later when she consulted me because her oldest child aged four years was reluctant to go to nursery school. It was possible to clear this problem up in one interview because the mother realized that she was having difficulty in separating herself from this child, to whom she felt very close. She had been aware that she had felt jealous and slighted when the child had at first very readily accepted the teacher and the other children (Chapter 8). I saw this patient again ten years later, a few months after her youngest child had started kindergarten. There had been no school-phobic problems with any of her children during the intervening years. Being aware of her tendency to hold on to her children, she had been able to handle herself admirably. She came this time for herself, because she had been feeling jittery during the past few months and realized that this was her reaction to "there being no children in the house." This case is also interesting as a twenty-one-year follow-up of an adolescent school phobia, but cannot be dealt with further within the framework of this chapter.

In cases of chronic induced phobia in an older child in the late latency or prepuberty period, the situation differs from that of the previously presented cases. It then becomes necessary to treat the child himself as well as concomitantly the parent (inducer). If the parent who needs the phobia of the child for his or her own neurotic reasons is unavailable for treatment, the prognosis for the child is poor because such parents will withdraw the child from treatment at the time when their equilibrium is threatened by the child's improvement (see Chapter 13). I would like to illustrate this briefly with the case of nine-year-old Harry, whose school phobia had become very intense during his last school year.

> In Harry's case, the pathological relationship was with his father, who gave the developmental history and brought the child for consultation and treatment. Mr. H. had been very close to Harry from infancy and had obviously been instrumental in Harry's developing severe reaction formations against anal-erotic and anal-sadistic impulses, as early as the age of two. The father was particularly proud of the fact that Harry had never displayed any overt manifestations of derivatives of anal impulses. He was delighted by the two-year-old child's "innate consideration and kindness." Harry never broke or destroyed anything and he was so clean that he never wiped himself because "he would become disgusted and nauseated." I learned later that for this reason Harry had never used the toilet in school for defecation. Harry was the older of two children. Two other siblings had died, one shortly after birth and the other in infancy when Harry was two years old. These events seemed to have played a part in the parents' latent anxiety about Harry and also, I believe, in Harry's phobic response to it. When Harry was not quite four his father left for the army. Sometime thereafter a baby sister was born who took up the mother's time and attention. At that time the family lived with the maternal grandparents, who genuinely cared for Harry. He did well during these two years when his father was away.

When Mr. H. returned, he resumed his preoccupation with Harry. The father seemed disappointed that Harry had "learned to get along without me" and that he liked school and being with other children. Harry's first neurotic reaction to his father's return manifested itself in a sleep disturbance, the dynamics of which will be discussed in connection with the manifest school phobia which he developed later. Harry's sleep disturbance seemed to have complemented his father's severe insomnia. Both Harry and his father would be up and together for parts of the night while the mother and sister slept in another room. Harry began to miss school when he developed frequent colds and complaints of sore throats. At seven and a half years he had a tonsillectomy. At the same time the family moved and Harry was transferred to a new school. He now showed a manifest reluctance to go to school and complained about the teachers. Mr. H., who could not tolerate any overt neurotic behavior in his son, now became very punitive and forceful with Harry. At this point Harry developed bellyaches and diarrhea. The diarrhea made it nearly impossible for him to remain in school, particularly because he had even earlier refused to use the toilet in school. Now he came running home from school several times a day to use the toilet. After a few weeks of this, Mr. H., feeling that the school authorities were not forceful enough with Harry, decided to take Harry to school himself and to stay with Harry to prevent him from running out. But as soon as the father left, Harry would run after him. Threats, beatings, bribes, changes of school were of no avail. During that year Harry ran away several times whenever an attempt was made to keep him in school forcefully. By this time the father had induced the school authorities to handle Harry rather harshly (Jarvis, 1964). The father did everything except follow the advice to seek psychiatric treatment for Harry.

From the history, the child's behavior, and my observations of father and child, I gained the impression that this father, prompted by his own intense neurotic needs, had induced a very severe school phobia in his son. Mr. H. openly devalued psychotherapy, which he considered a treatment for weaklings. He could not accept that his son was neurotic, which to him meant a weakling. What he wanted was a magical formula for returning Harry to school quickly. The mother was unavailable physically and emotionally. She was tied up with her baby daughter and entirely pushed into the background by her husband.

The psychological records, including a Rorschach taken when Harry was eight and a half years old, showed that he was struggling with tremendous repressed aggression and lived in terror of being overwhelmed by his impulses. A tendency to withdraw was noted, but there were no concrete evidences of disturbed thinking or deterioration in reality testing at that time. Clinical exploration indicated that a rapid deterioration of personality had taken place in the intervening half year. In defense against overwhelmingly strong destructive impulses (of a homicidal and suicidal nature) Harry was using somatic pathways for discharge. In addition to the bellyaches and diarrhea, he had also begun to wheeze as if he were developing asthma. His dreams, usually of a nightmarish character, were of such intensity and vividness that he often woke up confused and unable to differentiate between dream and reality. His dreams dealt with violence and death. In daytime, moreover, he seemed to have brief lapses of memory, which to me appeared like the beginning of petit mal. I found that there was a very close physical contact between Harry and his parents; his mother was still bathing him and cleaning him after bowel movements, and the father was both overly seductive and sadistic with him. Between Harry and his father there was a strong latent homosexual tie, which apparently covered up Harry's positive oedipal wishes and murderous impulses against the father. The intensity of the oedipal conflict and of his castration anxiety manifested itself in the severe sleep disturbance which Harry developed after his father's return home. Turning toward the seductive and sadistic father in (masochistic) submission was his attempt to deal with his intense aggressive impulses directed primarily against his father. The fear of loss of control and of something terrible happening (somebody getting killed) was an outstanding feature of his nightmares as well as of his school phobia. This was also expressed and acted out in the loss of control over his bowels. Both the waking up from the nightmares and the running home from school were attempts to gain control over an uncontrollable situation—his repressed impulses threatening to break through. The inescapable internal, instinctual danger was externalized in his sleep by the nightmares and in the daytime by the school phobia, so that he could escape the danger. This Harry did by staying up and avoiding sleep (nightmares = the phobic situation) and escaping the danger in sleep by waking up. In avoiding going to school and, when forced to go, in running from school, Harry used the same mechanisms.

After several weeks of treatment, during which Harry's panic lessened and he apparently accepted me as his therapist, Mr. H., feeling threatened by this, I believe, decided against psychotherapy and put Harry in a military school. Mr. H., who appeared to me to be a borderline psychotic with marked depressive and paranoid trends, was inaccessible to any psychotherapeutic interventions. His sadistic inclinations were scarcely concealed by his insistence on obedience and discipline. He once tied Harry to his bedpost for several days and on another occasion beat him mercilessly, commenting with pride that any soldier would have succumbed, but Harry did not budge. I felt that under the circumstances separation from the sick father was therapeutic in itself.

Chronic school phobia, whether of the induced or the traumatic (common) type, is an indication of a serious personality disturbance and is a difficult condition to treat effectively, requiring skill, patience, and time (see Chapter 8; also Coolidge et al., 1960; Greenbaum, 1964; Kahn and Nursten, 1962; Messer, 1964). Treatment should be regarded as successful only when it brings about favorable changes in the personality and character disturbances associated with chronic school phobia and not on the basis of whether the child does or does not return to school quickly—that is, the removal of the presenting symptom. The emphasis in the treatment of chronic school phobia has to be placed on the treatment of the total neurosis, of which the school phobia is only one manifestation, just as a persistent fever or cough may be only one symptom of a chronic progressive tuberculosis. The behavior of children with chronic school phobia of the induced type may resemble that of children with symbiotic schizophrenia, and there is a similarity in the dynamics of the parent-child relationship in these two conditions. In planning treatment of a child with chronic school phobia of the induced type it is important to keep this in mind (Chapter 22). Unless the pathological tie with the parent (inducer) can be resolved or at least appreciably modified, treatment will not be successful even though it succeeds in returning the child to school for shorter or even longer periods of time. There will be inevitable recurrences and severe setbacks, especially at those times when in the course of normal development the child's ability to relinquish the attachment to the original love objects and to form new relationships is being tested, that is, at puberty and adolescence. Here again, the similarity with schizophrenia as well as with children suffering from psychosomatic disorders is apparent (Chapter 3; M. Sperling, 1949d, 1951).

In all these instances we are dealing with children with unresolved symbiotic preoedipal fixations. Such children cannot resolve their oedipal conflicts and are unable to utilize the progressive forces of puberty and adolescence. Puberty and adolescence are critical phases for these youngsters because instead of progressing they may, under the influx of the biological and psychological stresses of these phases, regress to the preoedipal relationships (A. Freud, 1965). The onset or recurrence or intensification of phobic, psychotic, or psychosomatic manifestations is a frequent occurrence in puberty and adolescence (M. Sperling, 1955c). It cannot be emphasized enough that the aim of speedily removing the presenting symptom of school phobia before any appreciable change in the parent-child relationship and in the ego structure of the child himself has been achieved could be a disservice rather than a service to such a child. In these cases there is a resistance to treatment on the part of both the child and the parents because treatment is a threat to the continuation of the pathological relationships, and return to school is often used as a rationalization for discontinuing treatment. The chronicity of the case may be an indicator of the intensity of the need for the persistence of this relationship. I would like to illustrate this briefly with the case of fifteen-year-old Fred, who is rather typical of the more severe cases of this kind.

Fred's probic attachment to his mother had already manifested itself in nursery school. He had some difficulties in the early school years; but he still managed with shorter or longer absences until he was nine and a half, when he had a severe setback, developed psychosomatic symptoms, mainly nausea and vomiting, and stayed out of school for a prolonged period of time. He received brief psychiatric treatment of a supportive nature and medications and returned to school, though with many difficulties and rituals. His mother had to stay home and be available whenever he wanted to call her so that she could take him out of school when he felt sick. At thirteen he had what appeared to be an acute psychotic episode with some paranoid ideas accompanied by anorexia and weight loss. He returned to the psychiatrist who had treated him earlier. When the latter recommended hospitalization, the parents consulted another psychiatrist, who felt that he could treat Fred on an ambulatory basis. His school attendance was now very irregular, he was out for long stretches of time, and there was also a marked change in his personality. Fred was treated mainly with tranquilizers and was hospitalized at one time when he became more difficult at home. Since his intelligence was superior, he could keep up with his grades. Whenever he returned to school, the parents felt that the problem was solved, refusing to recognize the progressive deterioration of Fred's personality until he refused to go to school altogether.

Psychological tests, including Rorschach, taken when he was fourteen years of age revealed superior intelligence in a boy who was in a state of massive regression and failing defenses, especially the phobic and psychosomatic ones. In the case of a boy in such a precarious balance it was unwise to insist on his return to school, a factor that might further contribute to his deterioration.‡ Unable to cope with the realities of school, especially on a social level, and with the demands of adolescence, Fred was teased and made fun of by his classmates; this he experienced as persistent failure and continuous narcissistic injury, and it only increased his need for further regression and withdrawal from reality. His case would seem to illustrate particularly well the point I have tried to make earlier, namely, that a child with such psychopathology and without adequate treatment will react with severe exacerbation or even with a psychotic break to the stresses of puberty and adolescence. I was consulted when Fred was fifteen years old and the parents had been advised to place him in a hospital away from home. I was able to convince the mother to accept treatment for herself and psychoanalytically oriented psychotherapy for her son.

In my twenty-six years of child psychiatric practice I have seen quite a number of such cases and I have learned that proper assessment and treatment plans are essential for a successful outcome. I have found that in the case of prelatency children, indirect treatment, that is, treatment of the parent-inducer, is the treatment of choice and leads to excellent results, even in chronic cases. This approach may still be effective with latency children, although for this age group I favor the direct approach, that is, treatment of the child himself with prior or concomitant treatment of the parent (inducer). This method still works with puberty children, although in their case and particularly in that of adolescents I prefer to have minimal contact with the parents, especially the parent-inducer, during treatment of the youngster. My aim is to establish a therapeutic alliance with the parent(s) before I start treatment of the child. If the parent is in need of continued treatment, I refer the parent for therapy and make the

‡ In this connection a paper by Rodriguez et al. (1959) is of interest. These authors insist upon early return to school and do not hesitate "to invoke the legal authority of the school to compel attendance." They do not believe that school phobia in a child of latency and prepuberty age is a serious matter. Such thinking contributes to a neglect of early symptoms and their prognostic significance.

suggestion that the parent-child relationship should be specifically focused upon. If the parent later wishes to have further treatment for himself, this can then be arranged for in the conventional way as psychotherapy or psychoanalysis, whichever is advisable. The type of treatment to which I am referring here, in which the parent is treated as the senior partner in the pathological partnership with the child, is goal-directed and focused on his specific relationship to the child (Chapter 2; Part 5; M. Sperling, 1949d, 1951). In cases of older children and especially of adolescents, it is preferable to assign the child and the parent to different therapists, who have a similar orientation regarding the theoretical concepts and technical approaches, and who collaborate as a team (see Burlingham et al., 1955; Hellman et al., 1960; Levy, 1960; Sprince, 1962).

The differential diagnosis between induced chronic and common chronic school phobia is not always easy to make because once the school phobia has been in existence for some time the circumstances under which the acute onset occurred are usually not remembered, and if they are remembered, the accounts are distorted. Upon surface examination the children suffering from common chronic school phobia appear to be less disturbed than those suffering from induced chronic school phobia. In fact, if it were not for the presenting symptom, they would seem to be functioning well in other areas to the casual observer, and even to their families. On closer observation, however, it becomes evident that in these cases, too, the total personality is affected. The school phobia is used as a safety valve by means of which the child manages to maintain some sort of equilibrium. The school phobia in these cases has the function of keeping the neurosis localized to one area, while in the induced chronic school phobia the school phobia is one more overt symptom in a *manifest* total personality disturbance. This differentiation is of dynamic importance because in cases of common chronic school phobia it is obviously unwise to attempt the removal of the school phobia before working on the latent personality disturbance. In these cases the removal of the presenting symptom without sufficient therapeutic work endangers the precarious balance that is maintained with the help of the school phobia. Actually these children react to attempts to return them to school prematurely with panic and may develop transitory somatic symptoms as emergency discharges of anxiety.

In this connection I want to point again to the definite dynamic interrelation between certain psychosomatic disorders in children and school phobia. In fact, the onset of a psychosomatic illness can in some cases be traced back to the start of school, or to similar separation traumata which induce other children to develop overt school phobias. In consequence of their psychosomatic illness these children have a poor attendance record, with absences from school often ranging from months to years. I have found that at a certain phase in the treatment of these children, when the somatic symptoms begin to subside, the underlying phobia and symbiotic relationship with the mother emerge and must then be resolved before regular school attendance can be achieved and maintained. To this group belong children with ulcerative or mucous colitis and bronchial asthma, and others (M. Sperling, 1950c, 1952c, 1961, 1963).

Analytic study of children suffering from common chronic school phobia reveals that they acquired the disposition to react with a phobic response to traumatic situations early in childhood, but in these cases the object relationships and the instinctual and ego development during the oral and anal phases have been much more satisfactory than in the case of the induced type of chronic school phobia. In common school phobias, the conflicts mobilized by the trauma or series of traumatic experiences are mainly related to the oedipal phase. There are transitions between cases of induced and common chronic school phobia. If a common school phobia has been in existence for a long time, there will inevitably be character changes with emphasis on secondary gain from illness, as we find them in chronic traumatic neurosis of adults.

It is necessary to keep in mind that we are dealing with more or less severe personality disorders and that long-term therapy is required for a lasting result. The treatment of choice, in my opinion, for such a psychoneurosis is psychoanalysis, if possible, or psychoanalytically oriented psychotherapy. The aim in psychoanalysis is to analyze and to modify the main mechanisms of defense—in these cases, repression, isolation, projection, externalization, displacement, etc.—and to bring about structural changes in the ego and superego. The unconscious conflicts are then gradually brought to the fore, and the child whose ego has been strengthened by the therapeutic relationship is enabled to deal more appropriately with his conflicts and to find more suitable solutions for them in reality. It would be desirable, especially in view of the fact that there is some controversy concerning the applicability of psychoanalysis in puberty and early adolescence, to give a full account of the analytic treatment of such a case. It is impossible, however, to do this within the framework of this chapter. I shall have to limit myself to indicating the essential points concerning dynamics and technique. As an illustration I shall use material from the analytic treatment of a twelve-and-a-half-year-old boy, who had a common chronic school phobia.

Peter was referred because of a school phobia that had become increasingly evident over the previous two years. During the previous six months he had attended school only two days a week. His mother had to take him and call for him and be available for his calls from school to take him home in case he felt sick. For the past six weeks he had refused to go to school altogether. His attendance record had been poor for some time because of frequent colds, which turned to near-pneumonia, headaches, bellyaches, feeling faint, etc. On the surface he gave the appearance of a rather mature and well-adjusted boy. It soon became obvious that he had been fighting a losing battle against the spreading phobia and that he was in a state of constant anxiety, at times reaching panic proportions. He had been using counterphobic defenses and rationalizations in the attempt to conceal from others and himself the degree and intensity of his anxiety. He was afraid of doctors and dentists, injections, new places, elevators, water, getting lost, etc.

Psychoanalytic investigation revealed that there was repression of intense aggression and that his precarious balance was maintained mainly by reaction formations. There were occasional breakthroughs of destructive impulses, especially in self-destructive behavior. He was very accident-prone and had had innumerable accidents, some of a rather serious nature, prior to and continuing for some time during his analysis. Once he nearly blinded himself. He had obsessional thoughts of killing people, and since his father and he himself owned a collection of guns (for hunting), this was a matter of some concern. When cleaning a gun he often had fantasies that it accidentally fired and someone (a man), and less frequently he himself, was killed. Although it became apparent rather early in his analysis that his major problem stemmed from a very intense, unresolved oedipal conflict with repressed and displaced parricidal impulses, which gave a paranoid cast to his castration fears, this problem was not dealt with until late in the analysis. The anal-sadistic features were very marked and contributed to the severity of the oedipal conflict. Peter's personality was characterized by a high degree of narcissism and the persistence of the fantasy of omnipotence which made it dangerous for him to know his thoughts, feelings, and impulses. He also had a number of rituals and he carried a rabbit's foot with him as a magic charm.

I kept Peter out of school a term and a half in order to prevent repetition of the experience of failure to attend consistently and of continual narcissistic injuries resulting from it. I had the full cooperation of his parents and the school authorities in this matter. When Peter returned to school, his narcissism, his magical thinking, and his anxieties were considerably reduced due to the persistent analysis of his defenses. His attendance from then on was remarkable. He seemed to have developed a special immunity to colds from which he previously had so frequently suffered. It was not until the second year of his treatment that he could to some extent curb and bring into analysis a symptom which proved dynamically very significant and therapeutically more stubborn than his school phobia—namely, a persistent enuresis. Peter had been successfully bladder-trained at the age of two and became enuretic when he was not quite four years old, following a hernia operation and during a vacation in which he shared the parents' bedroom. He had been enuretic since then every single night. In the third year of treatment he formed a relationship to a girl which enabled us to analyze more fully his relationship to his mother and his attempt to transfer this relationship to the girlfriend, of whom he was very possessive and jealous. He no longer felt so dependent upon his mother. Through the school phobia he had managed to control and possess (the oedipal) mother in a preoedipal (anal-sadistic) way.

In the fourth and final year of treatment it was possible to analyze the oedipal conflict sufficiently for Peter to feel that to be a man did not mean to kill father and to be castrated, that is, to be killed in turn, and that he did not need his phobia which had been a regressive (anal-sadistic) way of possessing, that is, controlling, his mother. Peter had never been away from home, even for one night, until the end of the second year of analysis. He usually became sick in anticipation of such events and would have sleep disturbances and nightmares, indicating an acute intensification of separation anxiety. It was found that the acute exacerbation of Peter's school phobia at age twelve (Peter had shown milder signs of school phobia from the start of school, but these had been disregarded until his phobia became so intense that all concessions and manipulations failed to get Peter to school) had occurred at a time when his father had been away for several weeks and Peter had been left alone with his mother. During his treatment I could observe that Peter became very anxious whenever his wish to stay out of school (each time his father left for short trips) was revived. Neither Peter nor his environment had in any way connected this with his school phobia. This connection was made at an advanced stage of his treatment when this could be recognized and interpreted as an event that had acutely intensified his oedipal conflicts and as a consequence led to regression to the anal-sadistic stage. Peter had at first considered a college where he could live at home, but he later changed his mind and decided to live on campus.

The treatment of adolescents suffering from this type of school phobia can be limited to the adolescent, and no work with the parents is necessary. This is different in induced chronic school phobia, where the symbiotic tie between child and parent has to be modified before successful treatment of the child is possible. It is necessary, however, to insure the parents' willingness to accept long-term treatment because this is the only guarantee for a successful resolution of the child's neurosis. Peter's parents were genuinely concerned with helping him and supported my efforts without intruding or interfering with his treatment. In the first few months of Peter's treatment I spoke to his mother several times, mostly on the telephone, to help her to disentangle herself from Peter's controlling maneuvers. She obviously had neurotic, and particularly phobic, problems of her own, but these were neither interpreted nor dealt with by me. Because she behaved as though she and not Peter were responsible for his attending or not attending school she needed support and reassurance in order to relax her overcompensations and to let Peter carry this responsibility himself.

In the actual treatment of adolescents, the preoedipal conflicts and relationships should be dealt with first. Owing to the revival of the unresolved oedipal conflicts during puberty and the danger of a breakthrough into consciousness, repression has to be reinforced, and the lifting of this re-repression is strongly defended against. The anal fixations, especially the unresolved separation conflicts, also make the oedipal conflicts more pathogenic in these cases.

These dynamics and techniques also apply to adolescent girls suffering from chronic common school phobia. In such a case we usually find an overprotective, controlling mother and a seductive father, features which contribute to the intensification of the oedipal conflicts. The inevitable resentment and disappointment in both parents increase the girl's need for omnipotent control. The phobic attachment to the mother with its homosexual coloring covers up the underlying hostility and death wishes. In girls, agoraphobic features are more prominent, such as a fear of leaving the house, walking to school, crossing the street; the unconscious wish to run away, to have sexual adventures, to be raped (which in the final analysis reveals itself as a fear of death), comes out in the fear of getting lost, of being in crowds or in wide open spaces.

In acute cases it is often possible to connect the onset of the phobia with the precipitating event or events—usually those that trigger off such unconscious wishes and fears related to the oedipal conflict. While it may be possible in reestablishing this connection to make conscious some of the underlying sexual wishes and to relieve the anxiety to such an extent that a speedy return to school can be effected, this first aid (see Chapter 8) has to be followed up by further exploratory and interpretative work to prevent the phobic core from retaining its pathogenicity. The fact that some girls react in this specific way to certain experiences to which many others are exposed as well and to which they react differently indicates that there is a latent phobic disposition and that the trauma has a specific unconscious meaning and has been interpreted in this specific way (O. Sperling, 1950).

A frequent etiological factor in these cases is the identification with a phobic parent. In the case of a fourteen-year-old adolescent girl, Paula, who had a severe chronic school phobia and whom I treated in successful analysis for three and a half years, the mother was an agoraphobic. It is of interest that Paula behaved as if she were unaware of this fact, as if she tried to repress this knowledge. Her mother had been in therapy off and on during Paula's childhood and had returned to her therapist at the time of Paula's referral to me. There is a quality of secrecy and denial associated with the way agoraphobics deal with their handicaps. Paula applied the same tactics to her own phobia. I would like to repeat again that in the chronic cases of this type of school phobia one has to be careful with the interpretation of sexual material. One should first analyze and devalue the pathological defenses and the inordinate narcissism and need for omnipotent control. Futhermore, one has to resist the pressures exerted by the parents, the school, or even the patient for a quick return to school. This technique was applied in Paula's case.

I had an opportunity to see Paula some fifteen years later, when she consulted me because of problems in her marriage. I learned that she had gone to college, had finished graduate work, and was pursuing a career. She had two children, and there seemed to be some conflict between her career and her children. This conflict was related to her feelings about her mother. I learned that her mother was still phobic and manipulating and that her sister (who had always been held up to Paula as a model) had also developed agoraphobia. Paula was very critical of both her mother and her sister, but it appeared to me that her overemphasis on her career had a defensive function and that she was using it as a protection against her fear that she might repeat such a pattern with her own children. I am mentioning this here to indicate that such phobic patterns can be so persistent and pervasive that they affect whole families and are perpetuated through generations.

## Summary

In this chapter school phobias are comprehensively studied. Hopefully, a study of this kind should lead to a fuller understanding of some etiological, dynamic, and therapeutic factors that enable us to deal more effectively with these problems. I consider school phobia to be a neurosis characterized by fixation to the anal-sadistic phase of development, persistence of ambivalence, narcissism, and magical thinking (fantasy of omnipotence), and more closely related to the compulsion neuroses than to anxiety hysteria.

I have divided the phobias into acute and chronic and into induced and common (traumatic) school phobia. In the induced type, the traumatization is insidious and results mainly from a pathological parent-child relationship. In the common type, the acute onset follows a trauma or a series of traumata and resembles a traumatic neurosis with the presenting symptom of school phobia.

The indications for the type of treatment to be chosen depend upon the differential diagnosis and the age of the child at the onset of the school phobia, whether in prelatency, latency, or at puberty or adolescence. These factors determine whether the child or the parent(s) should be treated and, if both are to be treated, whether the parent should be treated prior to or concomitantly with the child, whether by the same or by a different therapist, and whether by psychoanalysis or short-term psychoanalytic psychotherapy. I questioned the value of symptomatic treatment and the emphasis on quick return of the school-phobic child to school without treating the total neurosis, of which the school phobia is one manifestation.

# 8
# Analytic First Aid in School Phobias

School phobias in children have attracted much psychiatric interest during the past two decades (Coolidge et al., 1957, 1960; Eisenberg, 1958; Gardner, 1952; Johnson et al., 1941; Klein 1945; Sperling, 1950c, 1951, 1952b). In some cases the onset of the phobia coincides with the start of school, which therefore appears to be the precipitating traumatic event. However, closer investigation reveals that a chronic phobic state already existed and was brought to crisis only when separation of mother and child was enforced by attendance at school. In other cases, children who have attended school without apparent difficulty for short or even long periods of time suddenly, or after a short initial struggle, develop a full-blown school phobia; often the child himself cannot plausibly relate his phobia to conditions at school. Dynamically this type of school phobia strikingly resembles traumatic neurosis, although trauma and effect seem disproportionate on surface observation. It may occur at any age, but I have encountered it most frequently in children at puberty and in adolescents. Biological changes and instinctual struggles inherent in adolescent development naturally make this age group more vulnerable.

Still other children develop a school phobia at the beginning of a new school year or term, or when faced by a change of school or teacher. In these cases both the child and those about him consider the phobia directly related to the school. However, these children are also chronically phobic and function so precariously that any event that rouses their basic conflict causes an acute exacerbation of the phobia. Because of their transitory character, these phobic states often remain untreated and may develop into permanent, crippling phobias. Brief periods of manifest school phobia, followed by various somatic complaints such as nausea, vomiting, bellyaches, diarrhea, headaches, or colds, to enumerate only a few, are found in other children. Here the somatic symptoms accomplish what the phobia failed to do: keep the child out of school, at least temporarily. This variation is discerned particularly in those children who are brought up with the attitude, "One does not give in to fear, but if one is sick one can't go to school." Some children develop somatic illness as an equivalent of phobia (see Chapter 3; Sperling, 1950c, 1952b).

Hence we find that the symptom of school phobia occurs in a variety of situations. Case reports have emphasized the hysterical, obsessive, and psychotic features of the phobia; Coolidge and Willer (1960) recommend differentiating neurotic from characterological school phobia. Yet, no matter how different the cases may appear clinically, the basic conflict underlying the symptom is the same, and the phobia demands prompt treatment based on psychoanalytic understanding.

I have studied fifty-eight children, ranging in age from two to sixteen years, nine of whom had lengthy analyses (from two to five years). But treatment of all the children in this group—even of those who had only a few interviews—was based on psychoanalytic principles. In some cases I treated the phobic couple (mother and child); in a few instances of young children I treated only the mother; in most cases, especially the older children and adolescents, I treated the sick child, using my initial talks with the mother to set up a relation with her that would permit undisturbed work with the child.

Freud, first in his study of phobia in a five-year-old child (1909) and later in The Problem of Anxiety (1936), established that a phobia is a true psychoneurotic symptom due to repression of positive and negative oedipal fantasies and wishes. Specific mechanisms enter into the formation of a phobia, the most important of which are externalization, displacement, and projection. By externalization, the danger which is instinctual, and hence internal and inescapable, is transformed into an external danger which can be avoided. Displacement removes the danger from the home, where the child has to live, to the school or the street or some other place. The conflict is displaced from the parents to the school authorities or classmates or others. Projection operates much more clearly in other forms of phobia, especially animal phobia, in which the threatening instinctual impulses are projected onto the phobic animal and give the illness a paranoid tinge (see Chapter 9).

Besides these mechanisms there occur distortion of original fantasies and wishes and condensation of contradictory fantasies and wishes from various levels of development. It seems probable that separation anxiety is so intense in children's phobias because separation unconsciously signifies death of the mother and, in turn, of the child. By separating or not separating from her, the child omnipotently controls his mother's life as well as his own. The strong fantasy of omnipotence, the high degree of ambivalence, and other features, clearly show that pregenital elements play a decisive role in the etiology and dynamics of phobia. The occurrence of phobias in children during the pregenital phase is further confirmation.

Phobic children often openly express their ideas about death. A six-year-old phobic girl asked her mother, "Who will take care of me when you die? Why don't you live with your mother? Who will take care of you when your mother dies?" A twelve-year-old phobic boy recalled the following episode experienced at age four. When his older brother showed him a globe and explained that it was a "picture of the world", he suddenly became terribly afraid of being separated from his mother and in panic ran to find her. He pleaded with her to promise him that if he should die she would hold his hand and die with him, and said if she should die he wanted to hold her hand and die with her.

Sometimes the phobia of the child covers up a phobia of the mother. The readiness of the mother to accommodate the phobic needs of her child is characteristic in these cases. I have described the function of the phobia as a life-saving device for both partners in such a relation (1951). A mother, after reporting that she had once momentarily lost sight of her child and that the child was almost killed, then stated that the child could not be without her and refused to stay with anyone else, even with the father. This made the mother indispensable and checked her unconscious impulse to run away (kill herself); she had to stay alive for her phobic child. In such a relationship the mother is the "life-saver", and indulgence of and abuse by the child is a small price to pay for such an important service. The balance of control, and with this the attitude of the mother, can change and the mother may become very intolerant of and even cruel to the child. This fantasy of magical control over life and death shared by mother and child, and expressed by both in their intense need and struggle for control over the other and over external situations, is very vulnerable. To the phobic child any situation that means that he is not in control can cause panic and this applies particularly to school, where the teacher, not the child, is in control.

That the same holds true for the mother is well illustrated by the following case. A child developed an intense phobia on the day after her mother visited the gynecologist who had advised against another pregnancy because of a gynecological condition. This advice unconsciously meant to the mother that she was not in control. She could not have another child and this made her child irreplaceable. Her anxiety manifested itself in an exaggerated need to watch and to hold onto her child, to which the child responded accordingly (see Chapter 3).

No matter what they are in reality, the precipitating events that touch off the acute anxiety, manifested in school phobia, are always events that unconsciously are interpreted by the child as a danger to his mother's life and his own life.

Understanding and accepting these fundamental dynamics

points the way to an effective approach to the problem. I do not believe in the "common-sense" approach to phobias; like any other true neurotic symptom, a phobia is not amenable to reason, persuasion, or punishment. Results achieved by such methods are short-lived and bring with them undesirable and often permanent pathological reactions and character changes. I also do not believe in the "self cures" of phobics. Phobic children learn to conceal their phobias and to protect themselves from anxiety-arousing situations at the expense of severe crippling of many functions.

Those who have treated persons with chronic phobia know how resistant they are to the mobilization of deeply buried anxieties. It is for this reason that we are particularly interested in dealing with phobic patients in the acute stages in order to prevent encapsulation of the process. Those who work with phobic children agree that it is important to get the child back to school as quickly as possible, but not all agree upon the method by which this is to be achieved. The method I recommend is based on psychoanalytic insight and operates by exposing to the patient as soon as possible the basic conflict underlying the phobia. This method works in alliance with the uncovering and against the repressive forces.

In our treatment of the phobic children we reconstruct in as much detail as possible the events immediately preceding, and dynamically related to, the onset of the phobic behavior. In most cases both the child and his parents offer numerous rationalizations and overlook the significant events, which have to be discovered by specific questioning. This phenomenon appears to be the result of a selective repressive tendency aimed at keeping vague those events that touch upon the repressed conflict of the child. The pathological effect of seemingly innocuous events results from their unconscious association with the child's basic conflict, which is thus activated. After establishing the unconscious significance of these events and their specific connections with the subsequent phobia and, if possible, with earlier phobic episodes, we interpret these connections and meanings convincingly to the child on the basis of the evidence obtained directly and from the mother. I have found this method particularly effective in acute cases where the anxiety can sometimes be relieved in one interview.

Three cases will demonstrate the procedure.

CASE 1.    A twelve-year-old girl had a school phobia of three weeks' duration. An interview with the mother revealed the following facts. Three weeks before the phobia began her teacher took her music book away from her in class. The patient was to play two piano pieces that afternoon and also was to have a piano lesson. She was upset by the teacher's action and, instead of eating lunch in school as usual, went home. When she found her mother was not at home, she called her father who told her that the mother had gone to the doctor for an injection for allergy. The patient then called the doctor's office but her mother had not yet arrived. As soon as the mother got to the doctor's office, she telephoned the child. The patient did not return to school that afternoon but the music book was sent to her after the mother called the teacher.

The next morning the child did not feel well and on arriving at school was sent to the nurse's office. Finally her mother was called to school, and after she and the nurse had talked with her the child went to class. For the next few days she vomited and felt sick in the morning and her mother walked with her to school. One morning she said that she felt better and that her mother need not accompany her to school. Nevertheless the mother went with her, saying that she was going shopping in that direction anyway. That day the patient became panicky in school and her mother was summoned again and took her home. For the two weeks since that time she had not returned to school.

I asked the mother if the patient had any reason to be concerned about her visit to the doctor. At first the mother said that she did not believe so as her daughter knew that she had gone only for an injection for allergy. But then she related the following event: on the Sunday before the incident in school the mother had fainted during a church ceremony while sitting next to the patient. She had fainted once before in the patient's presence, about five years before. At that time she had been suffering from a disease of the gall bladder for which she had received an injection on the day she fainted. The next day, the mother was operated upon. She recalled that at that period her daughter had insisted upon the mother taking her to school and remaining there with her. The patient was an only child and very close to her parents.

When I called for the patient in the waiting room I found her sitting on her father's lap, looking at a magazine with him. She followed me somewhat reluctantly but spoke freely in the interview. Adding to the mother's report, she told me that the teacher had been mean that day; she had taken magazines away from two other girls and then when the patient took her music book out during class had taken it away also. She went home because she was upset about the music book. When she found that her mother was not at home and the door was locked, she became anxious. (The mother had told me that she had said nothing to the patient about going to the doctor because she did not want to worry her. In my interview with the mother I had used this fact and her unwillingness to let her daughter walk to school alone to interpret to her the latent phobic relation between them.) From the patient's behavior it was obvious that she needed to know at all times where her mother was. I mentioned to her that her mother had told me about the fainting spell and asked if she had worried about it. I reminded her of the episode five years before. She said that she had not thought about it in this connection and that therefore she had not mentioned it.

I suggested to her that her mother's recent fainting had brought back fears which she must have had when her mother fainted and was operated upon when the patient was seven years old. I said that, without realizing it, she had been worried about her mother since the incident in church and that she came home for lunch because the incident in school had in some way increased her worry (teacher taking book away means not having control, and means that anything can happen). Not finding mother home and learning that she was at the doctor's office had intensified and confirmed her fear about mother being in danger, a fear of which she had not been consciously aware. I told her that children sometimes have angry feelings toward their mothers and, because they also believe in the magic power of their thoughts, they are afraid that something terrible may happen to mother. I assured her that thoughts and wishes are not dangerous and cannot kill anyone, but added that such thoughts can cause much fear in the child who has them and does not want to acknowledge them. I explained that children in such a situation are afraid that something may happen not only to mother but also to themselves. I suggested that she had become panicky the day her mother had accompanied her to school against her wish because this meant to her that her mother did not think it safe to let her go alone. This had intensified her fears about herself and about her mother to such a degree that she could no longer tolerate the separation from her mother and remain in school. I pointed out that this was really a conflict within herself which had to do with her feelings about mother and not a conflict with the teacher or the school. She had mentioned earlier in the interview her indecision about joining a club which some girls in her class were forming. I used this to suggest to her that she really wanted to be in school and with the girls and that now that she knew what was worrying her she would be able to do it.

Those who object to this direct approach should recall that Freud did the very same thing with Little Hans fifty-five years ago. He actually saw the child only once. The little boy was being analyzed by his father, who communicated what he learned to Freud, and Freud saw the boy only because an impasse was reached. On the basis of the father's information, Freud interpreted to the child his unconscious hostility and death wishes toward his father, and there was immediate improvement in his phobic behavior. The day after the interview Hans was able to leave the house by himself and to venture out in the street.

My patient, too, went back to school the day after her interview. That was in 1955. There was no recurrence of the phobia. In fact she graduated from high school in 1961 and her development and behavior have in general appeared to be very satisfactory.

In the interview with the mother I had pointed out that her own anxiety was transmitted to the patient, citing the incident of her accompanying the patient to school against her wish. She confirmed my interpretation with further evidence. In my concluding interview with the parents, I cited my observation of the father's attitude in the waiting room to show that both parents were keeping the patient in a relationship to them inappropriate and unhealthy for a girl of her age, and I suggested that they encourage activities for the patient outside the home.

CASE 2. A six-and-a-half-year-old girl presented an acute school phobia of two weeks' duration. There was no history of phobic behavior in the past. She had attended kindergarten for one year. Her mother described her as pleasant, friendly, and quite independent. In retrospect, the mother thought that the child seemed somewhat anxious before the outbreak of the phobia. She related this change to an illness—an infection of the finger which had developed into septicemia. The little girl had been quite ill and out of school for nearly three weeks. Her parents had been much concerned and the mother remarked to me that only the new antibiotics had saved her child's life. This illness had preceded the phobia by about six weeks. The paternal grandmother had died in a hospital after surgery just two weeks before the onset of the phobia.

The mother told me that the little girl had a congenital defect for which she would require plastic surgery in the future. The defect was not very noticeable, but the correction would be done purely for cosmetic improvement. The mother said that there had been no discussion about this matter lately, but it was obvious that the mother had strong feelings about it that appeared to be a mixture of guilt, anxiety, and overprotectiveness. After the grandmother's death, the child had remarked that this event had happened while she was in school. On one occasion she had asked her mother whether children also die. Her phobia started during school, on a day when for the first time her regular teacher was absent.

The little girl was interviewed in my playroom. She did not seem to be much interested in the materials for play. She knew that she came because of her fear of going to school. In reconstructing the events of her last day in school, I learned that she had heard someone saying that the teacher was in a hospital. She did not feel well that morning, but she was afraid to say anything to the substitute teacher until she felt so sick that the teacher noticed it. Since her mother could not be reached, her father came to take her home. The next morning she could not go back to school. I inquired what she knew about hospitals. She said that she was going to have an operation some day and that this would be done in a hospital.

The unconscious significance of the events preceding the outbreak of the phobia and their connection with the event that set off the acute anxiety attack in school now began to appear more clearly. Apparently the child's anxiety, mobilized by her recent serious illness, had been intensified by her mother's fear that the child might die. The grandmother's postsurgical death in a hospital had activated this anxiety which attached itself to the fears and fantasies about her own operation. Illness and operation are often unconsciously interpreted by children as a punishment for oedipal wishes and masturbation. The teacher's hospitalization apparently had shocked the child because of the unconscious association of grandmother, teacher, and mother, and meant that now her mother's and, with this, her own life were in acute danger. The fact that she was in school and really in a situation that she did not control (she had to stay in class until the teacher dismissed her) made school the phobic situation by displacement of the inescapable internal danger (omnipotent, unconscious death wishes) to the external danger of school. Further, the fact that her mother was not at home when she needed her so urgently, to make sure that mother was still alive, probably contributed to her need to stay home in order to guard her mother's life as well as her own.

I casually suggested that hearing of the teacher being in a hospital perhaps reminded her of her grandmother who had just died in a hospital, and added that children sometimes worry about what might happen at home while they are in school. She said, "My grandma died while I was in school." I said, "Maybe you were worried when you heard your teacher was sick and you wanted to be home and make sure that everything there, and your mommy, was all right. But in school you have to stay until the teacher lets you out. When you are sick you don't have to stay in school." She assured me that she really had felt sick. I said I knew that but pointed out to her that she was not sick at home except in the morning when she thought of going to school. I told her I could understand this because I knew that she had been very sick not so long ago and also that she was expecting an operation and probably worried about it without even being aware that she did so. I said I was sure she could see that this had nothing to do with school and assured her that her teacher would send her home should she really get sick in school. I suggested that we talk more about the operation, which was still far off, and offered to tell her exactly what was going to happen. (I had secured her parents' consent to my doing this.)

She returned to school the day after the interview. This was in March 1959. By 1961 there had been no recurrence of phobic behavior. In this connection Rose's recent paper is of interest; he reports on the remarkable effect of "analytic first aid," based on an awareness of analytic dynamic possibilities, in a case of acute phobia in a three-year-old child (1960).

CASE 3. A four-year-old girl developed a phobia at the start of playschool. When her mother took her to school the first day, the little girl seemed to enjoy the experience, and left her mother readily to play with the other children. The teacher and other mothers remarked about her mature behavior. The next day she appeared anxious and spent more time with her mother than with the group. After a few days of the same behavior, she refused to go to school, saying that she would go next year when she was older. The mother came to see me because she believed that her child's reluctance to go to school was in some way related to her own feelings. The mother as an adolescent had suffered from a severe school phobia which had required lengthy treatment. The little girl was an adopted child and the mother, because of her own phobia, had set out to bring her up as a secure and independent child, with apparent success in many areas. She had some doubts about sending her to nursery school. Realizing that this would be a desirable experience for the child, she decided to enroll her, unaware that she was overcompensating for a wish to keep the child at home. She had been very proud of her child's performance on the first day in school, yet had felt hurt by the child's readiness to leave her and to accept the teacher and the new situation. This case was handled indirectly through the mother. She wanted her child to be independent and to excel, but she unconsciously felt envious that her child, at four years of age, could leave her mother—an act she herself was still unwilling to perform. The mother remained in treatment for a considerable period of time, although her conflicts concerning her child had been worked out quickly and the child had returned to school. There were still many residues of her phobia to be resolved, especially her strong tie to her own mother.

Another case particularly clearly demonstrates the need for immediate analytic intervention in school phobias. The child developed an acute school phobia at the age of twelve and a half. One morning on hearing the air raid sirens at school she became panicky and wanted to run home. When I saw her, two years had passed during which several unsuccessful trials of various kinds of treatment had been made. She had been out of school for two years and even refused tutoring at home. She behaved in a schizophrenic fashion. She stayed home, watching people from behind the curtains, and if anyone rang the doorbell or came to the house she hid. Occasionally she ventured out of the house accompanied by her mother, who was not permitted to leave her even for an instant. When the mother left the house, the patient had to know exactly where she was going and when she would return, and then waited for her at the window. When she began analysis her mother had to sit in my waiting room in a chair next to the door of my office, and we could measure progress in the treatment by the increase in the distance between the chair in which the mother sat and the door of the office. After more than a year of analysis the mother was allowed to sit outside on a bench beside the parkway where my patient could see her from the window in my office. Though she had changed remarkably in many ways, the school phobia proved to be very resistant. It took almost two years of analysis to get her back to school.

Neither the dynamics of this case nor its treatment need here concern us; it is cited to emphasize that a school phobia can become such an integral part of the child's personality that it poses a very difficult therapeutic problem. This is why immediate analytic interpretation of the basic conflict and the establishment of the causal connections between the precipitating events and the manifest phobia is the method of choice in the management of acute school phobias.

Although it is sometimes possible by other methods to induce a child to return to school, these methods do not work satisfactorily in the long run and cause loss of valuable time during which the school phobia becomes encapsulated into the child's personality. If psychotherapy is planned, it is better to uncover the dynamics underlying the phobic behavior in the treatment, and when this is achieved the child will return to school voluntarily and assume responsibility for doing so himself. Any other method exempts the child from this responsibility and places it instead on parents, teachers, principal, truant officer, or therapist. In many successfully treated cases of school phobia I have had to oppose the demands of school personnel and parents for a speedy return of the child to school under his own conditions, such as being accompanied by a parent who stays at the school or being permitted to sit in the principal's office. Although the parents have claimed that such procedures worked, the proof of their futility is the fact that these children stayed out of school and were referred for treatment when the school phobia had already become chronic.

The problem of school phobia presents many difficulties to child guidance and community clinics. Most of all, it is important to make an accurate diagnosis. It must be emphasized that in this discussion only true school phobia is considered, not truancy, delinquency, or any other condition of which absence from school or irregular school attendance is a symptom. In these cases various other methods are useful and effective. None of these methods, however, work in the neurotic school phobias, which are actually a special form of anxiety neurosis.

# 9
# Animal Phobias in a Two-Year-Old Child

CASE PRESENTATION.  Linda was referred for treatment at the age of twenty-three months because of attacks of paroxysmal tachycardia for which no organic or any other cause could be found. The first attack occurred when she was seven months old. These attacks began with animal-like grunts which were different from any other cry. They occurred usually during the night and lasted for several hours. She often would be feverish during the attack and fall asleep toward the morning. During the attack she would assume a crouched position and fall asleep on her knees and elbows. Before an attack she would often complain of a bellyache. At nine months of age the attacks became more frequent (two or three times a week) whereupon the family doctor and the cardiologist advised hospitalization for the purpose of observation. Her pulse rate during these attacks was so rapid that it could not be counted. Although the child was very upset in the hospital, she did not have any attack there during her two-week stay. Because of the attacks a tonsillectomy was recommended and performed at the age of nineteen months. However, it did not affect the severity of the attacks nor the total behavior of the child. It rather increased the frequency of the attacks, which occurred now every few days. She was hospitalized again at twenty-one months; this time in a different hospital where she remained for three weeks. Again she had no attacks during her stay in the hospital. The consulting psychiatrist advised analysis for the child and psychiatric guidance for the parents.

The mother reported that toilet training had started very early, at the age of six months, and that Linda had been completely toilet-trained at nine months. After her second hospitalization Linda had regressed and both wet and soiled herself occasionally, especially before and during an attack. She often screamed when the mother attempted to change her wet clothes and at times she refused to go to the toilet. The mother reported that Linda had become cranky and irritable and was clinging to her. In addition, Linda exhibited another peculiar symptom. For no apparent reason Linda would become cranky and withdraw with her blanket into the corner of her crib or of her room. She would sit there in a crouched position as though she had cramps, constantly fingering her blanket, licking her lips and grunting. She would remain like this for hours, apparently removed from reality. Later on during the course of Linda's treatment when the mother had become more observant and had more insight into Linda's behavior, the mother could always detect a connection between this withdrawal and some frustration which Linda had experienced.

The mother could not understand why Linda was so timid and inhibited because she considered herself to be an unrestrained person and a progressive parent. Both parents were in the habit of walking around in the nude before the child, mornings and evenings. The mother was astonished when I suggested to her that they acquire and wear proper night attire. (Neither she nor her husband possessed any nightwear.) There was no toilet privacy and Linda had had sufficient opportunity to observe her parents in all their toilet functions. There was no doubt that the child had overheard and probably observed parental intercourse from a very early age on.

The onset of Linda's attacks seemed to coincide with toilet training and weaning from the bottle. Both occurred quite abruptly around the age of seven months. After the tonsillectomy Linda started wetting during the day, especially after an attack. This day wetting was a particular source of annoyance to the mother. On the other hand, Linda also seemed to show some compulsive traits; she was much concerned with cleanliness, picked up scraps of paper from the floor and always arranged things neatly and orderly.

When Linda started therapy she was twenty-three months old and her mother was in her seventh month of pregnancy. Linda was a physically well-developed child with an unusually well-developed language ability which greatly facilitated her analysis. She appeared to be very docile and eager to please. She always was spotlessly clean and very careful not to dirty herself. She also was very cautious in handling the toy material and never broke or tore any of the toys. Neither in her behavior nor in her play did she give any indication that she remembered her tonsillectomy or the hospitalizations. The only overt reaction to the tonsillectomy, according to the mother, had been a reluctance of Linda to take food which required chewing.

The birth of the brother occurred during the summer vacation (Linda was then twenty-six months old) and the mother reported that Linda had shown no overt reaction to this event. However, shortly after his birth she developed a severe anorexia and an acute sleep disturbance. She would wake up nightly and scream in fear "a doggy is biting my finger," "a kitty is biting my finger," or "a fish is biting my finger." It was almost impossible to calm her; she was up most of the night. I shall give the mother's report of one such night: "Linda was carrying on from twelve midnight right through until 7:00 A.M. [According to the mother's description she seemed neither fully asleep nor fully awake. It appeared as if she were acting out her nightmare.] She kept screaming out in her sleep, 'the fish are eating my fingers, the cats and dogs are biting me.' She didn't know where she was, she kept on saying, 'I want to go home.' She didn't know me and when I attempted to pick her up she screamed and almost jumped out of her bed. I kept on reassuring her that there were no animals in her room or in her crib or on her face. She seemed to be wiping off the fish from her face."

Linda carried over these phobias of fish, dogs and cats into the daytime. Once her mother brought a fish home; Linda screamed in terror. She was afraid to go out into the street for fear that she might see a dog or cat. In the analysis, a feeding game with dolls revealed how she dealt with oral-sadistic impulses. She was at first very fearful of feeding the doll, withdrawing her finger as soon as she came close to the doll's mouth. She was afraid that the doll would bite her finger and swallow it. The interpretation of the projection of her oral-sadistic impulses, namely, that she was the one who would want to bite and swallow something of which she was afraid, brought to the fore her jealousy of her baby brother. After this interpretation she began to speak about him and also became interested in anal play. The birth of the brother apparently had not only reactivated but also dangerously intensified her oral-sadistic impulses which had suffered a severe inhibition under the trauma of the tonsillectomy.

When her oral-sadistic impulses had been worked through, Linda's fears gradually subsided; she began to talk of her and her brother's genitals, referring to them as "toushies." Another factor which seemed to contribute greatly to Linda's oral conflict was her penis envy. This also was brought out in her play with the dolls. While she maintained that everybody had the same "toushies," she made the very correct distinction between the boy and the girl doll in the way in which she had them urinate, although both dolls had no genitalia and the difference in their sexes was indicated only in the way they were dressed and by the face and the hair. When I made a boy of clay with a penis she took the penis off but otherwise treated the clay doll as a boy. From her play with the dolls, it was obvious that she knew of the anatomical difference yet was denying the existence of a penis. This behavior was particularly surprising since she had had all the opportunity to observe genitals of her father, who had taken her with him to the toilet when he was urinating. It would seem that Linda had been and still was unable to tolerate consciously any idea of castration. The intensity of her penis envy, which she had completely repressed and which showed itself in her fear of having her finger bitten off, could be understood on the basis of the penis being cathected with oral libido. The fact that the baby was a boy had reactively intensified the impact of the earlier deprivations—weaning, training, tonsillectomy—which all were "losses" inflicted upon her by her mother. The denial of the existence of the penis and the displacement of the affect from it to her fingers meant that she still possessed all these lost objects—nipple, stools, penis, fingers—which she now feared would be taken away from her by oral-sadistic attacks. This was a projection of her own oral-sadistic impulses, and at the same time a way in which the objects she desired, particularly the penis, were protected from her oral-sadistic impulses.

The release and working through of these wishes and impulses brought on a very remarkable improvement of her sleep disturbance and anorexia. Occasionally she would still cry out at night and call her mother, whom she wanted to pet her and to reassure her. On such occasions she would sometimes say, "I don't like the pussy," or "Make the doggie go away," but would go back to sleep promptly. Sometimes she would wake up crying and say, "Don't go away, Mommy, I want to go with you," but she could be soothed by her mother and fall asleep again.

This waking up at night was different from her

"attacks," which had been the original cause for her referral for treatment. These attacks still occurred, though less frequently and for shorter periods. It was very surprising both to the mother and me that as soon as Linda had started her play sessions her attacks had diminished in frequency and intensity. After her first visit with me she did not have an attack for two weeks, while prior to that she had had two to three attacks a week. After half a year of treatment she had stopped wetting herself except immediately before the attacks. The mother now referred to these attacks as "disturbances." This indicated a significant change in the mother's attitude, namely, her acceptance of the emotional origin of her child's condition. The mother also told me that now she could get Linda to stop grunting during the attack. For instance, one night when Linda had awakened her and she was grunting and obviously starting a "disturbance," the mother asked her to stop grunting and to let her sleep. Linda said, "Alright, Mommy, go to sleep. I won't grunt any more." She actually stopped, but still called her mother several times before she fell asleep. Sometimes Linda would talk about her play with me when she awoke during the night saying that she was feeding my doll and enumerating all the food items she was giving her. This seemed to reassure her and put her to sleep and to prevent the onset of an attack. It seems that in doing so Linda was establishing a relationship with me which served to counteract her rising anxiety. The sources for this anxiety seem to lie in the early oral and anal deprivation, reinforced by the experience of the primal scene. It is noteworthy that of all the games which we played during the analysis, the feeding game retained its (symbolic) significance throughout most of the treatment.

All during this time I had not seen the child in such an attack except once, shortly after she had started treatment with me. The mother told me that Linda had been cranky that morning and had started to grunt. She showed all the signs of a developing attack. When I saw her she looked very unhappy, was whining and appeared to be fearful. She felt warm to the touch and had a very rapid pulse. When she saw me she brightened up and readily left her mother to come with me for her play session. The session apparently aborted the attack. I had the definite impression that Linda's attack was an equivalent of an acute anxiety attack in which the affect of anxiety was missing (though not completely), while all the physiological accompaniments of anxiety were exaggeratedly present. I learned from the mother in the course of Linda's treatment that Linda was able to shake off an attack on the days when she was told that she was coming to see me. This would seem to support my diagnosis of anxiety attacks and also indicate that Linda was experiencing relief of anxiety in her relationship with me. A further corroboration of this assumption and an impressive proof of the immediate therapeutic effect of the play sessions was furnished by an episode which occurred when Linda was about three years old.

According to the mother, Linda had been in very good spirits that morning and as usual was looking forward to her play session. When she and her mother were ready to leave, friends of the mother called. They offered to take them by car to my office so that they could spend the time together while Linda had her play session. Linda suddenly became very disturbed. She refused to leave, saying that she would go by train. She began to whine and complained about a bellyache. She was very upset when her mother picked her up and put her into the car. During the ride to my office, Linda had worked herself up to an attack of paroxysmal tachycardia of such severity as the mother had not observed before. The mother could not understand what had happened. Nothing she did or said could comfort Linda. Linda looked pitiful. She was doubled up on her mother's lap, yet not clinging to her mother but rather appeared to be pulling away from her. She appeared to be terrified and in a panic. She looked as if she were in a daze and she did not recognize me but continued to whimper when I talked to her. I kept saying to her again and again, "This is Mimie [the name by which my very young patients call me], Linda." After some time she seemed to come out of her daze and let me pick her up from her mother's lap and carry her to the playroom.

For the past few sessions we had been playing with paper dolls. The books, dolls, and plastic scissors were lying on the floor. Instead of taking them up as usual, she sat listlessly and avoided touching them. She seemed particularly afraid of the scissors which she had handled quite skillfully before. I started to cut out a dress. As I picked up one of the paper dolls to put the dress on it, a piece fell off. Linda was very frightened. I began to tear the doll up saying, "Nothing happens, we can even cut it up, nothing happens. It is only a paper doll." Her face lit up and she became more lively and accepted my suggestion to try to cut up the doll herself. After a while she took the scissors and at first fearfully, but then in a more determined way, began to cut the doll up. This was the first time that she had allowed herself a frank display of aggression in the play session. While cutting she became quite excited, saying with glee, "Cut up dolly, Linda cut up dolly." In the meantime her behavior had completely changed. When the session was over she walked out by herself very much to the surprise of her mother who did not know what had started nor what had ended Linda's attack. While I had some ideas with regard to the latter, it took me a long time until I was able to find out some facts which helped me to understand what had caused Linda's severe anxiety that day.

Linda became more aggressive in her play sessions now, however, without ever becoming destructive. She began to play with other children and even ventured out on her own onto the street. She became altogether more independent of her mother. She was going to nursery school and proved to be a very capable and bright child. Her anxiety attacks or "disturbances," as her mother called them, occurred very infrequently and had lost their original character. They now resembled the phobic clinging of older children in whom the association of phobic behavior with somatic symptoms, especially with stomachaches, is a rather frequent finding. These attacks manifested themselves by Linda's becoming moody at such times, complaining about a bellyache and clinging to her mother.

One day Linda spontaneously brought up the subject of the tonsillectomy. She told me that her friend had undergone a tonsillectomy and then said, "My tonsils have been cut out too." The mother also told me that Linda had spoken about the tonsillectomy to her and that she had mentioned some details which made it obvious to the mother that Linda remembered the actual event. Linda remembered that she had been taken to the hospital by car and that there had been other people who had come with them. The mother confirmed that Linda had been taken for the tonsillectomy by the same friends who had brought her to my office on the day when she had the severe, acute attack of panic. In the light of this information Linda's behavior that day, and particularly her pulling away from her mother, became more intelligible. Linda had displaced the repressed memory of the traumatic event to the car and to the friends of her mother. The circumstances on the day when they called for her had revived this repressed memory and as a result produced the panicky state.

Although Linda was doing very well now, I continued to see her because the enuresis had recurred at the age of three and a half years. Thus, I could follow up her development during the oedipal phase. It was remarkable how well Linda passed through this difficult phase. Between four and a half and five she liked to play with fingers which she herself made of clay. She would usually make a family consisting of the mother, father, the older child, a girl, and the little child, a boy, each with all the appropriate sexual attributes. One day she made a girl and said, "She is going to get married." Then she made a boy with a penis and said, "They are going to make a baby." Whenever Linda played family, she announced, "I'll be the big sister." That day when leaving she told her mother, "I'll be a mommy myself and have a baby." Linda is now eight years old and has continued to develop and to function adequately in every respect.

## Discussion

Forty-five years ago Freud (1909) developed some of the classical concepts of the phobias from the analysis of five-year-old Hans. Since then the technique of child analysis (and particularly that of play analysis) has enabled child analysts to study directly neurotic manifestations in children of preoedipal age. Bornstein (1935) found that a latent instinctual conflict which dated from the time of training, and which was reinforced by traumatic circumstances, led to the phobia of this child. Wulff (1927) described a similar observation in a child of one-and-a-half years of age. In this child the phobic behavior started at the time of toilet training and could be resolved through counseling of the parents. Hitschmann (1915, 1937), H. Deutsch (1929), and others emphasized the role of the aggressive impulses in the phobias.

I reported the case of Linda because it presented me with an opportunity to observe the formation and resolution of her phobias during the treatment process. Her case also seemed of interest for the study of the sources of anxiety and for that of symptom formation in a young child. Linda suffered from attacks of paroxysmal tachycardia. This diagnosis had been made originally by the family physician and the consulting cardiologist and was confirmed later on the occasion of the two (diagnostic) hospitalizations. In her analysis these attacks were found to be equivalents of severe anxiety (attacks). These attacks started at the time, when the coinciding experiences of weaning, toilet training and primal scene observation forced an abrupt repression of oral and anal impulses. The grunting and the position which Linda assumed during the attack and later on when she was able to talk, her complaints about bellyaches definitely pointed to the fact that she had conceived of intercourse as an anal act. Klein (1932) particularly has emphasized the traumatic effect of the observation of the parent's union in intercourse upon the young child and his reaction of rage to it. Linda's paroxysmal tachycardia would indicate a state of intense excitement, probably resulting from a mixture of fear, frustration and rage. The inhibition of the biting and chewing functions following the tonsillectomy would indicate that Linda had interpreted the operation as a punishment for her oral-sadistic impulses. It may be of interest to mention that Linda's brother when he was only two years old had become a terror to Linda and to the children in the neighborhood because he would bite them so fiercely that he would draw blood. Linda's father had suffered from a duodenal ulcer since adolescence and an unusually severe inhibition of aggression. After the tonsillectomy Linda was clinging to her mother while at the same time the periods of withdrawal with the blanket which obviously served to substitite for her mother became more frequent. This would indicate a further repression of aggressive impulses and of hostility toward her mother with the subsequent fear of loss of object relationship. In fact, during the periods of withdrawal Linda behaved as if she had lost her mother already. Early in Linda's treatment I found it necessary to suggest to the mother that she occupy herself with Linda constantly at such times when she was withdrawing and not to allow her, as the mother had in the past, to remain withdrawn for hours. Even though the mother complained that this was a very difficult task for her because Linda was very cranky and rejected her mother at such times, it proved to be an effective means of improving the relationship between Linda and her mother. The birth of the brother in this precarious situation was a trauma of such magnitude to Linda that it threatened to shatter completely her already very labile relationship with her mother. The birth of the brother seemed to confirm to Linda that her mother did not love her, that she had replaced her with the baby, whom she not only allowed all the pleasures which she had taken away from Linda but to whom, in addition, she had given something which she had denied to Linda, namely, the penis. These feelings had some justification in reality, because Linda's mother could not conceal her delight over having produced a boy child. She was a basically sincere and honest person and while feeling badly about it, she could not deny to herself that she had rejected Linda from birth on because of her sex. She had identified her with her own mother, grandmother and sister, all of whom she considered to be inferior and for whom she had little use. To be a female meant, for Linda's mother, to be weak, helpless and dependent. Her grandmother, mother and sister had not had any boys and had always depended upon a man and upon her for support in every way. Linda reminded her particularly of her grandmother, whom she had always hated. She could see where Linda was growing up to be just like this grandmother, whining, cranky and a nuisance to everyone.

Linda's severe anorexia following the birth of the brother could be understood as a depressive equivalent resulting from the repression of oral-sadistic impulses. Because the penis was cathected with oral libido, it became of vital importance to possess it —in accordance with the unconscious equation of penis-breast-mother. Much which otherwise would have had to be attributed to constitution could in Linda's case be found to be the result of earlier experiences. Because of our knowledge of the history preceding the onset of the acute phobias, Linda's predisposition to react to the birth of the brother in this particular way could be understood to be an acquired rather than an inherited constitutional quality.

In the face of this desperate situation, the denial of the existence of the desired objects and of the dangerous impulses proved to be insufficient. Linda was confronted with both an intolerable internal and an equally intolerable external reality. In this situation—the danger of the imminent breakthrough of the repressed impulses from within and the loss of object relationship with the mother and all its consequences, that is, depression or psychosis—the formation of the phobias proved to be a saving device. Similarly as the organism defends itself against the invasion of highly toxic agents, for instance in septicemia by localizing the process and externalizing it by the formation of abscesses, so in the phobias of Linda, the general invasion and complete disintegration of the psyche was prevented by localizing and externalizing the destructive energies of the pregenital impulses by means of projection, condensation and displacement.

1.   By the mechanism of projection an intolerable inner

danger stemming mainly from her own oral-sadistic impulses was transformed into an outer danger, namely, the fear of the biting animals. In this way she managed to escape from the otherwise inescapable danger in the waking state by (the mechanism of) avoidance and in the sleeping state by awakening.

2. By the mechanism of displacement the fear of the mother, who in Linda's unconscious figured as the castrator who deprived her of oral and anal pleasures and in addition replaced her with the baby brother to whom she gave a *penis*, was displaced onto the dog, cat and fish. Linda had used the mechanism of displacement in other similar situations. She had displaced the traumatic and repressed memory of the tonsillectomy in which the mother figured as the castrator onto the car and her mother's friends. Linda was very much afraid of noises, or more specifically, she had a fear of the noise of the vacuum cleaner, which could throw her into a panic. In analyzing Linda's reluctance to go to the bathroom, it was found that she was actually terrified by the noise of the flushing of the toilet. Neither she nor her mother had been aware of this fear, which she had at least partly displaced to the noise of the vacuum cleaner. From the noise of the vacuum cleaner she could escape by (the mechanism of) avoidance, by staying in her room and locking the door or running next door to the neighbors when the maid was using the vacuum cleaner. To be consciously so terrified of the toilet would have made her life even more painful. The vacuum cleaner lent itself particularly well to substitute for the toilet because of the fears she had, namely, the fear of the noise and the fear of being sucked in and to disappear in the toilet-vacuum cleaner.

3. By the mechanism of condensation all these impulses, wishes and fears primarily directed toward her mother and brother were condensed in her phobias in accordance with the unconscious identification of nipple-breast-mother-stool-penis-finger.

The analogy between the phobias and the dreams, which Lewin (1951) pointed out, would seem to me to hold true not only with regard to their structure but also with regard to their function. According to Freud (1900), the function of the dream is to insure sleep by allowing the repressed impulses and wishes to emerge, in a disguised form, in the dream. Projection is one of the most important mechanisms used in the formation of the dream. Why is it necessary to project these repressed impulses and why may the dreamer not (even in the sleeping state) experience these impulses and wishes as coming from within but only as dangers coming from the outside? Lewin (1951) states that the disturbing elements in the dream, "the wakers," are always projected outward because they originally came from the outside and were represented by the threatening father. Linda's case and numerous cases of phobias and phobic sleep disturbances in children which I have analyzed do not seem to confirm this statement. My experience in Linda's case would rather indicate that "the wakers" come from the child's own aggressive—pregenital —impulses which are directed toward the mother, the original object to satisfy or to frustrate these needs of the child.

The dangerous impulses that are dealt with by projection in the anxiety dreams as well as in the phobias are pregenital impulses. The danger comes from the increase in the destructive impulses when the balance between libido and aggression is shifted in favor of the latter, and is perceived by the child as intolerable anxiety. By the mechanism of projection, this danger from within is transformed into a danger in the outside, from which the dreamer can rescue himself (often only at the last moment) by anxious awakening. During the time when Linda suffered most from her phobias and nightmares, the mother was the only one who could comfort her, at least to some extent. Only later when her relationship with her mother was improved through the analysis could she accept also her father and others and did not insist upon the presence of her mother. Such behavior is commonly found in children who suffer from phobias and/or nightmares. Such children usually want the mother to comfort them and to take them to bed with her. The fact that the mother is present and comforting the child is reassuring and serves as a denial of the existence and effect of the dangerous, destructive impulses. In addition, the putting on of the light, looking around and recognizing that it was only a dream and that there is no immediate real danger serves to support the denial of the internal danger.

It seems to me that the real danger which is thus warded off is the danger of permanent loss of reality which would result from the sudden breakthrough of the destructive impulses (self- or object-directed) into consciousness. Dreaming is a state of loss of reality; however, this loss is limited to the sleeping state and is reversible. In the case of Linda, the structure of her nightmares and of her day phobias was identical and served the same purpose, namely, to prevent the break in object relations and with reality. By means of her phobias Linda managed to limit the loss of reality to the phobically feared objects proper while she could maintain the essential functions and relationships, particularly the most important relationship with her mother. The phobias in Linda's case, as one might put it, served to get her through the dangers of the Scylla and Charybdis of a depression on the one, or (paranoid) psychosis on the other hand.

# 10
# Spider Phobias and Spider Fantasies

Although spider phobias and spider fantasies are by no means a clinical rarity, only a few psychoanalysts have reported on them (Abraham, 1922; Azima and Wittkower, 1957; Gloyne, 1950; Little, 1966a, 1966b, 1967; Newman and Stoller, 1969; R. Sterba, 1950). To those who, like myself, have encountered these phenomena in work with patients, these contributions have been of great interest. There are no references in the literature to psychoanalytic observations of such phenomena in children, nor reports of follow-ups on patients in whom such phenomena have been observed during treatment.

I had an opportunity to study analytically spider phobias and fantasies in three children, two adolescents, and three adult patients. In one case I could observe a spider phobia in its early stages in a prelatency child and follow up the vicissitudes of this phobia during latency and adolescence. In one adolescent patient, the spider phobia and fantasies, which had been of long standing, came to light only at the beginning of the third year of analysis and reappeared toward the end of the fourth year, when they became a central point in her analysis. Two adult patients resorted to spider symbolism in critical emotional situations. In both, these remained single occurrences. In one patient it appeared as a nightmare and in the other patient as a kind of delusional experience. These and similar observations convinced me that the presence of spider phobias and fantasies may be of specific diagnostic and prognostic value. I therefore wish to take up this and other aspects of these phenomena that have not received sufficient consideration thus far. I should like to present case material upon which my thoughts and suggestions are based and shall begin with my youngest patient, four-year-old Ruth.

CASE 1.    Ruth was referred to me because of a severe sleep disturbance of some two years duration. From the age of one-and-a-half-years, following a tonsillectomy and the birth of a baby brother, Ruth was up every night for most of the night. She had frequent nightmares and was particularly frightened by one recurrent nightmare in which she saw a spider crawling on her bed wanting to take her to the hospital. She could not shake off the hallucinatory quality of this nightmare even after awakening. Once when talking to me about this nightmare, she showed me how the doctor had cut off her pussy "because I am very bad," adding, "I and my mommy have a big one. My brother and my daddy have a little one." "I could cut my brother's pussy off." Climbing up on me, she said, "I am the doctor and I'll cut your nose-pussy off."

In her play sessions Ruth also brought out her intense oedipal resentment against her mother. Her wish to kill her mother came out with particular clarity in a game which she played incessantly. In this game I was the mother who wanted to sleep, but Ruth would not let me. I would then be so sick that the doctor who came, and whose role Ruth played, would tell me that I would soon have to die because I did not get enough rest. The mother's constant complaint to Ruth was that she didn't let her sleep and rest. By her sleep disturbance Ruth managed to separate her parents at night, and because the mother had to take care of the baby, the father attended to Ruth during the night. This arrangement only intensified Ruth's oedipal conflicts and her sleep disturbance.

The mother had weaned Ruth abruptly at nine months of age and, in anticipation of the new baby, had accelerated her bladder and bowel training. Envy for the breast and penis, both of which she did not possess but which her mother gave to her little brother, had greatly intensified her oral-sadistic impulses. She dealt with this internal danger in a phobic way by externalization and projection onto the mother and displacement onto the spider. From her dreams, her play, and her verbalizations, it became clear that the spider represented the dangerous mother who had taken her to the hospital for a tonsillectomy as a punishment for her oral-sadistic impulses. But what had prompted the choice of the spider as the symbol of the dangerous mother?

In a similar situation, that is, following a tonsillectomy and the birth of a younger brother, I could study in a two-year-old child the onset of an animal phobia which first occurred only at night but then carried over into the daytime (Chapter 9). This little girl, Linda, was referred to me because of a sleep disturbance associated with attacks of paroxysmal tachycardia. Linda, too, suffered from intense breast and penis envy, and she, too, dealt with her oral-sadistic impulses directed against her mother's breast and her brother's penis in a phobic way by externalization and projection onto the mother, and displacing it first to a fish and then to cats and dogs. The first nightmare about a fish, in which she screamed that a fish was biting off her finger, occurred after Linda had watched her mother cutting off a fish's head. In Ruth's case, however, neither the child nor the mother could trace the onset of the acute spider phobia to an actual experience.

Play analysis brought, within a few months, such dramatic relief of Ruth's sleep disturbance that the parents, for whom this had been the only disturbing symptom, were ready to withdraw her from treatment. I had already at that time, more than twenty years ago, expressed the belief that severe early sleep disturbance even in the absence of other clinical symptoms, could be an early indication of possible psychotic development (Sperling, 1949, 1955b). The parents consented to let her stay in treatment for two more months until the family moved into a new house in another community. I tried to use this short time to bring about a modification of the relationship between Ruth and her mother, but the mother was not available for active participation in the treatment, and this goal could not be accomplished.

I heard from Ruth again when she was nine years old. According to the mother, Ruth had done very well up to about six months before, when a very marked and progressive deterioration in her behavior took place. She had a recurrence of the sleep disturbance with nightmares. She appeared withdrawn, she had unmotivated outbursts of temper and spoke incoherently. She could not concentrate in school, and the teacher had indicated that the school would not be able to keep her in her present condition. Ruth was obviously suffering from a schizophrenic disorder. This clinical impression was confirmed by psychological testing which in summary stated that this was a case of severe schizophrenia with marked paranoid features and a poor prognosis regarding therapy and recovery.

It is not possible, within the framework of this chapter, to deal with the dynamics of her illness or with the therapeutic techniques which led to a complete recovery with a follow-up to adulthood. For my present purposes, I have selected some fragments from her treatment during the schizophrenic phase which are directly related to the spider phobia of her early childhood. Among her many bizarre psychotic productions, a recurrent theme about a character which she called "Tiddy Ray" is of particular relevance. Tiddy Ray was a lady who devoured people. She did not eat with her mouth, but put people into a hole under her breast (Tiddy meant breast) or in the middle of her body. Tiddy Ray caught people who snooped around and came close to her. There were many elaborations with anal and phallic elements added, but the essential fantasy was a condensation and projection to Tiddy Ray of Ruth's oral-sadistic impulses. Ruth also had visual hallucinations; she saw Tiddy Ray and her gang hiding behind doorways or the venetian blinds signaling to the men to catch her.

In working through these fantasies, Ruth recalled her spider phobia and was now able to trace its onset. She remembered an incident when she was between two and three years of age. Some children with whom she played told her that spiders kill and eat people. She was not sure whether they had shown her a picture or had threatened her with a spider, but she knew that since then she had been terrified of spiders.

The spider fantasy which had played such a role in Ruth's fantasy life during childhood was a forerunner and the matrix for the later schizophrenic Tiddy Ray fantasies. The schizophrenic breakdown at eight and a half was preceded by the birth of another brother which to Ruth was a repetition of the trauma that had precipitated the sleep disturbance at age two.

The onset of puberty, when she began to develop secondary female characteristics, decidedly altered Ruth's already considerable conflict concerning her sexual identification into the direction of the male. She was awkward and tall and had a deep voice, which only increased her feelings that she was not a real girl. The birth of the brother had reactivated and intensified her penis envy and feelings that she could never please her mother as a girl, that is, without a penis. Ruth had already expressed in her play and fantasies at age four the displacement from mouth to genitals. She had experienced the tonsillectomy as an oral castration inflicted upon her by her mother. The spider, which expressed Ruth's oral-sadistic impulses directed toward her mother's breasts and her brother's penis, indicated her confusion of nipple with penis, and mouth with vagina. The oral-sadistic and the bisexual meanings of the spider were expressed later in the cannibalistic, persecutory, but human Tiddy Ray symbol. Exposure and working through of the spider phobia and of the underlying fantasies and impulses would seem to account for the change in the symbol used for the expression of her basic conflicts from all developmental levels (Chapter 6).

CASE 2.    Leslie was thirteen years old when she began treatment. Extremely infantile and withdrawn, she had great difficulty in school and socially. Many fears beset her and she daydreamed almost perpetually. She was suspicious and silent, and at first it was difficult to make contact with her. In the second year of treatment she began to reveal some of her fears and fantasies. She had a very marked preoccupation with spiders. She saw spiders, even when they were not there. She looked for spiders at night and searched her bed for them. Later in her analysis she revealed that she lay awake for hours during the night, afraid to close her eyes for fear a spider would fall into her mouth. She said she had the same feeling about spiders as she had about her mother. She disliked them intensely, but she looked for them all the time. "She is always on top of me," Leslie would say. She felt that her mother was always rushing her. She had a fantasy and a fear of spiders being on top of her. This was an important and elaborate fantasy which she revealed fully some three or four years later in her analysis.

She felt strongly about being touched by a spider. This was exactly how she felt about her mother touching her. Often when she found a spider, she crushed it with a vengeance. She would keep stepping on it even if it was dead on the first step. She talked about her feelings on watching her mother eat. The sight of her mother's teeth when she ate an apple, the crushing noise nauseated her. She also complained about a specific smell, especially when in the car with her mother, to which she was very sensitive and to which she reacted much as she did to the sight of a spider. When she saw a spider on the ceiling the other night, she thought about her parents and that they were together in their room while she was alone trying to do some homework. She suddenly felt very hungry and went into the kitchen to get some food. When she saw a spider she had the sensation of fear and immediately thought of her mother. She could feel a sensation on her skin like spider's feet or like fingers touching her. The sensation was a mixture of anxiety and sexual feelings. In her fantasy there were now an enormous number of spiders, and she had the feeling that the spider legs were tying her up so that she was in the power of the spider, "my domineering mother," she said.

Leslie had suffered from a very severe sleep disturbance since early childhood. She was afraid to fall asleep and kept herself awake by remaining on a spider watch practically all night. Analysis revealed that this sleep phobia had a protective function beyond the conscious fear of a spider falling into her mouth during sleep. To sleep in her state of mind was too dangerous because she might succumb to her thoughts and impulses and wake up crazy. As it was she had great difficulty in maintaining some sort of mental balance even in her waking state, and in her analysis she was still on guard against revealing the full extent of her "craziness."

Leslie was now sixteen years old and for the first time dating a boy. The resurgence of the spider feelings and fantasies at this time were related to her intense anxiety about going out with a boy. After her first date she was preoccupied with spiders all night. She had actually seen a spider, killed it, and then hallucinated spiders all over the place. She felt completely engulfed by them. Then she thought about what we had discussed about the spiders, namely, the spider symbolizing mother and her own homosexual desires for mother. She was afraid of boys and heterosexuality. The sensation of being touched by a spider was the same as being touched by her mother, and she was at this time phobically avoiding any physical contact with her mother.

She had fantasies of spiders coming toward her bed and attacking her. She also had fears and fantasies of being attacked by men. When she returned to her analysis after the summer vacation she noticed a change in her attitude toward spiders. "They have gone," she said. In explanation she added "maybe they have actually gone, but really I am not preoccupied with them anymore, but I am now preoccupied with wasps and bees." She was more afraid of the wasp than of the spider. Spiders she could kill, herself, but she was unable to do anything about a bee or wasp, and she had to call her mother for help. Her mother actually did once kill a wasp for her. She associated the wasp with her father. She was not afraid of bugs when they sat quietly and didn't move, only when they started moving and coming close to her, especially toward her face, or rather her mouth.

Her spider preoccupation returned in full force after a short time. She had a dream about a spider web over her head. It was not round like a spider web usually is, but straight, and went from one side of the room to the other. She thought of her mother and that this meant that her mother was on top of her. She was aware of the sexual meaning of this and of her wish for her mother to be with her at night when she felt lonely and frightened. She talked about the change in her feelings concerning her father and her mother. Although she still hated her mother, she felt closer to her now than to her father whom she regarded as weak and inadequate.

We were dealing now with her fears of growing up, of boys and heterosexuality, of being queer and of hating and needing her mother, and her feelings of being rejected. She had become aware that she was establishing with girls a similar relationship as with her mother. She had succeeded in graduating from high school and was now attending and living at a college, which made it possible for her to continue treatment. She had dated several boys casually, but had felt awkward and afraid. In dreams, she would be in bed with a girl when all the other girls slept with boys. She had changed roommates and felt that her new roommate got all the attention and was controlling her.

During this period of treatment (Leslie was now eighteen years old), she had been sleeping rather well and there had been no signs of any spider preoccupation. But now again her sleep became disturbed, she had nightmares of a paranoid, homosexual nature involving particularly her roommate. In these dreams, her roommate was coming into her bed to attack and kill her. In some dreams Leslie had posted signs in her bed, "Don't touch me. Don't do it." She was afraid to sleep because of what she might do during sleep to her roommate. She also had such thoughts and fears during the day. She felt very dependent upon this roommate and didn't dare to say anything to her. In fact, she had lost her voice on occasions, and even in her dreams could not talk, but had the written signs.

She had an unexpected date with a young man who was visiting. That night she looked for spiders again, and in her following session she was preoccupied with spiders. In class they had talked about a fable in which a man was transformed into a spider. She again had the sensations of soft spider legs touching her and spiders being all over her. She talked about not knowing what people really do in intercourse. She was very frightened of it because to her intercourse had something to do with strangling and killing. When she thought of her parents having intercourse, she thought of them having their legs wrapped around each other like spiders. She felt like killing her mother. She then remembered that it was not a man who was turned into a spider, but a woman who had been spinning. A goddess turned her into a spider hanging in the web. She had a recurrent fantasy in which she saw a spider caught in the web, hopelessly entangled and unable to escape. This fantasy she had had since childhood. She suddenly thought of a story a girl had told her about people who were turned inside out. In her next session she again talked about her roommate—her fear that this girl would attack and kill her or that she would attack and kill the roommate. She said that in her mind sex was tied up with attack and with spiders. It had something to do with being held down and unable to scream, with strangling and being strangled, but also with eating and being eaten. To squash a spider reminded her of a penis and the juice that comes out. Being eaten related to the vagina but also to having a spider in her mouth. Her roommate had told her that she once ate or swallowed a spider. But Leslie knew that her fear of spiders was very old and that even as a small child she could not sleep because she was afraid that a spider from the ceiling would fall into her mouth.

The release of these fantasies apparently facilitated the recollection of relevant early childhood experiences and related affects. She remembered how lonely and afraid she felt as a child. Unable to sleep, she would go into her parents' bedroom during the night and watch them silently. The silence also reminded her of a spider. She remembered the rage and humiliation she felt when her father once reprimanded her for pulling at her dog's penis. She thought of the clicking noise of her mother eating apples or chewing with her mouth open. Her roommate did this too, which made Leslie feel very uncomfortable. While talking about it she experienced sensations in her throat like choking, like having something stuck in her throat. The clicking noise had an association to licking, and she recalled that as a child she had been licking her dog and her dog licking her. She then thought of something that happened when she was two years old. She had been bitten on her mouth by the neighbor's dog. She had to be rushed to the hospital to get stitches and shots. Her mother recently spoke about it, so she knew this actually happened. Her mother had also mentioned that she had had a miscarriage around that time. When her mother said this, Leslie had a visual image of going upstairs into her parent's bedroom and seeing blood on a white sheet. Leslie knew that her mother had not wanted any more children, and she connected her fears of pregnancy and childbirth with this.

She had her menarche at twelve years of age. Her menses had been irregular and very painful until the latter part of her analysis when she had been able to work through some of her feelings concerning femininity and female functions. She recalled with much affect an experience when she was very young. She could see herself sitting on the floor and looking up at her mother. She could see the black pubic hair; she had the feeling that the origin of her spider phobia was related to this experience. Her parents always slept in the nude and would walk nude to the bathroom. She was always very much interested in looking. She talked about some of her activities during puberty. She and one particular girl used to get undressed and look and touch one another. Leslie had very strong voyeuristic impulses. Talking about this made her think of a spider who was silently and intently watching its prey—which is how Leslie had observed the primal scene as a small child.

Her fear of genital intercourse became more apparent when she began to date more frequently and engage in sex play. She was to see a gynecologist because of a vaginal discharge. She was very worried, afraid of what he might find. She considered the secretion an indication of something very bad, but was reluctant to speak about her thoughts and fantasies. She had felt nauseated on the way to her session and now her nausea returned. With signs of disgust and anxiety, she admitted to having the crazy idea that she had a horrible thing in her vagina, a spider which must have got into her vagina when she was very young and had just been staying there all this time. She had the idea that the secretion was the stuff that came out when squeezing a spider. She was afraid the gynecologist would find it, and yet she wished that he would remove the spider from her vagina because she considered this the cause of her fear of sexual intercourse. After she released this fantasy, her nausea cleared instantly. In her next session she reported that the vaginal discharge had stopped. We were able in subsequent sessions to work through her wishes for a hidden penis-nipple in her vagina-mouth which had been manifested in her spider fears and fantasies.

Leslie was suddenly able to understand her anxious

preoccupation with spiders, when she was called on to visit and help a young relative who had given birth to a baby. She managed to get a sore throat and thus avoid the visit. The thought of seeing the baby nursing (her relative was breast-feeding her child), as well as the thought of holding the baby, made her anxious and nauseated. Her oral-sadistic impulses and fears of eating and being eaten had been expressed in her spider preoccupation.

These excerpts from the analysis of an adolescent girl were selected to demonstrate that the spider symbol originated early in life, probably before the third year, together with the sleep disturbance. In Leslie's case, as with Ruth, the spider symbol contained the psychotic core of her personality. Leslie, too, had suffered an early injury to her mouth, the dog bite, and surgical intervention, and she too had externalized her dangerous oral-sadistic impulses, projected them onto her mother and displaced them to the spider. The spider had served to express her earliest as well as all subsequent conflicts. Because of this fixation and the intense narcissism, ambivalence, and hate associated with it, oedipal wishes and conflicts became particularly threatening and were expressed in the spider preoccupation. The spider had become the symbol for the primal scene (the parents wrapped around each other in intercourse) and for her bisexuality and homosexual wishes. Leslie's long analysis (six years) succeeded in bringing about an integration of her personality with resolution of the potentially psychotic core which had manifested itself in her spider preoccupation.

CASE 3.   In this connection, a dream from the treatment of the third patient, a severely phobic woman (and a transference fantasy of patient No. 4), are of particular interest. Patient No. 3 had been treated in early adolescence for a severe school phobia and behavior suggestive of psychosis. She made a remarkable recovery, returned to school, held a job, got married, and was even able to travel, but she had apparently not resolved the phobic core, that is, her relationship with her mother. She came for treatment after her youngest child had started school because she felt anxious and feared a return of the earlier phobic behavior. We found that she had in part transferred her relationship from her mother to her husband, and that raising three children had helped her to disguise the remnants of her phobia. When, in treatment, we were uncovering her resentment and death wishes against her husband and her oedipal conflicts and hatred for her parents which had been completely denied and overcompensated for by a very dependent and affectionate daughterly attitude, she had a nightmare about a big black spider. She had never before had any spider dreams or fantasies nor did she have a spider phobia. She thought of a clay sculpture she had seen the previous day that looked like a female genital, legs open and the vulva visible. It was an ugly thing and that was really what the spider reminded her of.

She talked about death and about being abandoned. Her husband had mentioned a pain in his chest and jokingly told her to prepare to take care of herself. She felt anxious that morning coming to her session and had asked her husband to follow her in his car, at least up to where the roads parted. When he pulled away in his car she had the feeling of being all alone and completely abandoned. While talking, she was putting her hand over her mouth and at that moment thought of the spider. She thought of anesthesia, a mask put over her mouth, the tonsillectomy, of suffocating, and of her mother. She was visibly shaken and expressed a fear of losing her mind. She thought of a psychotic relative who had recently been hospitalized. This led her to recall and to relive with much affect the very traumatic circumstances of her tonsillectomy at age eleven and a half. Her mother had taken her to the doctor for a physical checkup. Without the patient's knowledge, he recommended and arranged for a tonsillectomy to be performed the next day. When she got up that morning to go to school, her mother told her she was going to have a tonsillectomy and took her to the doctor's office. Her mother held her hand when the mask was put over her face, but she knew that her mother had left and the nurse had taken over before she became unconscious. "How could they do this to me," she cried in my office. "How could I trust anybody?" A few months after the tonsillectomy, her mother gave birth to a baby brother. It was shortly thereafter that she developed an incapacitating school phobia.

In subsequent sessions these associations were followed by memories and affects that led to the reconstruction of the events preceding the acute onset of the phobic behavior at age twelve. She had shown signs of phobic behavior from the age of three. When she was three years old a sister was born, and from that time on she had begun to cling to her mother. She had episodes of school phobia and reaction to changes, but was able to maintain herself until a brother was born when she was not quite twelve years old. She experienced the tonsillectomy which preceded the birth of her brother as an oral castration, inflicted upon her by her mother. This reactivated her intense breast and penis envy at the critical pubertal phase, when she was to relinquish both her preoedipal and oedipal hold on her mother in order to establish a proper sexual identification and accept herself as a female.

Her associations to the spider dream led her further back to early childhood. They used to spend summers in the country where she could overhear her parents quarrel and then have intercourse. She disliked this house, later rationalizing this with a dislike of some relatives who also vacationed there. She remembered seeing spiders there, but she never had any conscious preoccupation with or fear of spiders. The spider dream which eventually led to the resolution of the core of her severe and long-standing phobia, indicated that the spider symbol must have formed early about the time that her phobic clinging to her mother began, but it had been split off and remained latent until it was brought to the fore under the impact of analysis. She had never wanted to be pregnant and give birth to children because it was fraught with the idea of death. She had married a man she knew was sterile. She had adopted three children and had done a remarkable job with them, outdoing her mother without having been a "real" mother herself.

She had been talking about sensations in her vagina. She had a slight discharge and a fear that she might experience a burning sensation. She was unduly concerned about feeling as if she had a bubble there. We had talked in previous sessions about her penis envy and her bisexual wishes. She could now analyze these sensations herself and also understand why she had been so afraid and had avoided gynecological examinations. She left the session saying "I want to be a woman, not a spider." As with Leslie, the sensations in her vagina and the vaginal discharge completely disappeared after this session. The spider had been the symbol for her oral sadism (her intense breast and penis envy) and for her bisexuality, as well as for the primal scene and her oedipal hate. Multiple severe phobias and psychosomatic symptoms, especially nausea and headaches as defenses against the breakthrough of her destructive and perverse impulses, had enabled her to keep the potentially psychotic spider part of her personality under repression. Analysis mobilized, brought into focus, and resolved this danger.

CASE 4 highlights the role of psychosomatic symptoms as defenses against and expressions of pregenital oral and anal-sadistic impulses and of bisexuality. This material is from the analysis of an adolescent girl in treatment because of ulcerative colitis and anorexia nervosa. At the time of the episode reported here, the third year of her analysis, many of her fantasies underlying the ulcerative colitis and the anorexia nervosa had been brought to the fore. The somatic manifestations of the ulcerative colitis and anorexia had subsided, and she was dealing now with her symbiotic needs and wishes to engulf and completely control her objects. One of her basic colitis fantasies was of having little people in her colon. Cannibalistic and coprophagic fantasies and impulses had been a major dynamic factor both in her anorexia and the ulcerative colitis.

During one analytic session she suddenly saw in fantasy a spider pulling her strings one after another and eating her children. We had in previous sessions discussed her need to manipulate people like puppets and pull them on strings. She projected this need for magic control to her analyst and often suddenly sat up on the couch to watch me in paranoid fashion. She had fantasies of surprising me, of catching a glimpse of my magical "instruments." Sometimes, as she came into my office, she thought of "Come into my parlor," said the spider. Like Ruth, she felt she could never please her mother without a penis. She carried a boy's name, and as a child felt that she looked and was treated like a boy. Although she had clinging relationships with one girl at a time, she did not think that she could be a Lesbian. She considered herself a "homosexual," that is, a boy who likes boys, whereby she could merge and act out the fantasy of being both boy and girl in one.

She used to have an intense fear of crawling bugs, terrified lest the bugs eat her up. Once as a child she saw a bug crawling into her room. She screamed in terror, waiting for it to attack her. Her father, alarmed by her screams, came into the room, killed the bug, and threw it into the toilet. During her analysis she had many dreams of bugs, especially of leeches. She believed that leeches were poisonous, that they were not supposed to be pulled out or the poison would get into the body. They had to be cut out. At this phase of her analysis she had gained sufficient ego strength to be able to tolerate such fantasies consciously without fear of succumbing to them in reality, that is, of becoming manifestly psychotic.

In this case both the oral and anal fixations were particularly intense and played their respective parts in the somatic manifestations of anorexia and colitis and the unconscious fantasy life underlying these somatic symptoms. Her intense breast (a sister had been born when she was two years old) and penis envy, her pregnancy and birth fantasies, and her conflict of sexual identification and bisexuality had been elaborated mainly somatically, preventing their expression in overtly disturbed behavior.

CASE 5 again illustrates the use of the spider symbol as a transference manifestation in a pregenitally fixated patient who also employed somatic symptoms for the expression and release of her pregenital impulses and as defenses against a breakthrough of such impulses in a manifest psychosis. In this patient, the spider symbol also appeared during the later stages of her analysis when she had gained sufficient ego strength to tolerate and to deal with her fantasies and impulses consciously.

The patient, a thirty-five-year-old woman, had been in analysis because of severe, chronic ulcerative colitis. Concomitant with the subsiding of the somatic symptoms, her oral and anal sadistic impulses and fantasies came to the fore. She had dreams and fantasies about wild animals: tigers eating up people, cats swallowing birds (Sperling, 1960). By this time we had worked through some of her infantile sexual fantasies of oral impregnation and anal birth, her intense penis envy and primal-scene reactions, and were now analyzing her latent homosexual relationship with her mother. She had transferred this relationship in part to her husband and now to the analyst. During this phase of her analysis, fantasies about the analyst as a spider emerged. She had a fantasy that the analyst was in bed with her as a big spider engulfing and gobbling her up with a big mouth. She dreamed that she was at the analyst's office on a bed. The analyst was putting her arms around the patient's neck in a tricky way. The patient bit the analyst in the neck, near the jugular vein, and drew blood. Of interest is the fact that this patient had had bleeding with every bowel movement during her ulcerative colitis. Her mother had told her that she had been a difficult birth, that if it had taken any longer, the doctor would have had to cut her up into pieces. The patient had a fantasy that children, in order to get out of the amniotic bag, had to bite their way out. Sometimes when looking at the analyst she had the idea that the analyst was gobbling her up, pulling her thoughts and everything out of her and taking her inside into her body. She, similar to the adolescent patient, had fantasies that little people were in her colon. She had a very strong unresolved homosexual attachment to her mother and intense bisexual conflicts. One of her oral impregnation fantasies was that the baby got inside mother by being eaten up by mother, the same way that the patient would have wanted to obtain her husband's penis. She often expressed amazement that her husband was not afraid to put his penis into her mouth.

The experience with this patient would seem to support my belief that spider fantasies are not readily disclosed because they relate to the patient's most guarded and feared impulses. This may be a reason for the paucity of spider material in the psychoanalytic literature.

CASE 6. A seven-and-a-half-year-old boy was referred for treatment because of encopresis. The case was found to be not one of true encopresis, but of a peculiar bowel ritual. He had never defecated into a toilet. Instead he deposited his feces in a special place in the house, a corner of the bedroom near his mother's bed. His mother then inspected and disposed of them. But this behavior was not really why his mother had brought him for treatment. Peter also suffered from an intense phobia of black widow spiders. There had been some talk of black widow spiders having been seen, when his phobia began, but not in the vicinity of where he lived. He was also afraid of being poisoned by the fertilizer used on the lawn.

His mother impressed me as a borderline psychotic with marked paranoid trends. It was difficult to obtain information about Peter's early development. According to his mother it had been very satisfactory except for his refusal to use the toilet at home. Unfortunately, I could study Peter for only a few months because his mother withdrew him from treatment with the rationalization that he had sufficiently improved, and was no longer in need of treatment. The mother herself was not accessible to treatment and obviously was not able to tolerate the intrusion into her very pathological relationship with her son.

Peter's fears of being poisoned revealed themselves as manifestations of his pregnancy fantasies and of a very strong feminine identification. We had just begun to uncover wishes and fantasies of poisoning: that is, impregnating his sister and mother with his feces—fertilizer. The release of some of these fantasies had remarkably decreased his spider phobia and preoccupation with being poisoned, the behavior which had disturbed his mother much more than his encopresis. In fact, it appeared that Peter's special way of delivering his feces to his mother was in response to her pathological needs. There was no opportunity however, to investigate this further.

In Peter's case the anal elements and the anal significance of the spider symbol predominated. The black widow spider was the symbol of Peter's very strong but consciously rejected feminine identification and his anal (perverse and destructive) sexuality, externalized and projected upon his mother and displaced to the black widow spider. It would seem that in the male, the anal fixations and anality are the more significant factors in the genesis of bisexual and homosexual development.

This role of anality and of anal fixations in the choice of the spider symbol as a representation of the patient's bisexual orientation and pregenital sexuality is further illustrated with

CASE 7. Paul, whose long and successful analysis was conducted under my supervision, was diagnosed as a severely disturbed boy with flat affect and defective object relationships. He was a bed-rocker and very accident-prone. Paul was six years old when he started analysis. At the time of the episode to be reported here, he was in the fourth year of analysis.

He came in for his session sucking on an ice cream cone. He was holding it up so that it dripped into his mouth. This reminded him of sitting on the toilet and dropping feces. In this connection he thought of the many (repetitive) drawings he used to make of attacks from above and below, of planes dropping explosives and of anti-aircraft shooting up and destroying planes. For years his play and fantasy dealt primarily with machines rather than with humans. He then talked about an old fear of spiders coming up from the toilet. He once saw a movie of a giant spider. For a long time he was afraid that he would be bitten by a spider and be immobilized. This led him to talk about experiences with his mother. In order to prevent him from rocking, his mother used to tuck him in so tight that he could not free himself. He would wake up and become panicked. His mother's hand and fingers tucking him in, that is, immobilizing him, suddenly reminded him of a spider and it became clear to him that the giant spider he feared was his mother.

Paul's childhood had been inordinately traumatic. His mother had a depression when he was an infant, and when he was three years old, acted out severely before and after her divorce. His father, alternately seductively overindulgent and rejecting, also had many affairs. There had been actual seduction by an older brother, and sex play in which holding down and immobilizing the partner was a factor.

CASE 8 is a patient who will be described in detail elsewhere, in a study of vampire fantasies and vampiristic impulses. I shall confine myself here to relating an episode which took place in the third year of her analysis. Her mother had died when the patient was not yet six years old, and she was raised by an aunt. The episode relevant to spiders occurred the day of that aunt's funeral, which the patient did not attend. Her analysis revealed that she had not accepted her mother's death, and that she entertained fantasies of her mother returning to life. The night of the funeral, the patient was alone in the house, thinking about her aunt, when she saw a spider on the window. She was convinced that the spider was a reincarnation of her aunt. This patient had occasional acoustic and visual hallucinations all of which related to her fantasies about her dead mother.

## Discussion

As dissimilar as these cases may appear clinically, there are certain genetic and dynamic similarities between them which are of great significance for the thesis of this paper. All these patients experienced maternal rejection in their childhood, together with a high degree of overstimulation particularly in the visual spheres. In Cases 1 and 2, where the onset of the spider symbol and also of a severe sleep disturbance could be traced back to the age of two to three years, the maternal rejection was particularly marked. In Case 1, this could be clearly established during the second phase of treatment when she was overtly psychotic. Her mother confided that she had felt threatened and appalled by Ruth from birth on, that she had thought there was something wrong with her, that she was not like a real girl. These feelings related to the mother's unconscious rejection of her own femininity projected onto Ruth. Ruth's feelings that she could never please her mother as a girl, her intense rivalry with her brothers, her confusion and conflict over sexual identification, had some basis in her mother's unconscious feelings concerning her. The mother's identification of the child with an unconsciously hated and rejected part of herself is an important genetic factor in the development of psychosis in the child (see Chapters 21 and 22; and Sperling, 1955c). Severe, intractable sleep disturbance in a young child may sometimes be the first and only clinical indication of a later psychotic development (see Chapter 4; Sperling, 1949b).

In the case of Leslie, the mother's rejection was on a conscious level and quite apparent. The mother, sensing that her relationship with Leslie was very unsatisfactory and that Leslie was not developing properly, had sought treatment for herself when Leslie was not yet four years old. After a short period of treatment, the mother was advised to leave the care of the child to someone else. She could not accept this advice and broke off treatment. An attempt to treat Leslie when she was eight years old failed. She was found inaccessible and unresponsive. At the time her parents approached me, Leslie was ten years old, and the psychological testing suggested a schizophrenic development.

I worked with the mother for more than three years in preparatory analysis before undertaking to treat Leslie. In analyzing the mother, it could be established that Leslie represented to her not only the rejected "crazy" part of herself, but also of her own hated, psychotic mother. Leslie's mother had not wanted any children; Leslie was an unwilling concession made to her husband. Without the preparatory treatment of the mother, in which a modification of her attitudes and feelings toward Leslie could be achieved, Leslie, in my opinion, had no chance of recovery. As in Ruth's case, credit must be given to Leslie's mother; without her help the surprisingly successful outcome could not have been accomplished.

In Peter's case there were indications that he was identifying with his mother who appeared to be suffering from a paranoid psychosis. With Paul, the pregenital, especially the anal, fixations were marked, and the diagnosis pointed to the development of a severe narcissistic character disorder. The third patient, who had the single nightmare about a black spider, had used an incapacitating phobia with the mechanisms of denial (of the internal danger), of externalization, and of displacement—first to the school, then to any situation that entailed separation from mother—in defense against her overwhelmingly strong pregenital impulses. She, similarly to patients 2, 4, and 5, also had used somatic pathways for the immediate discharge of such impulses. Patients 2 and 3 primarily used nausea, severe headaches, and cramps, whereas patients 4 and 5 had ulcerative colitis and anorexia. When the phobic mechanisms as well as the somatic defenses were invalidated by analysis, the split-off pregenital and potentially psychotic core symbolized by the spider appeared. The spider was a highly condensed symbol containing the core fantasies and conflicts from various developmental levels, in particular, breast and penis envy, primal scene reactions (murderous and suicidal impulses), bisexual and homosexual wishes and fantasies. The spider also represented both the patient and the mother in these feared and deeply repressed aspects.

It is my contention that the use of the spider symbol by these patients in time of stress was an indication that they felt threatened by an imminent breakthrough of these warded-off pregenital, "crazy" perverse impulses. The spider fear, fantasy, or preoccupation served the function of preventing the flooding of the ego with these pregenital fantasies and impulses. By displacement to this specific symbol, a total break with reality was avoided. Here the similarity with the dynamic and economic function of single phobias and obsessions is apparent (Sperling 1952, 1967). Unless subjected to analysis, the psychotic core represented by the spider remains unchanged, and these fantasies and conflicts retain their pathogenicity, constituting a continuous threat to the patient's emotional equilibrium. In this connection, the patient described by Azima and Wittkower (1957) and the contribution by Newman and Stoller (1969) are of particular interest.

The patient of Azima and Wittkower was a man who suffered from an incapacitating fear of spiders and was treated with anaclitic therapy using drugs. The spider phobia dated back to childhood, but had been precipitated in an acute, intense form by the birth of a son. The material which the patient produced and his behavior during the regressed state was overtly psychotic, dealing mainly with oral-sadistic attacks and counterattacks upon the spider-mother-breasts, that is, with biting and being bitten, with devouring and being devoured.

Newman and Stoller's patient was a woman with hermaphroditic genitalia who, during a psychotic episode, developed the delusion that her genitalia were a spider. The authors found that the spider also represented the patient's mother and the patient herself as a hermaphrodite. This patient had been preoccupied with spiders from early childhood.

A review of the remaining literature on spider symbolism regarding the type of patients and problems encountered might be of interest. Abraham (1922) stressed the bisexual aspects of the spider symbol. His patient, who had fears of being transformed into a woman and his mother into a man, would, I believe, by present psychoanalytic criteria be considered a severe character disorder. Foulkes (1943) dealt specifically with this fantasy of sexual transformation. His patient developed a paranoia with a delusion of an operation which would transform her into a male. Sterba's paper (1950) is of particular interest because of his discussion of a short story by the German novelist, H. H. Ewers. The story deals with three men who succumb to an acute delusional spider psychosis and commit suicide by hanging. The last man, who kept a diary describing his delusion about a spider-woman, was found dead with a spider crushed between his teeth. Sterba's patient had attempted suicide by hanging. Little (1966a, 1966b, 1967) stressed the pregenital aspects of spider symbolism. The mother of one of his patients was a borderline psychotic; the mother of another patient had committed suicide. He mentioned a colleague who, after learning of his interest in spider phobias, confided that he had a spider phobia as a child which had not been uncovered in his personal analysis. I cite this as confirmation of my experience that spider phobias and spider fantasies are revealed only with great reluctance and usually late in treatment. Gloyne (1950) described mass hysterical reactions to the fear of being bitten by the tarantula during the Middle Ages, reactions characterized by a dancing mania leading to mass suicide. This tarantism, related to ancient cults and rites, was of a decidedly sexual character.

Most investigators would seem to agree that the spider is a representation of the dangerous (orally devouring and anally castrating) mother, and that the main problems of these patients seem to center around their sexual identifications and bisexuality. However, it has not been emphasized that this concept of the mother is the result of the child's projection of its own denied oral- and anal-sadistic impulses and of the specific relationship with the mother, nor have the roles of the childhood climate and of the traumatic experiences been sufficiently elaborated. There has been no convincing explanation of why these patients chose spider symbolism in particular for the expression of their conflicts and impulses. The type of patients and problems described in the literature on spider symbolism is not at all uncommon, nor is the sight of spiders; spider symbolism, however, seems to be rather uncommon. While preparing the discussion of this problem, I spoke to many colleagues with long and extensive clinical experience and was surprised by the apparent rarity of this phenomenon in clinical practice. I agree with Little's (1967) observation and thinking: that patients do not readily reveal their spider phobias, and because of the distaste attached to the subject (Little refers in this connection to Freud's [1919] paper "The Uncanny"), analysts do not seem particularly interested in it.

I should, therefore, like to point to some of the factors which in my opinion contribute to this specific symbol choice.

Even young children have a variety of choices available for the symbolic expression of dangerous impulses and wishes. The choice of insects, and in particular of spiders, is not only an indication of the nature of these impulses and the defenses adopted by the child's ego against them, but is also related to the developmental phases and the quality of the mother-child relationship at that time.

It is my contention that the choice of the spider symbol indicates a fixation to the pregenital and in particular to the anal-sadistic phase in a very ambivalent and predominantly hostile relationship to the mother, with an inability to separate from the hated mother. Here again, Leslie serves as a good illustration for the tenacity of such a relationship.

While she was at college (she was able to live away and function somewhat independently from mother by this time, although she still went home for weekends and telephoned her mother frequently), her parents went abroad. Leslie's separation anxiety had dominated the analysis for some time preceding this event, which occurred during a short holiday from school. The day before her parents departed, Leslie went out of town to visit a friend. In the past, whenever her parents had taken a trip, it was during the summer when Leslie was in camp. They always returned in time for visiting days. Leslie reduplicated this situation by visiting the friend. She could not tolerate the awareness of actual separation and the feeling of being left.

She returned to her parents' house with a friend the next day to fetch some things she had left in the study. While there she suffered a severe anxiety attack. She felt that a giant spider was coming out of the wall, engulfing her and tying her up with many legs, so she could never free herself and escape. She screamed in terror for her friend, who was in another room. The study, which adjoined the parents' bedroom, was a room which Leslie had not been allowed to use as a child, but to which she would sneak, especially at night, to listen to the noises from the parental bedroom, when the parents were "fighting." Because this room was infrequently used, it always contained spiders, or more spiders than other parts of the house. In Leslie's spider fantasies, the spiders, often in enormous numbers, came from this room. Her parents' leaving her had revived her unresolved separation conflict as well as the oedipal conflict and hate (for being excluded from parental intercourse), and had mobilized the regressive wish for inseparable union with mother. Leslie's birth fantasies were mainly anal, the fetus being expelled like feces and discarded into the toilet as worthless and undesirable—like a spider. When she visited a relative who was breast-feeding her baby, she had a recurrence of spider fantasies and expressed fears of holding and nursing a baby. In this connection, Little's (1967) patient, who masturbated by tying himself up with ropes, is of interest. This is not an uncommon and dangerous masturbatory practice of transvestites. The suicides by hanging in Ewers' story and the behavior of Sterba's patient would seem to be related to this.

Returning to the importance of anal fixations in spider symbolism, the fact that it is often combined with phobias and especially with a persistent phobic dependence on mother is of significance. These phobias originate during the anal phase as a result of unresolved separation conflicts and destructive impulses directed against the controlling mother (see Chapter 7). While the oral features are important in spider symbolism, they seem to overshadow and conceal the more significant anal features in this symbol choice.

The choice of the spider symbol is also an indication of the child's severely injured narcissism, which is especially vulnerable during the anal phase when sphincter and impulse control are to be acquired, and the hatred for this deprivation is projected on the spider-mother. The spider is also, as was pointed out earlier, repulsive, something which not only may but should be destroyed, which can be stepped on and crushed. This is exactly how Leslie felt as a child: crushed and stepped on. The spider reflects the patient's lack of self-esteem, which relates in part to impulses he considers repulsive and dangerous.

This was obvious in all patients, and particularly in Leslie. At age two, Leslie had been attacked and bitten on her mouth by the neighbor's dog. One might have expected that she would develop a dog phobia under these circumstances. At that time Leslie's parents owned a similar dog. Not only was Leslie not afraid of this dog, she always wanted and had a dog to whom she talked and with whom she liked to sleep. To Leslie, the dog possessed human status and represented her father. This became quite clear in her analysis when she expressed concern lest her dog, who was old, might die. She felt the same way about her father, who was considerably older than her mother. Leslie had felt rejected by her mother. She hated her mother and was afraid to express her hatred. This preoedipal hate was further intensified by oedipal hatred. Leslie had contempt for her mother. To her, the female genital was repulsive, dangerous, mysterious, and surrounded by hair—like a spider. The correspondenece here with Freud's (1922) interpretation of the Medusa head is worth noting. Leslie could not therefore identify herself or her mother with an animal who was loved and treated with affection, as her dog was treated by her family.

Preoccupation with smell is another important characteristic found in these patients. It has to do with their coprophilic and coprophagic impulses, and was present in all patients, particularly in patients 4 and 5, who had colitis. These impulses find indirect gratification in the pregenital practices which these patients prefer to genital activity. Direct gratification of these perverse impulses is warded off as "crazy," and finds expression in the spider symbolism. The frequent fear of such patients of a spider falling into their mouths, also most clearly expressed by Leslie, contains and expresses such coprophagic wishes and destructive (killing) impulses. The spider represents the anally devalued breast and penis and their excretions as poisonous and dangerous. In this connection, a patient described in Sperling (1968b) is of interest. This patient had an intense insect phobia, especially of insects flying into her mouth. She would eat the hair she pulled and experience the sensation of swallowing live insects, which to her meant sperm-feces. She, too, was anally fixated with many phobias and an intense phobic dependence on her mother.

## Summary

Psychoanalytic studies of patients who used spider symbolism for the expression of their repressed (perverse) impulses and conflicts revealed, as important genetic factors, pregenital, partic-

ularly anal, fixations and unresolved preoedipal relationships
with their mothers. The spider symbolism as well as the symptoms most frequently found associated with it, such as severe
sleep disturbances and phobias, are also an indication of unresolved separation conflicts and a high degree of ambivalence
which intensifies bisexuality and the problems of sexual identification. The mechanisms of defense employed in spider symbolism and in phobias are denial, externalization, projection, splitting, and displacement. They indicate the primitive, ambivalent,
narcissistic ego organization of this phase. The personalities of
these patients and of the mothers in cases where it was possible
to study them showed marked paranoid trends. They also used
psychosomatic symptoms in stress situations, either episodically
or more persistently for the immediate (somatic) discharge of
threatening impulses. The spider symbolism in most cases
remained latent and became manifest in traumatic life situations
and in analysis when the phobic and psychosomatic defenses
were invalidated. In the analytic situation the spider symbolism
was indicative of a specific mother transference.

I have tried to elaborate on some of the factors operating in
the genesis and choice of the spider symbolism and to deal more
fully with its dynamic and economic functions. I particularly
wanted to draw attention to the diagnostic and prognostic significance of spider symbolism in clinical practice.

# PART 4

# OBSESSIONAL NEUROSIS

# 11

# Notes on Obsessional Compulsive Neurosis in Children

Fully developed obsessional compulsive neurosis is usually not common in young children. Behavior indicative of such a development can, however, be seen already in children less than two years of age. Ritualistic and rigid behavior is common. If this is interfered with, the child may have manifest anxiety or temper tantrums. A one-and-a-half-year-old boy became very anxious when a drop of food would dirty his bib. Excessive cleanliness, ritualistic hand-washing, or excessive modesty are reaction formations against anal impulses and are frequent preoccupations in these children. The mothers in these cases are usually compulsive, restrictive, anally fixated women with exaggerated interests in anal functions. Usually they institute early toilet training with use of enemas and suppositories and they also restrict bodily activities and encourage passivity. The development of these children does not usually lead to obsessional compulsive neurosis in later life but rather to the development of anal character disorders. These children, like the adult patient with an obsessional compulsive character disorder, need, especially in situations of

219

stress, immediate outlets for discharge of the tension. Therefore, the mixture of obsessional compulsive neurosis with psychosomatic symptoms (pregenital conversions) is very frequent. There are occasional breakthroughs of the reaction formations mentioned before and a child who had been very clean can be messy and dirty, and immodest.

In cases where the magic attributed to thoughts and wishes is very strong and ritualistic behavior is much in evidence, the obsessional compulsive defenses often cover up a psychotic personality structure. In treatment one must be careful not to remove these defenses too quickly, that is, not before the magical thinking and the fear of loss of control have been invalidated in treatment. In this way the ego of the child is strengthened. The conversion reactions in these children are usually symptoms of the lower GI tract such as bellyaches, diarrhea, and various forms of colitis, but asthma, allergies, and other symptoms, especially of the respiratory system, are not uncommon.

In latency children, we sometimes see a mixture of obsessional compulsive neurosis with episodes of a breakthrough of the repressed anal impulsive. These children often suffer from chronic anxiety (fear of such a breakthrough) of the dangerous and forbidden anal aggressive and sexual impulse. This anxiety interferes with the child's ability to concentrate and to learn. Such children also form other inhibitions that interfere with their ability to express and to use aggression appropriately. In treatment one must be careful not to release too much aggression too soon. This would get the child in conflict with his environment, and may lead to destructive acting out and turning of aggression toward the self. In some cases it leads to a heightened accident proneness with self-injury, to disturbed sleep with nightmare, and in general to anxiety and phobic reactions that may also be directed toward the therapist.

## Rituals, Temper Tantrums, and Tics

Ritualistic behavior in children is an indication of the use of obsessional compulsive mechanisms to allay anxiety. This anxiety stems from repressed sexual and aggressive impulses and a fear of giving into the temptation to masturbate. Masturbation in these cases is so dangerous because of the destructive impulses and because of the prohibition of overt expression of sexuality and aggression. This anxiety may be particularly accentuated at nighttime, when the child is separated from his parents and left to his own devices. Some of these children develop sleep phobias and they try to delay going to sleep. As a protection against intruders such as robbers, burglars, monsters, killers, which usually represent the child's own dangerous impulses projected to external objects, these children use various defenses, among them ritualistic, obsessional, compulsive behavior (see Parts 2 and 3).

In some cases certain articles have to be arranged and have to stay in a certain order. Some of the children need to take fetishes, such as stuffed animals or dolls, with them into bed, a knife under the pillow or good-luck charms such as a rabbit's foot or amulets. If things are moved or disarranged the child will have an anxiety attack or a temper tantrum according to whether he is more inhibited or more aggressive. These children also need to touch certain articles compulsively, and use compulsive praying, particularly at night, in defense against unconscious death wishes directed against the parents and sibling(s). They often need to repeat certain words. The fear of attack is usually an indication of castration anxiety, but also of castrative wishes of the child directed against the father. These fears and the mechanisms of defense are in some cases an early indication of the development of paranoid trends. They can also develop into specific phobias. In addition they are an indication of the persistence of the fantasy of omnipotence and of ambivalence. Both are characteristic of anal phase fixation.

Characteristic mechanisms of defense in obsessional compulsive neurosis are displacement, projection, isolation. These children have an excessive need to control people and situations. Certain tics, especially those of touching, sniffing, compulsive repetition of obscene words, etc., are of similar origin (repressed sexual and aggressive impulses) and employ similar mechanisms. Fetishistic behavior such as taking specific articles into bed in order to be able to fall asleep are based on the need to undo separation and to establish control over the love (need) object which is represented by the fetish (see Chapter 15). One of my patients needed dirty, smelly panties of her mother in bed with her. Another patient, a little boy of five, used the panties of his mother soaked with his urine. Some children have pieces of fur, a blanket, or ribbon for the same purpose. Compulsive masturbation, twitchings of the body, certain circumscribed movements, fidgety behavior, and certain tics are also frequent manifestations.

CASE 1.     David was six-and-a-half years old when his mother consulted me. He had suffered from multiple tics for the past half-year. His mother, while concerned with his tics, obviously used this as an opportunity to seek help for herself. This was a very favorable circumstance for David because he benefited from his mother's treatment indirectly and required only brief direct treatment, since he was still young and his tics were of recent origin. In addition, treatment of his mother brought about a considerable improvement in her relationship with David, which had been an essential factor in the genesis and disappearance of his tics.

When David was three-and-a-half years old his mother's sister, who lived with the family, had a baby girl, and shortly after this aunt moved his mother became pregnant; she gave birth to a baby sister when David was four-and-a-half years old. He had shared the parental bedroom until his sister was born and had shown great interest in this event. He had frequently questioned about how babies grow, but the mother could not answer these questions. She was very irritable and restrictive, and when she observed him masturbating in the toilet she forbade him to do it. She also restricted his physical activities and did not let him play with other boys. He had to rest a lot, especially since his sleep was disturbed during this period and he would frequently wake up screaming that his legs hurt him. Medical and orthopedic examination was negative. The mother did not allow any overt manifestations of aggression. Once when he was angry and pinched her, she not only pinched back, but shook him in fury. It was around that time that he began to shake his head and developed facial tics. There was a change in his personality; he began to withdraw. She was ambivalent toward him, mostly angry, but she also had profound guilt feelings. She was aware that she did not permit him to discharge any angry or aggressive feelings and that she did not let him be a boy. She felt particularly guilty about a habit David had developed. He would touch his genital region and put his hand to his nose. Discussing this, she confided that she had the same habit until adolescence and sometimes would find herself still doing it now. She also had had tics until adolescence. She was not aware that she was still grimacing and twitching when she felt angry and frustrated, but David was very aware of his mother's facial expressions and mirrored them in his tics.

The mother had had a very traumatic childhood. She suffered from episodic depressions and was frigid in an unsatisfactory marriage. She hated her father, whom she felt had exploited her after her mother's death. She had carried over this hate to her husband and son, both of whom she was trying to emasculate. Her gradual understanding of her problems and relationships in treatment enabled her to become more tolerant and accepting of her husband and David. David was seen in therapy for about four months, during which time he expressed in play and verbally his hostility and resentment of his mother and jealousy of the little sister. According to the mother, David had shown no overt jealousy of his sister at home. We found that his tics developed after he had stopped masturbating rather abruptly due to his mother's intimidation and threats. He had impulses to hit, kick and kill his mother and his sister. These impulses had to be repressed because any overt attempt at expressing resentment and aggression toward his mother was met by her with increased rejection and restrictions. The changing feelings and attitude of the mother toward David made further direct treatment unnecessary. His tics had disappeared and he was allowed to lead the life of an active boy of his age. The mother remained in treatment for two years; during this time the satisfactory development of David could be followed closely.

# 12

# Children's Habits and Infantile Sexuality

Psychoanalytic psychology has effected a complete reorientation with regard to the role of the instinctive urges, primarily of sexual and aggressive drives, in the development of the individual. In preanalytic psychology, childhood was regarded as a more or less peaceful period of growth in which the instinctive urges, when they appeared, merely played the part of a disturbing element. In order to be able to diagnose and to assess properly the disturbed behavior in children, and particularly to assess the role of sex factors in such behavior, a familiarity with the principles of child development is essential. It is important to know when certain behavior is age-adequate and its manifestations should not be suppressed, and when it is not age-adequate and its manifestations are then an indication of either premature progressive, arrested, or regressive pathological development.

Psychoanalytic child psychology has introduced the concept of infantile sexuality and has taught us that infantile sexuality is not identical with adult sexuality and certainly not with genitality. To put it in a most simplified manner, infantile sexuality

225

means that important physiological functions, and those parts of the body serving these functions, are endowed with pleasure beyond their physiological purpose. This pertains particularly to food intake and elimination as well as to skin sensations. This infantile sexuality, which is the most important source of pleasure for the child, undergoes development in three stages until its maturity into genital sexuality. The pleasure which the child derives from its own body is called autoerotic and the activities by which it is obtained are referred to as autoerotic activities. Autoerotic activities—sucking during the oral phase, pleasure from excreting and excretion during the anal phase, and pleasure in touching and playing with the genital organs (infantile masturbation) during the phallic phase, when the genitals proper become the prime organs for obtaining sexual pleasure—are appropriate activities for a child during the course of its psychosexual development. The mouth and the anus are the most important erogenous zones during the early stages of development and retain their importance in a more sublimated way throughout life.

Even under optimal conditions of development, considerable amounts of sexual interest and energy will remain invested in infantile forms of sexuality. Kissing, touching, licking, holding, looking, smelling, etc., are essential ingredients of the forepleasure that in mature adults leads to the completion of a heterosexual relationship in sexual intercourse with the endpleasure obtained in orgasm. If major parts of sexual interests and energies have remained invested in infantile sexuality and erogenous zones serving it, particularly the mouth and the anus, this interferes with the assumption of the proper adult sexual role and function and may lead to various forms of sexual disturbances, particularly to those called perversion. A characteristic differentiation between adult, mature sexuality and perversion is the fact that the endpleasure, that is, the orgasm, in mature, adult sexuality is reached in heterosexual intercourse with the use of the genitals proper, while in perversions this is reached in some infantile manner without heterosexual intercourse. Infantile sexuality has a polymorph perverse character. It is important to understand that the manifestations of this infantile polymorph perverse sexuality are appropriate expressions of child behavior during certain stages of the child's development and that they should be considered pathological only if they persist in this form to a large extent in later childhood, in adolescence and in the behavior of adults. Sucking, for instance, in the infant, beyond its nutritional value, is a most important activity for deriving infantile sexual pleasure by using the mouth. If it retains, however, this exclusive importance beyond the first or second year of life, when other sources for gratification become available to the child, then it should be considered a pathological manifestation.

### Thumb-sucking

This leads me to the discussion of certain phenomena in children, called "habits," which are sometimes carried over into adulthood. Everyone knows that habits are quite difficult to give up and that they are a sort of characteristic of the particular child, or adult for that matter. But not everyone knows that infantile sexuality is the most important genetic and dynamic factor in habit formation and in the stubbornness with which these habits are retained. In 1878, long before the advent of Freud, a reputable Hungarian physician by the name of Lindner read a paper at the Royal Academy of Medicine in Budapest dealing with the evils and dangers of thumb-sucking and the sucking of teeth, tongue, and so forth. He recognized correctly that the most important factor in creating and supporting this habit was the satisfaction of some sexual needs. He considered this behavior as a disguised form of masturbation. Masturbation, according to the mores of that time, was regarded as a terrible sin, a perversion to be eradicated by all means. This was actually what Lindner advocated in his speech—the use of cruel, forceful, and sadistic means of preventing children and adults from practicing this habit. While Lindner's assumption that tongue-sucking and thumb-sucking in older children, that is, children beyond the age of three and certainly in adults, is a distorted form (a masturbatory equivalent) of deriving sexual gratification is valid today, our approach to this problem is quite different.

Today we know that such behavior is an indication of a disturbed psychosexual development of the child, beginning with the oral stage. Contrary to what one would expect, it is not an indication of deprivation but rather of overstimulation and particularly of inconsistency on the part of the parents, who tend to overstimulate the child at one time and in one area and to interfere with gratification at other times and in other areas. The interference usually starts when the behavior of the overstimulated child becomes more obviously sexual, especially during the phallic phases (three–five years) when infantile masturbation sets in. Most often parents try to suppress these obvious manifestations of heightened sexual interest of the child instead of recognizing them as indications of sexual overstimulation, especially when masturbation is excessive and compulsive, and eliminating the source of this overstimulation. Parents do not realize that little children have sexual feelings for which they do not have adequate outlets and that if unduly stimulated by exposure and overaffectionate and intimate body contact these feelings will have to be released through infantile sexual pathways, especially when the more appropriate sexual pathways are interfered with. Such children will develop or fall back on various oral or anal channels, thumb-sucking, nail-biting, hair-pulling, nose-picking, soiling, wetting, various tics, etc. I should like to illustrate with one case the personality and sexual disturbances that may result from disturbed sexual development in which infantile oral sexual drives retained their leading importance into adulthood. These oral sexual drives manifested themselves in a "habit" during childhood and adolescence.

This is the case of a woman of thirty years of age, referred to me by a gynecologist. She suffered from an intense fear of vaginal penetration and the gynecologist had been unable to perform an examination. She had been married for eight years but had never had sexual intercourse. She had been such a severe tongue- and thumb-sucker that she had to have oral surgery at age eighteen because of deformity of the upper jaw and teeth incurred through the excessive sucking, which had persisted into adolescence. Her parents had encouraged all forms of infantile sexuality, but any expression of genital sexuality, such as attempts at infantile masturbation, and later on heterosexual interests and masturbation in adolescence, had been repudiated by both parents as very dangerous to mental and physical health. She had intense fears of pregnancy and childbirth. Sexual intercourse was very dangerous to her because of the destructive oral and anal qualities such as cutting, biting, and tearing she ascribed to the male and female organs.

This case also indicates the value of an early assessment of such a habit in a child for possible prevention of the development of severe sexual and character disorders in later life. Her choice of a marriage partner who himself had sexual problems and was, therefore, satisfied with a marriage without genital intercourse was a pathological one and made it possible for her to continue with her husband the relationship of the child with her parents and in particular with her father.

I am citing this example, not because I believe that every case of excessive thumb-sucking leads to such serious pathological consequences in later life, but to draw attention to the fact that such a persistent "habit," even in the absence of other conspicuous behavior, should be taken as an indication of maldevelopment. I find it necessary to stress this point because there is a tendency especially among behaviorists to be concerned only with the behavior itself and not with its causes. To some pediatricians such a situation might be merely of concern as a future dental problem, as it had been in the case of this woman, rather than as a psychological one.

### Deviate Sexual Behavior

It is important to recognize the role of sexual factors in certain disturbed behavior in children even when this is not manifestly apparent as such. In cases where the sexual implications are more obvious, parents usually fail to acknowledge and report it. The cases of deviate sexual behavior in children that came to my attention were brought for treatment usually under much external pressure and with reluctance by the parents. In the treatment of an exhibitionist referred by the court, I was struck with the attitude of the parents, who had consistently disregarded manifestations of the perverse behavior of their son when he was an adolescent, although they had been brought to their attention, until he was apprehended (M. Sperling, 1947). I should like to illustrate with two examples such a situation in younger children (see also Chapter 13).

CASE 1. A six-and-a-half-year-old girl of above-average intelligence from an upper-middle-class home was referred to me by the school principal. This girl was in the habit of "attacking" other children. She would throw them to the floor and stick her tongue into their mouth and try to stick her finger into their anus. In treatment, it was found that she was a highly overstimulated child. Her father was in the habit of holding her on his lap, where she could feel his erect penis pushing against her behind. He liked to kiss her affectionately on the mouth when she could feel his tongue going into her mouth. The mother, herself a very anally fixated woman, was habitually giving her enemas and was overstimulating her in this area. Both parents were very restrictive of any overt expressions of sexual interest and had prohibited masturbatory activity as soon as it appeared between age four and five. At this age masturbation is a more appropriate autoerotic activity than is tongue-sucking or anal play. If a child at this age masturbates excessively and offensively in the presence of others, then it should be taken as an indication that this child is highly overstimulated. Instead of prohibiting masturbation, the pediatrician and the parents should look for the source of this overstimulation. Usually it is the parent's own behavior or seduction by older siblings, playmates or by other persons in the child's environment.

CASE 2. Another six-year-old girl, also referred by her school, was in the habit of seducing classmates by pulling their panties down and inspecting their genitals. She was stealing money from her mother and with the candy she bought for it, was bringing the children to conform with her needs. She too was a highly overstimulated child who, by behaving in this way, did with the other children what she experienced particularly with her older sister. Her mother was a very seductive, exhibitionistic, and voyeuristic woman. Her parents had just divorced and the child, who had been very attached to her father, felt abandoned by and resentful of him. She was identifying with him by taking the sexually aggressive (male) role. This girl, like many other sexually overstimulated children, exhibited various other habits, that is, symptoms resulting from the same source and indicating the development of a character disorder of the impulsive type. She was enuretic and obese; she stole and she suffered from bronchial asthma. (The successful treatment of her asthma is reported in M. Sperling, 1963.) Even at that early age the link with addiction and the possible development into a character disorder with acting-out behavior could be seen clearly and was interfered with by treatment of the patient and her mother.

## Fetishistic Behavior

There is other behavior in children in which sexual factors play an important role, but which even to the trained observer may not appear as obviously sexual. I am referring here to children who have an exaggerated attachment to articles of clothing, or a piece of bedding such as a pillow, a blanket, or other inanimate objects not particularly suitable as a child's plaything. The child must possess and use this article, the "fetish," in certain situations, especially before going to sleep or when alone or in a strange environment and even the presence of the mother will not comfort the child unless the fetish is available.

I had an opportunity to study in a number of cases of simultaneous treatment of mother and child the development and resolution of this phenomenon and to understand the sexual nature of this behavior. In these cases too, the child is rarely brought by the parents for this particular behavior unless there are other disturbing manifestations, such as difficulties in school, or difficult behavior at home, persistent bed-wetting, or the like. A case in which the pediatrician insisted that the parents consult with me because he found the behavior of the child so unusual is illustrative. This child's fetish was his mother's panties, which had to be saturated with his urine and he had to be able to bury his face into it as a condition for going to sleep. During the day he liked to hold the fetish to his face and smell it. The parents obviously had tolerated this behavior (which had been discovered only incidentally by the pediatrician) and did not feel that they or the child needed help with this situation.

The need for a childhood fetish indicates that there is a disturbance in the child's relationship with the mother. Gratification which is not obtainable from the mother is gained from the fetish-object. The fetish has the double function of making it possible for mother and child to separate in reality by magically undoing this separation. The role of the mother in the choice of the child's fetish may be illustrated with the example of a six-and-a-half-year-old boy. This boy would always carry a strip of silk stocking in his pocket to school and everywhere and also take it to bed with him. He would frequently finger it, especially when watching television and often put it into his pajama leg and rhythmically rub his scrotal region. The onset of this attachment dated back to the time when he was one-and-a-half-years old. The mother used to lie down with him at bedtime while he drank his bottle. He liked to stroke her legs while drinking and would fall asleep in this way. The mother then decided to absent herself and instead to offer him a silk stocking along with the bottle. He always carried a silk stocking with him and she had difficulty taking it away from him to wash it when it became smelly and dirty. When he grew bigger the mother became embarrassed by this habit and decided, in order to make it less obvious, to cut it into strips. Here the function of the fetish is quite obvious. He could do with the fetish what he could not do in reality with his mother.

The child's fetish is but a stage in a process that may or may not lead to adult fetishism. Some adult fetishism is a continuation of fetishistic behavior from childhood, sometimes with the same or a very similar fetish, sometimes with a succession of fetishes.

A fetish differs from other favorite articles treasured by children. At certain phases in their development, children may form an attachment to some inanimate object which is introduced by the mother for the purpose of gratifying certain specific needs of the child. Pacifiers or soft, stuffed animals are given with the correct expectation that the child will be able to give them up more easily than autoerotic gratifications. Adequate gratification of instinctual needs, by facilitating progress to subsequent phases of development and growth in object relations, enables the child to relinquish the gratifications of the earlier phases. Children at certain stages of their development often show strong preference for a special toy, but, although they may urgently need this toy at times, the need is not so compulsive nor persistent, nor the panic so overwhelming when it is unavailable or lost, as in the case of the fetishistic child. These phenomena and their relation to the transitional object are dealt with more extensively in Chapter 15.

The tenacity with which children hold on to this behavior is an indication that it serves in a disguised form the gratification of their sexual needs. Parents and physicians know of the difficulty of getting children to give up a habit such as thumb-sucking, nail-biting, or bed-wetting. Certain types of persistent bed-wetting that may continue into adolescence can be considered as masturbatory equivalents. They are an indication of disturbed sexual development and often the basis for sexual difficulties in adulthood. The infantile response to sexual stimulation in children is most frequently through the genitourinary and in some more anally fixated children through the gastrointestinal tract. It is well known that young children when excited or overstimulated wet and soil themselves. The urinary tract, especially in the male, is closely linked to the genitals and genital excitement. Freud considered bed-wetting as a sexual activity of childhood, to be followed by nocturnal emissions later on.

A few illustrations may indicate some of the concepts children have concerning the role of urination in impregnation and childbirth and their effects on the child's behavior. A little girl of seven was referred because of hyperactivity, lack of concentration, and inability to learn. Even in the classroom she was jumping around, often on other children. In addition, she was incontinent in both bladder and bowels. She was not retarded; in fact, she was rather brighter than her IQ of 115 would lead us to expect. In treatment it was found that her concept of intercourse and impregnation was that of the father jumping on mother and urinating and defecating on her.

Another six-year-old enuretic girl would occasionally playfully jump on her mother and wet herself in the process. This to her meant that she was making a baby for her mother. Another patient of mine, an adolescent girl, still clung to the idea that babies are made in the bathroom while urinating. A six-year-old enuretic boy with strong feminine tendencies expressed ideas that babies are born by urinating. He had fears that a baby might drown in the urine. At times he acted out these fantasies by taking little dolls into the bathroom and making a flood. Another patient, a young woman, derived the greatest excitement and could even bring on an orgasm by fantasizing that she was holding a man's penis while he was urinating or that she was watching men urinate. Voyeuristic and exhibitionistic tendencies are very prominent in urinary-fixated individuals and this patient had retained these wishes and fantasies from her early childhood. Such an infantile response to sexual excitement via the urinary system can continue until adulthood in certain individuals and lead to sexual disturbances and infantile behavior that could be classified as a form of urinary perversion. One of my adult patients not only had the wish but actually did urinate into his wife's vagina. Another patient responded to sexual stimulation with urinary urges and yet another adult patient when sexually excited or put under pressure would wet himself. One patient remembered that his mother would hold his penis tenderly for him when he was urinating as a little boy. This is what he expected a woman to do for him as an act of love. He was impotent, and the other patients mentioned suffered from sexual difficulties—periodic impotence, nocturnal emissions, and premature ejaculation. Another adult patient of mine was in the habit of using the bathroom each time before entering the office. Until this behavior was analyzed and understood as his way of devaluing and controlling the analyst, his analysis had remained sterile. This was how he discharged the sexual and aggressive impulses he directed at me.

These are conditions in which the dynamic role of sexual factors is not immediately obvious. In exhibitionistic, voyeuristic, or transvestite behavior, the sexual implications are readily apparent. In such cases one usually finds that the behavior is in some way that may not be obvious to others encouraged by the parents, usually by the mother (see Chapter 14). Although the roots for homosexual and lesbian behavior also go back to childhood, we cannot really speak of homosexuality or lesbianism before late adolescence or early adulthood, when a definite heterosexual object choice should be established.

Infantile sexuality is such an intrinsic part of human behavior that only a fraction of the multitude of pathological behaviors in which it is a genetic and dynamic factor could be touched upon in this chapter. I shall in passing simply mention its role in hysterical conversions in children and adolescents such as globus hystericus, nausea, vomiting and anorexia nervosa as well as in sleep disturbances, anxiety states, and learning difficulties.

In the management of such behavior it is insufficient and often harmful to remove only the symptomatic behavior without providing more appropriate outlets for the child's instinctual drives, both sexual and aggressive, and a more understanding environment that will encourage growth and a healthier development. Here I must emphasize the therapeutic and preventive value of simultaneous treatment of mother and child, whether conducted concomitantly, with analysis of the mother preceding the treatment of the child or in the case of very young children with only the mother being treated.

## The Relation of Children's Habits to Masturbation and Masturbatory Equivalents

The psychoanalytic concepts of infantile sexuality and of the psychosexual development of the child have given new dimensions and meaning to the manifestations of the sexual drive in children as well as in adults. They teach us that sucking in the infant serves not only the purpose of food intake but in addition and very importantly it is also a source for infantile sexual pleasure, and that this pleasure in sucking needs to be gratified so that the development of the oral instincts may proceed adequately. The lips, the mouth, and the tongue serve the first active contact with the object world and the experiences of the nursing period may well be decisive not only for the physical but also for the emotional and intellectual development of the child.

Thumb-sucking in infancy, if it is not excessive and if it is transient, is not a habit but an age-adequate autoerotic activity; so is a certain amount of anal play and interest in excretions during the anal phase, until about age three. Masturbation between ages three and five is the age-adequate manifestation of infantile sexuality and if not interfered with, and if there is no excessive environmental stimulation, will subside of its own. In this connection an experiment conducted by the Russian child analyst, Vera Schmidt (1924), with children raised away from home in an institution with trained personnel and under her supervision is of interest. These children were allowed expression of their instinctual drives, including masturbation, without threats and prohibitions. She reported that the children stopped masturbating spontaneously between ages five and six without guilt feelings. Those children where there was interference, especially on home visits, developed characterological symptoms such as lying, stealing, stubbornness and other undesirable traits. In the normal course of development the child around age six will enter the so-called latency period, where instinctual sexual urges become quiescent and the energies attached to them available for intellectual, social, and other pursuits. It has been my observation as well as that of others that some children living in a highly overstimulating environment do not have a real latency period.

Certain habits which develop during infancy in connection with feeding can be retained in an almost unchanged manner into adult life. They have been found to represent forms of infantile sexual gratification due either to excessive stimulation or to not enough stimulation of the components of the oral instinct, especially of touching and stroking. Too much as well as too little instinctual gratification contribute to fixation to this particular phase and mode of gratification. It is usually not a lack but rather overindulgence and in particular inconsistency in gratification that fosters the need for autoerotic gratification and fixation to this level of gratification.

In this regard Spitz's studies of autoerotism (1949) have been particularly enlightening, and have shown that certain auto-erotic activities, such as thumb-sucking and masturbation, origi-nate as a result of object relations and stimulations by external objects, while other types of autoerotic activities such as rocking and head-banging, to which he refers as malignant types, are indicative of defective or more grossly disturbed early object rela-tions. Thumb-sucking, which is often associated with twirling of the hair in infants and very young children, is still an age-ade-quate manifestation of oral instinctual gratification, but at the same time it is also an indication of a heightened need and of a special way of gratifying such needs. When it persists into later childhood or reoccurs at certain times in latency or in older chil-dren or adults then it has to be considered as serving the dis-charge of sexual energies and should be regarded as a masturba-tory equivalent. Thumb-sucking is a result of unsatisfied oral erotic drives expressing the child's need not for food but for suck-ing certain parts of the mother's body and establishing close body contact with her. A most outstanding illustration for this is the case of a psychotic seven-year-old-boy. He and his mother were treated in simultaneous analysis under my supervision. Among his many bizarre symptoms was also a severe eating dis-turbance. We found that in early infancy, when his mother was breast-feeding him, he would prefer to suck his thumb instead of taking the nipple. In the analysis of the mother this bizarre behavior could be understood and his feeding problem and other severe problems resolved. The mother related that as soon as her infant would take the nipple into his mouth she would pull it out, thus frustrating him extremely so that he refused to even try. She had then and still suffered from strong fears that he would bite and mutilate her breast. This was really a projection of her own oral-sadistic impulses onto her son. In the case of a little girl reported by Seitz (1950), who would not suck the bottle unless her lips were stroked by hair, it was found that she had been breast fed for several weeks by her mother who had hirsutism of the nipples.

During the anal phase, excretory functions, the holding in of feces or urine and then letting it out are associated with sexual pleasure. The rectum and anal sphincter and the bladder and the urethral sphincter are well suited to simulate the genital organs and their functions. Certain types of enuresis are a result of sexual overstimulation and are a form of perversion when they persist into adolescence and adulthood. Like all habits that serve the gratification of sexual instincts and are masturbatory equivalents, they are very resistant to treatment. Day wetting in particular is an indication of sexual excitement and in some girls may represent the equivalent of ejaculation. Enuresis usually stops when the sexual apparatus has developed and genital masturbation starts but this is not always so.

Nail-biting is usually a very stubborn habit and may often be the last symptom to yield to therapeutic intervention. This may be due to the fact that because of its fixation to the oral- and anal-sadistic phases of development it is a very important mode of gratifying perverse oral and anal impulses such as cannibalistic, necrophilic, and vampiristic impulses. Such impulses I have found particularly in patients who pick their skin around their nails until bloody and then suck the blood and eat the pickings of the skin with an absorption that indicates a high degree of withdrawal from reality at such times. There is a similarity in this behavior and in that of children who pick their noses and eat the pickings or who pull and eat their hair. The anal fixation also manifests itself in a need to smell the saliva and in fantasies that the long nails are dangerous weapons with which to scratch (bloody), to stab, and to kill the victim. Biting of the nails in such a case is a turning of the aggression against the self, and particularly in boys a form of self-castration. Boys are very ashamed of the nail-bitten hands. In this connection, the fact that nail-biting is more frequent in boys than in girls is of interest. Nail-biting does usually not occur before the age of three while thumb-sucking can be there from birth on. There is an increase in nail-biting with progressive age. Between the ages of three to five the figure is ten percent of the total population of this age group. In latency, between six to twelve it is thirty percent and in puberty and early adolescence it is forty percent (Wechsler, 1931).

It is inadvisable to focus on the removal of the symptom without first effecting some changes in the personality structure and object relationships of the child. The freeing of sexuality from its oral and anal fixations and redirecting it to the genitals, where it belongs, is an important prerequisite for successful treatment. The occurrence or reoccurrence of masturbation in such children should be regarded as a sign of progression. The gratification derived from the smell and the wetness of the saliva in nail-biting and thumb-sucking children is an indication of its displacement from the genitals to the fingers. It is also an indication of the child's conflictual feelings about his anal and genital organs and their functions. Thumb-sucking is a more oral-erotic, that is, benign, while nail-biting is a more oral- and anal-sadistic, that is, a more malignant, autoerotic activity. Both are masturbatory equivalents and very resistant to treatment. Anything can be given up more easily than a practice which serves the disguised gratification of sexual impulses.

Encopresis, although not as frequent as enuresis, is a fairly common habit of the anal phase. It is indicative of faulty training and of a faulty mother-child relationship. It is also indicative of a shift of sexual interest from the genitals to the rectum and the anus. This is encouraged by the mother's anal fixation, manifested in her interest in giving suppositories and enemas and in excessive handling of the child's anal region. In some cases it is a real perversion of both mother (and father) and of the child. The child may be in the habit of retaining feces in his pants and treating them like a fetish (see also Chapter 1).

# PART 5

# DEVIATE SEXUAL BEHAVIOR IN CHILDREN

# 13

# A Study of Deviate Sexual Behavior in Children by the Method of Simultaneous Analysis of Mother and Child

The method of simultaneous analysis of mother and child in which mother and child are treated psychoanalytically in separate sessions (preferably without the child knowing of the mother's analysis) by the same analyst was first applied by me in the treatment of psychosomatic diseases in children, especially ulcerative and mucous colitis, bronchial asthma and some skin disorders (M. Sperling, 1946, 1949a and c, 1952c, 1954).

In the treatment of these children, I found that at a certain phase during their analysis a seemingly unmotivated exacerbation or aggravation of their condition occurred or that their treatment was suddenly terminated, with or without a rationalization. I found that these occurrences were the result of an unconscious resistance of the mother to the treatment of her child. In adults, this resistance is manifest as such in the patient and can be handled directly; in children the resistance of the parents may come out through the child in various forms and often cannot be handled directly, that is, through the child alone.

I have found that this crucial phase in the treatment of the psychosomatically ill child is the time when the child, enabled by analysis, is attempting to dissolve the symbiotic relationship with the mother; the mother, because of her own unconscious needs, cannot accept this (M. Sperling, 1949a and d, 1951). Unless the mother can be helped through psychoanalytic intervention to understand and to overcome her resistance, she will not permit this basic change in the relationship. In spite of a very cooperative conscious attitude on the part of the mother, treatment of the child will not succeed. In these children, in whom resistance manifests itself in somatic symptoms that set in with amazing speed, it is essential that this resistance of the mother be spotted and analyzed at once. This can be done best by the analyst who treats the child, particularly in the case of younger children, where I have found that mother and child function as an inseparable unit which can be best understood and treated by one analyst. The shortcomings of the method of collaborative treatment, where mother and child are treated by two different analysts, lies in the fact that the subtle but decisive shades of the interplay between the unconscious of the mother and that of her child are missed even if there are lengthy and frequent conferences between the two analysts or team of workers (Bettelheim, 1955; Johnson and Szurek, 1952). Even in the treatment of these children in a clinic, where the handling of the mother was routinely delegated to another therapist, I found it necessary in many cases to treat mother and child myself, at least during certain phases of the treatment (see, for an example, M. Sperling, 1952b).

The analyst of the child must have the mother's complete acceptance and trust (this can be reliably established in the analytic relationship) if the treatment of the child is to be successful. The conscious attitudes of the mother are completely deceptive and unreliable in these cases. One modification of the method of simultaneous analysis of mother and child is the technique of treating the mother first, at least for a period of time, before embarking upon the treatment of the child, especially in the case of younger children up to eight or nine years of age. I have found that even in the cases of an acute and alarming illness such as ulcerative colitis, where the pressure of the situation is usually intensified by the attitude of the attending physicians urging hospitalization, surgery and other strictly medical procedures, adherence to the method of working first with and through the mother is extremely rewarding. In many cases, the acute symptoms subsided quickly and the children improved so remarkably that there was doubt in the parents' minds whether the child still needed direct treatment. This resistance can be handled very easily once a therapeutic relationship with the mother is established.

The great merit of the method of simultaneous analysis of mother and child, however, lies not in the fact that it represents an essential technical aid in the treatment of certain psychosomatic diseases in children, important as this may be, but that it proved to be a new and extremely rewarding approach to the study and understanding of a very important area of child development, namely, the psychology and psychopathology of the mother-child relationship. This method permitted the immediate observation of the interaction between the unconscious of the mother and her child, and of the ways in which the unconscious wishes of the mother were transmitted, received and reacted to by the child as well as of the changes in their mutual responses in the analytic process. With this a new understanding of the etiologic factors and the deep psychodynamics operating in certain psychosomatic diseases of children was gained. I have reported on the successful treatment of ulcerative colitis in children with this method and on my concepts of this illness based upon the insight gained with this method (M. Sperling, 1946, 1949c, 1952c, 1954, 1955b). This method also made it possible to study and to compare the conditions under which, in a situation of symbiotic mother-child relationship, a psychosomatic disorder occurred and in which situation a psychotic development was the outcome (M. Sperling, 1955b).

In the treatment of children with mucous colitis by this method, it is possible to recognize the specific behavior of the mothers of children with mucous colitis and to compare and to differentiate it from the behavior of mothers of children with ulcerative colitis (M. Sperling, 1952c). The study of a case of allergy and bronchial asthma with this method made it possible to observe in action the pathogenic effects of the mother-child relationship and to resolve them in the analytic process (M. Sperling, 1949a, 1954). The study of skin disorders such as pruritis, eczema and dermatitis, but particularly the study of a case of ulcers of the leg with this method, made it possible to understand the symbolic use of the skin and its ulcers by the child and his mother (M. Sperling, 1949a, 1954).

My application of this method to the study and treatment of severely disturbed children, whose bizarre, explosive and unpredictable behavior could not be fully understood nor sufficiently influenced in individual treatment, proved to be most fruitful. M. Mahler (1951), in discussing one of my papers stated, "By studying longitudinally in actual psychoanalytic treatment both partners of the mother-child unit, Dr. Sperling obtained insight into the specific and deep unconscious psychodynamic correlations between the psychopathology of mother and child." In the cases studied by this method, behavior which might have been ascribed to inherited factors could be demonstrated to be a reaction of the child to the mother's unconscious wishes (see Chapter 3). Similarly, it was possible to understand behavior in children which could have been ascribed to extrasensory perception had it not been studied by this method (M. Sperling, 1951). My research in this area would seem of particular interest for the understanding of the phenomena and psychodynamics in hypnosis, folie-à-deux, and child psychosis. In some cases, even of older children, where the child for various reasons was not available for treatment, the pathologic behavior of the child could be remarkably influenced through the psychoanalytic treatment of the mother alone (see Chapter 2).

In my discussion of the "Case of An Atypical Child" (see Gardner, 1949), I expressed my opinion that no permanent therapeutic results could be obtained with these children unless their mothers were treated psychoanalytically, preferably by the same analyst who treated the child, or, even better, were analyzed prior to the treatment of the child. I based my opinion on my findings, from the psychoanalytic studies of such a mother, that the mother unconsciously identifies the child with either an unconsciously hated and rejected part of herself or an unconsciously hated important object from childhood with whom she had not resolved her infantile conflict, and which instead was revived and continued with her child.

I have been interested for some years in the study of perversions in adults and of deviate sexual behavior in children. There are comparatively few contributions of deviate sexual behavior in children in the psychoanalytic and psychiatric literature (Arlow, 1954; M. Sperling, 1947; see also Bender and Paster, 1941; Buxbaum, 1935; Friend et al., 1954). This is rather surprising as severe character disorders and perversions are frequent psychiatric conditions in adults; they are difficult to treat and, from the etiologic and dynamic point of view, still present many problems. In the treatment of an adult exhibitionist, I was struck with the attitude of the parents, who had consistently disregarded the manifestations of the perverse behavior of my patient when he was an adolescent, although it had been brought to their attention, until he was apprehended and sentenced to treatment as it were (M. Sperling, 1947). In every instance of a case of deviate sexual behavior in a child which came to my attention, the child was brought for treatment under much external pressure and with great reluctance by the parents. The parents of these children appeared to be respectable, well-meaning people whose conduct seemed beyond reproach. The behavior of the children appeared almost paradoxically unrelated to that of their parents.

This chapter deals with research into deviate sexual behavior of children with the method of simultaneous analysis of mother and child. From the eleven cases of children with deviate sexual behavior I treated, fragments from the treatment of three cases will be presented to illustrate my method as a technique for research and treatment with its advantages and complications.

CASE 1. Treatment had been suggested for six-and-a-half-year-old Rhoda by the school because of certain behavior observed there. Rhoda had been found, on several occasions, with other girls in the toilet with her panties down, inspecting and touching their genitals. Rhoda had been bringing large amounts of candy to school as gifts for these girls. The candy she bought with money she took

from her mother's purse. Rhoda also suffered from persistent enuresis. Her mother had been told that she did not
require treatment for the enuresis and that she would
eventually outgrow it. Rhoda's parents had separated when
she was five years old.

Rhoda was a good-looking, but overweight, bright
youngster. For a considerable period of her analysis, Rhoda
would play school with me. She would push me, tie me,
want to hit me, yell at me, and, in general, treat me very
sadistically. Rhoda went to a private school where the
teachers were especially considerate. It was obvious that
this game did not repeat a school situation. On many occasions she would suddenly jump on me, get on top of me
and make movements as in intercourse. Rhoda very cau-
tiously began to reveal some of the activities that had gone
on between her and the other children. She had always
been the seducer. What she really was interested in, much
more than in looking, was to exhibit herself and to be
looked at. She also liked to treat the other girls roughly and
to hit them over their naked bodies.

After a year and a half of treatment, during which her
behavior in school had improved considerably but her analysis
did not seem to progress much further, her mother accepted my
suggestion that she undergo analysis herself. A condensed and
fragmentary account of the relevant material as it emerged in the
analysis follows.

Rhoda's mother had a very strong, unconscious homosexual attachment to her own mother, from whom she had
never separated. Mrs. A. (as we shall refer to Rhoda's
mother) had been a very pretty, bright and talented girl,
the pride of her mother. Her mother had controlled every
one of her steps. As a young girl, Mrs. A. had not been
interested in men; she was married at 25, after all her girl
friends had been married, to a man whom she supported
until he could establish himself. After her marriage she
continued to live with her mother, and for some years she

had spent her vacations with her mother, instead of with her husband. Analysis revealed that she had established with her husband the relationship which she had with her mother, only now she was taking the role of her mother. She had to know exactly where her husband was at all times, when he would come home, and would anxiously wait for him at the window should he be a few minutes late. She now also controlled her mother, who, after her husband's death, depended upon my patient. Mrs. A., a very soft-spoken woman, respected by everyone for her polite and kind behavior, would lose her temper frequently at home and have violent fights with her mother. During these scenes, both women would be in the nude, and "for an old woman she still has a very nice body," Mrs. A. would tell me. After such a scene, they would make up. Mrs. A. was treating Rhoda in a similar way to the way she behaved with her own mother. She would get very angry, yell at her, and hit her, also in the nude, as these scenes would take place in the bedroom or bathroom in the morning or at night. The sadistic and sexually attacking teacher whom Rhoda was impersonating could be identified now with certainty as her mother.

It could be seen that Rhoda was doing actively with other girls what her mother had been doing with her. Rhoda had been very disappointed and frustrated with her mother after the separation of her parents. She had hoped unconsciously to take her father's place with her mother, but, instead, her mother, who at that time was on the verge of a depression and completely preoccupied with herself, was totally inconsiderate and neglectful of Rhoda's needs. She did not spend much time with Rhoda; in fact, she was hardly ever at home during that year. This was the time when Rhoda's sexual aggressive behavior and the display of the scoptophilic, exhibitionist and sadistic impulses in school began.

The mother never admitted to herself and certainly could not have admitted to others how she felt about Rhoda and what was going on between them. She felt repulsion and strong attraction at the same time. She began to realize that she had unconsciously identified Rhoda with herself, although consciously she maintained that Rhoda was the image of her husband and that her unrestrained and impulsive behavior were the paternal characteristics.

In the analysis of the mother it became clear why Rhoda, after a year and a half, had come to an impasse in her analysis and did not make further progress. Mrs. A. felt that, in the matter of self-control, Rhoda was surpassing her. In fact, had she shown more control, she would have shamed her mother, who at that time was not ready to curb her own behavior. Later in the analysis when the mother began to curb this behavior toward Rhoda, Rhoda would often say, "We are getting modest these days," or "You are not kissing me as you used to."

It was found that Mrs. A.'s superego was peculiarly contradictory. On the one hand, it demanded very high moral, ethical and intellectual performance; she had to be very bright, altruistic, loyal and self-sacrificing. But, on the other hand, it permitted an almost complete abandonment of any standards and the acting out of crude sexual and sadistic impulses in reality. Only in the simultaneous psychoanalytic treatment of Rhoda and her mother could this behavior and its unconscious motivations be exposed and its effect upon Rhoda's psychosexual development and especially upon the structure of her superego be observed and understood. It became clear that this relationship with her mother had led to the establishment of a superego which not only did not prohibit, but, in fact, condoned her behavior. Rhoda had a very well-functioning ego; she showed no impairment of the sense of reality or other important and essential functions of the ego. She was very clever in her attempts to keep out of her analysis the significant material and to reveal as secrets, and with much fussing, the less significant behavior. In this respect, she behaved in her treatment like an adult pervert who is unwilling to give up his perversion. Even the enuresis in her case had the quality of a perversion as there was hardly any

guilt or shame but, on the contrary, much pleasure connected with it.

I had the opportunity to work with Rhoda analytically again
when she was sixteen years old and preparing to enter college.
The problem which brought her into treatment then was a
sudden marked drop in grades in her senior year of high school
and feelings of panic, especially during exams. It was found that
underlying these symptoms was a conflict of separation from her
mother. To graduate meant to go to college and to leave mother.
This analysis was very rewarding, particularly because it permitted the evaluation of the effects of the analytic treatment ren-
dered to her and her mother years ago. Significant additional
information and insight into the behavior she had exhibited as a
young child could be gained. This material, together with other
follow-up studies, will be reported at some future date.

CASE 2.   Jerry was eight and a half at the time he
entered treatment. His parents had been aware of his
behavior for some time but brought him for treatment only
after pressure from his school. Jerry had difficulty with
children as well as with adults. He habitually used filthy,
obscene language with adults. He was afraid of older boys
and boys of his age, but attacked younger children, especially girls. He had an insidious way of doing this, mostly a
sneak attack from behind. He would pinch them and poke
his fingers into the anal region. On one occasion, he had
jammed a pencil into a child's back and had injured the
child. He did not pay attention to the school work, being
busy molesting children, and consequently he was a permanent visitor in the principal's office. The parents disagreed upon methods for handling him: the father was for
strictness and punishment; the mother felt that her husband was too severe and, in fact, believed that he was
responsible for the child's behavior. She had resisted earlier
suggestions for treatment for Jerry, but now, under pressure from the school, was ready to accept it.

I learned from the mother that Jerry also suffered from

allergies of the upper respiratory system, a condition which she thought he had inherited from her. He had discontinued treatment by an allergist because he objected to injections and also because it was ineffective.

Jerry was a rather frail and innocent-looking youngster, with a long mane of hair hanging over his eyes. He didn't like to take haircuts, and so would go without one for months at a time. He had been told that I would treat him for his allergies with a new method, without injections, but would talk and play with him. He was a boy of superior intelligence and he was obviously curious about me and the playroom, and behaved in his first interview in a rather civil way. From the start of treatment and for some time after, Jerry would play only with the dolls during his sessions. He would make clothes for them and even bring some from home which he and his mother had made together. He was using a toy sewing machine, cooking utensils and everything that would interest girls. He wanted to sit very close to me and, in a rather obvious manner, made sexual advances toward me; for example, trying to put his head into my lap and toward my genitals. When he was rebuffed, he would go into fits, use obscene language worthy of a truck driver. He wanted to push me, jump at me, throw things at me. Then again, he would court me by bringing me cookies which he baked with his mother, and even flowers. His behavior alternated between overt sexual advances and abusive behavior and language when he was frustrated.

During the first few weeks of his treatment, there was a noticeable change in Jerry's behavior, particularly at school. It was the first time that his mother had not been called to the school for two weeks straight. However, there was a change now in his behavior in the waiting room. It was almost as if he were putting on an act. When I opened the door, he would begin to call me names, looking at me and at his mother, who sat there with a peculiar smile on her face as if she enjoyed the spectacle. He would run around the waiting room, unconcerned whether there were other people present, while his mother was looking at me to see how I would cope with such behavior. After a few minutes he would calm down spontaneously and storm into the playroom.

He became so abusive and physically aggressive with me that I felt I needed the help of his mother to keep him in treatment. The parents had indicated that they did not want to be involved in therapy themselves. The father had asked for treatment for Jerry upon the urging of a friend in whose judgment he had great trust. The mother had reluctantly consented and expressed skepticism about the advisability of such treatment. There had been such noticeable improvement in Jerry's behavior in school within the short period of treatment (three months) that I felt I could confront the mother with an ultimatum that either she undergo treatment also or I would terminate Jerry's treatment. I had learned from practical experience by this time that the treatment of a child with deviate sexual behavior is difficult and bound to fail unless the significant partner with whom the child has this relationship is willing to release the child from it.

This is a brief account of the picture as it shaped up in work with the mother. She had agreed to the treatment of the child because she did not think it would be possible for me to treat him. Although she was not conscious that this was a design on her part to break up his treatment, she was aware that Jerry's behavior in the waiting room had something to do with her feelings. It could be understood now that his behavior had the meaning of pacifying his mother, as if to indicate to her, "Don't worry; she (the analyst) is not taking me away from you; in fact, you see, I don't even want to go in with her." It also became clear that the mother was releasing her own hostility toward people through Jerry. He verbalized and did to people what she could not allow herself to say or do. This could be particularly well observed in Jerry's behavior toward me. Whenever she experienced an upsurge of resentment and hostility toward me, Jerry would become very difficult and

almost unmanageable in the playroom, on various occasions actually hitting me.

The mother felt very frustrated in her marriage, sexually and in every other way. She had always wanted a
double bed because she liked to snuggle up and enjoyed
the feeling of physical closeness during the night, but her
husband wanted twin beds and felt uncomfortable in her
close envelopment. She suffered from a sleep disturbance
of long standing. After her older son was born, she had
wanted her second child to be a daughter, but she felt now
that not even a daughter could have been more affectionate and loving to her than Jerry was. He was always with
her. Instead of playing with boys, he would spend his time
helping her cook, sew, with the dishes, the dinner table,
etc. For his fifth birthday she had bought Jerry a baby carriage and dolls because he liked it, she said. She was surprised at my questioning the advisability of such a birthday
gift for a boy: "Even if he liked it?" she asked. Jerry still
liked and collected dolls to this day. Before leaving for
school in the morning, he would always hug and kiss his
mother very affectionately and come running home at
lunch to repeat the performance and to have lunch with
her. She told me that he was in the habit of running over to
her and kissing her in the very same way as he observed in
love scenes on T.V. She never had any difficulties with him
when she was alone with him. The fighting and misbehav-
ior started when there were others around. He would
always fight for the seat next to her, and on such occasions
had often managed to pull the tablecloth and dishes off
when they were invited for dinner or were eating out.
People were afraid to invite her because of Jerry.

She could not remember having seen him masturbate.
Sexual matters were not discussed in her house; her husband and she were rather prudish people, she told me.
There was one thing about Jerry that really bothered her.
Sometimes, especially after a losing fight with his brother,
she would find Jerry sitting in his room and staring into
space. After such a fight with his brother recently, she told

Jerry to go to his room and to clean it up. When she came into his room, he just stood there. When she told him again, he just sat down and looked at her as if he were in a daze. He had a very peculiar expression on his face. She got scared and slapped him across the face to "snap him out of it." Her fears concerning his sanity came out more clearly later in her treatment when her own infantile fantasies and fears came to the fore. She, too, would often stare into space unaware of what she was thinking. At times, she would become panicky and find herself shivering and with goose-pimples all over her body without any apparent reason. Much later, when she had developed a strong transference relationship, she revealed that she had occasional visual and acoustic hallucinatory experiences. She also revealed that she had a fear that Jerry could kill her, or kill somebody, or himself. She had fantasies and fears of being sexually attacked. Her own destructive impulses could be dealt with only later in her treatment, which lasted for more than five years.

Her stepmother lived in the same building, but they were mostly not on speaking terms. On occasion, there were violent fights between them, at which Jerry was present.

With difficulty and reluctance, the mother was now beginning to discourage Jerry's affections toward her. On several occasions Jerry had gone off to school in the morning without kissing her, almost without taking notice of her. He now was not so punctual at lunch time and would spend some time with the other children. This was all very painful to the mother. In the course of having to frustrate herself, she was beginning to expose her husband. She was resentful that she, who had objected to Jerry's treatment, was involved in treatment herself, while the father went free, as it were. She thought that he was too strict and punitive. He liked to tease the children and they were afraid of him. When he was in a good mood, he liked to play with Jerry in certain ways, pinching and biting his behind and, as she put it, practically to stick his nose in

Jerry's anus. This type of play was practiced on Jerry also by the father's brother. Sometimes both men would get after Jerry, holding him down on the sofa and squeezing and pinching him playfully.

During this phase of treatment, Jerry began to show some phobic concerns regarding his mother. He became very anxious about her standing too close to the track on the subway, or about her walking downstairs and falling or hurting herself. He also complained that she didn't kiss him the same way she used to.

Jerry was still playing with dolls in his sessions, but he was less careful with them now. Once he tore off the head of one doll and wanted to rip her between the legs. While doing this, he told me that his mother had three girl's names ready for him. If he had only been a girl, he could have been Susan. To the interpretation of his hostile impulses toward his mother, he responded with outbursts of temper and verbal attacks upon me. He had fantasies of cutting my throat; he would put me into a bathrub so the blood would not drip on the floor. He would get my jewelry even if he had to cut off my ears for the pearls or my finger for the ring. He played out these fantasies with a doll, cutting her neck and stabbing her. He broke a little doll which he had liked very much into pieces.

He began to discuss the sexual differences with me. Boys, too, he said, have two holes, one in the back and one in the penis. He drew figures of male and female, making hair in the back of both. He erased it and said, "It is being cut off; when there is hair, bones can be moved even if there is only one hair." He had one such hair, he told me, and the doctor gave him something yellow over his face and cut it off. This happened when he was five years old, he said. "From the penis too, the skin is cut off," he explained, "or else urine couldn't come out. It would fill up and up to the throat and one would choke from it." These fantasies were in part an elaboration of his reaction to a tonsillectomy when he was five years old and to the death of a little boy in the neighborhood around that time. This boy supposedly died after an operation for spina bifida. These fantasies were of particular interest in connection with his allergies, but this subject cannot be dealt with here.

He was gradually losing interest in dolls. He joined the Cub Scouts and was playing with other boys. It was still very difficult for him to renounce gratification of the pleasures which he had so freely enjoyed with his mother. He began to show interest in books and particularly in painting. Upon his own request, he joined a painting class and actually enjoyed it and did very well in art work.

Through the treatment of the mother, some changes in her relationship with Jerry had been effected. It now became obvious that Jerry's relationship with his father was a highly pathologic one and that, for successful treatment, this would have to be changed also. Both Jerry and his father derived too much overt gratification from their physical contacts in fighting and teasing. In my limited contacts with the father, I had to be direct in forbidding him (with little success) this type of play with Jerry. It was possible, at the time when Jerry was eleven years old, to get the father into psychotherapy with the therapist who treated Jerry's brother.

In Jerry's case, both parents used him for the gratification of their own infantile sexual (perverse) needs. To the mother, Jerry had to substitute for the unsatisfactory husband, giving her the cuddling, kissing, physical proximity and all the attention and time she wanted, but did not get, from her husband. He also had to make up to her for the daughter she longed for. He used to bake, sew, and clean house with her and accompany her on her shopping trips.

Jerry knew exactly what his mother unconsciously expected of him. He behaved neither like a boy nor like a girl, nor was he very childlike. His mother hated men, but she also hated women and she did not like children because they required too much care. He was what she would have wanted to be. She had always been very self-conscious and timid. Although she was a bright and good pupil, she could never speak up in school nor anywhere else. She could not even ask questions. She had always been painfully aware of this shortcoming, but she had not been aware that she made up for it in an exaggerated way through Jerry. He said anything he felt like saying to people to whom she could have never opened her mouth. For this, she really admired him and he knew it. He was dependent upon her for sexual gratification and provocative with his father, whom he feared very much. Under these circumstances, this was the most satisfactory arrangement for him. In this way, he managed to have both parents busy themselves with him and oppose each other. At times when the parents were getting along well, they would go off together and leave Jerry to care for himself, often for the entire day. His mother, who was mostly very indulgent toward him, could also be very cruel with him at times. Such an attitude is typical for the dominant partner in a perverse relationship. In the analysis of the mother, it was found that she had a masochistic sexual perversion and she required for sexual gratification, pinching and hitting of her buttocks. At a later date in her analysis, the mother realized that she actually instigated fights between Jerry and his father because it gave her pleasure to see them both fight over her.

Jerry had not established a definite sexual identification. In this way, he could be the love object for both parents. The hate and contempt which he had for his mother were covered up by a compensatory overevaluation of her and turned against, and released, on other women. In the simultaneous treatment, it could be seen clearly that as long as the mother was maintaining this "love" relationship with him, the hatred and destructiveness were deflected from her and directed toward other people. For example, he once sprayed toilet water into the eyes of the maid when he was really angry at his mother. His mother suffered from an eye condition and was very sensitive about her eyes, which would become inflamed readily. He once "accidentally" killed the parakeet which belonged to his mother and which he liked too. He would damage and set fire to furnishings, cut upholstery, and so on when he was angry at his mother. She was spared aggression and treated with physical affection by him. The hate for the father was less repressed and only thinly covered up by the fear of him. These feelings expressed themselves in his behavior toward men; he liked to provoke them and often played nasty tricks on them; he once got the F.B.I. looking for his father's friend.

There was no superego conflict in his case. He had no guilt feelings about his behavior, nor did he have a wish to change it. His superego did not demand renunciation of his instinctual gratification nor ask him for control of behavior. Such behavior was not only permitted, but approved of, by the parents, especially the mother. In order to be free of internal conflict, he had to turn his aggression and hatred out and toward external objects. Every improvement in his relations with other people made for internal conflict, bringing back the hate to the superego, the incorporated parental images. This could be observed particularly clearly during one phase of his treatment when he had a positive relationship with me and did not release his destructiveness, but was repressing it. This was the time when he developed neurotic symptoms, such as phobias and nightmares.

His ego was not weak at all. He was very clever, almost shrewd, in manipulating people when he wanted to and when it served to gain the pleasures he desired. His sense of reality was not impaired nor was any essential function of the ego.

CASE 3.    Mrs. B consulted me about her thirteen-year-old daughter, Joan, who was a behavior problem. Joan was very critical of her mother, particularly in the presence of her mother's friends. It was obvious that the mother was using this difficulty with Joan to get treatment for herself. It was also obvious that she was afraid to admit, even to herself, that she was in need of psychiatric treatment. She had experienced a severe anxiety attack a year prior and now had a recurrence of this anxiety. She suffered from acute anxiety of panic proportions; she was afraid to be alone in the house; she was fearful to go near the window, and her sleep was very disturbed. She felt as if she were losing her mind. At times, when she was very anxious, she had experiences of a hallucinatory character. She would see her mother, who died when the patient was an adolescent of fifteen years, sitting on the bed, coming after her, and grabbing her from behind. She blamed her father for her mother's death. One night she and her mother had surprised the father in bed with the patient's older sister. Her mother, who had suffered from TB, died shortly after that.

Mrs. B's marriage was unsatisfactory. She complained about her husband's impotence but gradually came to recognize that she was frigid and only wanted foreplay and to stimulate her husband without gratifying him sexually. She had several friendships with women who obviously had strong homosexual leanings. She thought of having extramarital relationships with men, but she really wanted only to tease them. She claimed that the only satisfactory relationship was with her younger daughter, Judy, aged nine at the start of her mother's analysis.

For an entire year she had managed not to bring up her daughter, Judy, in the analysis. Gradually, with the development of a more positive transference and with the help of dreams, the relationship with this daughter was brought into the analysis. She began to reveal some of the activities between her and Judy which she had wanted to keep from my knowledge. Judy, by that time ten years old, was still coming into her mother's bed every morning after her father left and often would sleep with her mother all night. On such occasions, the father had to leave the bedroom and sleep in Judy's room. Judy liked to pet and kiss her mother's body. She had a certain way of doing it. Her mother told me that Judy would start from the top and go down to the bottom, petting and kissing her mother's vulva and then repeat this performance from the bottom up to the top. She would often tell her mother: "I don't want to get married when I grow up. I don't want a man to make sis with his penis into my vagina." Judy, who was a rather stout girl, according to her mother, liked to pull up the fat from her belly playfully, lifting it like an apron, and invite her mother to lick her vulva. The mother, who frequently had sensations of an imaginary penis, experiencing these sensations in that part of her body where she thought the penis should have been, on several occasions, when taking a bath together with Judy, hallucinated a penis also on Judy's body.

It was very difficult for her to curtail these activities with Judy. She felt rejected by her older daughter and by her husband. The only person from whom she received sexual gratification was Judy. Judy was the only one who really loved her, she felt. She was fearful of what analysis would do to this relationship; she could not afford to lose her. There was no chance of getting Judy into treatment. Even the slightest suggestion that Judy would require treatment was, at this point, totally unacceptable to her mother. After two years of analytic treatment, she could not yet discourage outright Judy's sexual approaches. Occasionally she would say to her, "Not today, I have a headache."

Nevertheless, there were definite changes in the behavior of her children. Joan became more amenable toward her mother, while Judy became more difficult. Judy began to have temper tantrums and, in a way, she was now behaving with her mother as Joan had before. At this point, the family had moved and Judy became friendly with a girl next door. Judy, who used to spend most of her time with her mother, now became inseparable from this girl. She became increasingly difficult and critical of her mother; she complained about the food, the house, her mother's appearance. The mother came close to a depression. She related that the change in Judy's behavior was so obvious that outsiders commented on it. She realized that she, herself, had become more critical of Judy and that she was jealous of Judy's girlfriend. She felt that Judy had replaced her with this friend and she suspected that the girls were having a homosexual relationship. She complained that whenever this girl visited Judy, the door to her room was kept closed. This was a source of great irritation to the mother since there had previously never been closed doors between mother and daughter. One day, when both girls were in Judy's room and the mother wanted to enter, Judy called out, "Don't come in!." The mother walked in and found the girls in a very suspicious position on the bed. At this point, she would have wanted immediate treatment for Judy, but it was obvious that Judy would not accept any suggestion for treatment. In fact, the mother still found herself at a loss at how to make such a suggestion to Judy. She discovered, in her analysis, that her wish for Judy to be treated was not geniune, but that she wanted to break up the friendship between the two girls and to win Judy back for herself.

Judy was now twelve and a half years old and preparing to leave for camp with her girlfriend. Shortly after, her mother called me from camp requesting an appointment for Judy. Judy and her friend had been expelled from camp for offensive behavior; they had been abusive to the counselor and camp director. Under the pressure of the situation, Judy had consented to see me. It was obvious that Judy was not ready for treatment; she felt indignant about it and considered it an imposition and intrusion into her private life. I saw her twice and tried to convey to her the feeling that the treatment was not a punishment for bad behavior, as she felt, nor something to be coerced into. I knew that I would have to wait for her and hoped that, through the continued analysis of her mother, Judy would eventually find her way into treatment. Later in her treatment, the mother, when analyzing her fears of insanity, recognized that she, too, had not been ready for Judy's treatment at the time she had brought her to me.

There was mental illness in the families of Judy's parents, a fact the mother was concealing from Judy. One day, to the mother's surprise, Judy asked her some questions about a relative who was in psychiatric treatment. At first, the mother wanted to evade the subject, but, realizing the implication, she managed to talk about it frankly. Judy asked how long this relative had been in treatment and whether it was helping him. The mother told her that she thought it did and that he was in his second year of treatment. Judy asked, "How long do you think it would take me?" When the mother said that she didn't know, but that it would probably take some time, Judy replied, "Why don't I start now?" Judy was fifteen and a half years old when she started psychoanalytic treatment with me.

Summarizing briefly the important aspects of this case, the fact that it took six years for Judy to get into treatment deserves some explanation. It is obvious, even from this very fragmentary report of the mother's analysis, that she had to be considered at least as a borderline case. It took over a year of treatment for her to get ready to talk about her relationship with Judy to me. It took another two years of treatment until she could get herself to discontinue the overt intimacies with Judy, and, even then, it was very difficult for her to tolerate the ensuing hostility from Judy and the threat of losing her as a love object.

As long as she had been willing to maintain this relationship with Judy, she not only permitted Judy these sexual gratifications without guilt but, at the same time, Judy's hatred against her mother (for being seduced by her and made dependent upon her for these gratifications) was kept in repression and was overcompensated for by the overt "love" relationship. This (pregenital) hatred and destructiveness, previously vented toward others, became now directed toward the frustrating and "unfaithful" mother who was withholding the gratification which she had offered before. The handling of this hate is a difficult technical problem in the treatment of these children; it requires the full cooperation and understanding of the parent with whom the child has had the relationship. If the child alone is treated, the parent may not be able to accept the turning away of the child and may become very cruel to the child. This happened with Jerry before and even for some time after his mother began treatment.

The change in the behavior of Joan toward her mother

could be attributed to the change in the relationship between the mother and Judy. Joan had often referred to them as the "lovers." The role of the father in such a family setting seems to be a typical one. If he is not an active partner in the relationship with the child, as in Jerry's case, he is conspicuous by his absence. In Rhoda's case, the father separated from his wife when Rhoda was five years old, but actually he had left Rhoda's mother for another woman shortly after Rhoda was born. Judy's parents had not lived together sexually for many years. In fact, there was hardly any family life in her home. The father would eat out with his business associates and the mother would have the two girls eat separately, preparing special dishes with great care for Judy. She realized, during the treatment, that she didn't want her husband home and did not want to feed him. Whenever she had to prepare a meal for him, she would burn or spill the food or have some mishap. According to the mother, "A dog deserved more consideration." This hatred for men and the right to exploit and abuse them was taken over by her daughters. Joan married a man whom she could treat as her mother treated her father. Judy had an opportunity to work through her feelings about men in her analysis.

## Discussion of Etiology, Dynamics and Therapy

Freud (1896), in his first concept concerning the etiology of hysteria, postulated the occurrence of actual sexual traumata as an etiologic factor. He later revised this concept by accepting fantasies, fictitious traumata and psychic reality as sufficient etiologic factors (1914). The concept of the traumatic etiology of the neuroses, although generally accepted, appears to be somewhat neglected in the clinical practice of psychoanalysis, where it is difficult and perhaps not always possible to establish the causal connection between trauma and illness. It appears to me that too much room has been left to the workings of fantasy life *independent* of experiences in external reality and to inherited factors in the etiology of the neuroses. I am referring here particularly to the Kleinian school of thought (Klein, 1932). An overemphasis on inherent factors in ego development also seems to me to constitute a similar danger of overlooking the role of actual experiences in ego and superego development (Hartmann, 1939; Rapaport, 1954).

While the instinctual life follows certain innate patterns of development in the child, it is a known and accepted fact in psychoanalytic theory and practice that these patterns of instinctual development in the child can be continually influenced and modified by the experiences of the child with his emotionally important objects (his parents), that is, through and by his object relationships. My investigation into deviate sexual behavior of children has been focussed particularly on this aspect. One of the reasons which prompted Freud to give up the seduction theory of hysteria is of interest in connection with this study: Freud spoke of his astonishment at being asked to believe that all his patients' fathers were given to sexual perversions (1914). It is difficult to assess correctly the etiologic value of certain childhood experiences in the lives of perverts from reconstruction from their analyses, especially if striking experiences of seduction are absent. But even if such experiences are found, we still question which factors promote the development of a perversion in one case, of hysteria or neurosis in another case, and seemingly undisturbed development into full genitality in many others. In this study, we are particularly concerned with defining those factors which encourage the development of deviate sexual behavior in children and which favor or determine that specific component instincts will take the lead.

In the simultaneous analysis of Rhoda and her mother, it was possible to establish with certainty that Rhoda's behavior was directly related to actual experiences and her relationship with her mother. It was also found that the onset of her behavior problems in school occurred at the time when she was disappointed in her mother and afraid of losing her as she had just lost her father (through separation). In identification with the lost object, she would have wanted to take his place with her mother. Disappointed in her mother, she turned toward other children as the active seducer, identifying herself with her mother in this aspect. Without this insight, her behavior could have been easily interpreted merely as an expression of her inner fantasy life and the significance of the specific relationship between Rhoda and her mother as the causal factor could have been overlooked.

Rhoda's deviate behavior manifested itself in a display of exhibitionistic, scoptophilic, and sadistic tendencies. There was also a marked tendency toward homosexual development, with a wish to take the male role. In the analysis of her enuresis, it was brought out that she unconsciously identified urine with semen and that she had fantasies of making babies for her mother by wetting. In her sexual games, she was always Bluie (the boy) while her partner, even if she was much older than herself, had to be Pinkie (the girl). In the analysis of her mother, it was found that these were exactly her perverse interests (exhibition-istic, scoptophilic, sadistic, and homosexual) and in the simulta-neous analysis it could be observed that and in which ways the mother stimulated specifically these partial instincts in Rhoda.

The manner in which Rhoda managed to keep out of her analysis certain activities between her mother and herself clearly indicated that she was aware of their sexual nature and that she sensed that analysis would interfere with them. This propensity of the child with deviate sexual behavior to protect the parent or older partner of this seductive relationship I have found with such consistency in the treatment of these children that I have come to consider it as typical. Only if for some reason the parent or older partner discontinues this relationship and the child is frustrated may the disappointment with the "unfaithful" partner express itself in hostility and abusive behavior toward this part-ner with a need to expose her unfavorably. From the technical point of view, these phases can be handled best if both partners are treated simultaneously. If only the mother is in analysis, this phase can be handled rather well, especially with younger chil-dren, as the withdrawal of these gratifications or the "weaning from the perverse relationship," as I would call it, can be done gradually and be replaced by a healthier and more genuinely affectionate motherly attitude. Even with older children, through analysis of the mother alone, the relationship between them can be improved to such a degree that the child eventually will accept direct treatment. This was demonstrated in the case of Judy, who, without the lengthy analysis of her mother, would not have entered and certainly would not have stayed in analysis. If the child alone is treated, this phase of the treatment when the child makes an attempt to free himself from his relationship may be dangerous for various reasons. It is the most frequent cause for failure of treatment because the mother (or parent with whom the child has this relationship) will not permit it and with some meager, or even without any, rationalization will withdraw the child from treatment. The mother, in such a situation, can become very cruel toward the child, and this may lead the child to serious destructive (self) acting out. To some extent, this was the case early in Jerry's treatment when the mother became quite cruel with him, and later on when the father's increased sadistic attitude toward him became a serious obstacle in his treatment, leading to much acting out and temporary interruption of it.*

Furthermore, analysis of the child alone does not reveal and certainly does not eliminate the pathologic attitude of the parent which has these particular effects upon the child's superego structure. The conduct of these mothers is usually exemplary. This was particularly true of Rhoda's mother. And yet Rhoda was stealing from her mother, wetting herself during the day and night, was overeating and manifesting the deviate sexual behavior described. In addition, she had a great need to cling physically to adults, especially women. This lack of instinctual control as well as the clinging to objects were very characteristic traits of her mother. Mrs. A. had overcompensated her very strong unconscious homosexuality with an exaggerated interest of a physically absorbing nature in men. The oral quality of her object relationship required the physical presence and preferably physical union with the object. She could not be alone. This need to reassure

* Johnson and Szurek (1952) have made similar observations in the treatment of children with antisocial behavior, and stress the need for collaborative therapy. They state that otherwise the guilt mustered up by the child in individual treatment will be dissolved by the unconscious permissiveness at home. They stress treatment of the significant parent and state that if this permissiveness is on a conscious level, treatment is usually impossible, and they consider treatment of the child alone in serious acting-out cases as dangerous. Cf. in this connection also Bettelheim (1955).

against object loss and make up for the lack in object relatedness by seeking close bodily contact was very apparent in Rhoda also.

Since, in my opinion, deviate sexual behavior in children is dynamically a disturbance of the superego resulting from the internalization of certain unconscious parental attitudes, I consider it an essential therapeutic requirement in the case of children to modify the unconscious attitudes of the objects from whom this superego is derived.† My material has amply demonstrated that these (more or less) unconscious perverse needs of the parent(s) present an irresistible temptation for the child and an insurmountable resistance in the treatment. If the "perverse relationship" is the only way in which the child can be close to the parent and receive gratification, he has no choice and this becomes the child's mode of object relationship.

The actual physical and emotional dependence of the child upon his parents makes for a transference in child analysis which is in some aspects different from that of adults. Only one of these aspects can be discussed within the framework of this chapter but this one is essential to an understanding of the therapeutic goals. The child knows what the analyst expects of him, namely, that he give up the deviate behavior, just as he knows what his parents and particularly the parent with whom he has this relationship expects of him, namely, that he continue the deviate behavior, even though the overt actions and verbalizations of this parent may not seem to indicate this. For a full cure of the child, which entails the reconstruction of his superego, it is essential that the analyst and the parents of the child see eye-to-eye on this matter; otherwise, the child will only be in conflict about whose leadership to follow (see also O. Sperling, 1950a). One outcome in this situation, if the unconscious needs of the parent have not been changed, may be a superficial compliance on the part of the child without a basic change in the structure of his superego. This situation in treatment is analogous to the situation when the parents of the child do not see eye-to-eye on

† I am referring in this connection particularly to the work of O. E. Sperling on the parasitic superego (1950a) and his concepts of the split in the superego (1956). I have reported similar observations concerning the superego structure in the treatment of children with pavor nocturnus type 1 in Chapter 4. (Cf. in this connection also M. Sperling, 1953a, Arlow, 1954, and Gillespie, 1956b).

the important issues of sexual adjustment. Just as the parents themselves have to be in true agreement concerning the important goals for the child, so have the parents and the analyst of the child to be united in their endeavors. I have found simultaneous analysis of mother and child to be an essential therapeutic technique in achieving this necessary unity.

One other advantage of simultaneous analysis of mother and child should be mentioned: it can be more goal-directed, especially with the mother, and focus on her relationship with this child. The objection might be raised that this is not in accordance with the rules of analysis. In these cases, however, the relationship with the child is the most pathognomonic feature of the mother's personality and consistent analysis of this aspect not only does not preclude but enhances the progress of analysis. The fact that the mother is aware of why she and her child are in analysis with the same analyst works as a stimulus for the analysis.

The question concerning the technical difficulty of having the mother in analysis simultaneously without the child's knowledge has come up. As far as the mother is concerned, there may occasionally be some difficulty in regard to her reliability on a conscious level, especially at the start of analysis. In such a case, or if the mother appears too sick to begin with, it is advisable to start with the mother alone and treat her, at least until a reliable therapeutic relationship has been established. If it is not possible to stimulate enough of a sincere wish in the mother to help her child so that one can rely on her, the chances for the child are poor. In Jerry's case it would have been preferable to work with the parents first, but to insist on this seemed too risky as it was obvious that they were uncooperative and looking for an easy way out. His treatment was fraught with difficulties and interruptions. But then again his prognosis, in view of the family situation, was a very unfavorable one from the start, and his development was leading into criminal psychopathy. He is now (1959) fifteen years old, in treatment, has maintained himself in school, has stayed at home and out of the courts. This, in his case, has to be considered as a satisfactory result so far.

In the sixteen years that I have been working with this

method, I have never had any difficulty in relation to the child. I have explained this phenomenon to myself on the basis that the changes in the mother conformed with the child's experiences in his analysis and therefore did not create any difficulty, conflict or confusion but, on the contrary, facilitated the progress of analysis by narrowing the gap between the attitudes of the mother (parents) and that of the analyst.

# 14

# The Analysis of a Boy with Transvestite Tendencies

There are comparatively few psychoanalytic studies of transvestitism. The classical concepts of this perversion have been developed by Fenichel (1930). According to Fenichel, the transvestite has not been able to give up the belief in the phallic nature of women and, in addition, he identifies himself with the phallic woman. Fenichel drew attention to an important accidental factor in transvestitism, namely, "that, as a rule, contemporaneously with the identification with the mother, there exists in another, more superficial psychic stratum a similar identification with *a little girl*." He believed that this identification occurs when "a sister has at an early period to a great extent become a mother-substitute." He assumed a special bisexual disposition in his patient, and wondered what the specific circumstances might be which lead to this outcome.

The psychoanalytic study of a child with overt transvestite behavior could provide an opportunity to learn more about the circumstances under which such behavior develops than is possible in the analysis of an adult transvestite, where significant childhood experiences are often not fully recovered and, at best, have to be reconstructed.

I had the opportunity to treat, in long analyses, two transvestite boys, one of prelatency and one of latency age. In both cases I had their mothers in analysis prior to treatment of the child. I have also treated two adolescents with marked transvestite behavior, and three adults with transvestite tendencies. Two had episodes of transvestite behavior prior and during the early part of their treatment. The third one, who had overt transvestite episodes in adolescence, had polymorph perversions, particularly exhibitionism and voyeurism.

Since, in my opinion, the presentation of detailed analytic material is indispensable for a convincing demonstration of the unconscious fantasies and conflicts underlying the clinical manifestations, I have decided to limit myself here to the report of one case, and I shall have to restrict myself to those parts which are essential to my thesis. I have selected the case of the prelatency child for three reasons: (1) his mother came into analysis for depression when he was six months old, and I could observe indirectly the development of the transvestite behavior from its very beginning; (2) he was only four years and ten months old when he began analysis, and the rich dream and fantasy material was obtained with unusual freshness; (3) I could follow up his development to adolescence.

## Case Presentation

### Preanalytic History

Of the wealth of material on Tommy obtained through his mother, only very little can be reported here. Up to the time he was two years old, the mother did not think that he presented any problems. She was too preoccupied with the difficulties of Tommy's sister, five years his senior. Because she felt that she had rushed her daughter's toilet training, she was reluctant to train Tommy, and when she did, she was ambivalent and inconsistent. Tommy was still enuretic when he came into analysis, and his enuresis proved to be a very stubborn symptom. An outstanding phenomenon in the analysis of the mother was her need to conglomerate both sexes in herself and in her children. She was a sturdy woman who wore a short, straight haircut and tailored clothes. Her husband was a small, frail-looking man with delicate features. Paula, Tommy's sister, was sturdy and strong like her mother. She was a tomboy. Tommy was frail-looking and small like his father. He liked to wear his sister's clothes, especially her panties, nightgowns, and pajamas. This, his mother thought, was very cute. This behavior had started when he was three years and four months old, shortly after an aunt, who had just given birth to a baby girl, had stayed at their house with the baby for several weeks. Tommy, who was very curious about this baby, seemed to be resentful and jealous of her. At that time he would say, "All people are born girls. Then they turn into boys. I was born a girl." He would frequently say: "When I was a girl . . . ." This fantasy, openly expressed at the age of three and afterward repressed, was one of the basic fantasies operating in his transvestite behavior, as will be seen later.

As a little boy he had had ample opportunity to see his mother in the nude. Observing her after a shower (when he was not quite three years old), he asked, pointing at her breasts, "What's that?" "My breasts," said the mother. "Will I have breasts when I grow up?" he asked. "No," said the mother, "you are a boy." "Take the brown stuff away and let me see your penis," he demanded. "I don't have a penis," the mother said. "What do you have?" "A vagina," she replied. "Will I have a vagina when I grow up?" he asked. "No, you are a boy," was her answer.

He started nursery school at four. He behaved very babyishly, disturbed the other children, and was considered a nuisance. He could not hold his own with the other little boys in his neighborhood and, instead of fighting, he would run away and play by himself. Even at the age of three and a half or four, he would help himself to money from his mother's purse and make up fantastic stories. This tendency to *pseudologia fantastica* became more pronounced later. He also had all kinds of accidents and continually hurt himself. A conversation he had with his mother at the age of four and a half when a classmate had a tonsillectomy indicated that he was, at that time, obviously struggling with castration anxiety.

> Tommy: How do they take out tonsils?
> Mother: They cut them out.
> Tommy (puts both hands over his mouth): I wouldn't let them.
> Mother: They put you to sleep. You don't feel it.
> Tommy: I won't go to sleep any more. Why do they have to cut them out?
> Mother: If they are diseased and make people sick . . . when they have a lot of colds.
> Tommy: I won't go outside any more so I won't catch cold.

While this discussion was going on, the mother was preparing carrots on the kitchen table. Tommy took a carrot and put it to his belly button, saying, "This is my tonsil."

> Mother: Tonsils are not in the belly button.
> Tommy: Oh, yes they are.

### Tommy's Analysis

Tommy's analysis started when he was four years and ten months old, shortly after his mother had finished her analysis. He exhibited a peculiar mixture of babyishness and alertness. On some days he would crawl from the waiting room into the playroom like a baby, talking like a baby. On other days he would come in a cowboy outfit and pretend to be riding into the playroom on his big horse. This was his first dream: He slept with his father, his mother slept in his sister's bed, and his sister in his bed. This dream, which was not interpreted to Tommy, gave immediate insight into Tommy's unconscious (fantasy) life. The role which he wanted and which, by the changes in the sleeping arrangement, he had managed to assume in his dream, was that of the mother and the sister. *He* slept in bed with his father in place of the mother, and, in his bed, in his place was his sister. As sometimes the first dream of an analytic patient contains the patient's basic conflict, which, in its full significance, may be understood and worked upon only much later in the analysis, so Tommy's first dream revealed some of his wishes and conflicts.

Tommy had a need to make his father into a "strong man." He would tell me that his father was an athlete and that he had been a gym teacher at one time and a famous fighter. Unfortunately, his father was nothing of the kind and, at that particular time, was in very poor physical health. When his father was in the hospital, Tommy glorified this by making him a "hero." However, when he drew a picture of his family for me, his mother appeared as the biggest person. Mother and sister seemed the important people in the family, father was "bossed" by mother.

He complained about his mother: "She never buys or gives me what I want." Actually, his mother bought and gave him things rather readily. Yet, there was a great deal of truth in his feelings, because she really did not want him to have "boyish" things, as she had not been able to let Paula have really "girlish" clothes and playthings. Once he asked his mother whether she would buy him a doll. She immediately agreed to it, but then he did not want one because "real boys don't play with dolls." Yet sometime later, Tommy became an ardent collector of dolls, thus picking up his mother's cues.

A dream about a snake in his bed which was spitting from its mouth at his sister and father, who first tried to run away but then were killed, brought into the analysis the aggressive, sexual aspects of his bed-wetting and also his jealousy of his father and sister as rivals for his mother. In connection with the dream Tommy began to talk about some of the activities between his sister and himself. Up to the age of five (Tommy was now six years old), they had been taking baths together, and his sister would ask him to make his penis wiggle. He was still frequently going into her bed at night.

There were noticeable changes in Tommy's behavior after some of this material had been worked through. He was becoming more agressive and was beginning to fight back with the boys. He had some dry periods, but this progress was not yet a sustained one. It was only then that the emergence of the positive oedipus complex manifested itself in Tommy's overt behavior. One could detect a quality of chivalry in his attitude toward his mother and sister. There was a lessening of the infantile behavior and a decrease in the overcompensatory cowboy and

Superman play. For a while Tommy almost behaved like a real little boy of his age, but his transvestite behavior continued; he was more careful, though, in concealing it. He was still wearing his sister's panties steadily. He also liked to put on her leotards and wanted to wear her jewelry and sometimes her discarded dresses. He was very observant of her development and would make remarks such as, "She will soon need to wear a girdle. Her nipples are getting big." He wondered why boys could not use makeup, and he sometimes liked to paint his eyebrows with an eyebrow pencil.

In the sessions he played a game in which he was shot by an imaginary attacker. He would drop to the floor shouting, "I have a bullet in my vagina." He had gone shopping with his mother and chose a red sports jacket. On the way home he said, "The boys will call me a girl." His mother suggested that he return the jacket, but he said, "What's wrong with being a girl?" He did not return the jacket. It was during this phase of analysis that he began to express thoughts about "whether girls never had a penis," and revealed this fantasy: "If there are girls in a car and boys are crossing the street and are run over and cut into halves, and the girls are also cut into halves, and then the halves get mixed up and the upper part of the girl is put together with the lower part of the boy, then in this way they would be half boy and half girl."

He had a dream in which he knocked over a big dinosaur. He told me that he had actually seen dinosaurs a long time ago when he had been to a museum with his parents. His reaction to seeing a dinosaur had come up in his mother's analysis. He had been particularly interested in the dinosaur's belly and had repeatedly asked, "Could I fit into its stomach?" "Could it eat me up?" When we discussed that he did not like his father and mother to sleep together and that he was angry that his father had his mommy (the big dinosaur), he replied, "But I have Koko and she is going to have babies." Koko was his cat to whom he was very attached. He considered her a member of the family, calling her by the family name. He behaved as though he considered himself the father of Koko's babies, but he also iden-tified himself with her. This was brought out in a dream about a cat which was in his bed, licking his face, jumping around, and pulling at him. While this was going on, everybody came into his room; his sister, his father and mother. The cat said, "Can't we have any privacy?" He told me that his mother did not like the cat to touch his face because of her dirty paws. The night preceding the dream, he had gone into his father's bed. I learned from the mother that he had been jumping around in the bed and, in the course of this horseplay, had touched his father's penis. The father, startled by this, had mentioned it to his wife.

Tommy was very much interested in babies and baby-making, and he told me that he had known for a long time that Koko would have kittens because her breasts felt big. His mother's friend was pregnant at that time and had told him about babies. He had asked, "What would happen to a baby if the food went in and hit the baby's head?" Although she had explained to him that there were two different places in the mother's belly, one for food and one for the baby, he had the idea that this would kill the baby. He had asked his mother whether she had urinated while giving birth. He had the fantasy that the baby could drown. He also thought that the baby came out through the navel. He asked me whether I had ever had a dead baby. His mother had told him that she had had one before he was born. He brought home two little dolls which he called "babies." He played with his friend and they were looking for the dolls' vaginas. When he went to the bathroom with his friend that afternoon, he wet all over the bathroom floor. He explained to his mother that it had happened because he had laughed so hysterically. Analysis revealed that he had acted out a fantasy of giving birth by urinating.

He played a game with puppets in the play session. The excitement with which he played and the fighting between the male and female puppets left no doubt about the sexual nature of this game. First the woman was attacking; she was a witch and she was lifting the male puppet up, saying, "Rise in the air," and then she would drop him. Then the male puppet attacked the female; he jumped upon her and threw her down. In the end, both puppets dropped from the edge of the little table on which the fight took place and were killed.

Sexual activity was dangerous for both the male and female (the parents). Nevertheless, Tommy seemed to come closer to an identification with the male. A story he invented about a lion was revealing: This lion, who was the king of the forest, felt that he needed a lioness to be his wife. He got the wife; they were king and queen and had six children. When the king became old, he devised a test to see who should be king. The young lions had to jump off a cliff. The first one drowned, four more shared his fate, the last one did okay and became King Tommy. King Tommy needed a wife; he went out of the jungle, came to a circus where he saw the most beautiful lioness, except for his mother. He married her and she began to eat a lot and had sixteen children and then the story repeated itself. Only one could be king and the others had to die.

During this phase, he would ask his mother such speculative questions as the following: "What would happen if you back out the car and my bike was in the driveway, and you hit it but it doesn't break?" He had a period of absent-mindedness; in his daydreams he was engaging in dangerous actions. He managed to injure himself in the most obvious ways. Once he actually cut himself deliberately with a knife. He was provocative in his behavior, inviting punishment upon himself. He was more careful, though, in concealing that he was wearing his sister's panties and nightgowns.

He reported the following dream: He was driving in a car with his friend, Fred. At first he could not drive and Fred was driving. But then he could drive. He went to live with Fred, who was married. It seemed to be safer not to *be* a man but instead to live with one (his father). His conscious attitude was much different. He would now make statements such as, "I'll grow up and I'll be a daddy," or "I'm glad I am a boy. I can plant the seed for the babies." To his father he said, "Now I know how you make babies." Earlier in his analysis he would say, "I won't get married. I don't want to be bossed." Talking to another boy he once said: "Girls are lucky. They grow up to marry a boy." The other boy replied, "Boys are lucky. When they grow up they marry a girl." He made up stories of clearly oedipal content and he wondered why he could not marry his sister.

Tommy began to display considerable interest in girls. He declared that he was in love with one little girl. He would say, "Now that I have a girlfriend, I don't have any fears any more." Similar to an adult patient, Tommy was attempting, with the exaggerated interest in girls, to demonstrate and to prove his masculinity as a cover-up and overcompensation for his feminine wishes. He now talked, although with reluctance, about the special games he played with the children. In these games the girls were included. They would pull their pants down and look at each other's bodies. Exhibitionism and voyeurism played a great part in his games, fantasies, and dreams. He had a fantasy that his girlfriend was at his house. He undressed her. All the boys from his class were looking, and he took a shot with the camera of her vagina. This theme (of voyeurism and exhibitionism) was repeated in innumerable fantasies and dreams. One dream sample: His girlfriend came into the house with her friend. His pants fell down in front of the girls. He awoke.

The analysis, now in its third year, took on a different flavor. He had stopped the bed-wetting and was making determined efforts to stop the transvestite activities. It was the most fruitful and decisive phase of his treatment, during which Tommy had settled down to work. While before he had been hyperactive in the playroom, he now became interested in his dreams and introspective. He disclosed his masturbation fantasies and practices. A phenomenon which he mentioned for the first time brought into the analysis his castration fears and his reactions to the sight of the vagina. Let me briefly reconstruct some of the events of this phase. Tommy had related several dreams about a ball. In one dream he had thrown a ball at the teacher. The teacher did not give him back the ball, but kept it. His associations made it clear that the ball represented his genital (he called his testicles penis balls) and that the teacher also represented myself (and his mother). In another dream his father had given him a ball, a very precious ball (there were only three or four such balls in the whole world, he said). The ball fell into the sewer. He went down into the sewer to get the ball. He got wet. He awoke dry. In association to this dream, he related the following two experiences. The night before the dream, a little girl cousin had slept over at his house. She had told him that when she touched her vagina with her finger, it smelled. They had played a game of touching each other's genitals. And then, with signs of great disturbance, he spoke of an experience which seemed to concern him very much. He said that he experienced things twice, as if the very same thing had happened before, and yet he knew that it had not happened. Tommy described in detail and with great affect a *déjà vu* experience. He was anxious and expressed fears about his sanity. "I think I am going cuckoo; maybe I should have my brain examined."*

I could show him that he was afraid of heterosexuality because this meant that he would lose his penis; the teacher, I, mother, would take it away from him if he were sexually aggressive. To be a girl would be preferable, but this idea was very frightening, because girls have a vagina, but no penis. Tommy proceeded to tell me that he liked the behind better than the front, in girls as well as in boys. He told me that wearing his sister's nightgown, he would slap himself on the behind and that this felt very good and gave him great pleasure. It tickled all the way down his legs. To my question as to when he had started this activity, Tommy answered by making up the following fantasy: "When I was born and came out of my mother's belly, she slapped me with a board which had a nail on it on my behind. That's why I like it." He said that the two people who slapped him on his behind in reality were his mother and his sister. I knew from the analysis of his mother that she had been in the habit of slapping him on his behind (her mother had done the same to her). He then revealed his leading masturbation fantasy and practice. He told me that he would put on his sister's dress and go into the crawling place in his house and imagine the king was beating him. This gave him the greatest pleasure.

There is a striking similarity between Tommy's behavior and that of adult transvestites observed and described by Boehm (1923), Fenichel (1930), and other investigators (Alexander,

* I have encountered *déjà vu* phenomena in two of my other transvestite patients (one latency and one adolescent boy). It is my impression that there is a specific connection between *déjà vu* and transvestitism. This is a subject which cannot be dealt with in this presentation but one which I intend to investigate further.

1928; Burchardt, 1961; Fessler, 1934; Greenberg and Rosenwald, 1958, 1960; Grotjahn, 1948; Gutheil, 1954; Hirschfeld and Tielke, 1912; Hora, 1953; Karpman, 1947; Lukianowitz, 1960; McKenzie and Schultz, 1961; Wilson, 1948). The leading fantasy is one of being beaten on the behind. In the cases of adult transvestites, the beating person is always a woman.

The origin of Tommy's beating fantasy could be traced back to age three and a half to four, the same age when he had expressed his fantasy of "All people are born girls." A fuller analysis of the genetic and dynamic function of these fantasies and their role in his transvestite behavior, and particularly of the dynamic function of the beating fantasy in relation to the primal scene and to the oedipal conflict, will be given in the discussion, following the case presentation. At this point, I want to draw attention to Tommy's masochistic needs, which manifested themselves in overt behavior and in his accident proneness. This is a feature characteristic of and prominent also in adult transvestites. Even when he was not really injured, Tommy sometimes would put on bandages and pretend that he had hurt himself. He once asked whether one could be punished for trying to commit suicide (he had once jumped out of a second-floor window "playing fire drill"). He wondered whether the punishment would be to be sent to a reform school and gave this as his version of what a reform school is like: "They give you a hammer and you break up stones six days a week. On Sunday as a special treat you get bread and castor oil. Every day you get bread and water. On Christmas everybody is excited and what do you get: a new hammer."

New and significant aspects of his transvestite behavior were brought into the analysis and could be understood with the help of dreams and his associations. I have in mind here a series of dreams, which Tommy termed "funny"-crazy dreams. In one dream, a boy in school had a bottle. He drank from it. He grew a vagina. He went into the boys' bathroom. His pants changed into a dress. His hair got long. He had no belt and the dress fell down. When he went back into the classroom, the vagina changed into a penis again. The girls took a hatchet and wanted to chop it off. He awoke at this point. In another dream he had a certain suit (he was actually to get a new suit and this time he had decided to buy a "real boy's suit"). It was a magic suit. By magic it made him what he was wearing. In the first dream it is a magic potion which transforms him from a boy into a girl. In the second dream this magical quality is clearly attributed to the clothing, to something that he could put on and wear on his body. This Tommy had been practicing in his transvestite behavior; by wearing his sister's panties underneath his own, he could maintain the illusion that he was both a boy and a girl at the same time. Similar to certain types of behavior in adults, who, although they use their genitals in their sexual activities, derive sexual gratification only with the help of pregenital fantasies (penis equals breast, vagina equals mouth and anus) and with special techniques (fellatio, cunnilingus), so Tommy, by his exaggerated interest in the genitals, was hiding the fact that, under the threat of castration, he had shifted his interest from the front to the rear and from below to above. He derived sexual gratification from stimulating his buttocks and anus and was very interested in looking at breasts.

The analysis of Tommy's persistent enuresis cannot be dealt with here except to indicate that pregenital fantasies entered into its dynamics. Urine, on one level, was milk and sperm, and, on another level, poison and feces. He had a dream about a boy who was born without a "tuschie." The b.m. (feces) kept coming out of his penis. He then became the boy in the dream. His pants fell off and his girlfriend said, "Wear a tuschie." Repressed memories from his traumatic oedipal phase were mobilized in the analysis of this dream. He did not remember the change in sleeping arrangements during the time his aunt and baby cousin stayed at their house (I knew from his mother that he had slept in the parental bedroom then), but he remembered that he would awaken in fear during the night and go into his parents' bedroom. This was later replaced by going into his sister's bed. He actually had suffered from a sleep disturbance which subsided when his enuresis became fully established. In the dream of a boy born without a "tuschie," Tommy's fantasy, "all people are born girls," returned in a different version. It was found that "tuschie" as well as "wear" had a double meaning. "Tuschie" meant not only the behind but also the front and was both the male and female genital; and "wear" was a play on words (a favorite game of Tommy's) and also meant "where?" In the dream, the calamity of a boy born without a "tuschie" proved to be no calamity because, first, he had a penis which took over such functions, and, secondly, he could remedy the situation easily by the transvestite mechanism of dealing with such a problem, i.e., by wearing a piece of clothing designed for intimate contact with a girl's body on his own body. In this way he magically acquired parts of or the whole body of a girl. This was the essence of his transvestite behavior. Since he was a boy and had a penis, he could, by wearing his sister's panties and nightgowns, gain in addition everything she (a girl) had. While in the manifest dream Tommy had the girl say, "Wear a tuschie," further analysis revealed that on a deeper level Tommy was asking the girl the fateful question, "Where is your tuschie-penis?"

Tommy's concept of the vagina was that it was an asset like the breasts and the pubic hair. The emphasis was shifted away from what girls did not have (and he could lose), namely, the penis, to what girls had or could grow later, namely, pubic hair, breasts, and babies. In the dream in which the magic potion transforms him into a girl, this is manifested by his growing a vagina, long hair (pubic hair), and by the change of the pants into a dress.

Tommy still insisted that men also grow breasts. He told me that he had seen the big breasts of his gym teacher (a cover for the big penis of his father). In the profile of a woman he drew, the equation of breast-penis was very obvious. The breast actually looked like a big penis. Concomitant with the flow of this material, there was a change in the character of Tommy's drawings. He was now drawing himself as a muscle man with tremendous biceps, but also with big breasts. He still wanted to have everything a man and a woman have.

There were marked changes in Tommy's behavior after the working through of this material. When he terminated his analysis at the age of nine, he had given up his transvestite activities completely, had settled down to work in school, had friends, and became interested in sports. He not only acted but he felt like a real boy. I saw Tommy again for a short period at age thirteen because of some difficulties he had in school. I found that his sexual development had progressed very satisfactorily and felt that I could leave him on his own. Tommy came to see me one year later just to report that he was doing very well. He had worked himself up to the upper third in his class and took pride in his achievement. He had grown and put on weight, and he was pleased with his appearance. He had made new friends, both boys and girls. He had become quite athletic and was a member of two teams in school. He had little conflict about masturbation and thought that he had less need for it than some of his friends. It appeared to me that Tommy showed a very good ability for sublimation. He had also taken up his music more seriously and obviously was doing very well at it. He had not only maintained but also consolidated these gains further when I saw him at age fifteen and last at age sixteen.

A few remarks about the technique of treatment seem indicated, particularly since no successfully treated case has been reported in the literature and because transvestite behavior is not a rare phenomenon in children or adults. That so few cases are known is due to the fact that parents usually do not ask for help unless the behavior of the child exposes them publicly and they are compelled to do so. Similarly, adult patients do not come for treatment because of their transvestite behavior (which they reveal reluctantly only later), but usually for accompanying symptoms, most often depression. It was my experience in many years of work with children with deviate sexual behavior that no satisfactory results could be obtained without concomitant treatment of the mother, and in some cases of both parents (see Chapter 13). A case such as Tommy's would have gone untreated or treatment might have been requested at a later time for other problems, e.g., learning and school problems, but not for his basic problem, had his mother not been in analysis. I have developed a technique whereby I preferably work with the mother first in preparation for the treatment of the child. This makes it possible to work with the child with very little contact with the mother, and also quickly to resolve resistances which otherwise might lead to withdrawal of the child from treatment.

The case report of Tommy may give the impression that he

was an easy patient to treat. He definitely was not. This was true also for the nine-year-old transvestite boy, whose mother was in treatment with me for three years prior to his analysis, which was successfully concluded after four years with three years of follow-up. In such a treatment, one gets a taste of the difficulties of treating adult perverts. It is essential for a successful outcome that the treatment be carried out in an atmosphere of instinctual deprivation. The analyst cannot be a party in the child's transvestite acting out in the treatment situation. The child has to know that he is in treatment because of the transvestite behavior, that the analysis will help him understand the reasons for it and enable him to give it up and find more satisfactory and more appropriate gratifications. It is essential also to establish with the mother of the child patient what I call the "superego alliance," which assures that the child has only one direction in which to go in his analysis. It also insures that the changes and gains made in the analysis will not be undone but maintained after treatment is terminated.

## Discussion

Although there seems to be a close relationship between transvestitism and fetishism on the one hand, and transvestitism and homosexuality on the other, transvestitism is a distinct perversion with its own well-delineated features. From the psychoanalytic point of view, the most significant difference lies in the choice of the love object, which in transvestitism is a heterosexual one. The transvestite, in order to achieve sexual gratification, has to have an article of female clothing, which is not limited to one fixed piece of clothing, on his body and in close proximity with it or certain parts of it. The fetishist, on the other hand, requires a very specific fixed article, the fetish, which may or may not be a piece of female clothing, which is not worn by the fetishist but usually by his love object. We would expect, therefore, to find different dynamic constellations in each of these conditions, and it would be possible to define specific factors which would account for these specific outcomes.

We know that bisexuality plays an important role not only

in transvestitism but also in other types of perversion as well as in the neurotic, psychotic, and even in the normal person (Freud, 1909; Kubie, 1954; Sperling, 1950d).

On the basis of clinical material, I shall attempt to identify certain factors which might account for the persistence and intensity of bisexuality and its specific outcome in transvestitism in certain cases. In the simultaneous analysis of children with deviate sexual behavior and their mothers, I have found that the relationship between mother and child, which I have described (Chapter 13) as the perverse type of object relationship, was a genetic factor in the pathological ego and superego functioning of the child. The fact that the parent-child relationship leads to specific superego pathology and thus is an important factor in the genesis of perversion has been noted by other observers (Gillespie, 1952; Johnson and Szurek, 1952; O. Sperling, 1951). The role of primitive mechanisms and identifications and of preoedipal conflicts particularly in fetishism has been stressed in numerous contributions (Bak, 1953; Balint, 1935; Friend et al., 1954; Gillespie, 1952; Greenacre, 1953; Socarides, 1960). From this point of view, the analyses of the mothers of the two boys with transvestite behavior are of interest. Only a few details of this material can be given here. Both women had older brothers who excelled intellectually, whom they envied, and with whom they had been in rivalry. Tommy's mother's brother died suddenly in his late teens, and she took up the education and career intended for him. She vied with both men and women, and it was equally important for her to be considered bright and efficient (like a man) and soft and attractive (like a woman). After the birth of her first child, she willingly gave up her career and devoted herself to her household and child. She recalled with great pleasure in her analysis an episode from childhood. Once, in a summer resort she met a boy on the first day of her arrival; this boy mistook her for a boy. She fooled him for an entire day about her true sex and enjoyed this experience tremendously.

The mother of the latency boy who showed transvestite behavior liked to wear slacks and short coats with big pockets. She never carried a (woman's) handbag. Her mother would say to her, "If you'll start wearing skirts, your boy would stop wearing dresses." The analysis of these mothers revealed that, unlike the latent homosexual, they did not suffer from an unconscious conflict concerning sexual identification; this type of behavior was rather a conscious playfulness and pretense of being both sexes in certain situations in the sense of a "controlled illusion" (O. Sperling, 1951). Both mothers encouraged similar behavior in their sons.

Friend and his collaborators (1954), in an interesting study of transvestitism in three boys, have noted the confusion of sexual roles in the families of these children. Yet such confusion of roles and similar family constellations are not uncommon findings in a great variety of neurotic disturbances. Even in those cases where the overt attitude of the mother would seem to encourage feminine behavior in her son, the development may lead rather to homosexuality or other forms of sexual deviation than to transvestitism. I have found that there was not a confusion of sexual roles, but rather a *fusion* of roles with an emphasis on being both male and female in one. Both mothers functioned adequately sexually and enjoyed being women. The role of a woman was not depreciated; in fact, certain feminine activities, and especially maternal functions, were highly valued. In comparison, the role of the man appeared to be less important in some respects because he was not entrusted with the care of the children. Both women considered themselves, and were regarded by their husbands, as intellectually superior and were the leaders of the family. The outstanding features of the mothers of these boys were their strong oral fixation and a bisexual orientation. The fathers did not seem to present any specific problems related to their sons' behavior. Tommy's father went into treatment shortly after Tommy began his analysis, as I understand, primarily for psychosomatic complaints. The father of the other boy appeared to function well and did not present any difficulties in the treatment of his son.

Tommy's bisexual wishes were aptly expressed in his fantasy of boys and girls being cut into halves and these halves being mixed up and put together again so that they were half boy and half girl. The nine-year-old patient referred to previously revealed an identical fantasy during one phase of his analysis. Boys and girls should be cut in half and the upper half of the girl put together with the lower part of the boy. A ten-year-old boy with transvestitite tendencies revealed the following fantasy: "It would be best to be half boy and half girl. One side should be a boy and the other side a girl." He explained that then he would not have to worry about getting married. He would be married from birth on. Possessing everything his mother had, he would not need her and would be able to take care of himself. He had also thought of a way in which this could be accomplished: a man and a woman would get together so closely that they would become like one. Their children would be born half boy and half girl.

What is the source of this intense wish of the transvestite to be not only male but also female? Fenichel (1930) put the emphasis on castration anxiety and on the identification with the phallic mother; yet the belief in the phallic mother as a denial of castration is a phenomenon met with frequently in conditions other than transvestitism. In fact, fetishism has been considered by Freud (1927) the classical perversion in which this particular feature, namely, that the fetish represents the illusory penis, is a decisive dynamic factor. Friend's study (1954), in which transvestite behavior had been observed in a one-and-a-half-year-old boy, seems to indicate that transvestite behavior can occur in the prephallic phases before castration anxiety proper is active. My experience from the analyses of children and adults with transvestite tendencies leads me to believe that, in addition to the specific mother(parent)-child relationship and castration anxiety, two factors have to be present which contribute to the persistence of bisexuality and would seem to account for the specific outcome in transvestite behavior.

In 1950 I introduced the concept of the pregenital father; that is, the father with breasts (equation of penis = breast). I could show that the particularly intense positive oedipal conflict of the girl, in certain cases, covered up for an unresolved negative oedipal conflict, whereby the pregenital father represented a mother with penis, breasts, and babies, from whom the girl expected everything that her mother had not given her. The intensity of the castration conflict and of the penis envy in the

patients described in this 1950 paper stemmed from their unresolved oral conflicts. They had cathected the penis with oral
libido and the intensity of the wish for a penis was derived from
an actual event: the birth of a younger brother which had been
experienced as a loss of mother to the baby. The primary source
for the fantasy of the loss of the penis (castration) in these cases
came from this loss and from the unwillingness to accept weaning, i.e., separation from mother. The cathexis of the penis with
oral libido was found to be a significant factor also in the dynamics of genital exhibitionism (M. Sperling, 1947).

We can now identify those two factors which, in my opinion, in a given situation, may account for the development of
transvestite behavior. The first factor is a strong oral fixation
with unresolved oral conflicts. Tommy's orality manifested itself
in his intense envy and greed. This is characteristic also of bisexual fantasies. To be both a man and a woman means to possess
everything that both have. A dream, which Tommy dreamed
under anesthesia when he had a tooth pulled, illustrates this orality. In this dream, in place of his teeth which had been pulled
out, the dentist gave him a crazy set of teeth over which he had
no control and which snapped at everything. The urgency and
impulsivity which characterizes oral personalities was also very
apparent in Tommy's behavior.

The second factor is the reaction to the primal scene, which,
in such a case, not only intensifies castration anxiety but is experienced as an abandonment by both parents and reactivates separation anxiety.

Tommy developed overt transvestite behavior at the age of
three, shortly after he had been confronted with the fact that girl
babies do not have a penis. Tommy had had ample opportunity
for sexual explorations in his play with his seductive sister and
his exhibitionistic mother. In his previous observations he had
seen his mother's pubic hair, her big buttocks and breasts; his
sister had long hair and was beginning to develop physically.
Growing long hair and breasts played an important part in his
dreams and fantasies of magical transformation into a girl. This
lent itself to support his fantasy that there was something hidden
("Take off your fuzz," he said to his mother once upon seeing

her nude) that eventually would develop and become visible. The shock effect of the sight of the baby girl came from the fact that he could plainly see that she had *nothing*: no penis, no hair, no breasts, no teeth. He counteracted with the confabulation, "All children are born girls." He could say, "I too was born a girl," because he was the actual possessor of a penis. That he was very much aware of this fact was brought out in a little incident which occurred about that time. He saw a little girl dancing; apparently he was envious that she could dance and said to her, "I have a penis and you don't, and I can urinate with my penis."

By the fantasy of "I too was born a girl," he could only gain. He could grow hair, breasts, and babies like his mother (aunt) and sister. By equating the (missing) penis of the baby with the as yet missing but later developing breasts, he could retain the fantasy of a female penis in a rationally acceptable form. The importance of the penis was displaced to the breast. Since he had a penis and girls did grow breasts, he could not only deny castration but support his bisexual fantasy.

Tommy was very curious about, but also very jealous of, the baby and of his mother who was very taken by the infant. He feared that he might be replaced by the baby. At that time his mother actually contemplated having another baby. He manifested regressive behavior particularly in speech and an intensification of his greed and envy. He wanted to have everything his mother and his sister had (he stole from his mother and sister but not from his father).

It seems to me that the emphasis in transvestite tendencies is equally as much on the man with breasts as it is on the woman with a penis. The fantasy material and the drawings of Tommy clearly indicated this. He persisted in the belief that men had breasts and that he, too, would grow them. He drew the breast of a woman in profile elongated and appearing like a big penis, and he would draw men with big penislike breasts.

Tommy expressed his positive oedipal wishes quite openly, especially in the displacement to his sister: "If I can't marry my mother, why can't I marry my sister?" he would ask. His dominant sexual orientation was heterosexual. The negative oedipal wishes were repressed and found expression and gratification in the transvestite behavior, especially in the beating fantasies and practice. Of interest is the fact that, although in reality his mother and sister were the ones who liked to slap him on his buttocks, in his fantasy he was beaten by the king. One adult patient with transvestite tendencies and with fantasies of being beaten by a woman remembered in his analysis a dream from childhood (during the oedipal phase). In this dream he was a slave and the king was beating him. He could permit himself the gratification of being beaten by a man only in a dream. In the beating fantasies which he developed in adolescence, the king was replaced by a woman. It would appear that hidden behind the woman in the manifest beating fantasies of transvestites is a man: the king-father; and that such a distortion may be a regular occurrence in the development of these fantasies. This patient, as my other patients with transvestite behavior, lived a full heterosexual life. He had never had any homosexual relationship and no conscious thoughts or fantasies of such a nature. Analysis, by bringing his unconscious passive homosexual wishes to the fore, did not transform him into a homosexual but, to the contrary, enabled him to gain more satisfaction and enjoyment from his heterosexual love relationship. I would not consider, as some authors seem to do (Friend et al., 1954), transvestite behavior as a defense against homosexuality or as a transitional phase in the development of homosexuality; I consider it a distinct perversion with a specific genesis, dynamics, and aim.

Reference has been made in the literature to transvestites who seek surgery so that they can actually live as women (Burchardt, 1961). In my opinion, this behavior alone would invalidate the diagnosis of transvestitism in these cases. The transvestite wants to be a man primarily and, at times, also a woman and have what a woman has. He does not want to be either one; he wants to be both. Tommy wanted to be his mother and he wanted to marry her; he wanted to be his sister and he wanted to marry her. He wanted to be the baby and he wanted to have babies. At the same time, he wanted to be a bigger boy and a father. He was the slave and the king. Yet, Tommy never really thought that he was a girl; he always knew that he just pretended.

The analysis of an adult patient with transvestite behavior revealed that the deeper meaning of this behavior was the reenactment of the primal scene. He, too, was playing both roles; the male and the female in one. It would seem that the transvestite patient is reenacting an *actual* trauma (the abandonment felt in reaction to the primal scene), and by himself representing both parents in the sexual embrace as one person with the attributes of both, he attempts to bring his conflict to a successful solution in the transvestite act.† This becomes particularly clear in the cases where the transvestite act takes place in front of a mirror (Greenacre, 1953). In this way the viewing of the primal scene and the unsolved puzzle of whether the parents in embrace are just one or two people is repeated. This would seem analogous to the hysterical fit in which Freud (1909b) recognized that the patient is playing both roles, the male and female, in sexual intercourse.

Not every "dressing up" of a little boy in girl's clothing can be considered as true transvestite behavior. In fact, the public masquerading of males in female clothing is more indicative of certain types of homosexuality than of transvestitism. Only if such dressing-up behavior continues through or originates during the oedipal phase, increases in intensity, and continues into latency and is practiced with a certain degree of secrecy as sexual activities would be, could it be considered as transvestite behavior. Tommy was careful to conceal those activities which were really important to him and became even more careful as he grew older. When he would put on his sister's dress during the daytime to indulge in his beating fantasy and practice, he would hide in the crawling space of the house or in other secret places. He would hide his sister's panties and nightgowns in his bureau drawers, and he did not want other children to know about his behavior. In order to differentiate whether such behavior indicates the beginning of a homosexual or of a transvestite develop-

---

† The need for episodic transvestite activity was clearly precipitated by a sudden reactivation and increase in separation anxiety in one patient. This activity had the earmarks of an emergency action, rather than one designed purely for the procurement of sexual pleasure and gratification. This behavior was similar to that observed in other types of perversion, but also in addicts and impulse-ridden (oral) characters (Bak, 1953; M. Sperling, 1947).

ment, it would be necessary to know the fantasies underlying it. The dominant fantasy of these children with transvestite behavior was the "half and half" fantasy, that is, to be half boy and half girl; a fantasy which would seem characteristic for transvestite behavior. Characteristic, also, was a certain plasticity, playfulness, and imagination which permitted displacement from the important to the less important, i.e., from the primary sex characteristics, the genitals proper, to the secondary sex characteristics, the breasts, the anus, pubic hair, and hair in general; from below to above, from the front to the rear, and from the body itself to the clothing and all the female accoutrements.

I found a striking richness of fantasy life and creative imagination in the children as well as in the adults. Tommy's parents permitted freedom of thought, playfulness, imagination, interchangeability of sexual roles and acting out of fantasies. He was a fantastic storyteller even at the age of three or four. He was able later (and I like to think that this was a result of his analysis) to sublimate these tendencies and actually wrote stories and poems. He could permit himself the controlled illusion of being *also* a girl in the transvestite act (O. Sperling, 1951).

In summary, it can be said that the equation of penis with breast and the emphasis upon the breast are special modes of dealing with castration anxiety, holding out the promise for gain rather than the danger of loss. To the concept of identification with the phallic mother, considered to be the basic mechanism in transvestite behavior, can be added the concept of the pregenital father, the man with breasts. Both are expressions of the fantasy of "half and half"; man and woman in one. In the final analysis, this fantasy and the transvestite activity are the result of the child's reaction to the trauma of the primal scene, expressing his feelings that the parents in embrace are one person with the attributes of both.

Tommy's behavior, while it could not be considered a perversion in the true sense, was an indication of a serious deviation in his psychosexual development, which, I believe, without therapeutic intervention, would have led to an actual perversion in later life. The nine-year-old boy, whose treatment was not reported in this paper, began his transvestite behavior at the age of three. Because of its persistence and increase, the family sought psychiatric treatment when he was five years old. He was in play therapy for one year, and his mother was seen once a week during this time. There was no improvement in the child's behavior, and, because it was felt that the mother could not be reached in therapy, the case was referred to me. I treated the mother for three years before I began his analysis, and I am convinced that I could not have been successful with him without this preparation. At the start of analysis, he was withdrawn, distrustful in a paranoid manner, had no friends, and did not function well in school. He was phobic and bizarre in many ways, and had frequent *déjà vu* experiences. His transvestite activities were now a well-guarded secret and not easily accessible in the analysis.

From the analysis of the adolescents and adults with transvestite behavior, I gained the impression that there had been certain experiences and certain behavior in their early lives to indicate the probability of transvestite behavior in the future, even though manifest and active transvestite practices may not have been present. In the case of one adult, an episode, which occurred when he was between three and four years of age, had a direct bearing on his transvestite behavior later. His first overt transvestite episode occurred in early adulthood, and was a reenactment of this early experience. This tendency, first noted during the oedipal phase, had remained latent through all these years, and emerged in a situation which unconsciously represented to him a repetition of the experience of that phase.

# 15

# Fetishism in Children

Some children display an exaggerated attachment to an article of clothing (usually not their own), or to a piece of bedding such as a pillow or blanket, or to some other inanimate object not particularly suitable as a child's plaything. The child must possess and use this article in certain situations, especially before going to sleep or when alone or in a strange environment. Even the presence of mother will not comfort some of these children unless this fetish is available when they need it. It is startling and puzzling to see an inanimate and seemingly valueless object preferred by the child to his mother. Mothers are usually embarrassed by this behavior and try to conceal it from outsiders and to minimize the degree of the child's attachment to the fetish.

In 1927, Friedjung, a psychoanalytically oriented Viennese pediatrician, published a short but very interesting observation of such fetishistic behavior in a sixteen-month-old boy. He had chanced to find the mother's used stocking or lingerie in the child's bed and was given significant information about the child's behavior, not by the mother, but by the grandmother and

295

the maid.

In 1930, Lorand reported on a four-year-old boy with shoe fetishism. Corroborating Freud's concept of the fetish as representing the "illusory" phallus of the mother, Lorand gave some description of the child's environment. His parents were exhibitionistic and the boy had unusually strong scoptophilia. He had slept with his mother until the age of three and still shared her bedroom and frequently her bed. He liked to climb all over her body, under her and other women's skirts, and often while sitting on his mother's lap, even in the presence of others, would reach for her breasts. Lorand discussed the very obvious castration anxiety of this boy, but made only casual mention of the attitude of his mother, who permitted this behavior but interfered with her son's attempts at masturbation even when he tried to conceal it. The boy had begun to curb this behavior, according to Lorand, under the influence of his superego. I believe his mother must have begun to restrict some of the previously uninhibited instinctual gratification. Lorand also refers to the mother's great interest in shoes, which may have played a role in the boy's choice of fetish.

Articles on fetishism in children are scarce, yet the condition is not rare. But even marked fetishistic inclinations in a child hardly ever cause parents to seek professional help (Chapter 13). Two cases referred to me primarily for their fetishistic behavior come to mind in this connection.

> The pediatrician of a four-year-old boy insisted upon consultation because of the child's unusual behavior, which the parents apparently tolerated. The child's fetish was his mother's panties, which had to be saturated thoroughly with his urine. He would go to sleep only if his face was buried in the fetish. During the day he liked to hold the fetish to his face and smell it. A seven-year-old boy used to lie face down on a certain spot in the living room, moving his body rhythmically and at the same time plucking wool from the carpet. This he did regularly before bedtime but also at other times during the day. Although this behavior was disturbing to his mother, neither she nor the mother of

the four-year-old boy accepted my and their doctors' advice that the children receive treatment.

Both Friedjung (1927) and Wulff (1946) discovered the fetishism by chance, confirming my own observation that parents often tacitly sanction this and other deviate sexual behavior and do not welcome outside intervention. Wulff, reviewing his own and Friedjung's cases, together with that of a twenty-month-old girl reported by Editha Sterba (1941), concluded that these phenomena are pathological and are closely related to fetishism in the adult. Wulff discusses Freud's (1927) concept of the fetish as a substitute for the missing penis of the mother (a position Freud also held in the case of the sixteen-month-old boy whom Friedjung had discussed with him) but concludes, "The abnormal manifestations in the young child in the preoedipal period are in their psychological structure nothing other than a simple reaction-formation to an inhibited or ungratified instinctual impulse, in which the inhibition or the forbidding of gratification comes from the external world." He draws attention to the significance of the fetish as a substitute for the mother's body in part or in whole, and discusses the relation of the fetish to sucking, to food, and to weaning. He states that "in the young child the fetish represents a substitute for the mother's body and in particular for the mother's breast." He adds, ". . . fetishistic manifestations in the young child are not at all uncommon, but the psychological structure of childhood fetishism, as of other pathological manifestations, is a different one" from that found in adult fetishism.

Wulff believes that study of the development of childhood fetishism could throw light on its probable connection with adult fetishism. He demonstrates convincingly the relation of the fetish to nursing and weaning, its oral origin, and its connection with eating and sucking. He points to the fact that only a specific property of the fetish is valued and gives a specific kind of gratification. If the fetish loses this property, it loses its value as a fetish. In other words it is not the object as a whole that is valued, and there is no emotional tie to the object itself but only to a specific quality such as texture or smell. He believes that, during the anal-sadistic phase, the fetish becomes a possession important as a whole object, valued not for only a single specific property. During the phallic phase, according to Wulff, the fetish becomes identified with the penis, and castration anxiety is carried over to the fetish.

In 1953, Winnicott described the "transitional object" as "an object that becomes vitally important to the child, even more important than the mother, an almost inseparable part of the child." He is correct in saying that some mothers "allow an infant special toys and expect them to become addicted to these toys" and that children use these toys in defense against anxiety. However, he considers these phenomena universal and part of "normal" emotional development. He objects to use "of the word fetish, [by which] Wulff has taken back to infancy something that belongs in ordinary theory to the sexual perversions." It seems to me that Winnicott has created much confusion by referring to these phenomena and these objects as transitional. I believe they are pathological manifestations of a specific disturbance in object relationship. Winnicott's concepts are not only fallacious but dangerous, because they lead to erroneous assessment of the meaning and function of fetishistic childhood phenomena and childhood fetishism.

Why should a child become so addicted to an intrinsically valueless article that it becomes more important to him than his mother? And why should a mother expect her child to become so attached to a toy as to feel that he cannot do without it? Winnicott correctly emphasized that these mothers are very careful of this object, taking it traveling with the child. Can it be that the mother has something to do with this behavior of her child, that she wants him to form such an attachment to an inanimate object, and in some way indicates this to him? It is fallacious to draw conclusions from observation of the behavior of the child and the manifest attitude of the mother without knowledge of the unconscious motivations of the mother, which can be obtained only by psychoanalytic study. Without such knowledge, certain behavior of the child either remains unintelligible or may be incorrectly interpreted. Even psychoanalysis of the child himself may give only incomplete understanding of the interplay between mother and child without psychoanalytic study of the mother; I have found deviate sexual behavior in children to require concomitant psychoanalysis if adequate understanding and therapeutic results are to be achieved (Chapter 13).

I have studied the onset and course of fetishistic behavior in a two-year-old boy, Martin, during three years of analysis of his mother. The case is of particular interest because his older brother, Leo, exhibited transvestite behavior. The analysis of the mother revealed that she had had different feelings for her two sons from their births. In her older son, who became very closely attached to her, she encouraged feminine behavior from the beginning. He exhibited all the traits she disliked in herself, particularly shyness. He was afraid to speak up, was withdrawn, and acted "funny." "Even though he had a penis," she said, "he was no better than a girl." In fact she thought him worse than a girl because he was clinging and fearful. With Martin she determined from the start to let him be a boy and independent of her. She even thought that Leo's penis looked different from Martin's, which was "a real male penis." Martin was a poor sleeper so his mother slept with him, not with her husband. Martin loved buttons; he liked to put one into his mouth to suck. This began in the following way: Martin liked to sit on his mother's lap and play with the buttons of her blouse and fondle her. One day his mother, deciding to stop this play, gave him a button, which Martin immediately put into his mouth and appropriated as a fetish. When it was lost, he became unhappy and would accept as a substitute only a button given to him by his mother. Her analysis revealed that she had not really accepted weaning. She was still in the habit of sucking on her teeth and gums, especially when she felt frustrated. She was consciously determined to wean Martin and to separate herself from him but she was unable to do so. The button represented to her the nipple, the breast, and a substitute for herself; by it she continued her "oral" relationship with Martin. When she understood this, his attachment to buttons weakened (it had lasted about six months).

He then developed an attachment to a blanket for several reasons. His mother now understood the meaning of the button; moreover, she was concerned that he might swallow it. (This concern she had had before, but it did not prevent her from giving him buttons.) What seemed decisive was the fact that her analysis made her aware of her part in Martin's sleep disturbance and of her use of it as a rationalization for sleeping with him. When she decided to separate herself from him at night, she offered him a blanket as substitute for herself. The special blanket she bought for him then became his second fetish. Martin clearly treated the blanket as his mother intended he should. He took possession of it, became inseparable from it, and dragged it with him about the house, often between his legs as if he were riding it. He liked to pick at the seams (it was a cotton-filled quilt), to pull the cotton out, to smell it, and to make little heaps. Martin was now at the height of the anal phase and approaching the phallic stage. By the time he was four years old, there were decisive changes in his mother's feelings and attitudes, and her unconscious needs interfered with him less. She became able to let his father, who had been conspicuously absent from the picture, play a part in the children's lives. In her analysis she liked to minimize the significance of the blanket, but she was very careful to take it wherever they went.

One day when Martin was four and a half, the family went on a trip to the country. Almost halfway, the mother remembered that she had forgotten the blanket. She wanted to turn back but Martin discouraged her. He was now hiding the blanket in a closet during the day when his friends came to play with him and used it only at night to sleep with. The mother reminded him to take the blanket when he went to camp for the first time (he was just five years old). She worried that he might not sleep, but Martin refused because the boys would laugh at him. His attitude pleased her but she later confirmed her need to hold on to him by means of the blanket. She told me that when she saw Martin touching a velvet ribbon as though he liked the feeling of the velvet, she thought of offering him the ribbon instead of the more obvious blanket but she thought better of it. She kept his blanket while he was at camp and when he returned he used it for a short time, then discarded it. Her analysis ended then, but she reports that Martin, now ten years old, has shown no fetishistic behavior and his development seems to have progressed satisfactorily.

This case is interesting for three principal reasons:

1.   It bears out Wulff's concepts concerning the origin and development of childhood fetishism. Martin's first fetish, the button, was no doubt of oral origin, representing the nipple or breast, the mother, or part of her. His second fetish, the blanket, had anal and also phallic meaning. It came to represent the whole mother as a possession and deflected anal-erotic and anal-sadistic impulses from her and from himself to the fetish. In this connection, his behavior during toilet training is of interest. For a long time he refused the toilet and defecated in a corner of his room or in his pants. When he was left in care of others he used the toilet. After his mother's very strongly repressed anal-erotic needs were exposed in her analysis, Martin gave up soiling and the blanket became his new fetish. Progress in the mother's analysis caused the fetish, in a way not wholly clear, to lose its significance for the child during the phallic phase and finally to be given up.

2.   This case demonstrates clearly the role of the mother in the genesis of fetishistic behavior and in the choice of fetish. This mother had an unconscious need for the type of relation with her child that seems conducive to fetishism. Unconsciously she resisted separation from her child and renunciation of the gratifications of bodily contact with him during his oral and anal phases. But she could not permit this relationship to be manifest because she had felt "exposed" by the behavior of her older son, for which she held herself responsible. The relation could, however, be established through the fetish which she introduced and which represented herself in part (oral) or as a whole (anal). The fetish must be something concrete and real. Aside from its symbolic meanings, it offers real gratification to such specific components of the oral, anal, and phallic instincts as looking, touching, and smelling.

It also permits deflection of destructive sadistic impulses

from the original object, mother, and from the self, to the fetish. The child can do with the fetish what he would like to do, but may not, with his mother's or his own body. The fetish must be replaceable. This is an important differentiation between fetishistic and autoerotic activity. When the fetish is a part of the child's own body, it is a replaceable part, usually the hair or nails. In both autoerotism and fetishism the fantasy of omnipotent control is a supreme factor, but use of the fetish is a sign that the child has not given up the external object represented by it and insists upon gratification in reality, even though this is only a substitute gratification.

It seems to me that the need for a fetish has something to do with the reality of the child's experiences. In the lives of these children there has been real seduction and actual overstimulation of these component instincts in the relationship with the parents, especially with the mother. Lorand's case of the little shoe fetishist and the cases of Stevenson (1954) come to mind. (Stevenson collected her cases in support of Winnicott's thesis of the normality of fetishistic behavior in children, which he terms "transitional phenomena"; yet the pathology in these cases is blatantly obvious, as is Stevenson's inexperience with the subject of fetishism, an inexperience she herself admits.) The reality or unreality of the experience plays an important part in determining whether development leads to perversion or to neurosis. The pervert seeks gratification in reality, whereas the neurotic accepts gratification in fantasy or symptoms. The fetish has the double function of making it possible for mother and child to separate in reality by magically undoing this separation. Thus the fetish enables both mother and child to maintain a facade of normality. Gratifications not obtainable from the mother are gained from the fetish. Formation of a fetish interferes with the processes of internalization and with development of the ego, and especially with development of the superego, which arises from internalized parental attitudes (see Chapter 13; see also: Gillespie, 1956a; Payne, 1939; O. Sperling, 1956). There is incomplete introjection of the parental images because of persistence of part-object relationship and deflection of unmodified sexual and aggressive impulses to the fetish. In this connection, it is interesting to compare children with a fetish to those with imaginary companions (O. Sperling, 1954). When there is an imaginary companion, the sexual and aggressive impulses have undergone modifications and are not deflected from the parents to a lifeless object. The imaginary companion, which like the fetish is a defense against separation anxiety, is endowed by the child with a personality even if it is an inanimate object.

Study of the disturbances in object relationships in childhood fetishism and their effects upon the formation of the superego in childhood might contribute greatly to our understanding of certain phenomena in perversion, addiction, and acting out, and might enhance our treatment of such patients. I have in mind particularly the corruptibility of the superego, the instability and unrealiability in object relationship, the insistence upon immediate gratification, and the resistance to change in mode of gratification. In the analyses of two adult fetishists I found that they had strong tendencies to alcoholism, gambling, and other impulsive and destructive acting out, especially when they were struggling with their fetishistic urges.

3.   This case demonstrates that the childhood fetish is an early indication of a specific disturbance in object relationship. If the child before the age of two becomes attached to an inanimate object in this way, we should be aware that he has not accepted weaning but has instead replaced the nipple, breast, or mother with the fetish. The mother's own unresolved conflict about weaning will interfere with her ability to help her child accomplish this essential task. When this happens, some mothers may knowingly or unknowingly encourage the adoption of a fetish by their children. Martin's mother did this. A specific fixation in object relationship is thus established; it affects development during the anal, phallic, and oedipal phases and influences regression in later life. This fixation is to a part-object, to specific parts of the mother's body, or to specific qualities of these parts. In essence this means that through the fetish, part-object relationship can be maintained and immediate, unmodified instinctual gratification can be achieved. I have expressed the opinion (Chapter 4) that certain sleep disturbances in children (especially during the first two years of life) are also an early indica-

tion of disturbance in object relationship, even in the absence of other manifestations. It is of interest that such sleep disturbances are frequently found in association with fetishistic behavior; the fetish serves to allay separation anxiety by providing the child with certain essential qualities of the missed object, or represents the missed object as a whole. When children beyond the third year of life still need a bottle, even if it is empty, at nap or bedtime, it indicates a problem in weaning. Certain bedtime rituals and sleep disturbances in adults are directly related to this problem. Sleep disturbance was a prominent symptom in two adult fetishists whom I analyzed.

The history of a boy who developed silk stocking fetishism at the age of one and a half convincingly demonstrates the role of his mother in the genesis of this fetish. She dated this attachment to his eighteenth month, when she used to lie down with him on the bed while he drank his bottle. He liked to stroke her legs while taking the bottle and would fall asleep doing so. She decided to absent herself and instead to offer him a silk stocking along with his bottle. Thereafter, Harry always carried the silk stocking with him. She had difficulty taking it away from him to wash it when it became smelly and dirty. When he grew bigger she became more and more embarrassed by his habit and decided, in order to make it less obvious to others, to cut the stocking into strips and offer him one. Harry is now six and a half and always carries a strip of silk stocking in his pocket to school and takes it to bed with him. Watching television, he fingers the strip and sometimes puts it into his pajama leg and rhythmically rubs his scrotal region. This makes his mother feel particularly uncomfortable. The case speaks for itself, showing clearly that the fetish has advantages for her as well as for the child. He can do with the fetish what he cannot do in reality with his mother. Harry can keep the fetish with him the whole night and at all times and thus undo separation from mother. The fetish sets the mother free and, as she says, it gives her a feeling of relief to know that the child has the fetish. It is as if she, through the fetish, were still with the child, and he dependent upon her as the instinctually gratifying object.

I agree with Wulff that childhood fetishism resembles fetishism in adults. The child's fetish is but a stage in a process that may or may not lead to adult fetishism. Some adult fetishism is a continuation of fetishistic behavior from childhood, sometimes with the same or very similar fetish, sometimes with a succession of fetishes. There may even be a long period of latency with sudden revival of the fetishistic tendency in certain situations with what may appear to be a new fetish.

This continuation of a fetish from childhood is exemplified by a thirty-two-year-old married woman who sought treatment because of depression, insomnia, and frigidity. Analysis disclosed that she alternated between two fetishes according to the intensity of her anxiety. One fetish was a little pillow which was found to be the direct continuation of a childhood fetish. As a young child she had suffered from severely disturbed sleep and for that reason often slept with her mother. She remembered sometimes actually holding her mother's breasts. Her mother, who slept on European-style bedding, would put the child close to her on a little pillow (*caprice*) on which the child would fall asleep. Her mother later gave her this pillow, which the patient always used and had remade several times. She was still using it at the time of her analysis and would often find herself with this pillow under her arm or under her face. When she was particularly depressed and sleepless, she would have to get out of bed and put on her mother's robe, which she kept in her possession.

In this brief account of the case, mention can be made only of the intense unconscious homosexual tie to her mother and her identification of her own body, particularly her head, with a phallus. She could not bring herself to wear a girdle at certain times, and she had never been able to wear hats. The pillow originally was a substitute for the mother's breast, but it also represented the mother's body and genitals. The patient's head represented a penis. She came close to transvestite behavior. Wrapped in her mother's robe, she was also enacting the primal scene in which she represented both parents (Chapter 14).

The inanimate fetish may be given up in some cases without resolving the fetishistic fixation, with the result that the person treats other people as if they were fetishes; he establishes fetishistic object relationships with them. The analyses of two adolescent girls illustrate the particular qualities of fetishistic object relationships.

A sixteen-year-old girl still kept her stuffed animals with her in bed as she used to have them in her crib. Her favorite animal was similar to one she remembered from very early childhood. Both had been given to her by her mother. At five, because of recurrent severe upper respiratory infection, she was sent with an elderly woman to live in the country. She took her stuffed kitten with her. She remained there for three years, during which time her parents visited her on weekends and spent the summers with her. She felt lonely and unhappy, and she developed a dominant fantasy which she called her "pump house" fantasy. There was a little pump house near the place where she lived. In this fantasy she and her stuffed kitten lived in a round pipe without windows and just big enough for her to fit in it with her little kitten on her lap. She found the idea of having been born from her mother's womb repulsive. She would take refuge in her stuffed kitten whenever she was unhappy or disappointed. It was only after many years of psychoanalysis that she was capable of actually loving live kittens and even then when in a rage would feel like smashing them. She had had recurrent nightmares since childhood of people being tortured and mutilated in the most sadistic fashion. Of particular interest was the quality of her object relationships as it began to unfold in analysis. She treated people as fetishes, exactly as she had treated her stuffed animals. She had an inordinate need for physical closeness and cuddling. A certain color and texture of the skin was extremely important to her. She had an intense need to possess and to control one person at all times and at all costs. If she suffered only the slightest disappointment by this person, she would go into deep depression with self-destructive acting out.

The other adolescent, also sixteen when she began analysis, had been a hair and fur fetishist from the age of three. She would pull her hair and eat it. She liked to pluck the hair of furs, and for this reason was feared by her mother's friends. At nine she suddenly stopped her hair-pulling and became extremely concerned with the appearance of her own hair. Analysis revealed that the sudden stopping of the hair pulling had followed her mother's hysterectomy, which had particular significance for my patient. Thenceforth, her primary concern was that every hair should stay in place, and she had her hair set weekly. In camp she avoided swimming and outdoor activities for the sake of her hair, and she always wore a little hat outdoors. She had never had any girlfriends and was very close to her mother. She was pretty and always exquisitely dressed. She dated older boys although she felt extremely uncomfortable and anxious when on a date. She was interested only in their genitals and had a compulsion to look at their flies. They were not "people" to her, and she used them for only one purpose: to stimulate her sexually. After going out with a boy, she would catalogue him by name with a brief description and the date. She always took something (a corsage, a napkin, a book of matches) from each boy to put into her file. It had to be something concrete, like the hair, which analysis had shown represented her mother's pubic hair and hidden penis, the baby, her father's penis, and her little brother's penis. Her brother was born when she was three years old; it was then that she started to pluck her hair.

Another patient, a forty-year-old woman with severe depression, had in play cut off her hair almost completely following the birth of her brother when she was three and a half years old. Later, after he was burned to death in an automobile accident, she began a fetishistic practice of plucking out her pubic hair, burning it with a match, smelling it, and then having an orgasm.

The parents of both adolescent girls, particularly those of the second, were seductive and exhibitionistic. Even when she was in analysis, her parents still walked around at home almost nude. She frequently slept with her parents. When she did not feel well, her father would lie down with her on her bed clad only in shorts. She had been allowed the closest contact with her parents' bodies, but her mother had actively interfered with her masturbation. The mother had also kept her from making friends by depreciating other girls. The patient was dressed like a doll and was treated like one: her feelings were not considered. She was used by her parents as a fetish for the gratification of their own needs, and she, in turn, was using other people as fetishes, having a relationship only with parts of the body, not with the whole person.

This brings up the question of fetishistic use of parts of one's own body. Although the hair, like the nails, is replaceable, thus satisfying a main requirement of the fetish, I hesitate to consider hair-pulling a true fetishistic activity. In this patient the dynamics were not quite the same as in true fetishism; her sexual and aggressive-destructive impulses had not been deflected from her parents but she had denied the existence of such impulses. The internalized parental images were not benevolent as they appeared in reality but were frustrating and destructive. Aggression was turned against the self in pulling and eating her own hair, among other symptoms. She also had anorexia, and she came for treatment because of pernicious vomiting.

Buxbaum (1960) describes the treatment of two girls who pulled out their hair. The parents, particularly the mothers, seem to resemble the ones described by me: exhibitionistic, seductive, narcissistic, and frustrating to the child. It is interesting that Winnicott's concepts seem to have influenced Buxbaum's thinking. She gave gifts to these children (dolls, a stuffed animal, an amulet) with the intention of deflecting their impulses from themselves to these articles. Just as Winnicott considers the transitional object a step toward development of true object relationship, Buxbaum seems to attribute the improvement in behavior of these children to the introduction of "transitional objects" in the form of these gifts. I am sure she will agree that the change in their object relationships was responsible for the change in their behavior, including their attitudes toward the gifts. The change, therefore, resulted from their relation with her as the genuinely interested and understanding therapist. Because of this and also because of the concomitant changes in the attitudes and feelings of their mothers—one mother was in treatment at the same time—these children were able to give up their previous behavior.

What I wish to emphasize here is that it is not the relation with an inanimate object, whether this object is called fetish or, as Winnicott prefers, transitional object, that promotes growth in object relationship. On the contrary, this morbid attachment to an inanimate object is an indication of an arrest in the development of object relationship and fixation to part-object relationship. It is the quality of the relation with his mother that determines how a child treats his objects, animate or inanimate, and whether he needs to cling to an inanimate object, whatever name be given to it. Buxbaum was aware that she was offering these gifts to the children as a substitute for herself. The attitude toward the gift is determined by the relation to the giver and to the true intentions of the giver, which children perceive clearly. This is also reflected in the behavior of children who incessantly ask for gifts only to discard them and never be satisfied; yet a strip of stocking will be treasured, clung to, preferred to any toy, even to the mother herself. Buxbaum and, I presume, also the children's mothers, wanted them to stop this behavior, not merely to displace it onto inanimate objects. These children certainly had toys and inanimate objects which they used destructively before they received therapy, but this had not prevented them from pulling their hair.

In hair-pulling, as in fetishistic use of a part or parts of the body, there has already been a displacement from the parts of the body forbidden by mother—the genital and anal areas—to another part of the body rather than to an external inanimate object. The psychodynamics in these cases are more closely related to those in psychotic depressions and psychosomatic disorders.

The need for omnipotent control exercised through the fetish, often shown only in such actions as carrying an amulet or a "magic" pill, serves to counteract the fear of loss of the part-object, needed not only for instinctual gratification (pleasure) but as a matter of life and death. This explains the panic reactions in childhood fetishism and the acting out of adult fetishists, which can be very destructive (Bak, 1953; Kronengold and Sterba, 1936).

When a mother, as I have shown above, directs her child to a fetish, the child's relation with the mother is split into two: a relation with the real mother and one with the fetish-mother. According to Freud (1938), the split in the ego serves to deny castration anxiety. The childhood fetish and the split in the object relations serve to deny the loss of the preoedipal mother; this denial is a defense against loss of the fantasy of omnipotent control, which at this phase of primary narcissism constitutes a threat to life. The fetish clearly serves as a substitute for the preoedipally gratifying mother and shows that a specific fixation in object relations has taken place. This fixation will affect the progressive development of object relations and may lead to the establishment of what I have described as fetishistic object relations. In such a relation, not the person as such but only a part of the body, or only a certain quality of that part, or only a certain gesture or bodily posture, are the compelling features of the object (Epstein, 1960; Grant, 1953; Hunter, 1954; Weissman, 1957).

Let us return to the problem of how a fetish differs from other favorite articles treasured by children. At certain phases in their development, children may form an attachment to some inanimate object which is introduced by the mother for the purpose of gratifying certain specific needs of the child. Pacifiers or soft stuffed animals are given with the correct expectation that the child will be able to give them up more easily than autoerotic gratifications. Adequate gratification of instinctual needs, by facilitating progress to subsequent phases of development and growth in object relations, enables the child to relinquish the gratifications of the earlier phases. Children at certain stages of their development often show strong preference for a special toy, but, although they may urgently need this toy at times, the need is not so compulsive nor persistent, nor the panic so overwhelming when it is unavailable or lost, as in the case of the fetishistic child. The child may become angry, tearful, and unhappy for some time, but this reaction is different from that of the child who loses a fetish. In psychotic children we sometimes find a clinging to inanimate objects in preference to the mother. But the attitude of the psychotic child toward this object is also different from that of the fetishist. Whereas the fetish is a very specific and highly cathected object, there seems to be little libidinal cathexis to the inanimate object for the psychotic child. Such clinging to a specific inanimate object by a psychotic child should make us suspect that it may be a fetish and that there may be transitions between fetishistic and psychotic behavior. (In the child who has an imaginary companion, the object is usually not a real one; when it is, it is not only libidinized but also endowed with a personality.)

Study of early fetish formation can contribute to our understanding of the role of object relationship in the vicissitudes of instinctual development of the child, particularly in his choice of defenses against separation anxiety. Separation anxiety is especially marked in phases in which real or threatened separation from mother or from part of her occurs: during weaning (when the child loses close contact with mother's body); at the height of the anal phase (when motility and ambivalence are developing and there is conflict over clinging to or letting go of feces, equivalent to mother); and at the oedipal phase (when mother is renounced as the sexually gratifying object). The ego of the young child, supported and directed by the auxiliary ego of his mother, adopts specific mechanisms for dealing with these anxieties. It is no coincidence that the phases in which the fetish is formed are these three traumatic stages in the life of the child. I have pointed to the close association of early sleep disturbance and fetishistic behavior in children. At night, when regressive tendencies are stronger and actual separation from the object takes place, need for the fetish and fetishistic activity increases. Both express separation anxiety and disturbed object relationship, and both are prevalent during these phases (Chapter 4).

Freud's concept of the fetish as representing the illusory penis of the mother does not seem to apply fully to childhood fetishism (1927). Although these children at an early age have had ample opportunity to see the genitalia of their parents, it seems that separation anxiety due to loss of the preoedipally gratifying mother is of greater importance than castration anxiety. The childhood fetish represents a pathological defense against separation from mother on the preoedipal (oral and anal) levels. The adult fetishist uses a fixed and more or less elaborate disguise—his fetishistic act—(Abraham, 1910; Friedjung, 1927; Grant, 1953; Kronengold and Sterba, 1936) to obtain at least partial gratification of the original wish; the child, like the adult, by gratifying his wish for possessing mother, represented by the fetish, manages to allay separation anxiety. The child's fetish and the fetish of the adult appear to be different stages of the same process, which may or may not lead to adult fetishism.*

* In this connection a paper by Dickes (1962) is of interest. In the treatment of adult patients with fetishistic behavior, he found that the precursors of the fetish go back to childhood. He also was impressed with the role of the parents in fetish formation.

# PART 6

# ENURESIS

# 16

# Notes on the Treatment of Enuresis

## The Treatment of Enuretics and of Patients with Character Disorders

Classical analysis in enuretics is usually a lengthy procedure. Enuretic children tend to react to the analytic procedure similarly to the way they reacted to the laissez-faire attitude of the parents, which these children correctly interpreted as a tacit permission for the enuresis. In the analysis, passivity on the part of the analyst is interpreted as a permission for the continuation of the enuresis. These children perceive keenly whether the parents really expect them to be able to control the wetting. They cannot be misled, either by the exaggerated concern about the enuresis which some parents show, nor by tactics such as rewards or punishment or by waking the child during the night. Mrs. A. could not tell her son not to wet since she herself had been an enuretic until adolescence, and did not think that he could stop it. Similarly, Mrs. B. told her twelve-year-old son not to worry

315

about his enuresis, that it would go away eventually. She was thus presenting the enuresis as something he could not actively control himself. She, too, had been a bed-wetter until late adolescence.

In the treatment of enuretics the emphasis is on the reconstruction of the superego, as in the treatment of character disorders. The ego of these patients is quite strong, inventive and persistent when it comes to the pursuit of gratification. It is the specific structure of the superego, which not only condones but in fact encourages such behavior, which has to be dealt with. One day after her session a patient of mine whose daughter was enuretic asked her child to leave open the door to her bedroom where she was playing with a little boy. This was unusual because her mother had always let them play behind closed doors, although she knew what games they were playing. This little girl, a persistently enuretic, aggressive child who seduced other children into playing sexual games, said to her mother later that day, "Today you were a good mommy."

As long as the enuresis continues unabated the sexual and aggressive impulses find discharge in this way and do not come into the analysis. The infantile sexual (perverse) urges are gratified and the sexual problems and conflicts are not fully exposed and are dealt with by the patient on a regressed (urinary) level. The transference nature of this behavior has to be analyzed and the patient has to be motivated to stop the enuresis at least temporarily. The technical procedures outlined here are based on the therapeutic experience with a large group of enuretic children and adolescents. A total of 104 cases was treated, 26 of these in analysis.

The feature common to all enuretics and impulse-ridden characters is their low tolerance for instinctual tension and the urge for immediate discharge of this tension in reality. Enuresis is not a disease; it is symptomatic behavior indicative of an underlying disturbance in personality and character according to J. Michaels (1955). The personality disturbances may show great variety and range from neurosis to character disorder, perversion, psychopathy and, in some cases, even psychosis. The genetic similarity between enuretics and impulse-ridden character disorders can be studied and understood more fully in long-term psychoanalytic treatment. Renunciation of direct, instinctual gratification is an important factor in making such a patient amenable to analysis. It was my experience that the persistence of the enuresis was an impediment to the therapeutic work. Headway in the analysis was made during the period when the enuresis was given up, even if only temporarily. These dry periods were associated with sleep disturbance, dream activity, and states of anxiety from undischarged aggressive and sexual impulses, which carried over also into the daytime. This made the patients more accessible to analysis than they had been during the state when direct instinctual gratification had been achieved through the persistent enuresis.

It is of interest to note how well even young children can rationalize enuresis. One episode from the simultaneous treatment of a five-year-old, persistently enuretic and severely disturbed boy and of his mother may serve as an illustration. When we discussed Paul's responsibility for controlling his impulses and stopping the wetting, he replied, "People sometimes do these things because they are unhappy. They do it to make themselves feel happier." When I explained to him that this was not really a good way, because he was only more unhappy afterward, he gave me an explanation of why he behaved that way, "My parents let me get away with too much. That was not good. Others punished me too much and that was not good. They should have stopped me when I was little." When I explained to him that these were rationalizations, and that in order to show up his parents he was making himself miserable, he replied "You know, I still have another reason. They want me to be different in one second," thus showing that he was well aware of the confusing ambivalent attitudes of his parents. I explained to him further that I had not rushed him; in fact, I had prevented his parents and Miss F., the principal, from doing so, until he himself would understand why he was behaving this way. To this he said "I know, I haven't made much effort." He wanted to be reassured by me, because actually he had made some effort, but not enough.

## Innervation of Bladder and Physiology of Micturition

Some knowledge of the innervation of the bladder and of the physiology of micturition will be helpful in understanding the close connection between sexual and urinary functions. It will also provide further evidence that the deep sleep and the weak bladder of the enuretic are but a myth perpetuated by the child, the parents, and the pediatrician. The bladder is innervated both by the autonomic nervous system and the cerebrospinal nerve center. The sympaticus takes care of the retention of urine by closing the inner sphincter and relaxing the bladder. The parasympatheticus takes care of the discharge of urine by opening the sphincter and contracting the bladder wall. The parasympatheticus, also called nervus erigens, serves the expulsion of urine and the transmission of certain sexual impulses. Contraction of the bladder wall and of the penis and clitoris are synchronous processes. This innervation explains why sexual impulses can be translated and perceived as urinary urge and vice versa. This is especially true for infantile sexuality that confines its expression to enuresis. It is a common observation that young boys, at the time when they are starting to ejaculate, show some confusion as to whether this is urination or ejaculation. There is a confusion between semen and urine.

The cerebrospinal nerve complex supplies innervation of the bladder and urethra and the external sphincter. The external sphincter controls voluntary micturition. This is how the voluntary regulation of urine retention or urine discharge takes place. The external sphincter which regulates the passage of urine is under the direction of the cerebrospinal nervous system. That means that it can and is regulated consciously and by will. If there is interference with the parasympathetic innervation, then ischuria, that is, an inability to urinate, occurs. If the sympathetic innervation is interfered with, urinary incontinence is the result.

## The Connection Between Sleep and Urination and the Myth of the Weak Bladder and Deep Sleep

During sleep the pupils are contracted. They dilate during awakening. If a child is picked up from sleep and the diaper is removed while the child is opening his eyes, urination occurs at the same time that the sleep-contracted pupils dilate. Observations of patients treated with sleep therapy extending over eight to ten days suffer from retention rather than involuntary wetting. With unconscious patients, the danger is urine retention. Characteristic for deep sleep are narrow pupils and increased tonus. It is a known fact that the bladder, even in a young child, can distend to hold up to double the amount of urine before the tension of the bladder walls leads to relaxation of the external sphincter and urine is passed. On the other hand it is known that emotional factors such as excitement and anxiety, as well as local irritations, can cause frequent and urgent urination in an almost empty bladder.

Urine production and discharge of urine are decreased during sleep. Production is reduced to a third and characteristic for night urine is a high concentration. Yet we find that enuretic children seem to have at their disposal almost unlimited quantities of urine. Exasperated parents who pick up the enuretic children, often several times a night, and are unable to achieve a dry bed are a proof of this. The child being put on the toilet during the night actually seems to preserve the bulk of his urine for the bed. In many of these cases the motive is resentment at the intentional disturbance of the sleep, and the enuresis in these cases is a punishment meted out to the parents, "revenge wetting."

The pediatrician Hamburger reported an episode in which he gave a fourteen-year-old enuretic boy an indifferent injection with the suggestion that now he might not be able to urinate. This boy had to be catheterized the next day. The deep sleep of the enuretic child is a defensive phenomenon. The same child who interrupts his sleep in order to wet the bed (crumpled pillows and sheets are one indication of this) will be deaf and insensitive to the attempts of the person who wants to waken him for the purpose of going to the bathroom to urinate. Often big children are carried by the parents to the toilet because "they are so sleepy that they cannot walk by themselves." Some children when awakened do not go to the toilet, but urinate in other places in defiance against being forced to urinate in a designated place. This is an expression of their rebellious attitude. The perpetuation of the myth of the deep sleep and the weak bladder is a convenient rationalization for both the parents and the child.

Children know that they are awake when urinating in bed and will tell the therapist about it when they have a positive relationship. They also enjoy the sensations of the warm urine and as one little girl put it, "it becomes unpleasant only when the urine cools off." They also know pretty well when they are going to wet.

Seven-year-old Richard told his mother that he was awake when he wet. He said that he woke up early in the morning but did not go to the toilet. Her neighbor's boy also wet, but got up at night and made his bed over completely. A colleague reports the following observations: his neighbor told him about her three enuretic boys, nine and a half, seven, and five years old. The nine-year-old boy slept with the mother. The other night he got up in the middle of the night, put a rubber sheet under the sheet, and then wet the bed.

As far as the weak bladder is concerned, we would expect enuresis to be more prevalent in girls, because they have the anatomically weaker bladder. However, this is not the case: the ratio between boys and girls is at least two to one. The dynamic factors which explain this are intense castration anxiety and unconscious feminine identifications in boys.

## The Myth of Heredity

Heredity as a predisposing factor in the etiology of enuresis is favored by both the medical profession and the parents. The term "familial" enuresis and the concept of the "irritable" bladder reflect this belief of inherited tendencies in enuresis. It is true that enuresis is more frequent in certain families, just as certain anal symptoms, for instance, soiling, diarrhea, or constipation, are seen more frequently in "anal" families. Yet what would seem to be an inherited constitution is found in analytic study to be the transmission of an attitude from the parents to the child rather than an organic inferiority. The significance of parental attitudes as decisive factors in shaping the personality of the child during the formative stages of its development is known from psychoanalytic child psychology. In my work with disturbed children and their parents the role of unconscious parental attitudes in character and symptom formation in children was clearly established. I should like to describe some of the most common types of attitudes encountered in the parents of enuretic children.

There are the parents who need to justify and rationalize their own childhood enuresis. In such families enuresis is accepted readily with the explanation, "The parent wet, the grandparent wet, the sister or brother wet and they got over it, so the child will get over it too in due time." That this feeling is perceived by the child and taken as license for wetting is well illustrated by the following.

A nine-year-old enuretic boy, who had made very good progress in his treatment, would relapse into bed-wetting at certain times. It was found that his episodes of bed-wetting coincided with his father's visits at home. (His father was in the Merchant Marine and came home periodically and for limited stay.) The father had not been in favor of his son's treatment (he had other problems in addition to the enuresis) because he felt that he, himself, had been enuretic until late adolescence and had overcome it without help. The trouble in such families starts when the child does not stop in due time, but continues to wet into adolescence. Especially with girls, where the onset of menstruation is expected to "break" the enuresis, mothers become greatly concerned when the enuresis persists.

Then there are the parents who have overcompensated for

their own "weaknesses" and now must see to it that their offspring develop "perfectly." In one case, that of a four-year-old girl, the father had been a bed-wetter and had exhibited other signs of inadequate instinctual control. He later on had completely denied this period of his life and had developed overcompensatory reaction formations. He had displaced his feelings of inadequacy onto his sister whom he considered as a person with "lack of control" and a "misfit." When his daughter was born, he feared that she might develop to be like his sister, and he set out from the start to prevent this. For bladder training, which started when she was one year old, he advised that his wife pick up the child and put her on the toilet hourly day and night, yet to no avail. His daughter was not only a bed-wetter, but she also wet during the day. At the age of four, whenever she would wet herself during the day, she would hit her mother and blame her for her mishap. At first glance this would seem unreasonable behavior, but from the standpoint of the child it proved to be very logical. Her sphincter conscience was still represented by the mother. She felt that it was her mother's job to know when she needed to urinate since the mother had always been in charge of the child's urinary functions.

Another type of parent is one who uses the child vicariously for the gratification of the parent's own unsatisfied, repressed infantile needs. These are usually mothers (but also fathers) who themselves had been trained very early and who had never been given a chance to live out their urethral impulses in infancy and early childhood. Their rationalization is that they do not want to deprive the child of the gratifications that they had been deprived of themselves. Because of the unconscious identification with the child in this area, there is an inability to consider the personality and actual needs of the child, and because of their resentment of their own mothers, they are ambivalent toward their child. This may lead to grotesque occurrences as the following: one boy discovered at the age of five, when he was in the country and for the first time lived in close contact with children of his age, that children do not wet their beds at night. His mother had never told him that. Another patient, who suffered from a severe obsessional compulsive neurosis had been trained for both bladder and bowel control very early and rigidly by her compulsive mother. When she started analysis with me her son was three and her daughter two years old. Both were incontinent and wet and soiled themselves during the day and night. She did not take them to the toilet mornings, and their wet and soiled cribs were accepted by her with a pleasure that could hardly escape her children. She made feeble attempts to sit them on the toilet together after their meals. They would sit there for a while, then return to their room and, with much jiggling and apparent pleasure, urinate and defecate in their cribs or on the floor. She claimed that her son insisted on urinating sitting down. She could not see why boys should urinate standing up. She felt that girls were more advanced and that her son should urinate the way his sister did. It took considerable time and analytic work to help her understand and curb the acting out of her pathological needs through her children. It was slow and arduous work with the mother but extremely beneficial for the children. Psychoanalytic treatment of the severely neurotic mother with emphasis on her relationship with her child is, in my opinion, the only way in which serious psychopathology in young children can be reversed and further pathological development prevented. Treatment of the child in such a case is ineffective unless the attitude of the mother can be modified.

In some cases, the child may represent to the parent (usually the mother) a sibling with whom she has not resolved an unconscious sibling rivalry. In such a case of unresolved unconscious conflict, toilet training is usually conducted in a very inconsistent manner. The conscious efforts of the parent at toilet training are defeated by the unconscious need that this child (the sibling rival) not acquire sphincter control. Such parents show great surprise when the enuretic child gives up the enuresis in therapy. It is as if they had not expected the child to be able to do so. A nine-year-old boy, who had been a persistent enuretic from infancy and whose mother remarked to him after a series of dry nights, "Now I know that you can keep dry," replied (correctly), "So you didn't think so before." Another six-year-old boy, also a persistent enuretic, said to his mother, who appeared to be pleased that he had had a series of dry nights, "I didn't know you wanted me to be dry." In another case, that of a ten-year-old girl who had been a persistent enuretic until the age of nine-and-a-half years, and who, upon her request, was going to camp for the first time, the following conversation took place: The mother was filling out the questionnaire of the camp and when she came to the question, "Is your child enuretic?"— "Does she need a rubber sheet?" asked her daughter what she should do about this question. The daughter replied that she had no intention of wetting in camp, that she did not need rubber sheets and that she did not think that her mother should make reference to her enuresis. The mother obliged but felt uneasy. When she visited her daughter in camp she was surprised and disappointed (she realized this herself) that the child had stayed dry. The mother knew that that meant that her daughter had decided to grow up and no longer needed the enuresis tying her to her mother.

# 17

# Dynamic Considerations and Treatment of Enuresis

Enuresis is a rather frequent medical problem for which pediatricians are called upon to give help and for which a variety of panaceas has been offered. Enuresis, as it will be discussed here, is referred to as idiopathic enuresis in textbooks of urology, and, according to the specialists, comprises 95 percent of all cases of enuresis (Campbell, 1951; Mindner, 1946). That is to say, in 95 percent of all enuretic children, medical experts, using all types of examinations, cannot detect any organic cause for the enuresis. Regarding the etiology, dynamics, and treatment, as well as the personality structure of the enuretic child, there is both confusion and controversy. This chapter will attempt to contribute to the clarification of these issues from the point of view of child psychiatrists and dynamically oriented pediatricians.

It will be helpful to define the use of the term enuresis as applying to a condition in which a child continues to wet himself consistently, either during the day (enuresis diurna), or at night (enuresis nocturna), or both, after he has passed the age when toilet training should be completed, that is, after the age of two and a half to three years. The relapse into consistent wetting, in a child of three years of age who had already achieved bladder control, would also come under the heading of enuresis. We would not consider as enuresis any case where the involuntary passing of urine occurs for accountable reasons, such as in epilepsy or in states of unconsciousness, inflammations of the bladder, local obstacles or irritations, malformations, etc.

It is essential in any discussion of enuresis to recognize that the voluntary control of micturition is a custom sanctioned by society and not an organic necessity. Toilet training is one of the child's first steps in learning to control bodily functions and toward the formation of a conscience. We know, from dynamic child psychology, that the formation of a conscience is based on the acceptance and internalization of parental wishes, as well as on the parents' prohibitions and interdictions. Ferenczi (1916) spoke of a "sphincter morale" as the forerunner of the conscience or prestage of the superego. In any case of enuresis, therefore, we must question what has gone wrong with the training and emotional development of the child at the time when instinctual control is learned, rather than what is organically wrong.

We find that the mentally superior child, as well as the mentally retarded child, is affected; the child who comes from a wealthy and cultured home, as well as the one from a poor and neglected environment. In fact, the following are excluded from consideration in this discussion:

1.  The group of mentally retarded children, who, because of their poorer equipment, will show retardation in most phases of their functioning. It is of interest and significance to learn from statistics that, even in mentally retarded children, enuresis is not more frequent than in other cases and is dependent upon the attitudes of the environment (Christoffel, 1944).

2.  Children who have not had the benefit of adequate training because they lost their mothers at an early age and were either institutionalized or changed foster homes frequently (it is known statistically that enuresis is a condition prevalent in orphanages, institutions or foster homes). It is also known, from statistics and reports of physicians and people in charge of insti-

tutions, that the incidence of enuresis on the enuretic wards depends upon the personality of the person in charge (Christoffel, 1944). It has been found that enuresis can disappear very quickly on an enuretic ward when a motherly nurse is in charge of it. The report from a Swiss orphanage, that the enuretic children would have a dry night on Sundays when tea was served to them in the evening, seems particularly interesting because it demonstrates clearly the ineffectiveness of fluid restriction (Christoffel, 1944). Also excluded are children of psychotic or psychopathic parents who obviously neglected to train their children, because they themselves did not accept the social or cultural restrictions of our society.

3. Those children with obvious anatomical malformations directly responsible for enuresis. The number of these children is negligible.

The group dealt with in this chapter is the major group with whom physicians have most frequent contact, namely, children of average and above-average intelligence who come from families where there is sufficient social awareness to institute bladder training.

To investigate enuresis from the medical standpoint is of little value. It becomes apparent that conclusions are based on the results of empirical methods and the etiology is really not known. With some of these methods there may be a symptomatic cure—the enuresis may cease, but the personality which produced it has not been treated. Disturbances in later life, particularly those of a psychosexual nature, in some individuals can often be traced back to enuresis in childhood. Certain types of sexual impotence, particularly premature ejaculation in men, and also certain types of frigidity in women, have been found to be directly related to the earlier enuresis in such individuals (Abraham, 1917; M. Sperling, 1950b). The connection between the psychosexual disturbance in later life and the earlier enuresis remains unrecognized by the patient himself, as well as by the untrained physician. It can be brought out only in psychoanalytically oriented treatment. That enuresis as a symptom is known to disappear in the majority of cases some time near puberty contributes to the fact that it is left largely untreated.

It is statistically known that the incidence of enuresis is much (two to one) higher among boys than among girls (Christoffel, 1944). In the medical literature this is noted as a fact, but no explanation is given. Despert (1944) explains the predominance of enuresis in boys as brought about by the confusion in the training period when the boy, unlike the girl, has to learn the sitting and the standing position for urination and defecation. In cases of mothers with unresolved conflicts concerning the sexual differences, this leads sometimes to grotesque training procedures with their male children and consequent enuresis of these boys. From the anatomical standpoint, we would expect the reverse to be true, that is, a higher incidence of enuresis among girls, since the proverbial weak bladder is anatomically present in girls. There are fewer muscle fibers, especially at the sphincter urethra, in the female.

It has been maintained, since time immemorial, that bedwetting occurs in deep sleep when control is relaxed. Parents, therefore, rely on the device of awakening the child so that it may urinate in the toilet. Physicians and parents know the poor results of this method. Children who are awakened in the night and taken to the toilet urinate only partially, finishing soon after in bed. It is known to observant pediatricians, nurses, and mothers that infants urinate, not in deep sleep, but on awakening (Christoffel, 1944). Bed-wetting is an activity carried out by the child in a state of partial awakening. The myth of deep sleep is perpetuated by the environment of the child, thereby transmitting from parent to child the concept that, since wetting occurs during deep sleep, control cannot be exercised. Were this so, how could suggestion of any sort be expected to work if the state of deep sleep precludes the possibility of control? It is interesting that many children can tell the night before whether they will be dry. The child himself is aware that wetting is somehow tied up with his feelings, and that not to wet means to forego the satisfaction of the impulse to wet.

Children frequently interpret being awakened as a punishment and resent it as an intentional disturbance of their sleep by their parents. In such cases, continued wetting is, to a great extent, a punishment meted out to the parents. One comes upon the paradox that advising the mother not to disturb the child at night, not to pick it up, will often yield positive results. Exhibitionistic needs of the child, especially when intensified by undue attention to his urinary functions by his parents, find gratification (negatively in a symptom) in the enuresis and are often a dynamic factor in its persistence. Some children want to be picked up by their mothers because it satisfies the child's need to be handled like an infant, and, at the same time, it frees the child from the responsibility of exercising control. By picking the child up, the parents transmit to the child their feeling that they do not think that the child could stay dry during the night. In working with such cases, it is necessary, before advising the mother to stop picking up the child, to guide her so that she can stop infantilizing the child and, instead, can encourage his natural desire to grow up and give up his needs for dependency, as indicated by the wish to be picked up.

Heredity as a predisposing factor in the establishment of enuresis is indicated by the term "familial enuresis" in cases with a family history (Bakwin, 1949). Physicians and parents accept enuresis, to a great extent, as an inherited tendency. In this way, the child is provided with a rationalization for the enuresis, thereby exempting him from the necessity for control, that is, his own responsibility in the matter. While it is true that enuresis is more in evidence in certain families, it is not the enuresis which is inherited. What would seem to be "heredity" is, in reality, the adoption of the tendency to forego the control of urinary impulses. It is the transmission of an attitude from parents to child, rather than an organic inferiority (Chapter 24). In some cases, enuresis may be a reaction to the overemphasis on this particular function and to bladder training, which has been initiated too early and exercised too rigidly by the parents.

How is bladder control achieved? We find that the normal infant regards its urine as something quite precious. This is true of all his excretions; he looks upon them as his first productions and possessions (Freud, 1905). It is a matter of common experience for mothers and nurses that, when the child is passed from person to person to be held, he is apt to wet the person he loves, as if he were giving a gift. The child gives freely to the mother of his most valuable possession. The good mother instinctively makes use of this mechanism, this giving for love, in the normal training procedure, thereby getting the child to give up its excretions at regular intervals in places designated for it. In this early stage, the relationship between mother and child deeply affects the child's ability to make the first rudimentary attempts at voluntary control. The mother who has regarded her child's excretions as love gifts is in a position to ask for control from her child (Winnicott, 1936). In this case, in order to please his mother, the child will forego the pleasure of wetting.

A change of nurse, illness of the mother, or birth of another sibling may bring on a relapse to wetting in a child who already had achieved control. This is to be understood as a reaction to disappointment in the mother or nurse and identification with the baby sibling. Where, basically, the relationship between the child and mother has been satisfactory before the arrival of the new sibling and the mother has not profoundly changed her feelings toward the child because she, e.g., prefers the new baby because of its sex, if bed-wetting occurs, it will be only a transitory symptom. In those cases where bed-wetting in reaction to the arrival of a sibling becomes a permanent symptom, it has to be taken as an indication of a disturbed mother-child relationship, even if other manifestations of this are missing.

The child, however adequate, should not be asked for control too early, because he must be given opportunities to live out his urethral impulses—the pleasure he derives from letting go of the urine when he feels the urge. In addition, psychoanalysis has taught us to understand the autoerotic pleasures derived from sensations of the skin—the warm, wet, ticklish irritations. In working with the younger child of two or three years, we can appreciate the importance of these skin pleasures, which are not only permissible, but seem to be essential to the child's well-being (Freud, 1905). Often, when an adult, concerned about the child's discomfort of being wet, questions him about it, the child (to the adult's surprise) is likely to say, "But I like the feeling of being wet." The fact that children rationalize their bed-wetting, often, by saying it happened because they felt cold, would seem to support the belief of those (and unfortunately there are still many in the medical profession) who see in micturition a mere reflex and do not comprehend the role of the instincts and emotions in all human functions, whether this be breathing, eating, excreting, or sleeping. Such thinking, or rather lack of thinking, has led to the invention and use of electric and other waking devices for the treatment of enuretic children (Davidson and Douglass, 1950; Mowrer and Mowrer, 1938). What the child means by this coldness is not the actual physical temperature of the room (these children wet on the hottest summer nights and do not wet in the coldest winter, once they have given up their enuresis), but the emotional feeling of being alone—anxious, resentful, and longing for mother, who sleeps with the father and not with the child. The enuresis then primarily serves to discharge such feelings and symbolically gratifies the erotic and hostile needs of the child. The skin sensations accompanying the wetting are, as has been pointed out, important sources for pleasure, and only after having been in the wet bed for some time may the child become uncomfortable and use this as a means for obtaining secondary gains from his wetting by waking and thus disturbing the parents, often with the premium of being taken into their bed and allowed to sleep there. These are sources of pleasure which an older child, who has other sources of satisfaction open to him, can more readily give up. However, when the child has been deprived of this pleasure and rigid emphasis has been placed on early bladder training, the child will achieve cleanliness quite quickly, but later may revert to bed-wetting with great tenacity. In this category belong the cases where the mother claims that her child has been bladder-trained at a very early age—sometimes from six months to a year old—only to revert to wetting at the time when bladder training should start; at the earliest, at the end of the first year. Such early conditioning is mistaken for the actual acquisition of bladder control. But we may speak of control only where the child's own will and conscious awareness of the situation are involved. It is around the end of the first year of life that the conscious will of the child comes into operation and expresses itself unmistakably.

In addition, from the standpoint of the anatomical and physiological development of the nerve centers and pathways, too early bladder training should be avoided. Despert (1944) pointed out that the bladder of an infant in the early months, before the higher cortical centers have been developed and myelinization has taken place, functions as a reflex organ. Training of a child with immature cortical pathways disturbs the function of personality and tends to overorganization and compulsive behavior.

Even with a child of two or three years, the methods of toilet training are full of hazards. Continued bed-wetting may become a very effective way, on the part of the child, of offsetting the mother's control. When he is hostile and angry because of the way in which he is being trained, a child does not give his mother a present of his urine. On the contrary, he spills his urine in spite of her, when and where he wishes, and not when his mother wants it. This also explains more adequately the ineffectiveness of picking the child up at night. The child feels coerced, and thus his desire to establish control over his mother by means of the bladder increases. The enuresis then becomes a reflection of the tensions being acted out between mother and child. It is as if the mother were commanding, "You must give me the urine now," and the child were replying, "I will give it to you when I am good and ready."

Leniency on the part of the parents has no ill effect upon the bladder training, provided this is a consistent attitude and the parents are genuinely interested in the child. Often enough, leniency is only a cover for disinterest, and, more often, particularly when overdone and alternating with attitudes of severity, it is an expression of unconscious hostility on the part of the parents. To this, the young child is very sensitive and invariably reacts with some form of rebellion, which is expressed openly or in symptoms (Chapter 24).

Enuresis is also, in a way, the child's method of exhibiting his genitals. He succeeds in drawing attention to this area of his body, even if negatively in the form of a symptom. We find enuresis most frequently in boys in whom there is an overly strong fear of injury to the genital, or where castration has been unconsciously accepted. Whether or not a real castration threat has been given in these cases is not the essential thing, since a fantasied threat is equally effective. The fear of castration is the reaction to the threat of punishment for masturbation, which has come under taboo. In these cases, the enuresis not only unconsciously serves as a substitute for the forbidden masturbation, but, like every neurotic symptom, it is composed of both the gratification of the forbidden impulse and the punishment for it. The unconscious meaning, to the boy, is that the genital organ has been injured, as if to say, "My penis is no good any more, it leaks." With this in mind, the higher incidence of enuresis in boys may be more readily comprehended. Enuresis, for this type of boy with a strong castration fear, represents an equivalent of masturbation. In reality, only boys have a legitimate castration fear, since they have a penis, which may be injured or lost altogether.

The psychodynamics of enuresis in girls often reveal the personality structure of a "tomboy," although this may not be apparent to the untrained observer. These girls tend to have sudden outbursts of temper equivalent to the sudden letting go of the bladder. The underlying character trait usually appears to be repressed aggression, which may come out as timidity accompanied by hostile, destructive behavior (Michaels, 1955; M. Sperling, 1950b).

A dominant factor in the establishment and maintenance of enuresis, for both sexes, is the element of sexual overstimulation. The enuretic child is usually sexually precocious; for him bedwetting is a disguised form of sexual activity (masturbation). A carefully detailed psychiatric history will, in almost every case, reveal the element of sexual overstimulation in one form or another. The overstimulation may occur in a concealed way; the parents may be completely unaware that, by their actions, they are perpetuating the very thing they would like to stop. To be more specific, such *helpfulness* as the mother's manual assistance, to a boy of eight or ten years, in urinating, or the physical closeness in picking up the child at night, and taking the child into the parents' bed when the bedclothes are wet, all tend to reinforce the mechanism that has established the enuresis. Often, the sexual overstimulation is much more overt and may even border on seduction. This has been known to happen with maids, relatives, and other people in the child's environment. Since the genital apparatus is still undeveloped, the excitement can express itself only in the urinary tract. Under the impact of guilt from the sexual stimulation and masturbation, the boy, in particular, is impeded in his normal sexual development, and remains fixed in this childish mode of expressing erotic feelings, as though he dared not use his penis for anything but urinating. This may lead to a period of nocturnal emissions and eventually to adult sexual maladjustment in the form of ejaculatio praecox and psychic impotence. When there is a real struggle with sex, an occasional attack of enuresis may occur as a retreat to an earlier form of erotic (urethral) expression. Usually enuresis disappears at puberty, with the assertion of sexual impulses expressed through the sexual organs. Reports from World War II have shown that enuresis was not uncommon among our soldiers, and was recognized as an indication of underlying sexual and emotional immaturity and treated psychiatrically (Levine, 1943–44). In girls, enuresis, continued into adult life, may serve as a rationalization for avoiding marriage. In such cases, the symptom covers up the underlying sexual maladjustment. In the history of frigidity in women, enuresis figures as a predominant childhood symptom.

## Conclusions and Treatment

A survey of the most frequent techniques employed in the treatment of enuresis clearly shows that the majority of physicians has not yet accepted enuresis as a symptom based on psychopathology and indicative of personality disorder, but insists on looking for and treating a nonexisting organic disorder. Enuresis is actually the (mis)use of a normal physiological function for psychological reasons, namely, for the gratification of instinctual needs of a sexual and aggressive nature. For the child and in the unconscious of the adult, urine and micturition have many symbolic meanings, particularly sexual and aggressive ones. These basic facts, known to us from the psychoanalysis of children and adults (Freud, 1905), are essential for an understanding of the dynamics of enuresis and of the enuretic child, and without acceptance of these facts, adequate treatment of enuresis is impossible (Chapters 16 and 24; Despert, 1944; Gerard, 1939; M. Sperling, 1949b, 1950b; Winnicott, 1936).

Another extremely important factor in enuresis, which I have tried to demonstrate, is the quality of the mother-child relationship. Emotional immaturity of the parents and their own difficulties in instinctual control, whether this is manifest or expressed in overcompensatory behavior, will affect the child's ability and willingness to acquire and to exercise such control himself. Enuresis is only one symptom in which this particular difficulty may manifest itself, as fever might be just one symptom of a patient with tuberculosis. The underlying disease in enuresis is a disturbance in personality and character. This disturbance in personality may show great variety. There is no specific personality of the enuretic. Yet there is a common denominator for all enuretics: an inability to tolerate instinctual and emotional tension with an urge for immediate discharge of this tension, and for immediate gratification. The vehicle through which this discharge and gratification are achieved is enuresis.

Frequently associated with enuresis are other manifestations of impulsive behavior: overeating, lying, stealing, pyromania, and delinquency, and those who act out their aggressive behavior more overtly (Healy and Bronner, 1936; Michaels, 1955). Thumb-sucking, nail-biting, stammering, passive, timid, or even withdrawn behavior are characteristic of those enuretics with repression of aggression. Since enuresis, in a dynamic sense, is a mode of discharge of instinctual energies through urination, our aim in treatment is to make available to the child these energies (sexual and aggressive impulses) so that he can use them in a socially acceptable and constructive way for himself in the pursuit of his life activities. The emphasis in treatment, therefore, should not be on waking the child, by whatever device, so that he may urinate into the toilet instead of into the bed. The emphasis has to be on training in instinctual control; that means that the enuretic child has to learn to be aware of and to tolerate his impulses and his feelings, such as loneliness, anxiety, resentment, excitement, sadness, etc., without discharging them immediately through urination, whether it be into the toilet or into the bed. Even a young child of two can sleep through the night without needing to urinate. Getting up at night once or several times in order to urinate is, for children and adults, symptomatic behavior. It is often the remnant of false training for urinary control, and, in many cases, a form of sleep disturbance. Transitory sleep disturbances with anxiety dreams and nightmares are a common phenomenon during the treatment of enuretics (M. Sperling, 1949b). The aim of the treatment is to encourage the child's ability and willingness for instinctual control and for personality growth in general. This, in many cases of enuresis, may be achieved in a relatively short psychotherapy through the relationship with the therapist. In many cases of enuretic children, it will also be necessary to deal with the environment of the child which was instrumental in producing this syndrome and which will continue to affect the child unfavorably unless it is modified. In the management of younger enuretic children, very good therapeutic results may be obtained by dealing with the environment or guiding the mother only (see Chapters 16 and 24). In any case, even where the enuresis is definitely a psychoneurotic symptom and not a sign of the child's total maladjustment, it is necessary to consider the mother-child relationship and to recognize the enuresis as a manifestation of a disturbance in the relationship between mother and child.

Now, a few words about what should not be done in treatment. All forms of diet therapy, such as highly spiced foods or limited liquid intake, are of no value. The beneficial effects, if any, come from the suggestive power of those who prescribe the diet. The same is true for medications. It is not the removal of the symptom of enuresis, whether this is achieved through pure suggestion or through diet or through a pill, that we are aiming for. What we want is to get the child to accept the responsibility for his sphincter control, and not to project this onto something outside, whatever this may be. Of interest in this connection are urological findings. Muellner (1960) found that the bladder control is a self-learned skill and that through the use of the (voluntary) mechanism, the child doubles its bladder capacity by the age of four and a half, as compared to what it was at the age of two. The enlarged bladder capacity insures night control of the urine. The removal of the symptom of enuresis, without providing other outlets for the child, leads to a replacement by other symptoms, which may not be as obvious to the environment as the enuresis is, and not even considered to be connected with the previous enuresis. These new symptoms are usually of characterological nature, manifesting themselves in behavior disorders more harmful to the child than enuresis (Michaels, 1955; M. Sperling, 1950b). It has been observed that after surgery undertaken to correct enuresis, either directly performed on the urinary tract or in more remote places, enuresis actually disappears, at least temporarily. In such cases, it is the shock of the operation which is interpreted by the child as the utmost in punishment for his "bad habit," which had this effect. For the surgeon this ends the case, but, from the standpoint of the psychiatrist, a more severe case has been created. Examinations of the urinary tract bear a similar psychological result. Greater discernment should therefore be exercised by physicians before embarking on routine cystoscopy or other procedures, such as prostatic massage, etc. The use of electric alarm devices in the treatment of enuresis is deplorable (Davidson and Douglass, 1950). It betrays the fact that those who advocate it are completely ignorant of the complexity of the human personality. The findings and suggestions presented in a condensed form in this chapter are the result of research and therapy with a large material (well over 100 cases) of enuretic children and adolescents, carried on in a child psychiatric clinic of a general hospital, The Jewish Hospital of Brooklyn, New York, for twelve years, and in my private practice for twenty-four years. It is hoped that a better familiarity with the dynamics operating in enuresis may be of value, especially to pediatricians, both for prevention and proper management of enuresis.

# 18

# Brief Psychoanalytic Intervention in a Case of Persistent Enuresis in a Pre-Adolescent Girl

Ruth was thirteen years old when she came for treatment. She had been a persistent bed-wetter since infancy. Her mother had tried everything from water-restriction and various diets to waking her up several times a night, but nothing had helped. She had hoped that Ruth would stop wetting when she would begin to menstruate. Ruth got her period at eleven and a half but continued to wet nightly. It was really Ruth who had now requested treatment and not her mother. It was the middle of June and Ruth had signed up for a camp to which she was very eager to go. She had been to camp the year before, but because she had wet nightly, she left after two weeks, "I couldn't take it any longer." Ruth had had repeated medical checkups because of the bed-wetting. Her mother had changed doctors frequently in the hope that she might find someone who could help Ruth with the enuresis. On several occasions the mother had raised the question about psychiatric treatment but had been discouraged by the physicians. It was the doctor who had seen Ruth for a medical checkup for camp who suggested psychiatric treatment and had referred her to me.

I had learned from the mother that Ruth had a brother three years her junior with whom Ruth was getting on very well. To the mother's satisfaction Ruth had never shown any obvious signs of sibling rivalry and there had been no change in the bed-wetting after the brother was born. Ruth had been consistently wetting from infancy and had never had a dry night yet.

In characterizing her children the mother described Ruth as an aggressive and active girl who was very much interested in athletics, while her son was a more retiring, passive child and no athlete at all. The mother also told me that she herself had been a bed-wetter up to her ninth year of age, when she suddenly stopped wetting during a stay in camp. She remembered clearly how it happened—it was during the first night in camp. She was so worried that she might wet herself that she stayed up all night determined to prevent herself from wetting. She succeeded and from that time on never wet the bed again. She still remembered the feeling of amused satisfaction after finding out that the child next to her in her bunk and many other children in camp were bed-wetters. A large factor in her determination not to wet had been her fear that she would be the only child to be exposed as a bed-wetter in camp. When Ruth had gone to camp for the first time a year before, the mother told her about her own experience in the hope that Ruth would do similarly. She was very disappointed when Ruth failed to do so and returned home because of the enuresis after a short stay.

Ruth was a well-developed, well-mannered, good-looking girl who observed me with guarded curiosity. She spoke very little about herself, as if she expected me to do all the talking. I had learned from the mother that after this first meeting Ruth had told her mother that I was looking at her as if I wanted to hypnotize her. She also told her mother that all during the session she was saying to herself (and she was probably so preoccupied with this that she could not think of anything else) "I won't let her hypnotize me." In the second meeting I discussed this with Ruth, interpreting to her that this was obviously what she would want me to do, namely, to hypnotize her. In this way she would have nothing to do with giving up her bed-wetting nor with finding out why she needed to wet nor would she be responsible for any recurrences. In short, she wanted to leave it all to me. I explained to her that this could not work like that—that whether she wet or stayed dry would have to be her responsibility—that all I could do was to help her to recognize that there was a part in her which wanted her to wet and that was why she did not succeed in her conscious efforts not to wet. Ruth had told me, of course, as most bed-wetting children do, that she did not want to wet but that she could not help it. How could she know what she did in her sleep?

At this point I discussed with her the myth of the deep sleep: I explained to her that bedwetting was not an activity carried out in deep sleep and that even a small child could hold its urine all night. She also knew, because she had been examined repeatedly, that there was nothing wrong with her urologically. I gave her a brief explanation about unconscious motivations which are responsible for the failure of conscious determination in a case when one is not aware of the unconscious need for certain actions. After this Ruth spent the rest of the session complaining about her father. He would not let her play with the boys, he did not let her go on the bike, he was very strict; in short, he did not let her do things that he considered activities which boys should pursue. He wanted her to be a very ladylike girl.

Before the third session the mother called to tell me that Ruth did not want to come. Ruth said that she was afraid of the hill which she had to pass coming in the car on the way to my office. The mother also told me that she herself felt very upset without knowing why. Immediately after that, she told me that Ruth had stopped wetting (for the first time in her life) and had said to her mother that she did not need me for bed-wetting anymore. I suggested to the mother to tell Ruth that she had spoken to me and that I felt that because Ruth was afraid of the hill she should come and talk to me about this fear. I suggested to the mother that she tell Ruth that I could help her also with some of the other problems that I knew she had. Ruth came and said "It's funny, when I decided to come I was not afraid of the hill anymore." I interpreted some of the meanings of this statement to her—first, that this was another resistance against treatment because now that she was not afraid of the hill anymore she did not need me for that either, and second, that once she had decided to come she did not need the fear of the hill, which was intended to stop her from coming here. She said that she could see that fear was a very strong means of stopping people from doing things. With surprise she suddenly remembered an incident that had occurred when she was six or seven years old. It related to her fear of the hill. At that time she had suffered an accident—the car in which she had been riding with her family fell down an embankment and upon awakening she found herself in a hospital. The only thing she remembered upon awakening in the hospital and immediately preceding the accident with the car was the wind blowing in by the window. It was the same feeling and fear she had experienced on the hill coming to me. It was a fear of the wind blowing through the window when the car was going downhill. Coming for treatment was associated with a situation of extreme danger, identical with losing her life. It had reawakened the repressed memory of an actual danger situation where she could have lost her life.

From my experience with the prolonged analyses of enuretic girls and their mothers I was able to understand the nature of these deeply unconscious fears stimulated by the treatment in both Ruth and her mother. The mother had told me that she too had been extremely anxious without knowing a reason when she should have been very happy because Ruth had stopped wetting. To give up wetting equaled giving up an unconscious male identification and her homosexual attachment to the mother, which had been maintained in this case by the wetting (the wet tie). This danger had obviously been sensed by both Ruth and her mother and was manifested in their anxiety, which reached almost panic proportions. I interpreted to Ruth that she felt threatened by treatment and that it appeared that this had mobilized an old fear, to warn her against danger, as if there was something very important that her unconscious wanted to guard and was afraid of, that she would find out and lose through treatment. I reassured her that there was no need to be afraid of her unconscious, which was only part of herself and could not do anything that she really did not want to do.

In the fourth and last session she again complained about her father, her brother and her boy cousin, who was the same age as she. For the first time she asked my advice in a real-life situation. Her predicament was the following: she was anxious to be accepted in a club and felt that this would be a social achievement for her because the members of this club were very discriminating. She was invited to attend a meeting of the club that night when her eligibility would be decided upon. Her cousin wanted to come with her to this meeting. She told me that she felt ashamed of him and considered him inferior, but that she was in a conflict because she did not want to hurt him. On the other hand she felt that bringing him along would spoil her chance of being accepted. I could show her that she was projecting some of her own feelings of inferiority and fears of not being eligible onto her cousin. Following this, Ruth brought out strong feelings about boys. In her first session Ruth had quite frankly stated that she would rather have been a boy than a girl. It was possible to show her that unconsciously she seemed to consider herself a boy and that for this reason she was overemphasizing in her behavior boyish traits and at the same time needed to feel that boys were inferior and to devalue her brother and his substitute, her cousin. I explained in this connection to her some of the concepts of the psychosexual development of little girls, pointing out to her that such feelings were universal with girls of a certain age. I suggested that there were some specific reasons why she still needed to hold on with such intensity to wishes that little girls have but eventually are able to overcome. She talked about the birth of her little brother when she was three years old. We discussed the fact that this was a very important age at which little girls are making observations regarding the anatomical differences and are very much aware of the lack of a penis and the wish for it. At the end of this session she said, "I have decided not to wet anymore and that's what I'll do."

After this session the mother called me the next day to tell me that Ruth had mentioned to her something about her vagina. The mother sounded extremely excited and said that she did not know how I could have known what had happened with Ruth when she was a little girl, but since I seemed to know, she felt that she had to tell me. She said that she had felt so guilty about it that she had been unable to talk to me about it at the time of her interview when she had arranged for Ruth's treatment.

When Ruth was three years old, shortly after her brother's birth the mother said that she was very annoyed with her bed-wetting and had told her that she must always urinate when she felt an urge or her vagina would burst. She had done this especially because whenever she picked her up, she did not urinate, saying she did not have to, but soon afterward she would wet her bed. In order to make this threat more impressive the mother had told her that her vagina was different and could not hold the urine. That the mother's threat had not fallen on deaf ears was borne out by the report of the teacher of the nursery school, which Ruth attended at the age of three. The mother remembered that the teacher spoke to her of Ruth's strange behavior during rest periods. Ruth would insist that she had to go to the toilet during rest period because her vagina was different and would burst if she did not. The mother felt very relieved after confessing this. It had obviously been burdening her all these years.

This telephone conversation took place the day before Ruth was leaving for camp. Ruth called me on her return from camp to tell me that she had a very good time, that she had remained dry during her camp stay and that she intended to maintain this good record.

This case shows that the unconscious wish to be a boy was supported in this peculiar way by a suggestion from the mother and proved to be the unconscious dynamic force for persistent enuresis in a girl of thirteen. It furthermore shows that on the basis of psychoanalytic insight gained from the treatment of enuretics, it was possible to clear in a shortcut, as it were, a condition which otherwise might require many years of psychoanalytic treatment. This case also illustrates some of the points made in Chapter 16 about the myths of deep sleep and the weak bladder, which in this case overnight turned into a rather strong bladder.

It also shows the important dynamic role of masculine identification in enuretic girls, and the tendency to homosexual attachment to the mother, with the enuresis permitting an undue physical closeness with a nearly adolescent girl. The retaining of urine while sitting on the toilet for bed-wetting later was not so much a revenge wetting in Ruth's case as a means of discharging incestuous perverse (homosexual) impulses directed at the mother by giving her a gift—the "wet tie," representing also an enormous ejaculation, with Ruth taking the male role.

# PART 7

# CHILD PSYCHOSIS

# 19
# Child Psychosis and Childhood Schizophrenia: Comments on Therapeutic Techniques, Current View and Treatment

My experiences from the treatment of children with psychosomatic disorders and in particular the method of simultaneous treatment of mother and child were of great help to me in the understanding of the mother-child relationship in child psychosis. I also made the observation that in some cases, especially of younger children, the most severe symptoms of the child often subsided without direct treatment of the child. I attribute this to the understanding the mother had gained and to the change in her attitude and handling of her child. I observed this phenomenon also in some older children, who refused or were unable to come for treatment themselves. In one twelve-year-old borderline patient a conversion reaction which had almost totally immobilized her cleared completely through indirect treatment, that is, treatment of the mother alone. In another, a thirteen-year-old girl with psychotic episodes yielded to brief psychoanalytic psychotherapeutic intervention with the child and of her mother (see Chapters 2 and 3).

The simultaneous treatment of mother and child made it

possible to understand and to resolve bizarre behavior of the child not explainable nor accessible to treatment otherwise. Psychoanalytic studies of mothers in the prenatal mental hygiene clinic of The Jewish Hospital of Brooklyn which I established in conjunction with the obstetrics service furnished additional insight into the role of the unconscious of the mother and the unconscious rapport between mother and child.

We found that in some cases the expected child was born into an emotionally predetermined environment. Some of the mothers had certain fixed ideas about this child prenatally, or even preconceptions, such as that the child would be born with specific defects, physical or mental, and a certain personality. In some cases the child was to be a replacement for a lost object, a child who had died (see Chapter 4). Or the child was to be a replacement for another object from the mother's past or present, as in the case of Paul, who was conceived for the purpose of replacing the mother's brother, who had been killed in an accident, and with whom she had an unresolved hostile relationship (see Chapter 3). The child can also represent certain repressed and rejected aspects of the mother's personality (see Chapter 9). In the case of Linda the child represented to her mother not only the rejected aspects of herself but also of her own mother. In those cases where the mother has unconscious doubt and fears concerning her own sanity this will be projected onto the child. The clinical material in this section provides illustrations for these and other situations and for their therapeutic management.

This brings me to some questions concerning the use of observational methods in such cases. The impressions gained by this method seem to me rather deceptive, because only the conscious attitudes are observed and the unconscious motivations for the pathological behavior remain obscured. When observations indicate that the child is developing a severe emotional illness or psychosis the application of the observational method without therapeutic interference may be questioned. This is like watching a child develop a physical malignancy. The damage may be irreparable if it is allowed to continue over an extended period of time without therapy. Furthermore, without treating the mother the child's behavior cannot only not be basically influenced but it cannot be fully understood, because the child in these cases is acting out and responding to the mother's unconscious needs and wishes, while the observational method deals only with the manifest attitudes of the mother and her child. It is therefore inadequate for the understanding of the genesis and of the dynamics of the child's behavior. For instance, if the child behaves toward the mother as if she were a persecutor, although in reality she does not manifest any such behavior, this is often considered by the observational investigator as a delusion on the part of the child. In the simultaneous psychoanalytic treatment of mothers and their psychotic children I have found that the child's attitude is perfectly justified in most cases as far as the psychic reality of the mother's and the child's relationship is concerned. Here again the case of Paul is most instructive. Paul represented to his mother the incarnation of the hated brother and was persecuted by her with the same vengeance and hate with which she had as a child persecuted her brother. When lifting a pot of hot water, she had the compulsive thought of pouring it over Paul and scalding him. When his teacher and principal, who liked him, came to dinner, she would provoke him to have a temper tantrum, break the china and expose himself at his worst. She would tell on him to his father as she used to tell on her brother to her parents. While speaking sweetly to him she often had the thought "Come into my parlor, said the spider." Unfortunately, then, there is a reality base to these delusions, although it may be exaggerated and distorted by the child and the feelings carried over from the mother to other people. Children in such a situation try to withdraw into daydreaming and to faraway places such as celestial bodies, into cosmic fantasies, the universe, to remove themselves from the disturbing and uncontrollable reality.

These children also have unusual symbols, reflecting their feelings concerning the primitive relationship with the object. They often use as symbols stone, wood, cosmic objects, inanimate objects, machines, ferocious animals, insects, snakes, spiders, to name only a few. The spider symbol is a symbol of the engulfing, constricting, destructive mother who is trying to immobilize her victim. I found this symbol quite frequently in latent or overtly psychotic children (see Chapter 10). The spider symbol is also a projection of the child's oral- and anal-sadistic impulses directed against the mother. These children feel as if they lived in an inhuman environment. One of my paranoid psychotic patients, now married and father of an adolescent son, lived for a very long time in an inhuman environment of stone and wood. He could magically make stone statues, wooden horses, etc., move or stop; this meant that he was in control. One can assess changes in feelings achieved in treatment before they become clinically apparent in changes of behavior by changes in the dream symbolism of these patients (see Chapter 6).

The narcissism of these children is intense and very vulnerable and has to be defended at all costs. The danger of trying to break it as mothers of psychotic children are doing is further regression and breaks with reality, with the child's withdrawal into psychosis or autistic behavior. In the case of an eight-year-old psychotic boy, his mother was furious when he withdrew into his psychotic fantasies and world. She told me that what made her so furious was the fact that she could not follow him there, while otherwise she would run after him wherever he went and enjoy tantalizing him. There was no lock on the toilet door. He could not escape her. The only way he could escape her was in his psychosis. With this knowledge his complaint about his mother persecuting him and his behavior, for instance, of running away from her, walking on the other side of the street, or hiding from her were bizarre and made no sense. Treatment of mother and son revealed that these were defensive maneuvers on the part of the patient and that they made a lot of sense. This brings up the question whether especially with young children, it is advisable to bring the child out of his psychosis without first effecting some changes in the environment that had precipitated and that is active in maintaining the child's psychosis.

Here a case reported by Mahler (1968) is of interest. This boy, Stanley, reacted to the outside noises and machinery, etc., with fright, in the same way as to his impulses, by which he obviously appeared to be overwhelmed. By his behavior he displayed that he had no control. It is of interest to compare this case with a psychotic patient of mine, seven-year-old Alec.

During a phase of his treatment Alec was making floods, turning on the faucet in the sink in the bathroom, letting it run and then running away himself. This was really a playing out of his feelings of being flooded by his impulses. After playing this water game for a couple of months in the bathroom I had succeeded in teaching him that he could stay and could turn off the faucet himself, that is, that he could achieve ego control. His mother played a significant role in his behavior. At the time when this was going on with Alec, his mother was training dogs and took a much greater interest in her dogs than in Alec. In the morning she would go out and walk the dogs and leave Alec alone in the house, knowing well what he would do—that he would turn on the faucet and make a flood. In this way, she was undermining what we were trying to achieve in therapy. In this case the mother was using her son as a means of revenge on her husband, who came from a very cultured and intellectual family, while she had no formal training and a poor background. Her husband was given to severe temper and at such times would berate the mother and hurt her where she was most vulnerable, in her narcissism, by telling her how he had lowered himself by marrying her. Her revenge was to be that this proud, scholarly man would have a son who was not only not an intellectual but a total misfit.

As mentioned before, some of these children protect themselves against the engulfing, destructive mother by dehumanizing her, as Ruth did (Chapter 10), by making her mother into a washing machine, a stove and other machines that could swallow her up and destroy her. This was also a projection of her own oral-sadistic impulses. In earlier childhood the mother had been represented by the spider symbol. Ruth's machine fantasies were similar to those of Mahler's patient Stanley, who feared that the wall telephone would take a bite out of him. To both of them the machine represented the mother. Mahler made the treatment of the child into a tripartite situation where all three, the mother, child and therapist were together "while the child's behavior is being observed by all three." This, in my opinion, is an unfavorable therapeutic situation because without understanding the unconscious rapport and the dynamics operating in this specific mother-child relationship, the observations will render only a distorted impression. The observer should be aware that the child is at a disadvantage in this situation because he cannot successfully compete with the mother for the attention of the therapist. The child will therefore compete negatively and show himself at his worst. This seemed to be the case in most situations described by Mahler.

The practice of anaclitic treatment with these children is inadvisable, because it encourages further regression and destructive behavior and weakens the child's ego. Instead, the therapist should attempt to strengthen the child's ego by putting limits and expecting him to follow some of these limits; thus he differentiates himself from the mother, who does not put any limits at all or does it in a very ambivalent way. This regimen has to be followed at home, and is possible only with the mother's genuine cooperation and not with a fake compliance. This is why I replaced the preparatory treatment of the child with the preparatory treatment of the mother in such cases. Mahler presupposes a "normal" autistic stage in the developmental stages of the child. In my opinion autism is always pathological, and denotes the mother's rejection of the child and the child's reaction to it. Autism is really a narcissistic victory of the child over the parent, at the highest price. An autistic stage in an infant is not compatible with the preservation of life. Autism, like fetishism (see Chapter 15), is a stage and a reaction to severely injured narcissism in the child. A child may become autistic if his symbiotic needs are severely frustrated and he may remain or become pathologically symbiotic if his needs for separation and self-assertion are frustrated.

# 20

# Tics and Psychosis: A Case Presentation

    I had the opportunity to observe a patient, who initially was presented with a tic syndrome and who later developed a psychosis for which he was hospitalized for more than two years in a psychiatric hospital, both during the initial phase and later after his discharge from the hospital, and to supervise the successful analytic treatment of his psychosis. This case is interesting also as a longitudinal study with a fifteen-year follow-up; during this period the patient remained well without tics and without psychosis, functioning on a high intellectual level and in a satisfactory marriage.

    Peter was eight and a half when he was referred to me because of facial and vocal tics and also because he was a withdrawn and rather fearful child. We found that his tics had developed following the birth of his sister when he was nearly six years old. His mother was depressed at that time and appeared to reject him. She needed much rest and Peter had to be quiet at all times for her sake and also in order not to wake the little sister. He was expected to play quietly by himself without bothering anybody. His father was working during the day and busy evenings helping his depressed wife with her chores. The mother was not able to follow through my suggestion for psychotherapy for Peter and for herself.

I learned later that because his tics and his behavior had become unbearable to the mother, Peter had been hospitalized. In the hospital his tics decreased gradually and disappeared but his behavior became more and more bizarre. He was much in demand as a patient for staff presentations because of his seemingly inexhaustible capacity for producing bizarre fantasies and behavior. He was diagnosed as a case of childhood schizophrenia and he remained in the hospital attending school there and going home for occasional weekends until he was twelve years old. At that time his parents consulted me again. They had to make a decision whether to take him home or transfer him to another hospital since the first hospital kept children only until age twelve. They decided to take him home and to accept my referral for psychoanalytic psychotherapy for Peter.

No account of his treatment, which extended over a period of four years, can be given here. What is of interest to us in this study is the fact that this patient, contrary to the predictions of Gilles de Tourette and others, did not deteriorate mentally, although he had a manifest psychosis and although his tic syndrome had all the characteristics of that described as Gilles de la Tourette. His vocal tics were really obscene four-letter words, which he did not fully articulate for fear of his mother's reaction, but intonated with hissing sounds. The muscular twitches, which had spread from his face to his shoulders and arms, were his way of expressing his aggressive and sexual impulses toward his sister, his mother and father, in symbolic exhibitionistic, confessional body actions (movements). This form of communication was then replaced by symbolic, exhibitionistic and confessional psychotic verbal productions, which secured for him the full interest and attention of the hospital staff. The element of scaring and shocking people by his sudden grimaces, muscular twitches and vocal emissions was retained in an attenuated way in his psychotic verbalizations. It was as if he had replaced the vocal and the muscular twitches with a kind of "mental" tic.

In his analytic treatment we found that he had actually enjoyed his exhibitionistic performances at the conferences and had taken pride in the production of his fantasies. It was necessary for his analyst to interfere with this form of exhibitionism by pointing out to him that he was not on exhibition and that she was neither impressed nor startled by this behavior. The analyst had continually to deal with his need to communicate and to confess his "crimes" both in his tics and in his psychosis, in a way that should not be understood by himself nor by those to whom it was directed. In connection with this case, an article by Brunn and Shapiro (1972) is of interest. The authors, after a review of the literature and an intensive six years' study of thirty-four patients with Tourette's Syndrome, found that Tourette had failed to differentiate this syndrome from other obscure diseases in his time. They found that although sounds or words eventually appear in all patients, coprolalia is not a necessary component of the syndrome and also that there is no mental deterioration in these patients.

# 21

# Reactive Schizophrenia in Children

From the group of child schizophrenias, I have chosen for discussion the syndrome which would be classified as paranoid schizophrenia. I have studied my material in three different ways: (1) by the method of direct psychoanalytic treatment of the child; (2) by the method of simultaneous treatment of the child and the mother; (3) by the method of indirect treatment of the child through the psychoanalysis of the mother. This chapter is concerned with the third aspect; fragments of the psychoanalyses of the mothers of two children with such a diagnosis are presented in the hope that it may help to shed some light upon the dynamics and genesis of certain forms of schizophrenia in children.

CASE 1. Mrs. A consulted me about her nine-year-old son Harry, for whom hospitalization in a psychiatric hospital had been advised. Harry had been treated by a psychiatrist (of the Board of Education) for the past year and a half, and his mother had been seen by a psychiatric social worker of the same agency. Harry's presenting symptoms were bizarre behavior, paranoid suspicions, fears and withdrawal. He masturbated openly and excessively. Although his IQ was 120 at the time, he had barely acquired the ability to read and write.

The mother felt very guilty, accusing herself of having "messed up the boy." In view of the severe disturbance of the mother, I felt that Harry would do better in a psychiatric hospital where he could receive treatment and attend school, both of which he resisted while living at home. Since Harry was spending weekends at home during the period that his mother was being treated by me, I had a good opportunity to observe the interaction between mother and son.

Mrs. A had misgivings before Harry was born. She didn't want a boy because her own brother had grown up to be "no good." She was determined to watch Harry very closely in order to prevent a similar outcome. When he was an infant, she stayed awake with him many hours each night, clutching him tightly to her. She realized, in her analysis, that she could not allow the boy to sleep because of her intense need to hold onto him in close bodily contact during the night. In this connection she revealed her favorite mode of masturbation, which she still practiced even in her married life. She would stand in front of a mirror, imagining that she had a penis. Sometimes she would stick a banana into her vagina and imagine that she had intercourse with a woman. When Harry was three years old, she felt that he was peculiar and difficult to manage. When he was four and a half, she could not stand his excessive masturbation and placed him in a boarding school. Because he was unhappy there, and the school would not keep him, she took him home after six months. After he had been home for a short period, she placed him in another boarding school. Harry adjusted to this school after some time, and was doing well. He showed remarkable ability in arithmetic. When he was seven and a half, she felt that he had stayed there long enough, brought him home, and placed him, against advice, in a public school. He could not function in the school. The children called him crazy, and he was referred by the school for psychiatric treatment. At first, he showed some improvement, which the mother attributed to the change in her attitude toward him. When the social worker assigned to her left the agency, Mrs. A had a very bad reaction and Harry's behavior deteriorated rapidly.

Mrs. A's outstanding feeling was that nobody cared for her, so that she had decided not to care for anyone. As a child, she had had no friends and had suffered from weekend and holiday depressions. She married in order to get away from home. She was contemptuous of her husband when he took her abuse, and furious when she couldn't "get a rise out of him." The marriage had deteriorated lately. She claimed that her husband was impotent. When she was first married, she worked for some time because her husband was ill. During this period when he was dependent upon her, she was satisfied, but resented it very much when he began to assert himself and to detach himself from her. She wanted a baby so that she would have something that would be only hers. She was aware that she was deliberately undermining Harry's relationship with his father, and could hardly conceal her satisfaction when the boy would be abusive to him. She had been taking Harry into bed with her and had been quite aware that she felt sexually stimulated by him. During the time when Harry came home for weekends and wanted to come into bed with her in the morning, she realized that although she told him, "Big boys don't go into their mothers' beds," through her behavior she was actually encouraging him to do what she was telling him not to do. She remembered an episode that had occurred before she had started treatment. Once when she was walking with Harry, he said to her, "Don't we look like husband and wife?" While she was disturbed about it, she experienced at the same time a feeling of gratification. She had a dream that she was riding on a train. Harry was sitting beside her; he was a grown man, yet was still with her. He began to act silly; took out his penis and exhibited himself publicly. (Harry had once actually done this in school.)

She could not bear it when Harry withdrew from her into his "fantasy world." Everywhere else she could follow him. There was actually no place where he could hide or run away from her, except into his fantasy world, where she could not follow him.

It soon became obvious that she was resentful and not willing to allow Harry to improve under therapy. Her behavior toward him when he came home for weekends was definitely aimed at upsetting his balance. Harry would often say, "I really don't know why I'm coming home to this crazy house." She had to admit to herself that his actions, queer as they appeared to the unfamiliar observer, made sense to her, since she understood that this was how Harry was defending himself against her. One day when she yelled at him and he said to her, "Leave me alone," she replied, "I won't, and what are you going to do about it?" She felt like a witch and knew that she wanted him to call her that, so that she would have a justification for her behavior toward him. Instead, Harry walked out and went to a distant swimming pool all by himself. He had escaped her. She felt very frustrated, and also felt that she wanted to "drive him crazy." After he left, she had the following fantasy: she was dead, having killed herself. Harry had been given to an institution, and when her family came to visit him he behaved idiotically. She was alone in the house and had to scream out loud "No, no" to stop this fantasy.

She could not tolerate Harry's attempts to detach himself from her. She would deliberately start an argument and tell him that she was stronger than he and that if she wanted to, she could send him to a reformatory. She provoked him, wanting him to lose control, which he did on occasions, when he would throw something at her. "You see," she said to me one day, "this is how I could even get him to kill me." There were always quarrels over the weekends about the movies. Harry wanted to go during the day, while she preferred the evening. They would fight about it on the street. She would leave him standing on the street and walk away, thinking, "Who is he to force me to do what he wants?" when they couldn't agree on the choice of the picture. She preferred the evenings because she wanted to go to a dance hall with a woman friend. She had become a frequent visitor of dance halls. Harry seemed to have sensed what she was doing. He once said to her, "If I go to the movies by myself, I feel you pushed me there because you don't want me to be around. If you go away, don't be surprised when you come back and find that I behaved silly. I will open the neighbors' doors and spit at them." He knew that she was concerned with keeping from her neighbors what was going on in her home.

Once when he masturbated in his room with the door open, she told him in a very annoyed tone of voice not to do such a nasty thing in her presence. He came toward her. She yelled and shrieked angrily at her husband, who was in the room and who, she felt, should have stopped Harry. Harry said to her, "If you yell, I'll show it to you," and he held his sore penis up to her face. The night before, she had a fantasy while Harry sat on the couch with her as she read the newspaper: Harry was giving her his penis; it was wrapped up in the newspaper.

Her hatred of men and consequent need to castrate them could only be mitigated by the complete submission of the male, who had to hand over his penis to her as Harry did in her fantasy. When she no longer could handle Harry as if he were her penis, designed to give her pleasure whenever she wanted it, she not only pushed him away as something she did not need, but she had to destroy him so that he could be of no use to himself nor to anyone else. He then became completely identified with her brother who had been "no good." Harry's acceptance of his mother's verdict was indicated in his overt behavior. His excessive masturbation and the withdrawal from reality were at the same time his means for survival. There was no use in fighting his mother, since any of his attempts met with her undiminished fury. She was extremely narcissistic and intolerant of any tension, and therefore had immediately to direct her destructiveness to the outside (for self-preservation). She was constantly on the brink of severe depression. Her attitude toward women was determined by her strong latent homosexuality, which in itself represented her compromise between her hate and need of women, that is, mother. In reality, her behavior with women was quite paranoid, and this, together with her hypersensitivity, also colored her transference.

After a year of psychoanalytic treatment (with a technique modified to the treatment of such a severe narcissistic neurosis), she said to me, after a conference with Harry's psychiatrist, "I know better than Harry's doctor or any psychiatrist what would help Harry; what he needs is a mother. I should bring him home and be a mother to him, but I can't." Harry stayed on at the hospital for another year and his mother remained in treatment with me. During this year, she allowed Harry to improve. It was felt by all concerned that Harry should not return home and he was placed in an institution, where he continued therapy and schooling. Neither he nor his mother could make a complete recovery; the damage had been too great. Mrs. A maintained contact with me through the years. Harry is now 15, and is able to function well within the protected environment in which he lives at present.

CASE 2. Mrs. B, the mother of a nine-year-old girl, Stella, consulted me, in view of the recommendation that the child be hospitalized. Stella had been treated for a year and a half by the psychiatrist who had made this recommendation, which was reinforced by a consultant psychiatrist. The presenting symptoms were negativistic behavior and severe temper tantrums (Stella on one occasion attacked the mother with a knife). The child had not responded to psychotherapy, and eventually refused to see her own or any other psychiatrist. The mother had conflicting feelings about hospitalization; even though she felt that

Stella was "insane" and "impossible to live with," at the same time she thought she was not really sick and that hospitalization would ruin her. The mother also had been under psychiatric treatment, during which she had suffered a "breakdown," with severe depression and suicidal attempt. She accepted treatment with me on the assumption that this would enable her to cope with Stella, and possibly enable Stella to resume psychiatric treatment.

Stella had been a very much wanted child, and the mother was extremely gratified by her, considering her beautiful, bright and gifted. According to the mother, nothing in Stella's early development deviated from the normal. Between two and three years of age, Stella had occasional temper tantrums. The mother and Stella had a very close relationship until Stella was four, when her sister was born. The mother stated that Stella had changed markedly and became a "nasty and difficult child," abusive of the mother. At this period, her temper tantrums and negativism became very pronounced. The mother showed overt preference for the younger child, rationalizing that it was difficult to be affectionate to an abusive child. She would often hold her younger child on her lap for hours. They would kiss and hug while Stella watched them. Analysis revealed that Stella had become identified in her mother's mind with Mrs. B's older sister, while Mrs. B herself identified with her younger child. Mrs. B had been very jealous of her sister and of the close relationship that existed with the mother, but had never been conscious of this. She now repeated with Stella actively what she had experienced passively as a child, with her sister and mother. Mrs. B's sister was considered pretty while she herself was always thought unattractive. In this connection, Mrs. B's reaction to interpretation of her latent homosexuality, in the course of treatment with a male psychiatrist, is significant, namely, that she reacted with depression. As is typical for a paranoid personality, it was very difficult for Mrs. B to gain insight into the unconscious motivations of her behavior, namely, that she was reenacting with Stella a situation in which Stella was the frustrated lover as Mrs. B would have wanted her older sister to have been in relationship to their mother.

The mother's manifest behavior toward Stella reflected her unconscious feelings. She actually fought with Stella as she would with a sister of whom she was jealous. For instance, they would fight as to who would sit next to the father in the car, what dress Stella should wear, or whether she could be present in company.

Stella's intense rage in the course of the temper tantrums and the physical and verbal attacks upon the mother could be understood as defenses on the girl's part against the mother's need for domination. This need of the mother resulted from her unconscious wish for passive homosexual surrender from the girl. The mother's urge to provoke Stella to rage and loss of control aimed at reducing the girl to submissiveness and having her beg for love like a penitent lover. One incident may illustrate this. One day the mother served corn. There were two large and two smaller pieces. The mother liked corn and took the biggest, and gave the other big one to the younger child. Stella wanted the big one, and took it. The mother insisted that she give it back. Stella began to scream, "You are a hog and a pig." The father had at first said that she could have the larger piece, but then sided with his wife. Stella ran into the bathroom and threw herself on the floor, screaming to her father, "Divorce her, divorce her right now." She would not come out of the bathroom. Later, her mother went to the bathroom, asking through the door, "Can I do something for you?" Stella said to her, "Apologize. Say 'I'm sorry,' and I want you to mean it." The mother said, "How can I mean it if you behave like that?" Stella then broke down, crying, "I love you, I love you. Why don't you love me?"

The mother constantly injected herself into the child's relationships, the aim being to prevent the child from having other close relationships. The child was first seen by a psychiatrist at seven years of age. The Rorschach at that time showed as outstanding features compulsive trends, marked oral emphasis and extreme negativism. The possibility of schizophrenia could not be entirely ruled out. Two years later, another Rorschach showed "signs of intellectual disorder in the manifest disregard for reality and the girl's emotional coldness and detachment, and finally in the bizarre quality of some of her projections." There were also present neurotic traits of a marked hysterical and somewhat compulsive nature. The diagnostic impressions suggested incipient schizophrenia with paranoid trends.

The behavior of the child, as well as the psychological findings, pointed to a progressive schizophrenic development. Although in the overt behavior she appeared to be fighting against her mother, unconsciously she was succumbing to her mother's wishes. This was also manifested in Stella's unwillingness to remain in treatment, which was only an answer to her mother's unwillingness to have her treated and to allow her to form a therapeutic relationship with the psychiatrist. Even after Mrs. B had had a year of treatment with me, and Stella once asked her whether she had not changed completely and for the better, the mother could not answer (although the change in Stella had been remarkable) because Mrs. B had not resolved her own confusion regarding her (sexual) role toward Stella.

The presentation of these two cases is in line with some of my previous presentations illustrating the response of the child to the unconscious of the mother in neurosis and in psychosomatic disorders. In these previous presentations, I could show that the symptoms of the child in each case meant that the child was carrying out the unconscious wish of the mother. In these two cases, the psychoanalytic study of the mother revealed a similar dynamic situation. Harry's and Stella's behavior could be understood as an unconscious obedience to the mothers' needs and wishes. These cases point up the necessity for psychoanalytic study of the personality of the mother, because unless we understand the unconscious of the mother, the behavior of the child remains inexplicable. And second, we cannot hope, through any method of treatment, permanently to change the child's behavior unless we can modify the unconscious of the mother.

As reflected in these cases, the mother made it impossible for the child to establish the proper sexual identification. In the first case, the mother castrates Harry, because she cannot tolerate "maleness." Although he seems to rebel against it in the open and excessive masturbation, this in itself is already an acceptance of castration which he carries out himself, even injuring his penis. This is further carried out by his failure to function on the intellectual and social level, in spite of good natural endowment. In the hospital, when he had an acute psychotic break, he would question, "Who am I? What am I?"

In the second case, Stella, although rebelling against it in her overt behavior, unconsciously cannot resist the mother's bid for passive homosexual surrender. This development could be interrupted only through the mitigation of the mother's latent paranoia.

The role of the father in both cases was similar; both were latent homosexuals, passive and dependent upon the wife (mother). There was therefore no interference from the father with the mother's drives in relationship to the child. The husband too was a child of the wife, and carried out and complemented the homosexual needs of his wife. In the life of the child, the father was really a shadow of the mother and did not attempt to rescue the child.

# 22

# Some Criteria on the Evaluation of the Treatment Potential of Schizophrenic Children

The clinical appraisal of the schizophrenic child (and of his environment) is particularly important to those child psychiatrists who treat schizophrenic children in an ambulatory setup. The treatment plan for a schizophrenic child will be primarily based upon the child's accessibility to therapy. A therapeutically useful diagnostic workup should include these aspects as well as an evaluation of the child's closest environment in this respect. The main objective of such a workup should be an evaluation of the child's chances for recovery through treatment.

The suggestions to be offered here are derived from my own experience in psychoanalytic work with schizophrenic children and from the supervision of work of others with such patients. A good number of these children were seen by us when their illness was at an advanced stage and when there was a very unfavorable prognosis regarding treatment possibility. It was possible, nevertheless, to treat these children very successfully with psychoanalytic psychotherapy or play therapy. On the basis of this experience, a reevaluation of some criteria for treatability would seem to be indicated.

All workers in the field agree that a very important factor in the evaluation of a schizophrenic child's accessibility to treatment is the child's ability to cathect objects, that is, the ability to form some object relationship with the therapist. It is also a well-known fact that this ability is impaired in varying degrees in the schizophrenic child. From this point of view, the prognosis for the autistic schizophrenic child would be considered more unfavorable than that for the symbiotic schizophrenic. Yet, in actual clinical work with schizophrenic children, this is not always the case. The clinging of the symbiotic schizophrenic child is in some cases a defensive cover for a very defective object relationship. It is a common experience that, with neurotic patients, the first contact is often decisive in setting up a therapeutic relationship between patient and therapist. This holds true, also, for the schizophrenic child, but this does not manifest itself in the same way as with the neurotic child, and concrete evidences may appear only later.

It is suggested that diagnostic interviews be conducted in the form of trial treatment with the focus upon the child's accessibility to therapy rather than upon diagnosis. It would hardly seem possible to determine, in one interview, a child's amenability for treatment. Also, the readiness of parents to subject their child to many brief contacts should be discouraged. The impressions gained thereby can be misleading, and such experiences may only further traumatize the child.

OLGA. A case in point is that of Olga, a nine-year-old girl with the typical history, clinical symptoms, and psychological records of malignant, progressive childhood schizophrenia. In her first interview, Olga sat in the furthest corner of the room, grimacing, and was obviously hallucinating. She did not seem to notice my presence at all. We spent two more sessions in the same way. She kept twitching her shoulders and grimacing while I kept looking at her pleasantly, smiling whenever I was able to catch her glance, without trying to establish verbal contact. (Her twitching and grimacing had indicated to me that she was trying, in this magical way, to shake off and to scare off dangerous intruders from the outside.) My patience was rewarded; in the fourth session, she smiled back at me faintly and I knew that we had established contact. In this case, the passive, silent approach proved successful. This child had been seen previously by other consultants and had been considered inaccessible to psychotherapy and institutionalization had been advised for her. I was consulted in order to help the parents in making a decision.

The approach has to be varied according to the situation. At times the situation may appear to be similar, but a careful evaluation will indicate the differences and make it possible to choose the most promising approach. It must be emphasized, also, that for the purpose of a correct evaluation, all data which can possibly be obtained, such as medical and psychological reports, hospital records, opinions of other doctors who had seen or had treated the child, and, of course, detailed developmental, social and school histories should be in the hand of the consultant, preferably before making arrangements to see the patient. I have found it very helpful to have a history of the child's development and illness, and any changes in the behavior which may have been apparent preceding the manifest onset of the illness, written by the mother, preferably before she is seen in consultation herself.

ARTHUR was four and a half years old when first seen by me. The report of the private nursery which he had attended indicated that he was unable to make contact with the group, also that he showed facial tics and appeared to be withdrawn. Psychological testing had been suggested by the nursery. During the psychological examination Arthur had been unresponsive, rocking back and forth in his chair. He could be roused from his stupor only by physical contact. He talked in nonsense syllables or neologisms, and after a short span would lapse into his detached state. Because of his extreme confusion and disorganization, no accurate estimate of his actual mental capacities could be made. But it was clear that he had at least average intelligence. The Rorschach showed poor, in fact, almost devastated reality testing and a good deal of deterioration. There was no evidence of any conventional modes of perception and thought. In summary, it was stated that Arthur was suffering from childhood schizophrenia. The classical signs included lack of object relationships, withdrawal, blunted affect, perseveration, echolalia, plasticity, and immobility. Familial history showed that one paternal uncle was hospitalized with a catatonic schizophrenia. The parents themselves did not evidence any overt emotional disturbance. Aside from the hereditary elements, the etiology was not clear and hospitalization in a psychiatric setting for observation and disposition had been advised. It was for this reason that the parents asked for a consultation. According to the mother's account of the developmental history, "when Arthur was born we lived with my father and my two brothers, and the infant got a great deal of attention. He was not allowed to cry and I always had to rock him to sleep. At two months, when it appeared that he might be a thumb-sucker—he sucked his thumb so that I almost thought he would lose it—I remedied the situation by giving him nipples with very small holes and in two weeks the thumb-sucking disappeared without recurrence." My reaction to this was: "This mother does not permit instinctual pleasure; she permits sucking only when it is for feeding."

When the infant was ten months old, she moved into her own apartment where the baby had his own room, and here she let him "cry it out," so that in a short time he went to sleep without rocking. At the age of two, and in his schizophrenic break, rocking was a most prominent phenomenon. Between a year and two years of age, Arthur would wake up screaming at night and his father would hold him in his arms and calm him down. The mother did not approve of this. Around age two, Arthur stopped crying at night but was up for many hours during the night and the mother could hear him rocking, violently, on his hands and knees, in his crib. Preceding the onset of the rocking,

Arthur, in order to make room for the visiting grandfather, had been moved into the parental bedroom for several months. The mother cannot remember exactly when he began to talk, but is sure that it was at least at the average age. He knew his nursery rhymes and could recite; in fact, the family "thought that he was quite smart." My reaction to this: "Mother does not seem to think so." He started to walk by himself at about twelve and a half months. He walked well but he never really ran. At one and a half he received a bicycle which he did not master well, and mother did not think that he really ever cared to ride it. He loved company and he also loved to be with children. He was completely toilet-trained at two. According to the mother, he trained himself and stopped wetting during the night before he did so during the day. When Arthur was one and a half, the mother went to work and hired a maid to take care of him. She would be out from 7:30 in the morning until 5:00. According to the mother, he did not seem to mind and only occasionally objected to his parents' leaving. (She would leave in the morning with her husband.) In retrospect, the mother thought that the first maid, who stayed for five months, was somewhat stern with the child. She reported a little incident that occurred: One evening the maid forgot something and returned after she had already said goodbye to Arthur. Arthur, at the time approximately two years old, pushed the maid over to the door saying, "Bye bye." After this there was a rapid succession of maids. Arthur had a bottle until the age of four. Mother never attempted to take the bottle away from him. He was content when he had the bottle and this was convenient for her. At four years of age, when he attended day camp in the country during the summer, he had asked to drink milk from a glass. After that, the mother stated, Arthur would drink from a glass even though he saw his baby brother drinking from a bottle.

Arthur was three years old when his brother was born. When his mother was in the hospital with the baby, Arthur developed a sore throat and had to stay at his grandfather's house for a week while his mother came home with the baby. The mother visited him daily and said that he didn't seem to mind not being at home. A week after the baby was born Arthur got lost one day. It was the first time that this had happened, and she was anxious because it had occurred on a street with much traffic. While she was in a store, Arthur had walked into the next building and had stayed there until he was found by his mother.

According to the mother, Arthur seemed to like the baby and was very helpful. He was also very observant of everything she did with the baby. He had a doll whom he treated as the baby and with whom he did everything exactly as his mother did with the baby. He even went to sleep with this doll. When he went to day camp, in the country, it became apparent that he had difficulties holding his own with the children. They would beat him up and he never hit back. He would run away and cry. He was very attentive to his mother and the baby. Since the father came only for weekends, Arthur slept with the mother in the bedroom. In order not to disturb the baby, he would talk in a whisper, whereas in the city, where he had his own room, he sang at the top of his lungs before going to sleep. "He seemed so unusually good," the mother stated. Toward the end of the summer he developed a habit of throwing his head up and grunting at the same time. It appeared as if he couldn't catch his breath. When she returned from the country she consulted her pediatrician about the head-throwing. The doctor suggested that she ignore it and make him feel more secure. After a few months this habit disappeared. She enrolled him in nursery school where he seemed to make a good adjustment at first.

He had many colds and had to have frequent injections. After attending nursery school for five months, he had a tonsillectomy. Mother said that she had prepared him for this by telling him that his tonsils would be taken out so he wouldn't get sick so often and that he would be given ether to put him to sleep. In the hospital, Arthur was taken to surgery by the nurse while the mother remained in the waiting room. After an hour of waiting, the mother was told that the doctor refused to operate on Arthur because he had had orange juice in the morning. He had been put in a gown and prepared for the tonsillectomy. The doctor arranged for the tonsillectomy in the afternoon, and Arthur was left at the hospital.

The mother did not see him until after he had been operated on. She learned from the nurse that he had been upset, had wanted to go home, and had cried for his mother. In the meantime, he had seen several other children enter the room after tonsillectomies. When she saw him, he had his hands tied to the sides of the crib. She thought that this was because he rocked so vigorously. He had to stay overnight while the other children who had had tonsillectomies earlier were taken home by their parents, When he came home, his baby brother had a cold, which Arthur contracted. He developed a fever and needed penicillin injections. It is interesting that the mother reported that after he had been home a week, he cried and asked her, "Why did they put me in a crib when the other big boys were in a bed?" The other children in the hospital, except the very young ones under two, had all been in beds.

It was shortly after the tonsillectomy that Arthur seemed to fall apart. The mother felt that Arthur had changed drastically on the day that she received the report of the psychological testing. She noticed that he became very despondent and was staring into space. He stopped talking and remained in this stuporous state.

From the developmental history, it appeared that this child had manifested signs of an early disturbance in object relationship by his disturbed sleep which later was replaced by excessive rocking. The mother was pleased that he gave up instinctual gratification without protest (as it would seem—prematurely), and that he had not shown any obvious signs of infantile sexuality (masturbation). According to the mother, he toilet-trained and weaned himself and had not protested her leaving him. It seemed to me that Arthur had indicated quite early that he also had a serious problem in using and expressing aggression. I learned later from the mother that there had also been a feeding problem, especially after weaning. Arthur did not chew well and, in order to speed up his feeding, she would place tiny pieces of food on his tongue so that he could swallow his food without chewing it. At the time that his brother was born Arthur apparently had tried to deal with his disappointment by identifying with the mother, playing mother with the baby doll. The mother later reported that, at that time, Arthur had expressed disappointment that she brought home only one baby. He spoke of two babies as if he had expected her to have two.

The summer preceding his acute schizophrenic break seemed to have been particularly trying. He went to day camp, leaving his mother with the baby brother, and at night it appeared that he assumed the role of the father, behaving like an adult. He slept in the same room with his mother and the baby and "he was very attentive and helpful to me, whispering in order not to disturb the baby." Weekends he was replaced by his father. He apparently was trying desperately to please his mother. He also gave up his bottle that summer. The head-throwing, twitching, and grunting which originated at that time could be interpreted, on the basis of our knowledge of children's reactions, as an indication of acute repression of aggression related to a traumatic oedipal phase. The unfortunate circumstances of the tonsillectomy made this an extremely traumatic experience for him, superimposed on his already very unbalanced state, and was apparently more than he could take. When he returned to the nursery school after the tonsillectomy, deterioration of his personality was so marked that an immediate psychological examination was advised.

The report of this examination left the mother hopeless, and the acute changes in Arthur's behavior, as observed and reported by the mother, indicated that he was very perceptive of her feelings. The psychological report emphasized the hereditary, organic etiology of the child's schizophrenia, leaving little or no hope for any psychotherapeutic approach to the problem. While undoubtedly this child had given evidence of atypical development prior to the onset of the acute schizophrenia, which resembled a catatonic state in an adult schizophrenic, it seemed to me that the role of chronic traumatization and of the unsatisfactory mother-child relationship as significant etiological factors in the child's condition were not recognized. For this reason I have presented the development data obtained from the mother in detail. It was on the basis of this information and of my thinking that I chose an approach to the case. I did not think that hospitalization was advisable, because I felt that it would only be taken by the child as a confirmation of his feelings of being given up and abandoned by his mother. This could only intensify the child's feelings of helplessness and act as a further motive for withdrawal from reality. I felt that an attempt should be made to reach the child and to interfere actively with his withdrawal. I also felt that it was essential to improve the mother-child relationship.

My approach to the parents was positive and encouraging. I especially praised the mother for her patience and astute observations in an attempt to enlist her help and cooperation for extramural treatment of Arthur. She was the leader of the family; her husband's position was weakened by the fact that his brother was a hospitalized schizophrenic, i.e., the unfavorable hereditary factors were on his side. I formed the definite impression that she was skeptical, and that she could not be involved in any treatment at this point. She appeared to have a compulsive personality with massive reaction formations and the facade of adequacy and normalcy were essential for the maintenance of her equilibrium. She agreed to give Arthur a chance for trial treatment and to supply further observations and reports of his behavior at home. Before my interview with Arthur, the mother informed me that there had been a change in his behavior; he seemed much better, almost cheerful, and was talking a great deal. He was difficult to understand because his speech was incoherent and he used many neologisms.

Arthur was a well-developed, handsome boy. He seemed disoriented and barely took any notice of his environment or of me. He left his mother in the waiting room without any protest and walked with me (I had taken him by the hand) into my playroom. He showed little interest in the toys; he was talking to himself. It appeared to me that he was hallucinating. He then crawled into the opening of the puppet stage and began to rock back and forth on his knees like a dervish. I sat on the floor next to him saying, "Arthur is afraid. He doesn't know where he is. Arthur is afraid. He doesn't know me. Arthur is rocking because he is afraid, like in the night when he is afraid and there is nobody there. I am here. I like Arthur. I like to play with Arthur." He didn't seem to listen but his swaying seemed to lessen. Suddenly his rocking increased violently and he was holding his hands over his eyes. I heard the noise of a (jet) plane. "Arthur is afraid of the noise," I said. "He doesn't know where it comes from. This is an airplane flying in the air. Arthur knows what an airplane is. Arthur must have seen many airplanes flying in the air. They make noise. Arthur doesn't like loud noises." He was talking, as it seemed, to himself. I clearly heard him say the word, "Light, Light." His mother had mentioned to me that, after he had come home from the hospital, he had talked a great deal about the light in the operating room. I remembered that I had seen, in nonpsychotic children who had undergone surgery, a strong reaction to the light over the operating table, which may have something to do with the feeling of being blindfolded before the anesthesia. I said, "This is not a hospital, Arthur. I know Arthur doesn't like hospitals and doctors. Your mother is outside. She is waiting for you. Let's go and see." I knew that he had heard me and understood because he had stopped rocking and got up immediately. I thought that I would not keep him too long for his first session and brought him back to his mother. There was no indication in his facial expression that he was relieved to see his mother and to leave me. He gave the impression of being oblivious to his environment and any changes in it. The mother reported that he was talking at home, that he was incoherent and difficult to understand, but it seemed to her that he was talking about the hospital and the children as she had heard him frequently mention these words. In the following two sessions Arthur's behavior was similar to that in the first session. He first crawled into his rocking space, but he stopped rocking and came to the play table and, upon my suggestion, made clay balls with me. I could occasionally make out a few words of what he was saying, which I used to try to break into his fantasies; for instance, when I heard him say the words, "country, boys," I said that the boys must have given him a hard time during the summer. The mother reported that he seemingly had taken notice of me. She heard him frequently mention the word, "lady" (on his way to my office). On his fourth visit, a hot summer day, Arthur was perspiring. He appeared very hot and uncomfortable. I washed his face with a cool washcloth and gave him a cold drink. I could hardly believe my ears when Arthur, in a clear voice and looking straight at me said, "I like you." Since private treatment for mother and child were out of the question, the best arrangement we could make for Arthur was placement in a day school for schizophrenic children where the child and mother could avail themselves of the services of professionally trained personnel.

The role of the parents in the total evaluation of treatment potential and final prognosis of a schizophrenic child is a factor of major importance. I have come to the conclusion that, unless at least one parent can be reached (emotionally) and can be relied upon, the chances for successful treatment are very poor. If, however, a reliable relationship with one parent can be established, a schizophrenic child can be treated successfully even in situations which would seem rather adverse.

JOHNNY, a six-year-old boy, was hospitalized with an acute upper respiratory infection. I saw him in consultation on the pediatric ward because the hospital personnel could not manage him. It was found that he had suffered from childhood schizophrenia since the age of two. The diagnosis had been established at the psychiatric department of a city hospital where the child had been admitted twice. The parents had been unable to follow through on the advice to institutionalize him. Both parents appeared to be very sick. The father was a weak, dependent, borderline schizophrenic; the mother was the stronger one, but she was also a latent psychotic. I was able to establish with the mother the kind of supportive relationship in which I became a mother figure to her and she, in turn, trusted her child to me. While it seemed essential for Arthur's mother to present and maintain a façade of health and adequacy at any cost, this mother displayed her helplessness and inadequacy and need for support in a most obvious way. She was immediately willing to accept me as a supporting mother, and to borrow the strength she herself lacked from me. Johnny was in ambulatory treatment at the Child Psychiatric Clinic (Jewish Hospital of Brooklyn), and I had an opportunity to follow up his development into adulthood. Several years after his treatment had been successfully terminated (he was almost twelve years old at that time), his mother developed an acute paranoia following a hysterectomy. She came to see me and, upon my advice, accepted hospitalization.

BILLY. Almost the reverse situation prevailed in the case of Billy, another schizophrenic boy. During his entire treatment (five and a half years) I saw his mother only once. This mother, in a paranoid manner, shied away from contact with psychiatrists. Realizing that she could not tolerate any involvement with her son's treatment nor accept any treatment herself, I left her alone and did not make any demands upon her. She continued to be seductive with her son and, in many ways, tried to interfere with his treatment. Yet, it was possible to keep the boy in therapy because the father, who had had treatment himself and was genuinely concerned in helping his son, was instrumental in the successful outcome of the therapy.

I have encountered the greatest difficulties with those cases where, on the surface, the environment of the child seemed to be adequate and the parents appeared to be intelligent, well-meaning, and successful people. I have found such parents to be particularly unreliable and unpredictable in their actions.

TIMMY, a five-year-old schizophrenic boy, was referred by the school he attended. Both parents were highly intelligent people, yet, although the child's behavior had obviously been schizophrenic for some time, they waited until the school insisted that he be seen by a psychiatrist. The mother had accepted referral because, for the pursuit of her activities, it was essential for her to have him in this school. The child responded very well to therapy, but at the time when he began to assert himself and to emerge as an individual, the mother withdrew him from treatment.

In the case where the parents unconsciously identify the psychotic child with either their own sibling, or parent, but particularly with their own denied psychotic personality, treatment of the child cannot be successful. Such parents cannot tolerate improvement of the child; the improvement threatens to upset their own precarious balance. They can maintain balance or sanity themselves only at the cost of the psychotic child. The attitude of such parents often is, "There is nothing wrong with us. We sacrifice ourselves for the child who, unfortunately, was born or for some unknown reason has become psychotic." These parents need, and invariably succeed in obtaining, an alibi for themselves by securing an organic diagnosis for the child. In such a case, it is essential to work with the one parent who has this unconscious identification, preferably prior to the treatment of the child.* Paradoxical as it may seem, the chances for successful treatment are better for children whose environment appears more overtly disturbed and traumatic.

BETTY. The case of Betty, a seven-year-old schizophrenic girl with bizarre behavior and marked retardation, comes to mind. She had lost her mother at the age of three, had lived for two years with a family where she was left almost entirely to the care of a senile grandfather. From the age of five, she had lived with her father, who had not

* A comprehensive presentation of the theories and of the techniques of treatment of childhood schizophrenia, which would have to be documented with detailed case material from the treatment of the child and, wherever necessary, also from the treatment of the mother, cannot be given within the framework of this communication.

remarried and who seemed to have strong, unconscious homosexual tendencies. Two elderly sisters of the father, one a simple schizophrenic and the other a spinster, lived with them. A third aunt, also a sister of the father, was in a state hospital. It was possible to utilize the genuine interest of the father to help his daughter to the extent that he changed his mode of living, and reserved several hours a day for his child. He also saw to it that the schizophrenic aunt, with whom the child spent most of the day, carried out suggestions made by me, especially that she discontinue sleeping with the child and handling her bodily. The child responded remarkably well to treatment. Some of her bizarre behavior could be understood as an imitation of, and an adaptation to, her unusual environment. In such cases, the child does not serve any specific unconscious purpose, but seems to be the by-product of the disturbed environment. If someone—as in this case, the father and one aunt—is genuinely interested in helping the child, the chances for recovery are good.

In view of the increasing demand upon child psychiatrists for treatment of schizophrenic children, the suggestions made here may be of some help in evaluating the suitability of cases.

# 23

# Equivalents of Depression in Children

It is commonly held that depression is a rare psychiatric condition in children (Hall, 1952; Despert, 1952; Bellak, 1952), as is evidenced by the paucity of references to this subject in psychiatric literature. This belief seems to be based on the assumption that depressive moods and ideas of self-destruction are foreign to the child's nature. The findings of my study, based on the psychoanalytic treatment of severe depressions (manic-depressive, schizophrenic, and neurotic types) in a number of adults and in fifteen children ranging in age from early infancy to adolescence, do not confirm this view (see M. Sperling, 1949a, 1950a and d). The depression, however, is not easily recognized because its overt manifestations are in most cases different from those in adults. As a result of incorrect diagnosis, these children are rarely seen by a psychiatrist. The pediatrician's treatment is in these cases ineffectively directed toward the presenting symptoms, while the underlying depression remains unrecognized and untreated.

It is well known that the severe forms of depression in

adults are often accompanied by somatic manifestations. In fact, the presence of somatic symptoms as well as the onset and course in certain types of depression (endogenous), which seem unrelated to external events, have been used in support of the concept of the constitutional and organic nature of such depressions (Jacobson, 1953).

Investigating the prevalent somatic manifestations in severe depression, we find most frequent and prominent disturbances of the digestive system. In fact, a certain type of anorexia and of abdominal complaints have been described as equivalents of depression in adults (Gero, 1953; Schick, 1941). My own findings in cases of severe ulcerative colitis revealed the close interrelation of melancholic depression and this illness (M. Sperling, 1946). Such findings indicating that oral conflicts are of dynamic importance are not surprising, but in accordance with the classical psychoanalytic concepts developed by Freud (1917), Abraham (1924, 1927), Rado (1928), Klein (1935), and others. Psychoanalysis has shown that the fixation and regression in depression is to the oral phases, particularly to the oral-sadistic phase of the psychosexual development.

Next in frequency among somatic manifestations are disturbances of sleep, especially the severe insomnia of agitated depression. In this connection, I am referring to my findings concerning the significance of early sleep disturbances in children as an oral symptom and indication of a severe disturbance in object relationship and possible forerunner of a later psychotic development (see Chapter 4). Pruritus, which is often generalized and intractable but may also be localized, is frequently found as a persistent symptom in depression and has recently been described as a depressive equivalent (Edwards, 1954). Migrainous type headaches are another somatic symptom associated with, and sometimes found as an equivalent of, depression (M. Sperling, 1952a). Motor retardation and the slowing up of vegetative functions are other well-known manifestations belonging to the clinical picture of depression.

In all the children with depression whom I have treated, two or more of these somatic manifestations were present in a very marked degree. The clinical picture, especially in the younger children, was that of a child suffering from an illness that primarily affected his food intake and sleep. The listlessness, moodiness, and general unhappiness of these children, often expressed in incessant crying, are not recognized by physicians as symptoms of depression, but are regarded as sequelae of the poor physical condition caused by an unknown illness. The case of an infant and that of a two-year-old child will be used to illustrate some of these points.

A child analyst is rarely consulted for an illness of an infant of four months, especially when nothing in the overt symptomatology points to a psychiatric disorder. The maternal grandmother of this infant was my patient, and she frequently mentioned how disturbed the entire family had been since the birth of the child. The infant appeared to be very restless, cried incessantly, did not take food, and vomited when food was forced upon her. She did not sleep and had to be carried around practically all night. "I don't think she wants to live," the grandmother would say to me. "She sighs like an old person and she never smiles."

I knew from my patient the unhappy events which had preceded the child's birth. She had been conceived in an extramarital affair and the mother had hoped for her parents' permission to divorce her husband and marry her lover. Her parents, however, opposed this plan because they considered the man a fortune hunter. The marriage broke up and the young mother returned to her parents' home with the child. The grandparents did not accept their granddaughter, and the grandfather had refused to see the child. The infant had been examined by several pediatricians, none of whom could determine her condition. Changes of formulas and sedation brought no relief. A baby nurse was in attendance. According to the grandmother, the situation had become increasingly worse, and at the suggestion of a consultant pediatrician an appointment had been made to have the infant X-rayed to find out whether an enlarged thymus was the cause of her trouble. At this point, the infant's mother came to see me at the suggestion of my patient.

The mother was basically a warm person, but she was

unhappy about the outcome of her love affair. When she realized that her parents would not permit her to marry her lover, it was too late for an abortion. Her parents were also unwilling for her to place the child for adoption. Her pervading feeling was that the child had ruined her life, was responsible for the loss of her husband, and for her present complete dependence upon her parents. She realized that she wished the infant out of the way, and wanted to have nothing to do with her. She could not even look at her. She knew that the nurse was very rough with the child but did not really mind. The young mother could be reached rather easily and helped to accept her child within a short time.

There was an instant and miraculous change in the child's behavior. No treatment had been instituted; in fact, at my suggestion, the X-ray examination had been canceled and sedatives had been discontinued. I attributed this change in the infant's behavior to a change in the mother's feelings and attitude toward her. The mother took over her care and the grandparents reconciled themselves to the situation; the grandmother, especially, gave much genuine affection to the child.*

I have remained in contact with the family for a number of years and have been able to follow the development of this child. Her mother remarried when the child was two years old. The new husband adopted her and, it appears, accepted her with great love. Thus she gained not only full status but also a loving father. The child is now nine years old. She seems to be a happy, healthy, well-functioning youngster.

The psychosomatic implications for the infant in a disturbed mother-child relationship have been recognized and described by a number of investigators (Benedek, 1949; Fries, 1954; Sperling, 1954; Spitz, 1951). That certain psychosomatic manifestations in early infancy represent the infantile form of a depressive reaction has not been recognized as yet. The clinical picture of "anaclitic depression" in infants, described by Spitz (1951), represents a severe disturbance of a psychotic nature,

* For further details, see Sperling (1949b). In this connection Ferenczi's paper, "The Unwelcome Child and His Death Instinct" (1929), seems of particular interest.

reversible only in its incipience. This type of depression is described as occurring in severely deprived infants of eight months or older, as a reaction to separation from the mother. In the children with whom I have worked, there was no apparent deprivation or separation from the mother.

Only close investigation revealed a certain quality of the mother-child relationship which would seem to play a specific role in the genesis of a depressive reaction in the child. The lack of genuine love for the child and acceptance of him is covered up by an overcompensatory concern and preoccupation with his bodily functions. In the atmosphere of such an emotional setting, certain experiences which the child ordinarily can assimilate into his growing personality assume an exaggerated traumatic significance and are reacted to as loss of the mother, even when in reality such a feeling on the part of the child would seem entirely unjustified. The similarity in the quality of the mother-child relationship in the cases of children with certain psychosomatic diseases and in those with somatic equivalents of depression is striking and thought-provoking, especially with regard to the problems of etiology, treatment, and prevention of the endogenous and psychotic types of depression of adults (Sperling, 1949d, 1955c).

The case of a two-year-old child may illustrate some of these points further. Actually this little girl had been referred to me for psychiatric investigation at the age of twenty-two months because of attacks of paroxysmal tachycardia, for which no cause could be established. She had been hospitalized twice for observation of this condition (see Chapter 9). At the age of twenty-six months, during my absence on summer vacation, the child developed a severe anorexia and sleep disturbance. She stopped eating and her sleep became fitful and interrupted by nightmares of hallucinatory quality. Her tendency to withdraw, previously evident, became more pronounced and she now spent hours in a crouched position in the corner of her room, fingering her blanket and clicking her tongue.

Play analysis disclosed that this behavior was the child's dramatic reaction to the birth of a baby brother. In a cooking game with dolls, she brought to the fore, and played and worked through, her intense repressed oral-sadistic impulses directed toward her mother and the baby brother. There had been no overt indication of her oral envy and jealousy of the baby. Her animal phobias, which she had developed together with the somatic symptoms, could be understood as projections of these repressed oral-sadistic impulses onto the familiar animals and could be resolved in play therapy. From a dynamic point of view, these phobias represented the child's attempt to rescue her very precarious relationship with her mother and to save herself from a psychosis by displacing onto the animals her oral-sadistic impulses. This case was characterized by two of the most conspicuous somatic features found in certain forms of depression in adults, namely, severe anorexia and insomnia. In addition, she suffered from motor retardation, withdrawal, moodiness, and phobias. Her phobias were of the nature of persecutory fears—a symptom which belongs in the clinical picture of the schizoid-paranoid form of depression in adults.

In addition to direct psychoanalytic play therapy with the child, treatment included work with the mother. The relationship between mother and child had been very precarious prior to the birth of the baby brother. The traumatic effect of this event was derived mainly from the disturbed mother-child relationship in which the birth of the baby brother meant to the child loss of the mother. The traumatic effect of this experience was enhanced by the fact that the analyst also had abandoned her (was on vacation) during this particularly trying period of her life. Her mother, in actuality, preferred the baby brother because of his sex. She had unconsciously identified her daughter with her own mother and grandmother, both of whom she considered "weak" and "inferior" and held in contempt. In treatment the mother discovered that she, too, had a "weak" female part, and that it was this rejected part of herself which she had denied and projected onto her daughter and which she was so vigorously suppressing now in her child. She did not want to see herself in her child, who strikingly resembled the mother and maternal grandmother, because she fancied herself as so different from her own mother. The mother herself had been a cry-baby, who had changed into an aggressive and controlling person in adolescence and married a very passive, ineffectual man. In this case the highly ambivalent feelings of the mother toward her child had become even more intense after the birth of the baby boy. The mother was openly triumphant over the fact that she had given birth to a boy, while her grandmother and mother had been unable to bear sons. This gave prestige and value to her life, while the sickly, moody daughter was an unfavorable reflection of herself.

When the child was unresponsive and moody, the mother had found it very difficult to be with her; in fact, she had considered it a relief when the child remained quietly by herself for long periods of time. At my suggestion, and supported through treatment, the mother now spent much time with the little girl, inventing games to stimulate the child's interest and thus prevent her from withdrawing. In the main, this new regime served to provide the child with the essential "emotional supplies" from her mother.

The recognition and treatment of depressive equivalents in a young child are of particular significance if one considers the difficulties encountered in the treatment of severe depression in adults. The case of a thirty-six-year-old woman treated psychoanalytically by me for five years is cited briefly to highlight this point. This patient had been suffering from recurrent depressions since adolescence and had had a psychotic break with depression after childbirth. In her analysis it was found that the prototype for these depressions had occurred when she was two years old and a baby brother had been born. At that time (confirmed by the patient's mother) she had changed from a happy and lively youngster to a moody and sick child, and had remained this way until she came for analysis (Sperling, 1950a).

These cases do not of course imply that the birth of a younger sibling necessarily causes a depression in the older child or even predisposes the older child to a depressive reaction. In certain cases, however, as discussed before, such an experience may have this specific traumatic effect upon the older child. Other events in early childhood, which to the child represent loss of the love object—such as illness or death of a parent, grandparent, or other parent substitutes, loss of a friend or even of a pet, which may have been the only love object with whom the child had a positive relationship—may have such traumatic effects and precipitate a depression (Keeler, 1954). The following case is an example.

An eight-year-old girl whom I treated for ulcerative colitis developed a severe attack of ulcerative colitis in reaction to the loss of her dog, which her mother had given away without the child's consent (Sperling, 1946). Later in her treatment, when she no longer had ulcerative colitis and the depressive mechanisms underlying this illness had become manifest, she reacted with some overt depressive symptoms to the loss of a second dog which had run away. Still later, she developed a brief depressive episode following the death of her grandfather. She had a particularly severe anorexia and was avoiding meat and meat products in an almost phobic way. In her analysis, it was found that this was a counterphobic attitude used in defense against very strong cannibalistic impulses. Such impulses had also been prominent in the dynamics of her earlier ulcerative colitis. It is noteworthy that the onset of the ulcerative colitis occurred when her father had been inducted into the army, and that an unusually severe anorexia had been an outstanding feature then. The death of the grandfather, unconsciously identified with the father, revived the trauma of the father's loss and called forth the same reaction, no longer in the form of ulcerative colitis but in the form of a depression with somatic symptoms. For a period of several weeks following the death of her grandfather, she also developed severe insomnia. She explained her not sleeping at all at night by saying, "Because it's so quiet, as if everybody were dead." Only during the day, when there was light and her mother could be heard in the kitchen, would she fall asleep. She was preoccupied with death, imagining that her dead grandfather was waiting for her in Heaven. She harbored intense unconscious death wishes against her father who stood between her and her mother, and she felt guilty for the death of her grandfather.

Anorexia and insomnia are the most prominent somatic equivalents found in depression. Severe general pruritus, with or without dermatitis, occurring especially during the night, is another somatic symptom frequently associated with depression.

A seven-year-old girl was referred to me for treatment because of a severe generalized pruritus with secondary skin irritation resulting from uncontrollable scratching, which was especially intense at night. On closer investigation, it was found that the child suffered from a depression with severe insomnia. The pruritus served to keep her awake during the night and, in addition, the scratching awakened her mother. The mother would then take her into her bed because the child claimed that this relieved the itching. This child was really afraid to fall asleep on account of her "horrible nightmares." She especially dreaded a recurrent dream in which she had a feeling of tightness, as if "I could not move or breathe," and had a feeling of being cold, like a "stone" or "ice."

The child's father, to whom she had been very attached, had died suddenly when she was six years old. The mother was a withdrawn, narcissistic woman who was herself depressed and unable to give warmth and affection to the child. The pruritus brought them into closer physical contact. It prompted the mother to have the child sleep with her, and on many occasions to take over the scratching for the child. They were actually meeting one another by way of the pruritus.

## Summary and Conclusions

My case material (of which only a small fraction could be presented here) demonstrates clearly two phenomena. I shall start with a discussion of the first one, namely, the prevalence of somatic symptomatology in the depression of young children. This is a phenomenon which has also been observed in the more severe depressions, particularly the so-called endogenous depressions of adults. The fact that the young child tends to express depression in somatic equivalents can be readily understood on the basis that the child is unable to tolerate painful sensations and impulses without immediate release. Such immediate "acting out" of impulses and emotions without awareness is possible only through bodily channels. Here the similarity between the dynamics of this type of depression and certain psychosomatic diseases becomes apparent. In both cases we find an immature ego structure coupled with a certain type of object relationship of a primitive nature. On the oral level, food and love object are equated and conflicts about object relationships may be experienced as conflicts about food and expressed as eating disturbances. "I don't want food," equals, in such a case, "I don't want mother."

The severe sleep disturbances found in these children also reflect their disturbed object relationships. It is the fear of losing the love object (in reality) which makes sleep dangerous for these children, and through their sleep disturbance they manage to secure the presence and even physical contact with the mother during the night. Yet food and sleep are as indispensable for the maintenance of life as is the care of a mother for the child. In a severe depression the adult patient regresses to the oral level with a revival of the earliest conflicts in which food and mother are unconsciously equated. Unconsciously, such a patient reacts like an infant, who feels helpless in the face of a frustrating reality. The profound disturbances of such vital and pleasurable functions as food intake and sleep in depression in children and certain depressions in adults can be understood on this basis.

The second finding, namely, that there is a high incidence of depression in children of all ages—contrary to the common belief—becomes evident if we consider some of the differences in clinical manifestations of depression in children and that in adults. This finding is also in accordance with the ubiquitous nature of depression (in adults) and with the basic psychoanalytic concepts concerning the traumatic etiology of the neuroses and psychoses and the role of early childhood experiences in the predisposition to mental illness. In this connection I am referring again to the psychoanalytic groundwork on this subject, especially Freud (1925) and Abraham (1924, 1927).

Melanie Klein postulates a "paranoid" and a "depressive" position as regular phenomena in infancy occurring at three and six months of age respectively. M. Klein does not relate these phenomena to traumatic experiences, but regards them as stages in personality development independent of actual life circumstances and of the quality of the mother-child relationship.

In conclusion, I would like to emphasize some of the practical applications of this study, particularly from the standpoint of prevention. A proper evaluation of certain conditions in children, leading to the correct diagnosis and effective therapy, might be significant steps toward a preventive approach to depressive illness in adulthood.

The orientation of pediatricians, who treat these children, to such a view would be essential. Treatment of equivalents of depression in a child cannot be limited to the treatment of the somatic manifestations; it must be directed primarily toward the child's reaction to the feeling of loss of his love object. These feelings are the result of the child's relationship with his mother or her substitute. To improve this relationship and to provide an emotionally suitable mother or mother substitute, I consider an essential part in the treatment of a young child suffering from depression or somatic equivalents of depressions.

I conclude that the predominantly somatic nature under which a depression manifests itself in childhood is retained and revived in certain depressions of adults. The traumatic nature of a depression in a child can be established rather easily and linked to specific experiences, while this is a difficult task in certain depressions of adults. This fact may have implications concerning current views about the etiology of certain types of depression in adults.

## Notes on Depression in Children

Increased accident-proneness is sometimes an indication of an underlying depression in older children. It occurs also in younger children following traumatic experiences, especially the loss of a love object. One of my patients, a six-year-old boy, had two rather serious accidents following the death of his mother. This, however, was not the reason for his referral. It had been noted in school that he had become inattentive and was daydreaming most of the time. One day while walking with his father he jumped into the lake although he could not swim, "just for fun." At another time he climbed into a parked delivery truck, released the brakes. The car started rolling but was stopped before crashing by the truck driver who ran out from the store. Another patient of mine, a seven-year-old boy, remembered during his treatment that he had swallowed a bottle of aspirin when he was three years old. He was rushed to the hospital and there was a lot of commotion about it. He came for treatment because he was an unhappy, awkward, rather passive boy who was holding on to his mother, much to her dismay. What is of interest here is that already at the age of three he seemed to have been fully aware of the suicidal implications of this act. A similar situation obtained in the case of Paul, who at the age of three and a half swallowed about ten thyroid pills while his mother was talking on the telephone, but was not unaware of what Paul was doing. The physician whom she called several hours later as much as accused her of intent to murder. Paul's mother had attempted suicide at age seven, on the day she was to return home with her father. She drank a disinfectant and was well aware that it was a poisonous substance. Her stomach had to be pumped and the return delayed. At the age of five, as a reaction to her brother's birth, she had "playfully and accidentally" cut off her hair completely. She had her first hypomanic episode after her brother was killed in a car accident; Paul was to his mother a replacement of this brother and carried her brother's name.

Another patient, a boy of age twelve, who came for treatment because of epilepsy, remembered several accidents with clearly suicidal intent from his early childhood. At one time, when he was about three years old, he climbed up to the medicine chest and tried to grab his father's razor blades with the intention of slitting his throat. At another time he swallowed a bottle of aspirin and had to be brought to the hospital. In both instances he knew quite well what he was doing. At a later age he would frequently bang his head against the wall with such force that he could be heard downstairs. This occurred especially when his parents were entertaining their friends and sent him up to his room.

# PART 8

# CONCLUSION

# 24

# Psychoanalytic Aspects of Discipline

*"Until the day dawns when the ideas are accepted that man is an indivisible whole, that psychiatry permeates the whole of medicine, and that students should be taught by the same men at the same time and on the same patients about the disorders of the mind as about the disease of the body, it is to be feared that the misunderstanding of the relations between mind and body will continue."*

—J. W. Todd in RATIONAL MEDICINE.

## Part 1

Not only to the general public, but also to psychiatrists and even psychoanalysts, is the concept of discipline enmeshed in considerable confusion. Lay critics of psychoanalysis have based their opposition, among other things, on the assumption that psychoanalysis aims at the elimination of disciplinary controls, with a consequent deterioration of the moral fiber of the individual. To "lose one's inhibitions" is considered by dilettantes to be the frivolous aim of psychoanalytic therapy and psychoanalysis is in this vein made the butt of numerous jokes.

The need for clarification of the dynamics of discipline as viewed from the standpoint of psychoanalytic theory and practice is of utmost importance in the present phase of child analysis, when therapeutic techniques have to be used in the handling not only of the classically inhibited patient, but also with the patient whose behavior disturbance is characterized by a *lack of inhibition*. Historically, psychoanalytic techniques were applied

397

to the neurotic, for whom the cathartic method was employed as a means of eliciting the repressed material. In the handling of disorders involving uninhibited (undisciplined) behavior of children, we have learned to use modified psychoanalytic techniques based on the understanding of the therapeutic role of the analyst, who functions as a support to the child's ego, and where the treatment method is not the acting out and release of repressed impulses but rather the integration of conflicting impulses into the ego, and a strengthening of its synthetic function.

Discipline has been equated with a repression of instinctual demands and has implicitly been repudiated as a component of sterile educational methods. Liberation of instincts is equated with lack of discipline and is erroneously regarded as the aim of psychoanalytic therapy. True discipline requires that the instinctual energy be at the service of the individual so that he is not afraid to use his impulses, and is independent of the pressure of the environment (parents, teachers) in the control of his impulses. When this is achieved, we have an internalization of superego commands, resulting in real discipline and personality growth. Psychoanalysis does not regard the release of impulses as a way of life, rather it aims at a liberation of impulses bound in repression so that they are made available to the individual for use in his life's pursuits.

It seems to me that the core of confusion regarding discipline lies in the fact that the defenses against repressed impulses (aggressive and sexual) and particularly reaction formation are looked upon as representing discipline. In reaction formation there is a transformation of the repressed impulses, usually into the opposite of the original instinctual drive: as for instance, over-concern for cleanliness is a compensation for the wish to be dirty, extreme kindness the disguised wish to be sadistic. The person is constantly on guard against the return of the repressed temptation and uses up his energy in order to maintain the repression. In lifting the inhibitions through analysis, the repressed energy is made available to the individual who in the course of treatment has developed sufficient confidence in his ability to maintain control, so that he can either suppress these impulses consciously or use them on a sublimated level.

Some of the modern trends in education and pediatrics reflect the misleading application of the concept of freedom, namely, release from discipline, e.g., in the exaggerated permissiveness of the progressive schools, nurseries and in the self-demand system for infants. In abandoning rigidity and authoritarianism, the tendency has been to abandon all restraint and, consequently, unduly severe responsibilities have been imposed, particularly on the younger child who needs to feel that there is a stronger person to support him in his struggle with his own impulses. The child feels safer when there is a ceiling to his impulses and becomes anxious when his forbidden impulses seek release. To give in to the child's demand is easier and pleasanter for the parent, who unconsciously feels that the child could not possibly tolerate the tensions which he has himself not mastered. The parents through identification with the child subtly transmit their fear or unwillingness to tolerate the force of their own impulses. Such parents may encourage in their child the lawlessness which is forbidden to them as adults and which they act out unconsciously in the child. Case histories provide ample material to illustrate the parent's provocation of the child to engage in destructive acts. The parent in such a case usually does not mete out punishment appropriate to the offense, but punishes the child for something inconsequential.

Where the mother has no faith in her ability to control her own (objectionable) impulses, she can have little expectation that the child can achieve control. Only absence of fear from one's own impulses and ability for self-control make it possible for parents and educators to give leadership to the child. The ability to tolerate the frustrating tensions in the early training periods may be viewed from the standpoint of the normal expectation set up by a mother who feels confident that even the young child can tolerate some measure of instinctual discomfort. She will then not fall back into overprotective pampering. The personality of parents and educators who themselves are afraid of their impulses is recognized in the undue harshness with which they ruthlessly suppress manifestations of impulses in children because they represent a threat to themselves; there is a fear in the adult that the act of the child may provoke a breakthrough of their own repressed impulses. The strict parents and judges are those who fear themselves and mete out punishment in accordance with the degree of panic elicited by the original feeling as reflected in the offender. To punish severely is to keep the impulse adequately repressed.

The inconsistency of undue severity and undue permissiveness reflects the weakness of the ego of the parents. Undue permissiveness and leniency of many parents is not interpreted by the child as a sign of love or respect for its democratic rights. On the contrary, the child rightly perceives this attitude as an indication of weakness in the parent and a certain lack of concern for the child. In the struggle to achieve true discipline, namely, control from within, not from the outside forces, there has to be a positive identification with the restraining or prohibiting personality. In order to help the child to achieve this, it is necessary, as a first step in transmitting standards of discipline, to strengthen and support his immature ego in its efforts to tolerate the tensions of the instinct without immediate release. It is in this area that so many parents fail.

It is also in this area of the early training of the child that the insight gained from psychoanalysis is of the utmost importance. While it is not possible to give parents a blueprint which would tell them how to handle each specific problem in a specific way, we can give to the parents and educators a basic understanding of the child's emotional struggles and a dynamic orientation toward the problem of discipline.

It was left to the genius of Freud to discover and to formulate for us, first in reconstruction from the analysis of adults and later from direct observations on children, the basic dynamic concepts of child development. This has effected a complete reorientation in child psychology with regard to the role of the instinctive urges in the development of the child. Psychoanalysis has shown that these innate drives are of the utmost importance in shaping the child's personality and character. Psychoanalysis has further taught us that the personality development of the child depends largely upon the interplay of these internal forces with the forces coming from the environment, particularly those coming from the most important people of the child's environment, his parents; in short, it has shown the significance of the parent-child relationship in the developing personality structure of the child. This is not to be understood, however, that the child merely mirrors the parental attitudes like a neutral agent, but rather that each child reacts to his environment in a specific way, dependent upon a complexity of factors, internal and external, of which the child's emotional relationship with the parents, reflected in the degree of his security, is a most important one.

It is not possible within the framework of this chapter to give a complete psychoanalytic exposé of child development, but it will be necessary to mention at least some important facts. From a dynamic point of view, the fusion of the two fundamental instincts—sex and aggression—is most important. These two instincts combine forces, thereby producing the characteristic manifestations of each of the child's developmental phases, eventually leading him into maturity. Any disturbance of the proper fusion of these instincts creates severe disturbances in the development of the child. From this it becomes clear that the proper handling of the aggressive and sexual impulses in children are of paramount importance. The fusion of sexual impulses with aggression makes it possible for the child to assert his rights to the possession of his love objects and for the mastery of reality in general. Without the admixture of aggression, sexuality would be ineffective; passivity and weak object relationships with impotence of the individual would be the result. On the other hand an insufficient admixture of sexual (libidinal) impulses with aggression would manifest itself in destructive and uncontrollable tendencies, making the child antisocial and criminal. It is precisely in the areas of sexuality and aggression that parents and educators make the most harmful blunders.

How much expression of such impulses to allow and how much to deny, when to allow and when to curb constitutes one of the most difficult tasks for parents and one in which even the most well-meaning parents will err unless they have a dynamic understanding and are not too much disturbed by their own emotional conflicts. This is the Scylla and Charybdis in training, where indulging the child without restraining his instinctual demands will make him unfit for living in a social group and a parasite and menace to society; while too early and too severe restrictions, by setting up massive repressions, will deprive the child of the energy that he needs for adequate functioning.

Yet the task of the parents in the education of the child in our society is to enable the child to tolerate a certain amount of frustration and also a necessary degree of control of impulses so that the child can live in a group and in conformity with required standards. Failure to achieve this essential adjustment of the child is a phenomenon so very frequent now that many child analysts have stated that child neuroses are disappearing in favor of severe behavior disorders and child delinquency. Parents who themselves do not accept and are unwilling to conform with the standards of our society are unable to achieve this in their children. Particularly difficult for the child is a situation where each parent takes a different attitude. In such a case the child behaves as if pulled all the time in opposite directions.

Tolerance for the expression of hostility and manifestations of infantile sexuality in children is very limited in parents who have difficulty in conceiving that their own offspring should at times hate them and should want to be destructive and dirty. This is even so with many so-called progressive parents, who have an intellectual acceptance of these expressions but reject them emotionally because they experience them as a danger and threat to their own repressed, objectionable impulses. This rejection may be masked by a liberal use of terminology and lengthy technical explanations given to the children and by what would appear to be free and uninhibited behavior. Yet the child is not deceived by the pseudo-freedom, but very keenly senses the parental anxieties, which are a result of incomplete repressions. Children often feel seduced by their parents' behavior, for instance, the indiscriminate bodily display in which many parents indulge for "the sake of the child," "so that he will not be bashful" or the close physical contact which many parents maintain, even with older children, under the slogan "love your child." Such practices only overstimulate and increase the child's own anxiety and certainly do not support him in the struggle with his own impulses.

One mother, who had difficulty in disciplining her twelve-year-old son, was amazed to find that her son experienced taking showers together as a seduction. Even then she could not get herself frankly to tell him that this was not proper, but would try to avoid it by excusing herself with a headache. She had found nothing wrong with his affectionate kissing her on the mouth and in this situation also resorted to excuses, such as he shouldn't do it because of lipstick. Another mother, who complained that her three-and-a-half-year-old son would not allow her any privacy, was astounded to find that it was really she herself who did not allow him to have any privacy. She was a woman with very strong anal impulses, and would not allow her son to use the bathroom alone. She was startled to find how well he understood and respected her privacy when she allowed him to have his. In her analysis, it was revealed that she was afraid to be alone in the bathroom because of a fear that she might faint during defecation.

For a real understanding and acceptance of the child's instinctual nature, not only an intellectual but an emotional acceptance of psychoanalytic concepts is necessary. Without this, much of the behavior of the child, especially when it is motivated by unconscious drives, remains unintelligible and inaccessible to change. It is obvious that child training and education and pedagogy in general have gained and have still much more to gain from psychoanalysis. This does not mean that psychoanalysis is to take the place of ordinary child-rearing. Psychoanalysis cannot substitute for this, not only for practical but also for theoretical reasons. Psychoanalysis is a method of investigation and treatment of the mentally sick. Training and discipline however, are methods for the healthy child who is still in the process of growth. Through correct application of psychoanalytic thinking, training and discipline should be practiced so that the child can remain healthy during these formative processes and yet with the understanding help of his parents and educators, acquire the internal controls and the inner freedom that are necessary to make him a happy child and later a mature adult.

## Part 2: Case Presentations

A variety of situations, some of a more simple and some of a more complex nature, will be presented to illustrate the points made in Part One.

Eight-year-old Martin was a severe behavior problem, a terror in school and in the neighborhood. His mother suffered from a functional heart condition which she attributed to the excitement which Martin caused her. At home he was rather well-behaved and affectionate with his mother and his three years younger brother. Psychoanalytic investigation revealed that Martin was acting out his unconscious, very intense resentment of his mother with his teachers. In this way, he managed (similarily to the way a phobic would) to live comparatively free from anxiety with the real objects of his hostility. In this case, guidance of the mother alone, who was willing and cooperative, would have been insufficient, without the child's understanding of the unconscious motive for his behavior. It was possible to interpret comparatively easily to the child why he was acting in this way, and with the changed attitude of the mother, who allowed Martin to verbalize some of his feelings regarding the brother, the vicious cycle could be reversed.

In another, on the surface, very similar situation, the dynamics were somewhat different and required more intensive work, especially with the mother. Eight-year-old Robert was constantly in trouble with the neighbors and in school, but he was also disobedient and difficult at home. The mother claimed that she could get him to do things only with corporal punishment. Robert, who to some degree was openly expressing his hostility toward his younger brother and his resentment of his mother, was also a nail-biter and although of superior intelligence not able to apply himself in school. He was a very insecure child who felt rejected by his mother. It was brought out that his mother had identified Robert with her husband in the traits which she resented very much in him and punished in her child, using Robert as a substitute for her husband. The marriage was unsatisfactory. The mother was unconsciously castrating both her husband and Robert, while the younger boy was spared because he submitted passively to her. Robert tried to resolve his difficulties in a masochistic fashion. Some very insecure children develop such an attitude as a reaction to the unpredictable and explosive behavior of the mother, who in excitement threatens to leave the child, give him away, kill herself, etc. Through their provocative or negativistic behavior they try to bring on the very reaction in the parents that they fear most. They have an unconscious need to "make" them lose control and the parents usually comply very promptly. The parents, as a result of their own helplessness, now try to assert their control over the child at all costs. When this happens the parents have lost the battle, because the child now unconsciously operates by the masochistic formula, "I must be in control of the situation. So they can't do anything to me unless I want them to." This control over the parents is then proven by "I can get them angry when I want to and even though they punish me, it is because I want them to." There is no way out of this vicious cycle for either child or parent unless they are helped to recognize why and how they got into it and unless the parents are willing to make the first step to stop it. It is a difficult situation for the parents, who expect the child to change instantly, while the child, from his previous experience, has learned to mistrust the stability of the parents and will try through provocation to test them again and again until he is convinced. Psychoanalytic insight made it possible to recognize the different underlying dynamics and mechanisms used by these two children and to resolve them, although on surface observation the two cases appeared to be very similar.

Another typical, difficult situation for parents and therapists, yet inevitable in the course of therapeutic reeducation of a child, is the transitory phase of the freeing of repressed, destructive energy in the treatment of the neurotically inhibited child. In such a case the analyst sometimes has to take over the role of the parents in order to achieve at a belated date with the child what his real parents failed to achieve. Anna Freud, in discussing the technique of child analysis, states that the child analyst in some cases also has educational functions which should be carried out, preferably in conjunction with the parents. In order to get the child ready for this, a part of the neurosis or character deformation first has to be removed. This implies work with and transformation of the unconscious of the child, for which neither parents nor educators are equipped and for which the therapist himself requires special training. This makes it obvious that our ordinary means of education are not sufficient in such cases.

The analyst has to be able to establish a relationship with the child that enables the child to make a positive identification with his analyst in the important therapeutic aspects and to be willing to accept discipline from him. Only then will the analyst be able to convey the feeling to the child that the child can tolerate his destructive impulses in consciousness without having to act them out instantly. There seems to be a naive belief that psychoanalytic therapy with a child is permission given by the analyst to the child to act out all of his impulses. If this were so, such a therapy would certainly not only not help the child, but would increase his internal and external difficulties. Being at the mercy of his impulses, he would only get into more serious conflicts with his environment in his attempts to act them out. The child must feel that the analyst, while understanding his urges and his need to release them, will stand by and not let him be overwhelmed by them. If the child does not feel safeguarded in this way by his analyst, he will be anxious and distrustful, looking upon the analyst as a person who seduces him into being "bad" and thus gets him into conflict with himself and his environment. Also the child always, and rightly so, interprets complete permissiveness of the adult as weakness, and as a result may become increasingly destructive in order to test how far he can go without being stopped. Every analyst has had the experience in treating children that his permissiveness is felt as a threat by the child. The child, like the adult patient, wants the analyst to be as afraid as the child himself is of his impulses, so that the analyst will not insist upon bringing these dangerous impulses to the fore. The analyst must not fail in this test, because it is this specific experience which so many children have never had in actual life with their parents, who are afraid of their child's impulses.

Misinterpretation of psychoanalytic principles and mistaking an intermediary phase of treatment for the goal of analysis led to such attitudes in education as held for instance by Neill, who advocates complete abandoning of inhibitions and unrestrained behavior for children. There are cases in which for purposes of therapy it may be necessary for the therapist to withstand the incessant provocations of the child, which are aimed to break down the therapist so that he finally will become angry and retaliate, and thus confirm the child's belief that all adults are the same, unreliable, sadistic and punitive, and that therefore the child's antisocial behavior is justified and need not be changed.

I have in mind here the treatment of destructive juvenile delinquents, especially Aichorn's remarkable experiences with such children. It must also be borne in mind that the treatment of destructive juvenile delinquents is best carried out in a controlled environment, and with a person sure of his own feelings and his control over himself. What seems to me the basic therapeutic principle here, as well as in any psychoanalytically oriented psychotherapy, is the fact that the therapist has to prove himself to the child as a person different from anyone else the child has known before. He must be neither afraid to allow nor to restrict if necessary; at any rate he must be one who understands the child and the unconscious motivation for this behavior and who can be patient enough to tolerate the child's behavior, so that through him the child eventually can be helped to understand his own behavior and to change it actively. Parents, of course, often have a valid cause when they complain, "You only treat the child, but I have to live with him", but while the parents' plight is a difficult one, we must remind them that what the child is today is in most cases the result of years of faulty upbringing and that the parents themselves have a very hard time changing even their most obvious attitudes toward the child.

In fact, I have often marveled at how many children

change through treatment, in spite of their parents. I think that this is probably due to the fact that the identifications in children are not too rigidly established and that the child therefore can still modify these, or establish new ones if a suitable object is presented. With younger children it is desirable to provide suitable objects for identification in the child's parents, and therefore work with the parents, especially in behavior and disciplinary problems of the young child, is the treatment of choice. But even with older children and adolescents, it is sometimes necessary and possible through psychoanalytic treatment of the parent to modify the child's identification with this parent by turning him into a more suitable love object for the child (see Chapter 2).

A clear understanding of these points seems to me very important and I should therefore like to illustrate this with a case.

Seven-year-old Peter was a very good boy. He had been a model child up to his fifth year. The parents had been very pleased with him but became worried when he did not behave like a regular boy. He did not fight with children but ran away instead. He was fearful during the day and suffered from night terrors. His condition became aggravated when a sister was born when he was five and a half. He showed no signs of jealousy. In fact, his parents were delighted with his attitude toward his sister. He loved her so dearly that he would not accept anything without sharing it with her. Peter's parents were compulsive personalities with very high standards. His training had been strict and discipline in his case meant to deny the existence of any "badness." After he realized that he did not need to impress me with his gentlemanlike manners and that I neither approved nor disapproved of his actions, his behavior changed very much in the playroom. He began not only to throw things around but insisted that he could hurt me and that I had to pick everything up for him. While it was necessary to allow him to bring to the fore and to release his repressed aggressive impulses, at the same time, his behavior had to be interpreted and it had to be made clear to him that I was not his mother, whom he wanted to abuse and punish for sleeping with father and having the baby. It was necessary to insist that he did not deliberately destroy things, and that he help me clean up the mess. It was also necessary to guide the parents so that they should not restrict him too severely as they had before but yet not allow unrestrained behavior. It is the acceptance of the existence of such feelings in the child without condemnation which is essential, and not the acting out of them. The child has to learn to tolerate them in consciousness and to acquire control over them, instead of either acting them out or repressing them. This is only possible with parents who are tolerant of such feelings but not of such behavior. Peter for instance, had never been allowed to smear or to play with finger-paint. Upon my suggestion, his parents now let him do this, but because they felt guilty for having restricted him severely in the past, they did not think of stopping him when he wanted to smear the walls with it or throw clay around but had to be told not to allow him to do this.

These are cases which usually do not require intensive therapy. The situation is quite different in cases where the parents themselves have a deep-seated emotional conflict, of which they are not aware, about the child. Parents of this type may give the untrained observer the impression of well-organized and successful people. There is one conspicuous element, namely that in spite of their concentrated and sincere efforts with the child, they fail in their tasks as parents. In these cases, the children are attuned to the "unconscious" of the parents and react to this and not to the apparent appropriate conscious attitudes. Many cases in which all educational and disciplinary measures fail in spite of sincere conscious efforts, can be understood and corrected on this basis. I should like to give some examples:

Paula's mother, at the time when this episode occurred, was working out in her analysis, her inability to let go of the child and particularly to allow her to go to camp. She was just beginning to become conscious of this and as a result had decided to make arrangements for camp, and made an appointment for the camp director to visit the home. Upon this visit it depended whether Paula, who was then seven years old usually a well-behaved child, would be accepted for camp. As soon as the camp director entered the home, Paula's behavior changed very strangely. She became wild and unmanageable, climbing up the living room furniture, which she had never done before, and behaving so badly that the mother did not expect that she would be accepted for camp. Paula, who wanted to go to camp, did not know why she had behaved in this way, but her mother was able to understand in her analysis, that the child had acted out the mother's unconscious wish. Incidentally, Paula did go to camp that summer and made a very good camper.*

How important the understanding of the dynamics is in such a situation for the proper handling of it, the following case may demonstrate:

The mother of Dickie, who was six and a half, came for a consultation because he was unmanageable and very destructive. She was very much disturbed because hospitalization of the child in a psychiatric hospital had been recommended, and she wanted my opinion before committing the child. I learned that Dickie's difficult behavior had started a year before and had become increasingly worse. In the therapeutic interviews with the mother, it was found that she had an unresolved conflict regarding the adoption of a four-year-old girl who had come to live with the family a year before. The little girl was the child of her deceased brother, fully orphaned, and she felt a moral obligation to adopt her, yet she had been undecided and very disturbed for many months preceding the adoption. It was revealed that to her, to adopt the child meant to harm her son and

---

* Cases of such strange, explosive behavior in children, either of an episodic or permanent character, are described in Chapter 3.

to disown him in her affections. She did not feel that she was able, nor wanted to, care for two children. Of these feelings she had been vaguely aware, but she had been completely unconscious of the major disturbing force, which transmitted itself to Dickie and prompted his behavior. It was brought out that she unconsciously needed the child's disturbance, his unmanageable and destructive behavior, which was especially directed toward the little girl, in order to prove that the two children could not be together. This would provide the mother with a rationalization that she could not keep them both. To have to send Dickie to a psychiatric hospital because of the little girl was to convince her that she had to give up the little girl for Dickie's sake. Dickie himself proved to be an insecure child, very dependent upon his mother. He had never had any particular behavior difficulties prior to this. The mother's recognition of her conflict and her decision that she could keep both children after all, had a remarkable effect upon her own behavior and consequently upon Dickie. Without any direct treatment of Dickie, the very distressing situation resolved itself. In fact, Dickie and his little adopted sister got along very well after the mother had "allowed" them to do so.

Where the parents unconsciously identify the child with a hated sibling, or an unconsciously hated, objectionable part of their own personality, very severe behavior disorders in the children are the result, often leading to extreme destructive and self-destructive behavior as well as schizophrenic symptoms. The parents in such a situation cannot function as parents as much as they try and their failings and guilt feelings only further incapacitate them.

The mother of five-year-old Paul, who unconsciously identified him with her hated brother, never knew when to help him or when to discipline him. One day, while looking out of the window she saw Paul being attacked by a gang of older boys; panic-stricken, she did not know what to do, whether to help him and to pamper him in this way or whether to let him fight his own battles. She decided to call a friend (a mother substitute) and to ask her what to do in this situation. By this time, Paul had come into the house, beaten and with his clothes torn. He did not say anything and kept away from her. Paul was always difficult when he was with his mother, would break things, mess, and spill. In her analysis, the mother was able to understand that her inability to handle her son was a result of her unconsciously looking upon him as her rival brother. For instance, in the incident just mentioned, she had unconsciously enjoyed his being beaten by the boys as she had as a child wished and enjoyed this when it happened to her brother. When she brought him for therapy under the pressure of the school, she wondered how it would be possible for me to treat him because he was so destructive. Yet, in the play analysis, Paul was very easygoing once he had found out that I would not let him go wild, but protected him from his own destructiveness. He felt safe with me, but in constant anxiety with his mother, who unconsciously stimulated him to behave in this fashion. His father was not very helpful to him. When Paul picked flowers in a public garden, his father not only did not stop him but argued with the attendant who had intervened. One day when Paul, while riding on his bike, almost knocked over two pedestrians, the father in Paul's presence maintained that it was not Paul's responsibility to watch out for his own and other people's safety, but it was up to them to watch out for themselves. He encouraged Paul, who then was a consistent day and night wetter, not to hold back when he felt an urge to urinate, but to relieve himself no matter what the circumstances were. In this case intensive psychoanalytic treatment of the mother and the child was necessary.

With my last example, I intend to demonstrate the deleterious effects which the unconscious conflict of the mother had upon her nine-year-old daughter. From birth on this mother had looked upon the child as a problem, but came for help when the child was nine years old. By then, Dora had been lying, stealing, and failing in her schoolwork. The mother had been carrying on a merciless struggle with her daughter, practically since infancy, with the rationalization that she had to suppress Dora's need to be dirty and to overheat, and later on, her delinquent tendencies. It was found that the mother unconsciously had identified Dora with her own repressed objectionable impulses, and thus in projection was fighting these impulses in the child. The mother herself, until late adolescence, had been fat. She also had profound guilt feelings about masturbation and having indulged in dirty sex play. She was constantly fighting with an impulse to overeat and to be dirty and the display of such behavior in her daughter represented a threat to her own balance. The mother had severe guilt feelings about her older sister, who had had a nervous breakdown and had committed suicide. She had been unaware that she, as a result of her guilt, unconsciously expected the same fate for herself. In the psychoanalysis of the mother, it was revealed that she had an intense hatred of her own mother and sister because her mother, after the sudden death of her husband, had placed my patient into an orphanage while she kept the older sister. My patient never forgave her mother and sister for this. Unconsciously, she felt responsible for her sister's insanity and death. Repetition compulsion forced her to reenact and repeat this unresolved conflict with her own child. She was very unhappy when she gave birth to a girl, because she had the misgiving that the same thing that happened to her sister would happen to her child and that she would have a miserable life like her mother, with whom she had identified in the "suffering." The psychoanalytic treatment of the mother, by resolving this conflict, brought about a remarkable change in Dora's behavior.

## Conclusions

Psychoanalysis not only made it possible to understand the dynamics of these conditions but also provided the tools for correcting them. I am not referring here only to psychoanalysis as a method of treatment, although in some of these cases, it had to be applied. Psychoanalysis rather teaches us about the basic requirements under which discipline, in the psychoanalytic sense, namely, inner freedom and internal control, can develop. These internal controls develop only as a result of positive identification with suitable parent figures. Psychoanalysis has shown us that in the special relationship which the child forms at a certain age, the so-called oedipal phase, the child, by directing his demands for gratification of his instinctual needs onto the parents, becomes a highly sensitive object for educational methods if the parents or their advisors know how to use them. It is during this phase that the child develops from an auto-erotic and asocial into an object-related, that is social, being. It is also during this phase that the child, by identification with his parents and by internalization of parental wishes and interdictions, forms the structure of the mind referred to as superego. One of the functions of the superego is to regulate behavior.

It is obvious that because of the child's instinctual nature, denials and prohibitions are unavoidable in his training and education. If however, a basic understanding allows for proper timing and dosing, these will not mean coercion, but rather give support to the child and prevent him from developing fears of his own impulses which are incompatible with inner freedom. In this way psychoanalysis points up the basic requirements in education and the importance of training in psychoanalytic principles for those to whom the education of children is entrusted.

Psychoanalytic studies in sociology indicate that the unconscious rapport that exists between child and parents also exists between the masses and the leader. I am referring to the work of the Committee on Social Issues of the American Psychoanalytic Association and particularly to a paper by Otto E. Sperling (1950b), who could demonstrate that the unconscious rapport between the leader and his followers—the obedience of the masses to the unconscious of the leader—operated as a dynamic force in the outbreak of riots. In rioting, the followers were carrying out the leader's unconscious wish rather than reacting to his spoken commands.

This is an aspect of great significance and throws new light upon the phenomena of mass discipline and mass disorder. Freud (1922) prepared the ground for such work, in the same way as he recognized and anticipated the value of psychoanalysis for the future of education.

# Bibliography

## ABBREVIATIONS

*Almanach: Almanach der Psychoanalyse,* Internationaler Psycho-analytisch Verlag, Vienna.

*Bull.: Bulletin of the American Psychoanalytic Association,* International University Press, New York.

*Psa. and Soc. Sc.: Psychoanalysis and Social Sciences.* International University Press, New York.

*Paed.: Zeitschrift für Psychoanalytisch Paedagogik,* Internationaler Psychoanalytisch Verlag, Vienna.

Abraham, K. 1910. Remarks on the psychoanalysis of a case of foot and corset fetishism. *Selected Papers on Psychoanalysis,* pp. 125–36. New York: Basic Books, 1953.

———. 1911. Notes on the psychoanalytical investigation and treatment of manic depressive insanity. *Selected Papers,* pp. 137–56. London: Hogarth Press, 1927.

———. 1917. Ejaculatio praecox. *Selected Papers,* pp. 280–98. London: Hogarth Press, 1942.

———. 1922. The spider as a dream symbol. *Selected Papers on Psychoanalysis,* pp. 326–32. New York: Basic Books, 1953.

———. 1924. A short study of the development of the libido. *Selected Papers,* pp. 418–502. London: Hogarth Press, 1942.

Aichhorn, A. 1935. *Wayward Youth.* New York: Viking.

Alexander, F. 1928. Ein Fall von masochistischem Transvestitismus als Selbstheilungsversuch. *Almanach.*

Arlow, J. 1954. Perversion: theoretical and therapeutic aspects. *J. Amer. Psa. Assoc.* 2:336–45.

Azima, H., and Wittkower, E. D. 1957. Anaclitic therapy employing drugs: a case of spider phobia with Isakower phenomenon. *Psa. Q.* 26:190–205.

Bak, R. C. 1953. Fetishism. *J. Amer. Psa. Assoc.* 1:285–98.

Bakwin, H. 1949. Enuresis in children. *J. Pediat.* 34:249.

Balint, A. 1932. Die Psychoanalyse des Kinderszimmers. *Z. Pad.* 6:49–130.

———. 1937. Die Grundlagen unseres Erziehungssystems. *Z. Pad.* 11:98–101.

Balint, M. 1935. A contribution on fetishism. *Int. J. Psa.* 16:481–83.

Baruch, D. W. 1949. *New Ways in Discipline.* New York: Whittlesey House.

Bellak, L. 1952. *Manic Depressive Psychosis and Allied Conditions.* New York: Grune & Stratton.

Bender, L., and Paster, S. 1941. Homosexual trends in children. *Amer. J. Orthopsychiat.* 11:730–43.

Benedek, T. 1949. The psychosomatic implications of primary unit: mother-child. *Amer. J. Orthopsychiat.* 19:642–54.

Bernfeld, S. 1928. *Sisyphos, oder die Grenzen der Erziehung.* Vienna: Int. Psa. Verlag.

———. 1935. The psychoanalytic psychology of the young child. *Psa. Q.* 4:3–15.

Bettelheim, Bruno. 1950. *Love is Not Enough.* Glencoe: Free Press.

———. 1955. *Truants from Life: The Rehabilitation of Emotionally Disturbed Children.* Glencoe: Free Press.

Boehm, F. 1923. Bemerkungen uber Transvestitismus. *Z Psa.* 9:497–509.

Bornstein, B. 1935. Phobia in a two and a half year old child. *Psa. Q.* 4:93–119.

Bornstein, S. 1933. Ein Beitrag zur Psychoanalyse des Paedogogen. *Paed.* 7:314–21.

———. 1937. Missverstandnisse in der psychoanalytischen Padogogik. *Z. Pad.* 11:81–90.

Broughton, R. J. 1968. Sleep disorders: disorders of arousal? *Science* 159:1070–78.

Brunn, R. D., and Shapiro, 1972. Differential diagnosis of Gilles de la Tourette syndrome. *J. Nerv. Ment. Dis.* 155:328–34.

Burchardt, J. M. 1961. Struktur und Soziologie des Transvestitismus und Transsexualismus. *Beitrage zur Sexualforschung* 21:1–69 Hamburg: F. Enke.

Burlingham, D. 1935. Child analysis and the mother. *Psa. Q.* 4:69–92.

———. 1937. Problem des psychoanalytischen Erziehers. *Z. Pad.* 11:91–7.

———, Goldberger, A., and Lussier, A. 1955. Simultaneous analysis of mother and child. *Psa. Study of the Child* 10:165–86. New York: Int. Univ. Press.

Buxbaum, E. 1935. Exhibitionistic onanism in a 10-year-old boy. *Psa. Q.* 4:161–89.

———. 1960. Hair pulling and fetishism. *Psa. Study of the Child* 15:243–60. New York: Int. Univ. Press.

Campbell, M. D. 1951. *Clinical Pediatric Urology.* Philadelphia: Saunders.

Christoffel, H. 1944. *Trieb und Kultur,* pp. 199–201. Basel: B. Schwabe.

Coolidge, J. C., Hahn, P. B., and Peck, A. L. 1957. School phobia: neurotic crisis or way of life? *Amer. J. Orthopsychiat.* 27:296–306.

———, Willer, M. L., Tessman, E., and Waldfogel, S. 1960. School phobia in adolescence: a manifestation of severe character disturbance. *Amer. J. Orthopsychiat.* 30:599–607.

Davidson, J. R., and Douglass, E. 1950. Nocturnal enuresis: a special approach to treatment. *Brit. Med. J.* 1:1345–47.

Dement, W. 1964. Experimental dream studies. *Science and Psa.* 7:129–84. New York: Grune & Stratton.

Deutsch, H. 1929. The genesis of agoraphobia. *Int. J. Psa.* 10:51–69.

Despert, J. L. 1944. Urinary control and enuresis. *Psychosom. Med.* 6:294–307.

———. 1952. Suicide and depression in children. *Nerv. Child* 9.

Dickes, R. 1962. Fetishistic behavior: a contribution to its complex behavior and significance. *Psa. Q.* 31:446–48.

Edwards, K. C. S. 1954. Pruritus and melancholia. *Brit. Med. J.* 2:1557–79.

Eisenberg, L. 1958. School phobia: diagnosis, genesis and clinical management. *Ped. Clin. N. Amer.* 5:645–66.

Ekstein, R. 1954. The space child's time machine. *Amer. J. Orthopsychiat.* 24:492–506.

Epstein, A.W. 1960. Fetishism. *J. Nerv. Ment. Dis.* 130:107–19.

Fenichel, O. 1930. The psychology of transvestitism. *Collected Papers* 1: New York: Norton, 1953.

———. 1942. Symposium on neurotic disturbances of sleep. *Int. J. Psa.* 23:49.

Ferenczi, S. 1916. *Contributions to Psychoanalysis.* Boston: Badger.

————. 1929. The unwelcome child and his death instinct. *Int. J. Psa.* 10:125–29.

Fessler, L. 1934. Ein Fall von posttraumatischen Transvestitismus. *Arch. Psychiat. & Nervenkrank.* 100.

Fisher, C., and Dement, W. C. 1963. Studies on the psychopathology of sleep and dreams. *Amer. J. Psychiat.* 119:1160–68.

————, and Dement, W. C. 1969. The psychophysiological study of nightmares. Freud 19th Anniversary Lecture, New York Academy of Medicine, April, 1969.

Foulkes, S. H. 1943. The idea of a change of sex in women. *Int. J. Psa.* 24:53–56.

Fraiberg, S. 1950. On the sleep disturbances of early childhood. *Psa. Study of the Child* 5:285–309. New York: Int. Univ. Press.

Freud, A. 1928. *Introduction to the Technique of Child Analysis.* New York: Nerv. and Ment. Dis. Pub. Co.

————. 1935. *Introduction to Psychoanalysis for Teachers and Parents.* New York: Emerson Books.

————. 1935. Psychoanalysis and the training of the young child. *Psa. Q.* 4:15–25.

————. 1936. *The Psychoanalytical Treatment of Children.* London: Imago Pub. Co.

————. 1949. Notes on aggression. *Bull. Menninger Clin.* 13:143–52.

————. 1965. *Normality and Pathology in Childhood.* New York: Int. Univ. Press.

Freud, S. 1896. The etiology of hysteria. *Collected Papers,* 1:193–219. London: Hogarth, 1946.

————. 1900. The interpretation of dreams. *Standard Ed.* 3 & 4. London: Hogarth, 1953.

————. 1905. Three essays on the theory of sexuality. *Standard Ed.* 7:123–243. London: Hogarth, 1953.

————. 1909a. Analysis of a phobia in a five-year-old boy. *Standard Ed.* 10:3–149. London: Hogarth, 1955.

————. 1909b. Some general remarks on hysterical attacks. *Standard Ed.* 9:London: Hogarth, 1959.

————. 1911. Psychoanalytic notes on an autobiographical account of a case of paranoia (Dementia paranoides). *Collected Papers* 12:3–82. London: Hogarth, 1958.

————. 1914. On the history of the psychoanalytic movement. *Collected Papers* 1:287–359. London: Hogarth, 1946.

———. 1917. Mourning and melancholia. *Collected Papers* 4:152–70. London: Hogarth, 1925.

———. 1919. The uncanny. *Standard Ed.* 17:217–52. London: Hogarth, 1955.

———. 1920. Beyond the pleasure principle. *Standard Ed.* 18:1–64. London: Hogarth, 1955.

———. 1922a. *Group Psychology and the Analysis of the Ego.* London: Int. Psa. Pub. Co.

———. 1922b. Medusa's head. *Standard Ed.* 18:273–74. London: Hogarth, 1955.

———. 1927. Fetishism. *Collected Papers* 5:198–204. London: Hogarth, 1950.

———. 1930. *Civilization and Its Discontents.* London: Hogarth.

———. 1933. *New Introductory Lectures on Psychoanalysis.* New York: Garden City Pub. Co.

———. 1936. The problem of anxiety. *Standard Ed.* 20:77–175. London: Hogarth, 1959.

———. 1938. Splitting of the ego in the defensive process. *Collected Papers* 5:372–75. London: Hogarth, 1950.

Friedjung, J. K. 1924. Beitrag zum Verständnis der Einschlafstörungen der Kinder. *Wien. Med. Wochenschr.* 74:1002-3.

———. 1927–28. Wäsche-Fetischismus in einem Einjährigen. *Z. psa. Päd.* 2:25–26, 235–36.

Friend, R.M., Schiddel, L., Klein, B., and Dunaeff D. 1954. Observations on the development of transvestitism in boys. *Amer. J. Orthopsychiat.* 24:563–75.

Fries, M. 1945. The child's ego development and the training of adults in his environment. *Psa. Q.* 14:85–112.

———. 1954. Psychosomatic relationship between mother and infant. *Psychosom. Med.* 6:157.

———. Film on "The Interaction between Child and Environment." New York University Film Library.

Garma, A. 1956. The meaning and genesis of fetishism. *Int. J. Psa.* 37:414–15.

Gardner, G. E. 1949. Panel: Report from the James Jackson Putnam Children's Center, Boston. Amer. Psa. Assoc. Midwinter meeting *Bull.* 5:33–36.

———. 1952. The child with school phobia. Presented at the 38th Annual Convention of the National League to Promote School Attendance, Boston, Oct.

Garvey, W .P., and Hegrenes, J. R. 1966. Desensitization techniques in the treatment of school phobia. *Amer. J. Orthopsychiat.* 36:147–52.

Gerard, M. W. 1939. Enuresis: a study in etiology. *Amer. J. Orthopsychiat.* 9:48–58.

Gero, G. 1953. An equivalent of depression: anorexia. *Affective Disorders.* New York: Int. Univ. Press.

Gesell, A. 1943. *Infant and Child in the Culture Today.* New York: Harper.

Gillespie, W. H. 1952. Notes on the analysis of sexual perversions. *Int. J. Psa.* 33:397–402.

———. 1956a. The general theory of perversion. *Int. J. Psa.* 37:396–403.

———. 1956b. The structure and aetiology of sexual perversion. *Perversions, Psychodynamics and Therapy,* pp. 28–41. Ed. S. Lorand. New York: Random House.

Gloyne, H. F. 1950. Tarantism, mass hysterical reaction to spider bite in the Middle Ages. *Amer. Imago* 7:29–42.

Grant, V. W. 1953. A case study of fetishism. *J. Abnormal Soc. Psychol.* 48:142–48.

Greenacre, P. 1953. Certain relationships between fetishism and faulty development of the body image. *Psa. Study of the Child* 8:79–98. New York: Int. Univ. Press.

Greenbaum, R. S. 1964. Treatment of school phobias: theory and practice. *Amer. J. Psychother.* 18:616–34.

Greenberg, N. H., and Rosenwald, A. K. 1958. Transvestitism and pruritus perinei. *Psychosom. Med.* 20: 145–50.

———, and Rosenwald, A. K. 1960. A study in transsexualism. *Psychiat. Q.* 34:204–235.

Grotjahn, M. 1948. Transvestite fantasy expressed in a drawing. *Psa. Q.* 17:340–45.

Gutheil, E. A. 1954. The psychologic background of transsexualism and transvestitism. *Amer. J. Psychother.* 8:231–39.

Hall, M. B. 1952. Our present knowledge about manic-depressive states in childhood. *Nerv. Child* 9.

Hartmann, H. 1939. Ich-Psychologie und Anpassungsproblem. *Int. Z. Psa. u. Imago* 24:62–135.

Healy, W., and Bronner, A. F. 1936. *Delinquents and Criminals.* New York: Macmillan.

Hellman, I., Friedmann, O., and Shepheard, E. 1960. Simultaneous analysis of mother and child. *Psa. Study of the Child* 15:359–77. New York: Int. Univ. Press.

Hirschfeld, M., and Tielke, M. 1912. *Der erotische Drang zur Verkleidung.* Berlin: Pulvermacher.

Hitschmann, E. 1915. Ein Fall von Zwangbefurchtung vom Tode des gleichgeschlechtlichen Elternteils. *Int. Z. Psa.* 3:105.

———. 1937. Bemerkungen über Platzangst und andere neurotische Angstzustände. *Int. Z Psa.* 23:393–401.

Homburger, E. 1935. Psychoanalysis and the future of education. *Psa. Q.* 4:50–69.

Hora, T. 1953. The structural analysis of transvestitism. *Psa. Rev.* 40:268–74.

Hunter, D. 1954. Object-relation changes in the analysis of a fetishist. *Int. J. Psa.* 35:302–12.

Jacobson, E. 1953. Contribution to the metapsychology of cyclothymic depression. *Affective Disorders.* New York: Int. Univ. Press.

Jarvis, V. 1964. Countertransference in the management of school phobias. *Psa. Q.* 33:411–19.

Jekels, L., 1945. A bioanalytical contribution to the problem of sleep and wakefulness. *Psa. Q.* 14:169–89.

Johnson, A. M. 1949. Sanctions for superego lacunae of adolescents. *Searchlights on Delinquency.* pp. 225–45. Ed. K.R. Eissler. New York: Int. Univ. Press.

———, Falstein, E. I., Szurek, S. A., and Svendsen, M. 1941. School phobia. *Amer. J. Orthopsychiat.* 11:702–11.

———, and Fishback, D. 1944. Analysis of a disturbed adolescent girl and collaborative treatment of the mother. *Amer. J. Orthopsychiat.* 14:195.

———, and Szurek, S. A. 1952. Genesis of anti-social acting out in children and adults. *Psa. Q.* 21:323–43.

Jones, E. 1931. *On the Nightmare.* New York: Norton.

Kahn, J. H., and Nursten, J. P. 1962. School refusal: a comprehensive view of school phobia and other failures of school attendance. *Amer. J. Orthopsychiat.* 32:707–18.

Karpman, B. 1947. Dream life in a case of transvestitism with particular attention to the problem of latent homosexuality. *J. Nerv. Ment. Dis.* 106:292–337.

Keeler, W. R. 1954. Children's reaction to the death of a parent.

*Depression.* Eds. P.H. Hoch and J. Zubin. New York: Grune & Stratton.

Klein, E. 1945. The reluctance to go to school. *Psa. Study of the Child* 1:263–79. New York: Int. Univ. Press.

——. 1929. *Personification in the Play of Children: Contributions to Psycho-Analysis,* pp. 215–26. London: Hogarth, 1948.

Klein, M. 1932. *The Psycho-Analysis of Children.* London: Hogarth.

——. 1935. Contribution to the psychogenesis of manic-depressive states. *Contributions to Psychoanalysis,* pp. 282–310. London: Hogarth, 1948.

——. 1940. Mourning in its relations to manic-depressive states. Ibid. pp. 311–38.

——. 1946. Notes on some schizoid mechanisms. *Developments in Psychoanalysis,* pp. 292–320. London: Hogarth, 1952.

Kris, E. 1950. Notes on the development and on some current problems of psychoanalytic child psychology. *Psa. Study of the Child* 5:24–46. New York: Int. Univ. Press.

Kronengold, E., and Sterba, R. 1936. Two cases of fetishism. *Psa. Q.* 5:63–70.

Kubie, L. S. 1954. The drive to become both sexes. Presented at the Amer. Psa. Assoc., St. Louis.


Leavitt, A. 1964. Treatment of an adolescent with school phobia. *J. Amer. Child Psychosom. Med.* 11:377–85.

Levine, A. 1943–44. Enuresis in the Navy. *Amer. J. Psychiat.* 100:320.

Levy, K. 1960. Simultaneous analysis of a mother and her adolescent daughter. *Psa. Study of the Child* 15:378–91. New York: Int. Univ. Press.

Lewin, B.D. 1952. Phobic symptoms and dream interpretation. *Psa. Q.* 21:295–322.

Lindner, 1879. The sucking of fingers, lips, etc. in children (pleasure-sucking). *J. f. Kinderheilkunde,* repr. *Psa. P.* 8 (1934), 117–38.

Little, R. B. 1966a. Oral aggression in spider legends. *Amer. Imago* 23:169–79.

——. 1966b. Umbilical cord symbolism of the spider's dropline. *Psa. Q.* 35:587–90.

——. 1967. Spider phobias. *Psa. Q.* 36:51–60.

Lorand, S. 1930. Fetishism in statu nascendi. *Int. J. Psa.* 11:419–27.

Lowrey, L. G. 1939. Trends in therapy. *Amer. J. Orthopsychiat.* 9:669.

———. 1948. General developments and trends. *Amer. J. Orthopsychiat.* 18:381.

Lukianowitz, N. 1960. Two cases of transvestism. *Psychiat. Q.* 34:517–37.

Mahler, M. 1951. Discussion of Sperling, Melitta: The neurotic child and his mother: A psychoanalytic study. *Amer. J. Orthopsychiat.* 21:363–4.

———. 1968. On Human Symbiosis and the Vicissitudes of Individuation p. 101. New York: Int. Univ. Press.

McKenzie, R. E. and Schulz, I. 1961. Study of a transvestite: evaluation and treatment. *Amer. J. Psychother.* 15:267–80.

Meng, H. 1945. *Zwang und Freiheit in der Erziehung.* Bern: H. Huber.

Messer, A. A. 1964. Family treatment of a school phobic child. *Arch. Gen. Psychiat.* 11:548–55.

Michaels, J. 1955. *Disorders of Character.* Springfield: Thomas.

Mindner, J. 1946. *Lehrbuch der Urologie.* Bern: H. Huber.

Mowrer, O. H., and Mowrer, W. M. 1938. Enuresis: a method for its study and treatment. *Amer. J. Orthopsychiat.* 8:436.

Murray, E.J. 1959. Conflict and repression during sleep deprivation. *ASP.* 59:95–101.

Muellner, S. R. 1960. Development of urinary control in children. *J. Amer. Med. Assoc.* 120:1256–61.


Neill, A. S. 1949. *The Problem Family.* New York: Hermitage Press.

Newman, L. E., and Stoller, R. J. 1969. Spider symbolism and bisexuality. *J. Amer. Psa. Assoc.* 17:862–72.


Payne, S. 1939. Some observations on the ego development of the fetishist. *Int. J. Psa.* 20:161–70.


Rado, S. 1928. The problem of melancholia. *Int. J. Psa.* 9:420–38.

Rapaport, D. 1954. The autonomy of the ego. *Psychoanalytic Psychiatry and Psychology,* pp. 248–58. Eds. R. P. Knight and C. R. Friedman. New York: Int. Univ. Press.

Redl, F. 1932. Erziehungsberatung, Erziehungshilfe, Erziehungsbehandlung. *Z. Pad.* 6:523–32.

Ribble, M. 1943. *The Rights of Infants.* New York: Columbia U. P.

Rodriguez, A., Rodriguez, M., and Eisenberg, L. 1959. The outcome of school phobia: a follow-up study based on 41 cases. *Amer. J. Psychiat.* 116:540–44.

Rose, G. J. 1960. Analytic first aid for a three-year-old. *Amer. J. Orthopsychiat.* 30:200–201.

Sachs, H. 1942. The community of daydreams. *The Creative Unconscious,* pp. 11–54. Cambridge, Mass.: Sci.-Art Press.

Sachs, L. J. 1957. On changes in identification from machine to cripple. *Psa. Study of the Child* 12:346–75. New York: Int. Univ. Press.

Sadger, I. 1920. *Sleep walking and moon walking.* New York: Nerv. & Ment. Dis. Publ. Co.

Schick, A. 1947. On a physical form of periodic depression. *Psa. Rev.* 34:432–42.

Schmidt, V. 1924. *Psychoanalytic Education in Soviet Russia.* Report on the Experimental Children's Home in Moscow. Vienna: Int. P. Verlag.

Seitz, P. F. D. 1950. Psychocutaneous conditioning during the first two weeks of life. *Psychosom. Med.* 12:187–8.

Simmel, E. 1942. Symposium on neurotic disturbances of sleep. *Int. J. Psa.* 23:65–68.

Socarides, C. W. 1960. The development of a fetishistic perversion. *J. Amer. Psa. Assoc.* 8:281–311.

Sperling, M. 1946. A psychoanalytic study of ulcerative colitis in children. *Psa. Q.* 15:302-29.

———. 1947. The analysis of an exhibitionist. *Int. J. Psa.* 27:32–45.

——— .1949a. Analysis of a case of recurrent ulcer of the leg. *Psa. Study of the Child* 3/4:391–408.

———. 1949b. Neurotic sleep disturbances in children. *Nerv. Child* 8:28–46.

———. 1949c. Problems in analysis of children with psychosomatic disorders. *Q. J. Child Behavior* 1:12–17.

———. 1949d. The role of the mother in psychosomatic disorders in children. *Psychosom. Med.* 11:377–85.

———. 1950a. A contribution to the psychodynamics of depression in women. *Samiksa* 4:86–101.

———. 1950b. Enuresis. Seminar on psychiatric problems in the practice of medicine. *Jewish Hosp. of Brooklyn,* 8–17.

———. 1950c. Mucous colitis associated with phobias. *Psa. Q.* 19:318–26.

———. 1950d. The structure of envy in depression of women. Proceedings of a symposium on feminine psychology, New York Med. Coll.

———. 1951. The neurotic child and his mother. *Amer. J. Orthopsychiat.* 21:351–64.

———. 1952a. A psychoanalytic study of migraine and psychogenic headache. *Psa. Rev.* 39:152–63.

———. 1952b. Psychogenic diarrhea and phobia in a six-and-a-half-year-old girl. *Amer. J. Orthopsychiat.* 22:838–48.

———. 1952c. Psychotherapeutic techniques in psychosomatic medicine. *Specialized Techniques in Psychotherapy*, pp. 279–301. Eds. G. Bychowski and J. L. Despert. New York: Basic Books.

———. 1953a. Psychoanalytic observation of deviate sexual behavior in children. Presented at Amer. Psa. Assoc. Midwinter meeting.

———. 1953b. Psychodynamics and treatment of petit mal in children. *Int. J. Psa.* 34:1–5.

———. 1954. Psychosomatic medicine and pediatrics. *Recent Developments in Psychosomatic Medicine.* Eds. R. Cleghorn and E. Wittkower. London: Pitman.

———. 1955a. Etiology and treatment of sleep disturbances in children. *Psa. Q.* 24:358–68.

———. 1955b. Observations from the treatment of children suffering from nonbloody diarrhea or mucous colitis. *J. Hillside Hosp.* 4:25–31.

———. 1955c. Psychosis and psychosomatic illness. *Int. J. Psa.* 36:320–27.

———. 1955d. Roundtable on childhood schizophrenia. Amer. Psychiat. Assoc., Atlantic City, May 12.

———. 1958. Pavor nocturnus. *J. Amer. Psla. Assoc.* 6:79–94.

——— .1960. Unconscious fantasy life and object relationships in ulcerative colitis. *Int. J. Psa.* 41:450–55.

———. 1961. Psychosomatic disorders. *Adolescents: Psychoanalytic Approach to Problems and Therapy*, pp. 202–16. Eds. S. Lorand and H. I. Schneer. New York: Hoeber.

———. 1963. A psychoanalytic study of bronchial asthma in children. *The Asthmatic Child*, pp. 138–65. Ed. H. I. Schneer. New York: Harper & Row.

———. 1968a. Acting-out behavior and psychosomatic symptoms: clinical and theoretical aspects. *Int. J. Psa.* 49:250–53.

———. 1968b. Trichotillomania, trichophagy and cyclic vomiting: a contribution to the psychopathology of female sexuality. *Int. J. Psa.* 49:682–90.

———. 1969a. Migraine headaches, altered states of consciousness and accident proneness: a clinical contribution to the death instinct theory. *Psa. Forum* 3:69–83. New York: Jason Aronson.

——. 1969b. Ulcerative colitis in children. *J. Amer. Acad. Child Psychiat.* 8:336–52.

——. 1973. Conversion hysteria and conversion symptoms: a revision of classifications and concepts. *J. Amer. Psa. Assoc.* 21:745–771.

Sperling, O. 1950a. The interpretation of the trauma as a command. *Psa. Q.* 19:352–70.

——. 1950b. The misunderstanding between the leader and his followers. Presented at Amer. Psa. Assoc. Midwinter meeting, New York.

—— .1951. Illusions, naive or controlled. *Psa. Q.* 20:204–14.

——. 1954. An imaginary companion, representing a prestige of the superego. *Psa. Study of the Child* 9:252–58. New York: Int. Univ. Press.

——. 1955. Some observations on failure of leadership. *Psa. & Soc. Sci.* 4:83–93. New York State Univ. Press.

——. 1956. Psychodynamics of group perversions. *Psa. Q.* 25:56–65.

Spitz, R. A. 1946. Anaclitic depression. *Psa. Study of the Child* 2:313–42. New York: Int. Univ. Press.

——. 1951. The psychogenic diseases in infancy: an attempt at their etiological classification. *Psa. Study of the Child* 6:255–78. New York: Int. Univ. Press.

——. 1954. Infantile depression and the general adaptation syndrome. *Depression.* New York: Grune & Stratton.

Sprince, M. P. 1962. The development of a preoedipal partnership between an adolescent girl and her mother. *Psa. Study of the Child* 17:418–50. New York: Int. Univ. Press.

Sterba, E. 1941. An important factor in eating disturbances of childhood. *Psa. Q.* 10:370–71.

Sterba, R. 1950. On spiders, hanging and oral sadism. *Amer. Imago* 7:21–28.

Stevenson, O. 1954. The first treasured possession. *Psa. Study of the Child* 9:199–217. New York: Int. Univ. Press.

Suttenfield, V. 1954. School phobia: a study of five cases. *Amer. J. Orthopsychiat.* 24:368–80.

Szurek, S., Johnson, A., and Falstein, E. I. 1942. Collaborative psychiatric therapy of parent-child problems. *Amer. J. Orthopsychiat.* 13:511.

Talbot, M. 1957. Panic in school phobia. *Amer. J. Orthopsychiat.* 27:286–95.

Tausk, V. 1919. On the origin of the "influencing machine" in schizophrenia. *Psa. Q.* 2(1933):519–56.

Waelder, J. 1935. Analyse eines Falles von Pavor nocturnus. *Z. Psa. Paed.* 9:1–70.

Waldfogel, S., Coolidge, J. C., and Hahn, P. B. 1957. The development, meaning and management of school phobia. *Amer. J. Orthopsychiat.* 27:754–80.

Wechsler, David, 1931. The incidence and significance of fingernail biting in children. *Psa. Rev.* 18:201–209.

Weissman, P. 1957. Some aspects of sexual activity in a fetishist. *Psa. Q.* 26:494–507.

Wilson, G. W. 1948. A further contribution to the study of olfactory repression with particular reference to transvestitism. *Psa. Q.* 17:322–39.

Winnicott, D. W. 1936. Enuresis. *Brit. Med. J.* 2:903.

———. 1953. Transitional objects and transitional phenomena. *Int. J. Psa.* 34:89–93.

Wulff, M. 1927. A phobia in a child of eighteen months. *Int. J. Psa.* 9:354–59.

———. 1946. Fetishism and object choice in early childhood. *Psa. Q.* 15:450–71.

# Acknowledgments

The author wishes to thank the publishers of the books and periodicals enumerated below for permission to reprint the following articles:

Chapter one is a small part of the article "The Clinical Effects of Parental Neurosis on the Child," by Anthony and Benedek (eds.), *Parenthood*, Little, Brown and Company, Inc., Boston, 1970.

Chapter 2: "Indirect Treatment of Psychoneurotic and Psychosomatic Disorders in Children," *The Quarterly Journal of Child Behavior*, 1950, 2:250–266.

Chapter 3: "Children's Interpretation and Reaction to the Unconscious of Their Mothers," *The International Journal of Psychoanalysis*, 1950, 31:36–41.

Chapter 4: "Sleep Disturbances in Children," *Modern Perspectives in International Child Psychiatry*, John G. Howells (ed.), Oliver & Boyd, Edinburgh, 1969.

Chapter 5: "The Diagnostic and Prognostic Significance of Childrens' Dreams and Sleep," *Currents in Psychoanalysis*, I. Marcus (ed.), International University Press, New York, 1971.

Chapter 6: "Dream Symbols and the Significance of their Changes During Analysis," *Journal of the Hillside Hospital*, 1961, 10:261–266.

431

Chapter 7: "School Phobias: Classification, Dynamics and Treatment," *Psychoanalytic Study of the Child*, 22:375–401.

Chapter 8: "Analytic First Aid in School Phobias," *Psychoanalytic Quarterly*, 1961, 30:504–518.

Chapter 9: "Animal Phobias in a Two-Year-Old Child," *Psychoanalytic Study of the Child*, 1952, 7:115–125.

Chapter 10: "Spider Phobias and Spider Fantasies," *Journal of the American Psychoanalytic Association*, 1971, 19:472–498.

Chapter 13: "Deviate Sexual Behavior in Children," *Dynamic Psychopathology in Childhood*, Lucie Jessner, M.D., and Eleanor Pavenstedt, M.D. (eds.), Grune & Stratton, Inc., New York, 1959.

Chapter 14: "The Analysis of a Boy with Transvestite Tendencies," *The Psychoanalytic Study of the Child*, 1964, 19:470–493.

Chapter 15, "Fetishism in Children," *Psychoanalytic Quarterly*, 1963, 32:374–392.

Chapter 17, "Dynamic Considerations and Treatment of Enuresis," *Journal of the American Academy of Child Psychiatry*, 1965, 4:19–31.

Chapter 21: "Reactive Schizophrenia in Children," *The American Journal of Orthopsychiatry*, 1954, 24:507–512.

Chapter 22: "Some Criteria on the Evaluation of the Treatment Potential of Schizophrenic Children," *Journal of the American Academy of Child Psychiatry*, 1963, 2:593–604.

Chapter 23: "Equivalents of Depression in Children," *Journal of the Hillside Hospital*, 1959, 8:138–147.

Chapter 24: "Psychoanalytic Aspects of Discipline," *The Nervous Child*, 1951, 9:174–186.

The articles "Introduction" and "Concepts and Therapeutic Techniques" and Chapters 11, 12, 16, 18, 19 and 20 were written specifically for this book in 1970–73.

# Biographical Sketch of Dr. Melitta Sperling

Born to parents who tried to free themselves from the stranglehold of their extreme Orthodox Jewish environment, Dr. Sperling decided early to fight superstitions and self-inflicted suffering. Another influence was an aunt who was a physician; in identification with her, Dr. Sperling made the fight against death and physical suffering a second life goal. It was later in her life that she succeeded in combining these goals by demonstrating that the same self-destructive tendencies can express themselves alternatingly in neurotic symptoms and in behavior disorders.

After graduating from the Medical School of the University of Vienna, she interned in the Vienna General Hospital. She wanted to become a pediatrician but, as part of her rotating internship, she also had to serve three months in the Psychiatric Department, very much against her will. There she met the undersigned, a resident in psychiatry. I tried to comfort her about this "misfortune." It would appear I succeeded in my attempt because she remained in psychiatry for two years, and at the end of our residencies, we married.

In Vienna, Dr. Sperling began her psychoanalytic training but interrupted it because of two pregnancies. Her son, Dr. George Sper-

433

ling, is a prominent experimental psychologist. Her daughter, Eva S. Cockcroft, is an artist. Dr. Sperling had four grandchildren.

In 1938, Dr. Sperling had to flee Austria to begin life as a refugee in America. While continuing her psychoanalytic training at the New York Psychoanalytic Institute, she worked in the Pediatric Department of the Jewish Hospital of Brooklyn. There she saw children die of ulcerative colitis, and decided to establish a psychoanalytically oriented child psychiatry clinic.

During the fifteen years that she worked at the clinic, she developed and established a specific technique in the treatment of psychosomatic disorders: Strict adherence to psychoanalytic neutrality (no gifts, no feeding, no special sympathy) and prevention of the splitting of the transference by weaning the patient away from drugs, and if possible, from specialists and family physicians, during his psychoanalysis. She emphasized that the psychoanalyst is the primary treating physician and that other physicians are only occasional consultants.

Dr. Sperling was a Clinical Professor of Psychiatry at the State University of New York, Downstate Medical Center, and a training analyst and supervisor at the Division of Psychoanalytic Education. In her teaching as well as in her own practice, she emphasized the obligation of the physician to not only study the patient, but to cure him. Only in the effective interaction between physician and patient would it be possible to penetrate the inevitable resistances and to get to the truth.

Her previous training in medicine enabled her to look critically at internists and surgeons instead of accepting their authority in the treatment of her patients, and so to establish a proper place for psychoanalysis. She could do so because her therapeutic successes convinced her that her technique was right.

It is out of these experiences and insights that the papers in this volume were written, and they are offered posthumously in this book as a tribute to her dedicated work and memory.

OTTO SPERLING, M.D.